# Signs of Recognition

# Signs of Recognition

*Powers and Hazards of Representation in an Indonesian Society*

Webb Keane

UNIVERSITY OF CALIFORNIA PRESS
*Berkeley* · *Los Angeles* · *London*

University of California Press
Berkeley and Los Angeles, California

University of California Press
London, England

Copyright © 1997 by
The Regents of the University of California

Library of Congress Cataloging-in-Publication Data

Keane, Webb, 1955–
    Signs of recognition: powers and hazards of representation in an
Indonesian society / Webb Keane.
        p.    cm.
    Includes bibliographical references and index.
    ISBN 0–520–20474–3 (cloth: alk. paper). — ISBN 0–520–20475–1
(pbk.: alk. paper)
    1. Anakalang (Indonesian people)—Rites and ceremonies.
2. Anakalang (Indonesian people)—Social conditions.   3. Anakalang
(Indonesian people)—Psychology.   4. Social structure—Indonesia—
Sumba Island.   5. Interpersonal relations—Indonesia—Sumba Island.
6. Representation (Philosophy).   7. Anakalang dialect—Semantics.
8. Anakalang dialect—Discourse analysis.   9. Sumba Island
(Indonesia)—Social life and customs.   I. Title.
DS632.A52K43   1997
306′.09598′6—dc20
                                                    96–18064
                                                    CIP

Printed in the United States of America

1   2   3   4   5   6   7   8   9

*For my parents*

# Contents

# Illustrations

# Preface

This book is a study of representational practices in Anakalang, a society on the island of Sumba, in eastern Indonesia. Its purpose is to examine the nature of representation as both action and objectification. To do so, it treats verbal and material representations as embodied forms that occur in encounters between persons. But these forms, and the understandings that Anakalangese bring to them, are also deeply implicated in powers, identities, and sources of authority that lie far beyond the concrete "here and now" and the living individuals who put them into play. In the tensions between their immediacy and their imputed transcendence, representational practices introduce important dilemmas and sources of dynamism into the heart of Anakalangese social, religious, and political life. In particular, I argue, there is an intrinsic but seldom obvious relationship between the formal display of cultural or cosmological order and the risks of social interaction. Although the specific configurations these dilemmas take are, of course, peculiarly Anakalangese and located at a particular historical juncture, I suggest that they also inflect certain endemic features of representation insofar as it is a component of action in a world full of other people.

In the process of approaching representations as both action and objectification, and as both concretely present and transcendent of their context, this book also seeks to challenge some of the ways in which contemporary studies of the symbolic and material dimensions of social life often talk past one another. It examines the verbal and material representations, especially poetic speech and exchange valuables, whose transaction lies at the heart of Anakalangese public events. Understood as "practices," representations do not exist only in the abstract—as, for example, some disembodied "discourse." Rather, that they take concrete forms, situated in activities, is critical to their signifying, performative, and even causal capacities. These capacities are not restricted to the expression and communication of meaning, as commonly understood. One consequence of their embodied character is that even the most controlled representational practices are thoroughly implicated in the hazards—and thus the politics, economics, and historicity—of social existence.

The primary focus of this book is on the kinds of public events that form the heart of contemporary Anakalangese life, especially as I knew it in the 1980s and 1990s. These interactions are critical scenes for the workings and failures of power, the building and erosion of reputations, the construction and crumbling of gendered subjects, the reproduction and splintering of collective agency, the consolidation and dissolution of relations of domination and dependency, the accumulation and dispersal of wealth, and the quest for spiritual efficacy and authority. In looking at these scenes, the book pays close attention to a number of tensions inherent to representations in their roles as media of action and in their relationship to everyday activities. These include the ways in which speech is both bound to and yet exceeds the context of speaking and the ambiguities entailed by the effort to use valuable or useful goods as sign vehicles. The accompanying ambiguities and slippages present important dilemmas for people in Anakalang as they strive to construct their public identities and exercise—or elude—power. By analyzing representations as social practices, this book explores the tensions between power and hazard, order and action, expression and economics. In the process, it suggests that in these tensions lie fault lines that may be revealed at moments of historical pressure.

This book is a somewhat hybrid work, moving as it does along the intersections among the studies of language, exchange, material culture, and social organization. In particular, although my approach draws heavily on the lessons of linguistic anthropology, and takes seriously its concern with form, it aims to work with rather than replicate the research that is being done there. I examine many of the same materials but often toward a somewhat more interpretive goal. Where a linguistic anthropologist might ask, for example, what are the verbal devices that reproduce authority, I ask what the use of these devices tells us about the nature of authority. In the process, I hope that the insights won from the close analysis of language can be brought back to illuminate certain problems of society and culture.

The reader who wishes more ethnographic background on Anakalang can refer to my dissertation (Keane 1990). The present book is both narrower in ethnographic scope and broader in theoretical intent. In addition to the limits imposed by mortality and attention span, it is in the very nature of the argument that I am making here that I recognize this to be a partial account, not a model of a total culture or self-contained society. The first chapter introduces the theoretical problems this book addresses, and explains what I mean by the words "representation," "recognition," and "hazard." There I lay out a case for treating interaction and objectification together, as components of representational practices. The second chapter outlines some essential historical, economic, and social organizational background. This discussion is guided by relevance to the themes I wish to highlight here, not by the goal of ethnographic or historical completeness in the abstract. For example, my treatments of gender and slavery are meant primarily to introduce processes of transformation, displacement, and delegation on which I will then elaborate in looking at objects and speech. The next four chapters analyze the media of representation. Chapter 3 concerns the interpretation and value of material objects and their problematic nature as representatives and representations of those who produce, transact, and possess them. That chapter introduces the transformations by which the circuit of household production and consumption can provide material resources for social, temporal, and semiotic expansions of agency. Chapters 4 and 5 examine the poetic, semantic, and pragmatic character of ritual speech and the dilemmas these can involve. Chapter 6 describes the performances that bring objects and speech together. There I pay special attention to the distribution of speaking parts and  their role in creating a collective speaking subject, an agent that transcends particular living individuals, and the kinds of vulnerability to which such subjects are prone. The two chapters that follow concern some social, economic, and political ramifications of representational practices. Chapter 7 is about the character of the action that these practices undertake and the nature of their risks. It discusses the ways in which formal action can and cannot be said to "follow rules" and some of the socioeconomic entailments of formality. Chapter 8 describes the ways in which Anakalangese conceptualize the stakes and hazards of interaction and seek to reserve a core of stability apart from the vicissitudes of interaction. The conclusion briefly notes some of the implications of this analysis for the concepts of objectification, voice, agency, and historical experience.

Anakalang is located on Sumba, an island about the size of Jamaica, lying about halfway between Bali and Timor, in the Indonesian province of East Nusa Tenggara. The island is divided among some five to twenty closely related ethnolinguistic domains (depending on what linguistic and cultural criteria one uses) with identities of varying distinctness. Within the ethnographic spectrum of Sumba, Anakalang forms a transition zone between the societies to its east and west. Linguistically part of east Sumba, it lies in the regency (*kabupaten*) of West Sumba. Anakalang is geographically, economically, and in some ways culturally closer to its western neighbors (thus I only capitalize "East" and "West" Sumba when referring to administrative units).

I have lived on Sumba for some twenty-four months, over the course of a preliminary visit in 1985, a twenty-two-month stay in 1986–1987, and a trip in 1993. Anakalangese are justifiably proud of their rather aristocratic generosity toward visitors, of which I was the constant, and at times overwhelmed, beneficiary—something that can only be hinted at in the acknowledgments. My relatively easy entry into Anakalang had a great deal to do not only with my hosts' courtesy, goodwill, and curiosity, but also, inevitably, with international and local structures of authority, with my identification with America and Jakarta, as a foreign expert in "culture" (Indo. *kebudayaan*), and with the letters I bore from governmental officials. All of this tended at first to put me in the position of someone who was to be given normative, synoptic accounts of marriage customs, clan histories, and the like, and then, I expect, sent quickly on my way. To my discomfort, in my first weeks in Anakalang several local officials arranged meetings with priests (*ratu*) and "experts in customary law" (Indo. *ahli adat*) for me. Imagining I was going to take a subtler and more "natural" approach, I was at first somewhat dismayed by this procedure. When I became familiar with the formality that marks even routine visiting in Anakalang, however, I realized any other way of introducing myself would have been inappropriate. Although these beginnings meant I had to struggle against certain expectations about what I should be studying and how I should be going about it, they also meant that my presence soon became known across Anakalang. When I did not quickly go away, the nature of the conversations in which I was involved slowly changed. Still, it may be that many Anakalangese will in the end be disappointed that I have not produced a book that looks quite like what they had expected, a definitive compilation of custom or a permanent record of clan histories. But the task of Sumbanese self-portrayal belongs to others, and is well under way (see, e.g., Kapita 1976a, 1976b, 1979, 1987; Sabarua 1976). I hope that those Anakalangese who read this book will, at least, not find the portrait to be alien or unfair. I hope as well that it will make evident something that lay behind my choice of Anakalang, that poetic speech and ceremonial exchange are extraordinarily vital parts of contemporary life, not idealized customs recollected in tranquility.

For most of my time in Sumba in the 1980s and in 1993, I lived in the large household (containing at times as many as twenty-two people) of Pak Tinas Sabarua and his wife, Ibu Mariana R. Kahi Kawurung. Ama Yati and Ina Yati, as I knew them, provided a comfortable base for my forays, although these often ranged more widely in both geographic and social terms than made them feel comfortable. Far from "traditional," their household was a contemporary melange. Ama Yati had been to university in Kupang, the provincial capital, on Timor, one brother was a schoolteacher off on the east coast (and author of Sabarua 1976), two others were studying in Kupang. After a brief stint in government work, Ama Yati was reshaping himself as master of an estate, a figure in the local politics of exchange, a modernizer, and a leader in the local church. In 1993 he was elected head of the Desa Anajiaka. His wife, an elementary schoolteacher, was the daughter of an important local power broker and a strong, assertive, and often intimidating figure in her own right. Within the household, we negotiated for me a somewhat complex, never fully stable, position, part younger brother (thus son, uncle, and affine as well), part distinguished visitor, part student. Much of my practical sense of Anakalangese life begins with our collective push and tug among the demands of kinship, hospitality, and research.

With a base in this household, I began in earnest the slow business of studying the language of Anakalang, relieved many afternoons by visits to acquaintances. By the end of my first year, I had become a regular visitor in a number of villages within a four-kilometer circuit of Anajiaka, especially within the Desa of Wai Rasa, Anakalang, Malinjak, and Umbu Mamiyuk. Many individuals also invited me to accompany them to the events in which they participated (and in which I was occasionally subjected to the demand for brief, embarrassing, public performances). I established especially close ties in two other places, Kaboduku (Desa Makatakeri) and Deru (Desa Umbu Pabal), and much of my perspective on Anakalang comes from the intersecting lines of sight from these very different sources. People in Kaboduku tend to consider themselves to be both keepers of true Anakalangese culture and more cosmopolitan than others. The village, which had been the base of the Dutch-appointed rulers of Anakalang, is still linked to many of the most powerful people in West Sumba and is currently the gateway to the sacred village of Lai Tarung, and an occasional tourist destination. Deru can be used as the collective name for a small cluster of villages on the eastern border of Anakalang, in Parewatana. By dialect somewhat distinct, Parewatana is closely linked to Anakalang proper by geographic proximity and ties of marriage, economics, and ritual (in this book, at the few points where there are significant distinctions between them, I will always refer to Anakalang). In contrast to Kaboduku, Deru is at the margins, relatively poor, obscure, and more difficult to get to. Outsiders who know about these villages often fear them, acknowledging them to be an active center of ancestral ritual and, in particular, to house the powers of lightning. Because of Deru's distance from Anajiaka, I often stayed there for several days on end (which allowed me to experience households very different from my own). Through a complex mix of accident, affinity, and negotiation, three elderly ratus (Umbu Pàda Buli Yora in Kaboduku, Umbu Kàna Dapa Namung and Umbu Dewa Damaràka in Deru) ended up taking particular responsibility for me, and developed into teachers, each with quite distinct styles and perspectives but all sharing a love of ritual speech. At the same time, I made a constant effort not to be confined to the company of guardians of tradition and counted as companions a number of cattle thieves, cynics, gospel teachers, ministers, petty traders, former slaves, schoolteachers, a high official or two, a good number of rogues (including some of the most talented ritual speakers I know), and at least one reputed witch. Within my household I found the warmth, wisecracks, gossip, and worries of a mother and several sisters and sisters-in-law. Elsewhere I attracted the pitying and protective attention of several self-appointed mothers and grandmothers. Nonetheless, a good part of my conversations tended to be dominated by men, since outside of my own household those were the people with whom it was proper for me to be alone. This has certainly inflected the perspective from which I write.

An important part of my work in Anakalang consisted of the effort to take part attentively in ordinary life. I did not want my interest in formal events to cause me to lose sight of the ongoing flow of daily work and the other activities out of which they arise. I spent a great deal of time participating in everyday household activities, and I frequently accompanied Ama and Ina Yati on visits or as a member of their entourage at exchanges, feasts, wedding parties, funerals, church gatherings, and the like. The other side of my work was more formal in nature. I had not been long in Anakalang when I was swept into the unrelenting round of marriage negotiations, rituals, divinations, feasts, funerals, conferences, and more casual politicking that takes up so much time during the long periods when agricultural work is not pressing. Most formal events last all night, often several nights in a row, and I was astonished at the stamina that the men and women around me possessed (and that I so pathetically lacked). These were mostly public events and matters of local pride, and my plan to tape record them was so strongly encouraged that there were times when, having run out of tape, I had to pretend to record to avoid giving offense. In contrast to this openness about formal occasions, Anakalangese have a strong sense of propriety; they saw little point in recording ordinary conversation or offstage talk, matters they consider to be full of errors to which I should be paying no attention. I managed to record a certain amount of informal talk, but I never tried to do so without the speakers' knowledge. All Anakalangese from whom I asked permission to publish their names granted it. Since I discuss several sensitive incidents, however, I have decided to use pseudonyms for persons, villages, and kabisu, except where a matter of public record or to identify the source of a recorded performance or canonical text, such as a myth.

Two men, Bapak U. S. Kababa (Pak Ande) and Umbu Siwa Djurumana (Umbu Pàda's son), did most of the transcribing of tapes. Both had completed high school, Pak Ande having also spent time at university in Java and subsequently working with a Dutch development expert. They were very intelligent and scrupulous at the task, but neither could claim much expertise on ritual speech. We thus ran into many questions of esoteric vocabulary and obscure metaphor. This was the result of the predictable problem, that those who were most knowledgeable about ritual speech either could not write or were too much in demand to take on such a time-consuming chore. My work on the tapes therefore involved at least two steps, as I took completed transcriptions on my visits and worked over them either with the speakers themselves or other participants in the event. With most of these men, the deference my youth and inexperience owed them carried at least as much weight as the status accorded to my foreign origins and scientific project. As a result, such visits usually tacked back and forth among directed task, casual conversation, and a vast number of competing demands on my hosts' time and attention. Frustrating as this may have been at times, it was for me a recurrent reminder of the priorities Anakalangese needed to keep in view, as well as a constant source of unexpected insights and puzzles.

Although my understanding of Anakalang is informed by my research in the Dutch colonial archives and the extensive published materials on Sumba, this book is primarily about life in Anakalang as I witnessed it in the 1980s and 1990s (for some historical perspectives, see Keane 1995b, 1996, in press). My concern with the circumstances and concrete details of performances and actions renders it difficult either to work at secondhand from earlier writings (which, for Anakalang itself, are scanty) or to rely more than occasionally on comparisons to other parts of Sumba and neighboring islands. Nonetheless, this book should not be taken for an account of an "ethnographic present," in the sense of a portrayal of a timeless and self-contained system. To the extent that I do describe practices that have a certain logic to them, it is a logic whose entailments include underdetermined significances, uncertain outcomes, and unforeclosed possibilities.

In particular, I attempt to show the intertwining of the causal and logical relations among, for example, acts of signification, the forms they take, their material conditions of possibility, and their political consequences. This nexus of causality and logic means that even the most ritually bounded of activities are implicated in that which lies "outside" them, including the market for cattle on Java, the institutional competition between clan and local government, the coercive powers of the state, the assertions of the church, and the structures of formal education. It is no longer realistic (if it ever was) to treat a place like Anakalang as an autonomous unity; it is simultaneously encompassed within a series of larger wholes (ethnographic region, nation, state, global church, international economy, transnational flows of cultural goods) and "internally" divided by varying effects of and allegiances to that "exterior." On the other hand, if we should no longer be surprised to discover that Anakalang is part of Indonesia, I do not believe this justifies privileging the perspective of centers of power, whether we find them in Kupang, Jakarta, the Hague, or Washington. Surely it would be as reductive (and unmanageable) to locate the "final instance" in the largest possible context as was the classic positivistic attempt to ground all explanation in fundamental units. It would be an injustice to deny the sphere of reference within which Anakalangese themselves situate so many of their most strenuous endeavors. To recognize that practices are situated is to recognize that not all dimensions of all practices are appropriately understood at the same level.

# Acknowledgments

Much of this book is about debt, the burdens and pleasures of which, as the people of Anakalang have taught me, are inseparable, inescapable, and, ultimately, unending. The thanks recorded here are only the shadow of what remains unreciprocated.

Fieldwork on Sumba (1985–1987 and 1993) and archival research in the Netherlands (1988) were made possible by financial support from Fulbright-Hays Dissertation Fellowships, the Joint Committee on Southeast Asia of the Social Science Research Council and the American Council of Learned Societies, with funds from the National Endowment for the Humanities and the Ford Foundation, the Wenner-Gren Foundation for Anthropological Research, and the Southeast Asia Council of the Association for Asian Studies, with funds from the Luce Foundation. The sponsorship I received from the Lembaga Ilmu Pengetahuan Indonesia and the Universitas Nusa Cendana (Kupang) was extended with courtesy, efficiency, and a true spirit of cooperation. I wish also to acknowledge the earlier support of a University of Chicago Special Humanities Fellowship, National Resource Fellowships, and, for writing the dissertation, a fellowship from the Charlotte W. Newcombe Foundation. Much of the present book was written while I held a National Endowment for the Humanities Fellowship for University Teachers.

From the very beginning of my interest in Sumba I have benefited from the unflagging collegiality of James Fox, Janet Hoskins, and Joel Kuipers. I received advice and assistance over the course of research from Marie Jeanne Adams, Sander Adelaar, Farchan Bulkin, James

Collins, Larry and Lucy Fisher, Gregory Forth, Eugene Galbraith, Jan Hostetler, Umbu Hina Kapita, Edgar Keller, Leng Kep and his family, Makoto Koike, Yos Lelaona, the Lomi family, Henk Mahenu, A. W. F. Miedema, Rodney Needham, Suzanne Siskel, Elizabeth Traube, Laurence van Veldhuizen, Jacqueline Vel, and the late Taro Goh, whose death during his own fieldwork has been a terrible loss.

The book draws on materials I first analyzed in a dissertation (Keane 1990). The members of my dissertation committee, Marshall Sahlins, Michael Silverstein, and Valerio Valeri, were exemplary in their combination of support, criticism, and restraint. Each has had a profound and distinctive influence on my work, if not always finally evident in shapes that each might immediately recognize. Janet Hoskins and Susan McKinnon also made valuable comments on the dissertation. Of the many contributions made by others at the University of Chicago to the present book, I must mention the work of Nancy Munn. Cornell University's Indonesian language program and Modern Indonesia Project provided a marvelous environment and challenged me to think about Indonesia in ways with which I am still wrestling. Of particular importance have been many conversations with James Siegel. During periodic stays in Ann Arbor, I have found a remarkable community of interlocutors at the University of Michigan whose goodwill and warmth never dull their critical edge. The Department of Anthropology at the University of Pennsylvania has been generous and flexible when it mattered most.

Along the way, various attempts to formulate the ideas presented here have passed under the critical eyes of Arjun Appadurai, Richard Bauman, Charles Briggs, Jean Comaroff, John Comaroff, Joseph Errington, Robert Foster, William Hanks, Judith Irvine, Liisa Malkki, Francesca Merlan, and Daniel Miller. Conversations over the years with Nicholas Dirks, Marilyn Ivy, John Pemberton, Rafael Sánchez, and Patricia Spyer have been an unfailing source of pleasure and provocation. The manuscript was read in its entirety by Don Brenneis, Kenneth George, Joel Kuipers, and John Pemberton, and in parts by E. Valentine Daniel, Brinkley Messick, Patricia Spyer, and Greg Urban. I am deeply indebted for their comments. Stanley Holwitz and his colleagues have made the production of the book look easy, and Matthew Tomlinson added a keen editorial eye and prepared the index. I shudder to think what this book, whatever its present failings, would look like without Adela Pinch, who, despite the demands of her own book, has read it countless times, and on whose subtle insight, sure feel for language, and good sense I have constantly relied.

Parts of chapter 3 appeared in somewhat different form in Keane 1994 (reprinted by permission of the Royal Anthropological Institute of Great Britain and Ireland) and parts of chapter 6 in Keane 1991 (reprinted by permission of the American Anthropological Association, not for further reproduction). I had assistance in producing the maps from Renwei Huang. Figure 3 is reproduced by permission of the Museum für Volkerkunde, Basel, with thanks to Dr. Urs Ramseyer. All the other photographs and figures 6 and 10 are mine.

For a description of my fieldwork and the contributions of certain individuals, see the preface. I have learned much from even fleeting encounters, but must name here some of those who went beyond the call of the extraordinary generosity that in Sumba counts as ordinary good manners. I had a home thanks to Bapak Augustinas U. Sabarua, Ibu Mariana R. Kahi Kawurung, Bapak Guti Sabarua, and Rambu Ngoma, as well as Bapak Yonatan Sabarua, Rambu Wasak, Andreas, Niko, Rambu Dapa Teba, Rambu Loba, Rambu Joru, Rambu Rikka, and Bapak Alex Tomas. My research was especially dependent on the patience and efforts of Bapak U.S. Kababa, Umbu Dewa Damaràka, Umbu Pàda Buli Yora, Ubu Kàna Dapa Namung, and Umbu Siwa Djurumanu. I must also acknowledge the kind assistance of many officials at Propinsi, Kabupaten, Kecamatan, and Desa levels. Among the many others to be mentioned are Kepala Desa A.U. Radda, Bapak Cornelis Ora Seka Iki, Umbu Dati Nyanyi, Umbu Djama Tagumara, Umbu Djima, Umbu Djowa Ubu ni Api, Kepala Desa Umbu Eda, Umbu Gàba, Bapak Gani Wulang, Umbu Hama Dota, Umbu Hami Leli Dima, Rambu Hida Laidu, Umbu Kabalu, Bapak S. Kadiwangu, Rambu Kadunga Regi, Umbu Kalla, Umbu Kuala Ngara Ata, Umbu Laiya Sobang, Umbu Lobu, Rambu L. P. W. Loḍang, Umbu Neka, Ratu Ngongu, Umbu Pila Ngala Ḍeta, Umbu Raisi Suruk, Kepala Desa Umbu Rauta Karebu, Kepala Desa Umbu Sunga, and Rambu Weli Rawa. I would like to thank the ratus of Parewatana collectively for permitting me to accompany them where reasonable caution dictated otherwise.

> ḍa ma kawukugeya na rabi rara
> ḍa ma wogeya na wini tana tàdungu

# A Note on Orthography, Transcription, and Vocabulary

Anakalangese (*na hilu Anakalang*) is a distinct dialect within the cluster of (more or less) mutually intelligible language varieties of eastern Sumba. There is a great deal of microregional and possibly generational variation within Anakalangese. The language of Parewatana is further distinguished from Anakalangese by the preference for certain lexical items and some phonological variants. These do not, however, interfere with communication: I have even seen a spokesman from Parewatana using his own dialect to serve one group of Anakalangese in addressing another. Anakalangese is rarely written and there is no standardized orthography, nor has it received linguistic analysis except for some brief comments (Onvlee [1936] 1973c) and lexical cross-references (Onvlee 1984). In my transcriptions I make no effort to standardize across the dialectal and idiolectal variations I recorded, although I do defer to those few personal names that have acquired an accepted written form (e.g., Umbu Sappy Pateduk instead of Ubu Sàpi Pateduk). The subscript (.) marks implosive consonants. A useful weighing of the pros and cons of Sumbanese orthography, with particular reference to the west Sumbanese language of Weyewa, is given by Joel C. Kuipers (1990: xviii–xxiii), and I concur with him in most respects. I differ slightly, however, in my treatment of vowels, in which I follow the east Sumbanese transcriptions of Lois Onvlee and Oe. Kapita. Kuipers doubles consonants except when this would result in doubled digraphs (e.g., /ngng/), in which case he accents the preceding vowel. In the interest of treating vowels consistently while also avoiding doubled digraphs, I retain the accent across the board. (Kuipers rightly refers to indigenous writing habits in making his choice; in Anakalang, however, I have already been obliged to deviate from local writing since, as far as I know, it never indicates the phonemic distinction between implosive and other consonants.) For most Anakalangese, /h/ and /s/ are not phonemically distinct and may co-occur in the speech of a single speaker.

CONSONANTS

| | bilabial | alveolar | alveopalatal | palatal | velar | glottal |
|---|---|---|---|---|---|---|
| stop | | | | | | |
|    voiced | b | d | | | g | |
|    v. impl. | ḅ | | ḍ | | | |
|    voiceless | p | t | | | k | |
| fricative | | s | j | | | h |
| nasal | m | n | | | ng | |
| lateral | | l | r | | | |
| semivowel | w | | | y | | |

For the vowels (a, e, i, o, u) and diphthongs (au, ai) see discussions in Kuipers (1990) and Onvlee ([1936] 1973c). Canonical stress is on the penultimate syllable of the root, unaffected by affixation. The abbreviation "Indo." indicates words and expressions in Indonesian and the local variants of Malay.

Anakalangese pronouns do not indicate gender. The first-person plural does indicate whether the addressee is included or excluded, which I note where relevant.

In transcribing ritual speech my chief concern has been to keep the poetic units visible, sometimes at the expense of intonation and breath groups (for the issues raised by transcription choices, see Hymes [1977] 1981, Ochs 1979). The three principal units that I indicate are the line, the couplet, and the stanza (for further discussion of these units, in Weyewa, a west Sumbanese language, see Kuipers 1990, although my definition of stanza is narrower than his). By stanza, I mean a set of intercalated couplets, the two lines of each couplet being separated by at least one line of another couplet. In these cases, couplets are indicated by indentation: the components of the first couplet are flush left, the next couplet indented one step, those of the third couplet two steps, and so forth. Unpaired phrases, such as "and another thing" (*higulna*), receive their own line, and back-channel cues are placed in parentheses. Throughout the text, double quotation marks enclose verbatim reported speech, mostly from tape recordings, and single quotation marks indicate statements for which I can offer a close report (from notes taken at the time or shortly thereafter) but cannot vouch for word-for-word accuracy.

In the interests of making the book accessible to the nonspecialist, I have limited the use of Anakalangese vocabulary. This poses, of course, real ethnographic problems, tempting both author and reader to accept a closer semantic correspondence between Anakalangese and English than is warranted. I have retained a few terms whose importance and problematic translatability I wish to underscore. These, and the places where they are most fully discussed, are:

| | |
|---|---|
| dewa | soul, spirit, fate, fortune (chap. 8) |
| desa | Indonesian administrative unit at the "village" level |
| horung | formal negotiation between affines (chap. 6) |
| kaḅisu | clan (chap. 2) |
| kajiàla | ritual speech of negotiation (chap. 4) |
| mamuli | omega-shaped metal valuable (chap. 3) |
| ngàba wini | affines of the husband's side |
| pata | patterned way of doing things; ancestral custom (chap. 7) |
| Rabu (Rambu) | honorific term of address and reference for women |
| ratu | priest, ritual specialist |
| Ubu (Umbu) | honorific term of address and reference for men |
| wunang | ritual spokesman and negotiator (chap. 6) |
| yera | affines of the wife's side |

# CHAPTER ONE

# Introduction

*Representation, Recognition, and Hazard*

But then how ridiculous would be the effect of names on things, if they were exactly the same with them! For they would be the doubles of them, and no one would be able to determine which were the names and which were the realities.

Plato, Cratylus, 432

Late one night in September 1986, I was in the high hilltop village of Prai Maleru. It was several days into a ritual sponsored by Sulung, an important and elderly ritual specialist (*ratu*), to inter his parents' bones in a new tomb. This was an occasion for him not only to fulfill his own long outstanding obligations to his parents but also to call in the debts others owed him, to put forth an autobiographical justification in a long series of orations, and, incidentally, to lay claim to a bit of disputed land just below the village. Each night, old women sat in the front room by the bundles of bones, talking quietly, occasionally bursting into stylized but wrenching keening songs. Several neighboring houses were crammed with scores of visitors, drawn by obligations, the opportunity to make their own demands of the host, the pleasure of the dances, the appeal of the oratory, the company, and the feasting. Outside, in the plaza in front of the house, gongs played, a weary singer grew hoarse, and men danced while young women watched and encouraged them with periodic ululations. On the veranda, ratu Sulung rested between orations. Inside, I huddled with several other men around the hearth against the chill of the dry-season night. Ubu Kaledi, a local government official, was doing most of the talking. His clan (*kabisu*), an important exchange partner of ratu Sulung's, had also been involved in a long series of disputes with ratu Sulung's kabisu. Tensions were exacerbated by personal differences. Ratu Sulung was a vehement, foul-mouthed, and often obstreperous opponent of the rising forces of Christianity. Ubu Kaledi, in contrast, was involved in an uncomfortable effort to lay claim simultaneously to the prestige of modernity, government office, and church membership and to the status of the ritual title to which he believed himself heir.

I was being lulled to sleep by the familiar course of the talk as the men rehashed old disputes about cattle promised and received, differences of opinion about ritual procedures, insults alleged, reputations impugned, the baroque twists of matrimonial politics. In the midst of this, I perked up, realizing that Ubu Kaledi had turned to a rare topic in these circles, national politics. His interest in the national scene was unusual in Anakalang, where, in the words of the American politician Tip O'Neill, "all politics is local" and where for many people "Indonesia" is a distant abstraction. Even more unusual were his heterodox opinions. He began holding forth on the alleged Communist coup attempt of 1965, which led to a convulsion of killings in many parts of the country, the downfall of Sukarno, and the birth of the present New Order regime of President Soeharto. In contrast to the official line, he maintained that the coup was really a matter of rivalries within the military. Musing on the nasty goings-on in Jakarta, he commented 'That's the way it always is, it's all *politik*,' using an Indonesian word that usually connotes the disorder that arises out of self-interested intrigue and factionalism. He then drew an analogy from close to home: 'It's like here in Anakalang: when we *kajiàla*, that's politik.'

The analogy was startling, and is emblematic of a problem that lies at the heart of this book. Ubu Kaledi here used *kajiàla* (negotiation speech) to refer to the full range of ritual speech. This is a highly formal register that stands in marked contrast to everyday ways of talking. It is defined in particular by indirection, density of metaphor, and strict poetic form. Said to have been handed down unchanged from the ancestors, ritual speech is required for all significant interactions, both among the living and between the living and the dead. Its performance style, poetic structure, and ancestral origins all give it the aura of eternal, harmonious order. Even Anakalangese who identify themselves with modernity, Christianity, and the state usually place enormous value in ritual speech, which they describe as central to local identity, ancient wisdom, collective values and social solidarity, and the sense of order that enables them to resist the chaos threatened by contemporary life. In other words, ritual speech should stand for everything that opposes the national scene, modernity, factionalism, and disorder of politik. Likewise, ritual speech exemplifies the ethnographic image that places like

Anakalang often present to the outside world as vestigial reserves of ritualized, traditional order (see Keane 1995a). And yet here was Ubu Kaledi, whose most vigorous efforts and ambitions hinged on masterful use of ritual speech, identifying it with the discreditable activities of politik. Notice that he was not suggesting that ritual speech disguises or overcomes politik. In this, and other casual comments, he was suggesting a stronger, even an inherent, relationship between that which is most highly valued and orderly and that which is most devalued and disorderly.

At one level, this conjunction of ritual, politics, and disorder should not be surprising. As Clifford Geertz ([1959] 1973a) pointed out long ago in his account of a troubled Javanese funeral (and as the violence of the European Reformation might remind us), rituals are well suited to express or catalyze political tensions. To the extent that rituals are public and consequential, their forms, materials, personnel, and timing can all serve as tools of strategy and themselves become bones of contention. But analyses of ritual and politics often approach the two as involving distinct principles. Thus, for Geertz, the problems in the Javanese funeral arise from a lag between cultural persistence and rapid social change, a peasant ritual clashing with an urban context ([1959] 1973a: 169). Other approaches treat ritual as a medium for conflicts that are "really" about something else, be it, for example, factional strife, control over resources, structures of domination, or resistance to hegemonic discourses. But this book begins with a somewhat different concern, with the way in which the potentials for slippage and conflict might be immanent in ritual form itself. Moreover, these potentials are not necessarily confined to ritual. The formality, consequentiality, and reflexivity of ritual bring to the fore certain dilemmas implicit in the very nature of representation—dilemmas that, I suggest, are thoroughly implicated with general problems of power, authority, and agency.

I was intrigued by Ubu Kaledi's view of things, because over time my own experience of the high and often tense formality of social relations in Anakalang seemed to bear it out. It seems I was not alone in the sense that ritual events bear disturbing undercurrents. When I returned to Anakalang in 1993, there was much talk about government restrictions (as yet not entirely successful) on certain kinds of ceremonial events. Responding to the state's ever-growing pressure for economic rationalization, the regent considered feasting to be at once backward and a hindrance to the economic development of the island. The butchering of cattle was wasteful, the sacrifice of chickens an affront to religious modernity. In seeking to control the local enthusiasm for slaughter and the public distribution of meat, the state was tackling a problem that had preoccupied Dutch Calvinist missionaries since their arrival on Sumba in the early decades of the century. Viewed from the theological perspective of the church, the central events of Sumbanese life involve people in a tangled confusion of subjects and objects (see Keane 1996, n.d.). The Sumbanese seem at once to fetishize the material world and objectify the human. Both the project of religious conversion and the project of modernization, in these views, require that words, things, and persons be sorted out and restored to their proper places. The church seeks to prevent Christians from consuming meat butchered at certain events and criticizes local ritual speech as insincere, as words that are not spoken from the heart. In their conversations, whether they laud or criticize the government's policy, many Anakalangese speak in terms similar to those used by the government: that the present era is dominated by "economic thinking" (Indo. *pikiran ekonomis*), a time of rampant individualism whose slogan is "as long as I (get mine)" (*mali nyuwa*). *Ekonomis*, like its coordinate, *politik*, has much more negative connotations than the English equivalent: it suggests antisocial stinginess, a ruthless and vulgar calculating of costs and benefits.

In its effort to limit excessive expenditure, the state attacks one side of the problem. In its attempt to control the meanings of objects, the church takes on another. The complex nature of the problem is shown by the double nature of the prohibitions: to ban events in which animals are slaughtered is also to ban certain speech performances. Although the state's primary concern is economic rationalization, its intervention can also be interpreted as a challenge to the authority of ritual speech (Kuipers 1990: 1). To focus exclusively on either the material or the verbal dimension is to miss the importance of their conjunction. What is distinctive about the situation is precisely the ambiguity induced by the fact that prohibitions on speech and on material expenditure are inseparable, and that the powers of speech are entangled with those of objects. Their mutual involvement and its ramifications lie at the heart of the central problems—and promises—posed for Sumbanese by the state, the church, and the "modernities" that they project. But what is it about the nature of power, the shape of agency, the value of words, and the meaning of things that makes this nexus so compelling in the first place? What can this particular configuration of words and things tell us about representation and power more generally? Why should the appearance of order be so implicated in the tumult of conflict? The purpose of this book is to explore some of these questions, by looking at the media—words, things, and performers—through which Anakalangese seek to exercise power in scenes of encounter. The troubled relations among politik, ekonomis, and high moral value—a configuration hardly unique to Sumba—are neither obvious nor trivial. To understand this is to begin to understand the intertwining of words and things, of meaning and economy, and of agents, powers, and representations. It means going beyond the mimetic and normative aspects of ritual, to explore the relationship between representation and the conflictual, contingent, and risky character of social life.

## REPRESENTATION, AGENCY, AND MATERIALITY

When Ubu Kaledi is calling poetic speech "politics" and the regent is curbing sacrifices, both are responding to the powers, ambiguities, and potential dangers of the most ritualized forms of action. Ritual speech and the accompanying material practices (exchange, sacrifice, and offerings) are the central components of events usually associated with high formality, shared cultural values, and traditional ceremonialism. And yet these anecdotes suggest that the appearance of well-regulated order is at best incomplete. I wish to raise this doubt about the status of ritual order for reasons both empirical and theoretical. The project that gave birth to this book was inspired in part by the remarkable abundance of formal self-portrayal, in many societies of Indonesia, something that has often been commented on (Keane 1995a: 102) and that gave rise to some of the strongest treatments of culture as text (Geertz 1973c), theater (Geertz 1980), or structuralist schema (Lévi-Strauss [1956] 1963; Needham 1980)—both within anthropology and in the continuing interventions of the Indonesian state. The questions this self-portrayal might provoke can be better understood in light of three features of recent developments in the study of culture and society.

The first feature is a conflicted attitude toward ritual in particular and normative cultural accounts in general. Many anthropologists are increasingly uneasy with the assumption that ritual holds the key by which an entire culture, as a set of meanings borne by an untroubled consensus, can be unlocked. On the one hand, it is evident that certain ritualized activities are embedded within larger practical contexts. This recognition has given rise to important bodies of work on the political workings, within ritual frames, of exchange (Appadurai 1986; Ferguson

1985; Strathern 1988; Thomas 1991; Weiner 1992) and speech (Bloch 1975; Brenneis and Myers 1984; Duranti 1994; Hill and Irvine 1992; Lindstrom 1992; Watson-Gegeo and White 1990). On the other hand, as anthropologists have become increasingly attentive to problems of agency, contending interests, and disjunctive perspectives, they have learned to be suspicious of official depictions of order. Some of this suspicion is epistemological, an alertness to the schematizing and reifying effects of what people *say* about what they *do*. The epistemological problems posed by reification may be inseparable from their political effects (Asad 1986; Bourdieu [1972] 1977; Foucault [1969] 1972). Even the simple norms of everyday propriety, among the least dramatic elements of any cultural account, may serve particular interests or forces of domination (Scott 1990). If the normative is the language of political hegemony, then ritual should be hegemony's most powerful instrument, its authoritativeness bearing some relation (echoing, reproducing, or disguising) to the distribution of political authority within society (Bloch 1986). Rituals, moreover, may be subject to manipulation by the colonial and postcolonial state precisely because of their apparent role in reproducing order. Suspicion of the normative, the official, and the verbalized has opened up new vistas as anthropologists seek out the marginal, the everyday, and the contested (in Indonesia, see Steedly 1993 and Tsing 1993) and rethink the complex status of "traditional ritual" in the contemporary nation (Pemberton 1994).

At the same time, the reevaluation of ritual and other public forums has perhaps led us to become inattentive to the dynamism and the aporia that they may bear within them. In turning away from the study of ritual "order," we may be taking its apparently static surfaces and claims to authority too much at face value. It is pertinent to consider here the concept of formality. Regardless of whether one treats ritual as the key to cultural meanings or as an instrument of political hegemony, in doing so one may be collapsing together several distinct kinds of "formality." Judith Irvine (1979) points out that "formality" can refer to highly structured representations, or to an emphasis on stereotypical performance roles, or to a heightened focus on the given situation. Formality often induces explicit talk about rules and norms, with all the reflexivity to which that can give rise. Not only are these different sorts of formality not identical, they may even work at cross-purposes. As this book examines the multiple dimensions of ritualized action, it will show how they are implicated with another set of distinctions. Cultural and linguistic approaches to "power" occasionally treat power as synonymous with authority and status and their various representations. The distinctions among these can be important, however, especially when the effort to weave them together is a far from untroubled business.

A second feature of much contemporary work in society and culture  is the concern with agency. A common effect of this concern, as Sherry Ortner (1984) has pointed out, is to privilege the individual as the presumed locus of agency. But the ways of acting and talking that I discuss in this book challenge this common Western inclination to locate agency (see Strathern 1988), or, for that matter, "voice" (Vološinov [1930] 1973), in biologically distinct individuals. By placing formal action at the center of this work, I follow a wide array of Anakalangese (young, old, male, female, high ranking and low, disgruntled and complacent) who situate the most public, most socially consequential, most powerful (and for some, most oppressive) matters in what might be called "scenes of encounter." Preeminent among these are events in which two groups confront, speak to, and exchange objects with each other.[1] These scenes of encounter work to display and tap into an agency that is assumed to transcend the particular individuals present and the temporal moment in which they act. This project takes effort and is fallible. Indeed, I will suggest that to the extent that the most authoritative agents in Anakalang are entities such as clans, they constitute an imputed subject that exceeds the capacity of particular living persons to inhabit in a fully stable and definitive manner.

The practices that give life to authoritative agency in Anakalang conjoin both senses of the word "representation," depiction (representation *as* something) and delegation (representation *by* someone or something) (Pitkin 1967: 69; see also Peirce 2.273).[2] Participants in scenes of encounter stage complex performances about who they are (such as *like? Kinship?* named clans), who they are to each other (such as descendants or affines), and who they are together (such as self-respecting people allied in authoritative performances). In the process, they engage, challenge, or otherwise presume the existence of particular sorts of interlocutors, to the exclusion of other sorts. In scenes of encounter and the events that support them, participants *interactively* define themselves and each other (something that also has quieter entailments for power differences within each group). The relevant locus of agency—living individual, disembodied ancestor, household, faction, clan, interclan alliance—is subject to ongoing construction and transformation. It is liable to shift, subject to the strategies and miscues of the interaction, reflecting a more general set of possibilities, as individuals can be split "into a variety of presences" (Hill and Irvine 1992: 7; see also Strathern 1988) or assembled into a collective subject (Merlan and Rumsey 1991). Much of the work of power aims at, and is registered in, such transformations or constrictions of agency.

A third feature of many current approaches to the study of culture is the privileged place they give to discourses and representations. This concentration on representations often seems to work against some of the more vigorous concepts of practice I have already mentioned, to the extent that the latter includes causes and consequences that elude intentions and consciousness. Bearing this problem in mind, I begin with the central, and I hope uncontentious, assumption that representations exist as things and acts in the world. They are enunciated in speech events, enacted in rites, embodied in clothing, and portrayed in physical media; they circulate as goods and live in the form of human delegates. A medium of representation is not only something that stands "between" those things that it mediates, it is also a "thing" in its own right. I want to stress the importance of the ambiguity introduced by the embodied character of representations. This implication can be found, for example, in Charles S. Peirce's definition that representation is

> an object which stands for another so that an experience of the former affords us a knowledge of the latter. There are three essential conditions to which every representation must conform. It must in the first place like any other object have *qualities independent of its meaning*. . . . In the 2nd place a representation must have a *real causal connection* with its object. . . . In the third place, every representation *addresses itself to a mind* (Peirce 1986: 62; emphasis mine).

Both symbolic anthropology and its critics have paid the greatest attention to the third of these conditions. In contrast, I will be especially concerned with developing the implications of the first two. This book treats representations both as entities with their own, particular, formal properties (such as poetic structure and material qualities) and as kinds of practice, distinct and yet inseparable from the full range of people's projects and everyday activities. It examines words, things, and performances together as coordinated media of authoritative, potentially powerful, action. As a result, it works at the unstable boundary at which the "symbolic" and the "material" meet, reinforcing or undermining one another. In the process, the book explores the complex and sometimes contradictory relations among signification and causation, agency and contingency.

If representations and power are not to be reduced one to the other, it is important to pay attention to a variety of hazards. For if representations are really part of the action, then they are also implicated in the vicissitudes to which action is prone (see Sahlins 1985: ix). But this implication is not mere accident: representations, I suggest, do not only include reflections of the actions they serve, they also hint at the nature and the sources of potential *failure* as well. In Anakalang, this potential for failure embodies and sometimes conflates dilemmas of several distinct sorts. In part, it reflects the way in which authority, legitimate agency, and the various sources of social and economic power do not necessarily cohere.[3] To bring them effectively together takes ongoing effort. In particular, it requires that words and things be coordinated in public events. Much of the politics and even the cosmology of representations in Anakalang concerns this effort, the resistances it generates, and the hazards to which it is prone. But the effort and hazard are not matters of which people are fully conscious, and the politics are not to be found in a set of choices clearly laid out before autonomous strategizing agents. Hazard arises in part out of the complex relations between discourse and material economy, in part out of the political dialectic of solidarity and challenge. The latter is brought to sharp focus in the agonism and mutual dependence that pervade public interaction. This interaction is mediated by formal representations that reflect, in turn, a fundamental tension between text and context, repetition and act. This study examines representational practices for evidence of the limits, contradictions, and risks of action. Some of the sources of these problems are to be found in the practical conditions of possibility and consequence to which they are bound. Some, however, are reflected in the very nature of representational media themselves.

In the rest of this chapter, I explain my use of the words "representation," "recognition," and "hazard" and propose a dialectical approach to the semiotic and material economies they involve. Hazard, I suggest, is critical for understanding the powers, resistances, and experiences that representational practices produce and the historical fates to which they contribute.

## ORDINARY OBJECTIFICATION

Historically, the study of "representation as" has tended to center on mimesis. Mimesis, for example, is central to the original formulation of "collective representations" (Durkheim and Mauss [1903] 1963) whose influence on current approaches remains strong even where unacknowledged or opposed. Durkheim and Mauss postulate that classes of things in the world reflect preexisting classes of social groups. Often manifest in such concrete forms as the spatial disposition of dwellings, collective representations are objectifications that serve the self-knowledge of members of society. Their principal value lies in their isomorphism with the true or desired state of things.

But if we treat words, things, and performances together as media of action, the mimetic function is only part of the story. Mimesis does not disappear, but it is resituated as one component of a practical and semiotic complex. To see why it might be productive to resituate mimesis, it is useful briefly to look at its role in two important analyses of pre- (or early) colonial Indonesian societies. Clifford Geertz and Benedict Anderson both respond to the prominence of ritual and formality in societies in which they are clearly inseparable from questions of power. In his account of the "theatre state," Geertz echoes Durkheim and Mauss's basic theme: "What the Balinese state did for Balinese society was to cast into sensible form a concept of what, together, they were supposed to make of themselves" (1980: 102).[4] Geertz asserts that ritual representations do not just portray a conceptual order but provide an exemplar for society and a foundation for relations of authority within it. Wary of the temptations of functionalism, he is careful not to seek a final explanation in either purposeful actions or causal effects. Rather, the power of representations lies ultimately in mimesis: "by the mere act of providing a model . . . the court shapes the world around it into at least a rough approximation of its own excellence" (1980: 13).

My interest here is not with whether this is or is not a good portrayal of the historical Bali but rather with the questions this might raise about how we think about representation. What sort of "shaping" might a "model" provide? Some insight is provided by Anderson's ([1972] 1990) influential account of charismatic power in Java. According to Anderson, Javanese traditionally conceived of power as something that exists independent of those who hold it. Thus the possession of charismatic power hinged not on being asserted but on evidence of its presence, that is, on signs. A practical paradox inhabits this model of power, which, as in Geertz's account, eschews appeals to intentional action. Since the signs of power are supposed to be manifestations of what they signify, the possessor of power should not appear to act *intentionally*, that is, to desire, seek, or hold onto it: "the grasp for Power may mean its loss and the withdrawal from Power its acquisition" (Anderson [1972] 1990: 67).[5] As a result, charisma depends on *others*. For example, "being *thought* to have such [power-laden] objects . . . at one's disposal is just as politically advantageous as actually having or making serious use of them" (Anderson [1972] 1990: 27; emphasis in original). This places the leader at the mercy of the follower's interpretations of signs.

Anderson sees the power of representations ultimately to depend on Javanese ideas about their sources—because the signs of power are *generated* by a source that at some level remains (ambiguously) distinct from them, they serve as *evidence* of its existence: "the charismatic leader's Power is revealed rather than demonstrated" ([1972] 1990: 74). As I understand this assertion, the difference between revealing and demonstrating power is a difference in imputed agency. A "demonstrated" sign occurs by virtue of an intention to communicate (and by virtue of being seen to intend to do so, what H. P. Grice [1957] calls a "non-natural meaning").[6] In reading such a sign, we look for the intentions of a sign user in the background. By contrast, a "revealed" sign is one that should be taken to have a "natural" meaning; that is, it is really linked to what it signifies by causation or proximity, the way clouds "mean" rain. Herein lies the semiotic side of the quandary of charismatic power. Like many kinds of authority, its legitimacy hinges on signs that can be interpreted as "natural."

To the extent that these accounts exclude the "traffic" in power from the field of legitimate authority (Geertz 1980: 132), however, they also threaten to reproduce functionalism's opposition between ideas and actions.[7] To separate symbolism from action risks making the former puzzling (what do we gain from privileging *this* domain of human life?), irrelevant (why don't we just look for how things "really" happen?), omnipotent (how could things ever turn out otherwise?), or historically fragile (what happens as soon as a follower's belief wavers?). Such questions mark out the split between those who find the interpretation of images and texts to provide a sufficient account of society and its politics (as in some versions of Cultural Studies) and those who would see "through" representations to get to the real action (as in some versions of Marxism).

To take representations seriously, I suggest, we should not have to treat them in isolation from, or as subordinated to, the other activities of society. Even the most transcendental images occur in particular social and ontological spaces, facing audiences, making use of performers and their skills, presupposing certain assumptions about how actions occur and what sorts of beings inhabit the world, and requiring economic and social resources. Thus, for instance, to the extent that charisma is mediated by signs, this suggests that charisma cannot be entirely divorced from action. But to include action in an account of representations should not require us to return to bare functionalism or to reduce the symbolic to the material. A more realistic approach might be one that seeks to keep both dimensions in mutually irreducible play with each other. To begin, I ask how representations, if they are not only mimetic, are embedded within ordinary action and party to its vicissitudes.

A first step might be to reconsider the character of representation, seen as objectification. Since for Durkheim, objectification is the concrete embodiment of an idea, it has become a commonplace to criticize the Durkheimian tradition for excessive intellectualism and for situating ideas at a timeless, static plane. But the foundational accounts of Hegel and Marx portray objectification as a necessary moment in action, not as at odds with it. This is evident in the Hegelian treatment of the subject's self-constitution. In the dialectic of Lordship and Bondage, for example, this self-constitution occurs in an active process of challenge and response. That is, a subject objectifies itself *with respect to an other*: "self-consciousness exists in and for itself when, and by the fact that, it so exists for another; that is, it exists only in being acknowledged" (Hegel [1807] 1977: 111). In the Hegelian concept, objectification thus is not a simple matter of self-contemplation but is inherently implicated in action. Moreover, it develops out of interaction with others.

A basic concept of interaction plays a fundamental role in work ranging from that of Marx and Georg Simmel to such diverse contemporary projects as the linguistic analysis of conversation (e.g., Duranti and Goodman 1992) or the rethinking of gender (Butler 1990) and of multiculturalism (Taylor 1992). For my purposes in this introduction, I will here draw selectively from a point of intersection between pragmatist and phenomenological traditions. Alfred Schutz ([1932] 1967: 61) begins with a phenomenological reading of Max Weber's model of intentional action: "the meaning of any action is its corresponding projected act." As a result, intentional action already contains within it a split between subject and object, *prior* to any encounter with another person. This is a function of its temporal structure. Intentional action, being oriented to the future, represents to itself an *already completed* act ([1932] 1967: 59–61). In this moment of imagination, self-consciousness takes the acting self as an object of perception, distinct from the perceiving self ([1932] 1967: 58): to move actively into the future necessarily entails self-objectification.[8]

But the internal split entailed in self-objectification is thoroughly implicated in the subject's active engagement with a social universe of others. Consider, for example, the role played by the public, shared signs of language in George Herbert Mead's version of interaction. The reflexive character of interaction arises out of the need to anticipate the other's response to one's own gesture, as the fencer's challenge anticipates a riposte (Mead 1934: 43). In the fullest form of social interaction, however, this anticipation is not limited to the gesture itself. Action includes a distinct moment of self-consciousness. This self-consciousness is predicated on the existence of the other person. It is only through the perspective of the *other* that I can experience myself as an object, thus as a complete self (1934: 136–138). But I do not take on the other's position directly. My ability to see myself from your position is mediated by *signs*, especially language.[9] Language supplies a missing element in two ways. Because speech is an objective medium outside of me, I am able to hear myself just as you can, whereas I cannot, for example, directly see my face (1934: 65). Because speech uses symbols that we both share, it has the same effect on me as it has on you (1934: 46). Thus representations do not simply *express* some autonomous inner or ideal meaning. Moreover, the fact that they have material form, and that they draw on collective resources, makes them crucial conditions of possibility for *actions*. For me to act, I must be an object to myself, but for me to be an object to myself, I must have both a medium and an audience (1934: 141–142).

As the Hegelian model suggests, self-consciousness is not a neutral matter of epistemology. Since each party to interaction is also evaluating and acting on the other, self-consciousness is open to contestation. This agonistic potential of everyday interaction is implicit, for example, in the work of Erving Goffman (1956), who distinguishes between demeanor (behavior that shows the respect that I owe to myself) and deference (behavior that shows the respect I owe to others). Deference and demeanor suggest that there is a micropolitics to the interdependence of self and other. Not only does my deferential behavior say something about who I think you are, but so too does my demeanor. The way in which I handle myself displays my self-respect, but the respect with which I feel I must handle myself in front of you can imply a statement about you as well (this is why *my* state of undress might offend *you*). Conversely, the deference I show you simultaneously displays my interactive skills and my social knowledge (Errington 1988). In showing that I know your value, I am also putting forward a claim about my own—a claim, however, that depends on your response for its affirmation.

## RECOGNITION

Critics of the interactionism that developed out of Schutz and Mead point to how it overemphasizes individual spontaneity and self-knowledge at the expense of institutions, history, difference, power, and the vagaries of consciousness (Bourdieu [1972] 1977: 81; Giddens 1979: 254). But if we focus on recognition, it becomes apparent that the very nature of interaction calls for an account of society and power. To begin with the ordinary nondialectical sense of "recognition," people recognize actions and identities in terms of things of which they *already* have some understanding. Objectification depends on an act of comparison in which the new event can be *recognized* as an instance of something that is already known (Schutz [1932] 1967: 84). One synthesizes one's perceptions in relation to previous experience, and gives them a name: one sees, for instance, a swinging ax, flying woodchips, a man in motion, as a unity, namely, a woodcutter engaged in the act of cutting wood (Schutz [1932] 1967: 110–111). This requires both prior knowledge of the world and a language, which provides an interpretive scheme.[10] Similarly, for Mead, experience is mediated by recognition. Moreover, we recognize things insofar as they are *repeatable*: "[When] something is recognized, there is a universal character given in the experience itself which is at least capable of an indefinite number of repetitions" (Mead 1934: 84). Thus recognition entails an inherently temporal dimension, objectifying the moment with glances both retrospective and prospective.

But as the role of language in Schutz's woodcutter example suggests, what counts as repeatable is at least in part social, not a direct precipitate of experience. For Schutz and Mead, recognizable types exist as a relatively unproblematic background of shared common knowledge (Schutz [1932] 1967: 170). To the extent that a recognizable type is repeatable, it exists independently of the particularities of time, place, power, and subjective idiosyncrasies. Rather like Durkheim's (1915: 434), collective representations, they are communicable only by virtue of being types and thus, implicitly, by being publicly available.

In this account, I depend on you to recognize me or my actions as instances of certain types. This means, in principle, that recognition cannot be entirely in my hands. It is subject to the playing out of the in-teraction *between* us and thus begins to take on a more dialectical and potentially power-laden quality than that of a simple embodying of an existing type. Thus I depend on you to recognize that my identity (wood-cutter, stranger, or neighbor) and my actions (making a living, trespass-ing, or borrowing) are indeed of a certain type and not some other. The outcome depends on interaction that is not fully in the control of either party. What's more, whether I get you to accept my action as that of a stranger or a neighbor may depend on our past history, respective power, and standing relative to one another and thus to institutions (such as courts) and categories (such as gender). As James Scott (1985: 291) ob-serves, in reference to the politics of peasant resistance, the "English poacher in the eighteenth century *may* have been resisting gentry's claim to property in wild game, but he was just as surely interested in rabbit stew." The ambiguity is not settled simply by appealing to the poacher's intentions, especially once he has been caught by the gamekeeper. This suggests not only <u>that interaction presupposes social knowledge but also that it is mediated by relations of authority</u> (even as it contributes to them—a circularity to which I will return in later chapters). As a re-sult, the questions of "what" is going on and "who" is doing it are po-tentially subject to contestation, the definition of the situation itself, in-deed, what even counts as "experience," becoming an object of politics (Rosaldo 1973; Scott 1991). <u>In this light, "recognition" as a known type becomes involved with the social and political dynamics of "recog-nition" as acknowledgment or affirmation.</u> When collective agency and ancestral identity are at stake, the two may be inseparable.

To the extent that the construction and evaluation of one social iden-tity depends on the actions of others, that identity may be contestable. It is useful here to recall the dilemma that Hegel describes in his ac-count of Lordship and Bondage. It is not sufficient for the Lord to ob-tain recognition from the Bondsman. An other from whom all agency is removed is incapable of the real act of granting recognition. In such a case, any such recognition would seem ultimately to emanate from the Lord's own desires, and thus would suffer the same disabilities that An-derson describes for the possessor of charisma, who cannot appear to strive for power. At this point recognition takes on a dialectical mean-ing: the Lord wishes to see himself in the recognition of the Bondsman, whose recognition comes from seeing himself in the Lord. That is, the Bondsman can only fully acknowledge the free activity of the Lord to the extent that he himself acts freely. Yet the Bondsman's freedom is curtailed precisely by the Lord's own freedom, which the Lord asserts by limiting that of the Bondsman.

By referring to the dialectic of Lordship and Bondage, I do not intend to take on Hegel's metaphysical assumptions or become embroiled in the debates to which they have given rise. What interests me about his account is the way in which it captures an aspect of the dynamic and the quandary of agency as Anakalangese publicly construct it. In particular, the logic of this dialectic can be seen in the character of Anakalangese scenes of encounter. As has often been remarked, the gift can carry a profoundly ambivalent charge, simultaneously honoring and challenging the recipient. Even from a setting as different as nineteenth-century America, Emerson remarks "we do not quite forgive a giver" ([1844] 1983: 94). Often, as in Anakalang, one reason that the challenge in itself confers honor is because it presupposes that the other is the type of person who is worthy of challenging and able to respond (see Bourdieu [1972] 1977: 12). In anticipating a response, the challenge takes the first step in the elicitation of mutual recognition (a step that is not complete until further steps are taken, which in Anakalang is not a forgone conclusion). The dynamic of challenge and response places both parties in uncertain mutual dependence. Viewed from the side of the giver, to make too overwhelming a gift fails to create honor for oneself, because it removes the possibility of response from the recipient. From the side of the recipient, without the challenge offered by an initial gift, one lacks even the practical capacity to express one's agency through a response. To this extent, the most authoritative kinds of agency are out of the hands of any single party. They are not attributes of either party but are jointly (though not necessarily equally) constructed.

## FORM AND REFLECTION

Anakalangese representational practices take the form of highly stylized versions of the self/other dialectic. But why pay special attention to formal events? After all, if the self/other dialectic has any generality, it is found in all sorts of practices of the most ordinary sort, such as daily greetings, the dealings of parents with children, and even the cooperation among gardeners. Most of the empirical studies that have come out of interactive models have focused on the micropolitics of everyday, face-to-face encounters among small numbers of people (e.g., Goodwin 1990; Grimshaw 1990). This book asks, however, What does it mean to formalize interaction in major public events? What might the pragmatics and materiality of representations reveal about the relations between ritualized and more mundane activities?

One common effect of formal frames is to induce self-consciousness (Bateson [1955] 1972). They provoke people to be aware of rules to be followed (and thus of the repeatability of past acts), of behavior to avoid (and thus of possible consequences), and of the disjunction between representation and represented. If the sorts of self-reference that formal action brings about were no more than a set of official propositions or normalizing imperatives, however, they would be a very poor guide to the full range of things people do, fear, and desire. To create a frame often implies something about what is outside the frame as well. In Anakalang, for example, to use ritual speech is, among other things, to display the fact that you are *not* speaking in colloquial styles. In the process, the formal frame attempts to give meaning to, confine, or transform what it *excludes* (not just colloquial speech but, as will become apparent, everyday labor, female and youthful speakers, the marketplace, even the state). In their self-referentiality, Anakalangese formal events resemble the Elizabethan theater in which the "distinction between the theatre and the world . . . was not one that went without saying; on the contrary, it was constantly said" (Greenblatt [1988] 1994: 514). By insisting too much, as it were, the frame invites the watcher to imagine its vulnerability to breaking and to appreciate the difficulty of sustaining it.

Anakalangese scenes of encounter dramatize certain ideas about the nature of the self/other dialectic. In particular, this takes the form of objectification and self-reference, persistently speaking, by both explicit and implicit means, of "what is going on here" and "who is doing it." In its public and formal character, this self-reference is not simply a guide for self-understanding. Anakalangese scenes of encounter take place before the evaluating gaze of a wider world of living contemporaries and even the dead. It is under this gaze that the two senses of "recognition" come together. There are many ways to respond to the challenges of any given exchange, but they are evaluated, in part, with reference to shared ideas about proper ways of acting. The politics of Anakalangese interaction are not simply a matter of gift and counter-gift, performance and counterperformance. They also make constant, often contested, and never unproblematically secured, reference to the ancestral authority that they invoke.[11]

To invoke the authority of ancestral types of action presents a host of problems. For one thing, ancestors, however "present" they may be in some sense, are not "here" in the same way as the living performers (although in what ways they are absent will vary according to local ontologies; Anakalangese, for example, are not subject to possession by ancestral spirits as some people are), nor is their authority invested in the living as the law in a judge at the bench. When Anakalangese act *like* ancestors, they know they have not (entirely) *become* ancestors. This places a great deal of weight on the ability of their acts to shape the context in which they occur. This ability, which is never guaranteed, is a function of several dimensions of the activity. For one thing, as concrete actions, they impose material and organizational requirements on people. As I will suggest below, in discussing "indexicality," these requirements can neither be fully separated from nor entirely encompassed within the semiotic character of actions. To be fully authoritative and efficacious, participants strive to be taken by others as replicating the *forms* (ritual speech, ceremonial exchange, certain structures of performance) created by the ancestors. To this extent, ritualized action is indeed mimetic, as in the Durkheimian view, but the mimetic quality alone is insufficient to account for its power. Ritual also, for example, contains a language of self-reference that presupposes that participants act on their *historical* ties to the ancestral sources of authority. These ties are the actual links of inheritance, transferral, or even conquest by which people lay claim to the knowledge and possessions with which they are able to act. When most successful, ritual performance works by a circular logic in which it creatively *brings about* a context and set of identities that it portrays as *already* existing. But, as I argue, this outcome is fraught with both logical dilemmas and practical hazards, and it cannot be understood by looking at its efficacy and successes alone. It is perhaps only in highly legalistic frameworks that people can easily distinguish between conventional effects (oaths of office, wedding vows) and causal outcomes (good harvests, healthy children). When Anakalangese engage in "speech acts," the potentials for performative infelicities and material misfortunes go hand in hand.

## CAUSATION AND SIGNIFICATION

The interactive model asserts that if representational acts are to endow people with authority, those acts and actors must be recognized by others—as true to form, and as proper to who those actors really are. It is this combination of sociality with meaning, and the alternative to

Machiavellian or Hobbesian models of power that it seems to provide, that leads both Anderson and Geertz to place such great weight on the content of representations. Yet their recurrent parenthetical allusions to "trafficking" and other offstage machinations lend to both accounts a sense of incompleteness. If we are to take seriously the power of representational practice, and if this power is not to vanish the moment people (men and women, juniors and seniors, experts and laity, nobles and dependents, Christians and ancestral ritualists) differ in their points of view or their beliefs, it might be fruitful to seek a more dialectical relation between signs and socioeconomic circumstances. Such is the complex web that links representation and resources, that the former cannot be reduced simply to being a reflection of or disguise for the latter. A first element in this dialectic is provided by the intersection of causation and signification in semiotics. This asks us to look not just at content but at form as well.

The effectiveness of signs, whether verbal or material, depends in part on *how* people take them to signify. Some of the implications of how they signify can be shown by way of Peirce's semiotic trichotomy of icon, index, and symbol. These terms distinguish among the ways in which a given sign can be connected to that which it signifies. An icon, such as a diagram or painting, signifies by virtue of an imputed resemblance to the original.[12] An index signifies by virtue of a real relationship of causation or contiguity to its object. In Peirce's example, a bullet hole in the wall indexes the fact of a gun actually having been fired. The index finger serves its function by pointing in the real direction in question. A symbol signifies only by virtue of a social convention, as in what Saussurean linguists call the "arbitrary" relation between words and their referents.

Icon, index, and symbol thus are not simply properties of signs as things in the world. They reflect our own understanding of how any given sign works. This is not a mere epistemological quibble. Part of the authority and power of signs of social status or divine power lies in how people take those signs to be related to their objects. For example, one way of interpreting the efficacy that Geertz imputes to Balinese representations is in terms of iconism. It might be that the mimetic, that is, iconic, relation between ritual, palace, cosmos, and society can be explained as manifestations of a single animating source. But in that case, a convinced audience understands that iconism to be causally produced: it should not, for example, be seen to be the result of shrewd political calculation. Like the resemblance between a photograph and its subject, *iconism* can be persuasive in such a case because it *indexes* (what Balinese take to be) an existential connection between sign and signified.[13]

As this example suggests, indexes are of particular importance in linking representations to their contexts and conditions of possibility. Like the signs of charismatic authority, they seem "natural," that is, not the result of intentional action.[14] So, one effect may be that the more natural a sign of charisma seems, the more irresistible the authority of its bearer, to the extent that people take it to manifest that person's real essence. Conversely, to the extent that people recognize that a sign is a symbol, they may be more prone to seek out the intentions and agency of a sign *user*. At the same time, some circumstances (mishearings, puns, the role distance induced by official jargon, the aura of a sacred vocabulary) can foreground the fact that conventional signs are drawn from sources that lie beyond the speaker's intentions. As I will argue in this book, in this distance between speaker and speech may lie elements not only of authority's sources but also of its elusiveness.

## SPEECH AND POLITICAL ECONOMY

At the practical and conceptual base of authoritative actions Anakalangese insist on a simple but critical requirement: words and things must be transacted together. The requirement is a local peculiarity, but the problems it seeks to master, of weaving together and containing power, value, authority, performative efficacy, material resources, and communication, are widespread concomitants of representational practice. In an effort to untangle this set of problems, I have tried to keep speech and valuable goods and the performances by which they are transacted within a single field of vision. As a result, much of this book is concerned with both ritual speech and ceremonial exchange. These are topics with long histories in anthropology that have usually been treated as distinct fields of study. Both ritual speech and ceremonial exchange are especially prominent in contemporary Sumbanese societies. Detailed studies of speech (see especially Forth 1988 in Rindi; Hoskins 1988 in Kodi; Kuipers 1986, 1988, 1990 in Weyewa) and exchange (Hoskins 1993a, 1993b in Kodi; Mitchell 1981 in Wanukaka) are now available. My own project is enormously aided by this wealth of recent research. What the present book proposes to contribute to these twin fields of study is an exploration of the space *between* them.

To do so leads me to ask interpretive questions about the form and content of representational media and about the society within which they function. Consider, for instance, Macaulay's remark, somewhere, that "parliamentary government is government by speaking." If we look at the workings of parliamentary debate, we might ask a nested series of questions: How does rhetorical form contribute to the outcome of debates? What is it about Parliament that makes debate there powerful? What kind of agent and subject does the structure of Parliament presume and reproduce? What is it about the power of Parliament that makes some ways of talking more effective than others? And how does the power of Parliament differ from that of, say, the church, the throne, the army, or the stock exchange? A similar nested set of questions can be asked of material goods, whose economic value, semiotic meaning, and social power are not inherent but are functions, in part, of *how* they are transacted, held onto, put to use, and so forth. For this reason, partly ethnographic and partly theoretical in origin, I have chosen to speak of "representations" in this book, rather than signs, language, performance, exchange, or ritual. In particular, I wish to avoid privileging words or things or performances a priori. Rather, I am interested in their imbrications, ambiguities, and mutual tensions.

What the interactive model of a self/other dialectic introduces is the link between representation, action, and the presence of other persons. In particular, the role taken by the other party provides a crucial link between cultural expression and social organization. Addressed to audiences, given to recipients, eliciting interlocutors, representations both presuppose and give life to particular sorts of agents, kinds of beings, and forms of relationship. It is a sociology and a cosmology that provide us with an account of possible others and the terms under which representation can and must take place. It is local assumptions about the nature of representations that help determine how they work. The relation between the forms of representational media and their historical and material conditions of possibility provides us with access to the full range of powers to which representational practices aspire. But "context" is not simply a given background necessary for the interpretation of speech events or material transactions. Part of what is at stake in the dynamism of scenes of encounter is the ongoing business of reconfiguring the nature of the setting, event, and participants.

Anakalangese scenes of encounter articulate people's knowledge and skill with their social and economic resources. They do so in ways that entail and construct a public realm. The participants in an encounter act in full awareness of the fact that others, members of a wider social world, are watching and evaluating their deeds. This reflexive character of formal action depends on recognition, which exposes intentions to denial, thereby introducing an irreducibly political dynamic into representational practices. The very media of representation introduce elements of slippage into scenes of encounter. Words can be ambiguous, their authorship, efficacy, and pertinence disputed. Objects can be damaged, lost, diverted away from their rightful recipients, their value debated, their meanings confused. Alert to slippage and aware of the potential for cross-purposes within groups and the challenges between them, Anakalangese embark on even highly formal events with a sense of risk. But this vulnerability need not be mere happenstance, something that might be weeded out of a good depiction of how formal action works. Rather, I propose that formal action provides its own (albeit highly partial) account of this vulnerability: it does so not simply in order to control risk but also to *instigate* it. If action is real, it must be subject to failure. If it is valuable and powerful, it must display itself as overcoming failure. For all its formality, by placing so much weight on such problematic means, ritualized action contributes to as much as it constrains the gamble of action. This means we must pay careful attention to the *media* of representation—to the form of words, the shape of things, the ways in which words are spoken and gifts given, and who does what—as well as to the social and economic conditions for their possibility.

Over the course of this book I will explore how the iconic, indexical, and symbolic dimensions of representational practices—whether verbal, material, or performative—are crucial to their capacity to construct authority and give agents access to various sources of power. Representational practices work in complex ways to link the logical aspects of signification with the causal. To be valid, words must be spoken in tandem with material transactions. The efficacy of material goods rests both on their character as conventional signs and on their economic weight and practical utility—components whose relations are unstable. The requirement that words and things be transacted together means that the authority of speech and the economic power conveyed through goods should each index the other. But by virtue of simple causality, exchange also indexes the real presence of supporters and material goods in the background and all the political strategies, demographic accidents, and economic circumstances that that presence involves. Yet until strategy, demography, and economics are transformed through representational practice, they provide imperfect foundations for the authority or even identity of those who wield them. The meaning and value of objects are never reducible to the resources they index. The most powerful forms of representational practice hinge on the complex play between logical and causal relations and between what enters and what eludes signification. There is no reason in principle to draw from this the reductivist conclusion that political economy itself is either an efficient or a final cause of representations. The nexus of signification and causation suggests that we are not faced with a stark choice between two reductionisms, either (to rephrase Geertz 1980: 13) pomp serving power or power, pomp.

## THE DIFFICULTIES OF REPRESENTATION AND THE HAZARDS OF ENCOUNTER

The care with which anthropologists have shown the workings of rituals, exchange, and even hegemony has perhaps led them to overemphasize their efficacy. In Anakalang, representational practices are subject to the hazards of semiotic difficulty, economic weakness, political conflict, and ancestral ire. Like many ritualists, Anakalangese practitioners commonly describe their own actions as mere "shadows," incomplete remnants of the more powerful capacities of their ancestors. Perfect ritual knowledge, truly authoritative speech, genuine wealth, and exchange partners who never fail you are always out of reach in the near or distant past. This perception at once insulates an idealized past from the corrosive effects of current imperfection and contributes to a broader vision of time, as a continual falling away from a better world. But Anakalangese are also aware of more immediate sources of hazard, such as what James Scott (1985) calls the footdragging resistance of subordinates, as well as the arrogance of superiors, the obduracy of affines, the stinginess of allies, and the obscurity of ancestors. Their awareness of shortcomings is in part a way of recognizing the temporal dimension of action, in which neither other people's memory of past events nor outcomes in the future are settled. The forms their awareness can take are important to how they undertake ritual actions.[15]

To the extent that they find themselves compelled to represent themselves to one another, Anakalangese must be concerned with the social force of signs, the effort to control that force, and the slippage to which signs are prone. The difficulty of representation seems to localize the more diffuse uncertainties of politics and even the contingencies of life in general. But this concern is also grounded in the difficulties that ritualized media impose on action. Ritual speech, for example, creates authority by enacting icons of imputed ancestral originals. By appealing to absent sources of authority, however, those who use ritual speech wield an agency that is ambiguously divided between the living and the dead. They cannot claim full authorship of the words they speak.[16] The materiality of objects and the social constraints on circulation prevent even the wealthiest Anakalangese from full mastery over the goods they transact. The relative autonomy of both verbal and material signs is at once a source of their authority and a threat to those who use them. This threat is concretized in people's anxieties both about ancestral vengeance for errors and the fact that political outcomes are unforeseeable. These anxieties seem to reflect a more general quandary of agency, arising out of people's ongoing effort to take on an authority that rests on the skillful weaving together of tactical moves and ancestral models.

Ritual speech exemplifies the problem of agency because of the way it foregrounds the ambiguous authorship of spoken words: they must be attributable at once to the speaker and the ancestors (see chapter 4). As a result, it is especially prone to what Austin ([1955] 1975: 14) calls the "infelicities" of performative language, some implications of which are drawn out by Derrida ([1972] 1982). Performatives seem to express the intentions of speakers (it is not just anyone, but *I* who hereby wed thee). But their institutional force depends on certain conventions ("I hereby do thee wed" is by social and legal convention how one weds somebody). That is, they rely on an inherent property of language, what Derrida calls its "iterability." By virtue of being conventional, they must be repeatable by other speakers on other occasions (I cannot wed thee if the act of wedding someone is unique and never to be done by and to others as well). But insofar as performative words can be repeated by others, they can be said (or, for that matter, heard) out of context, quoted, or used in a "nonserious" manner (say, jokingly or in a play). By accentuating these properties, ritual speech compels speakers to be aware that their words are not fully in their control but are vulnerable to misunderstanding, misattribution, or misfire. Although this vulnerability is placed in the foreground by the particular attributes of ritual speech, it expresses the more general characteristics of representation. Recall that Mead privileges language because of its peculiarly intersubjective character, that, in part, it is speech that allows us to hear ourselves as others hear us. Derrida ([1967] 1973: 86–87) also draws attention to this property of speech in his particular version of the claim that language cannot be reduced to being the outward expression of an inward intention to convey meanings. Rather, the intelligibility of representations depends on having the character of "writing" ([1967] 1973: 93), on being detachable from particular speakers and acts of speaking. To the extent that people's intentional acts are mediated by representation, they are liable to encounter various effects of the gap between intention and representational resources. Among these effects is ambiguity about agency. In everyday talk these effects are rarely at issue. The smooth flow of conversation relies on the participants sharing certain default assumptions about context, authorship, and cooperation (Sacks, Schegloff, and Jefferson 1974; Duranti and Goodwin 1992). When ambiguity does obtrude, it is subject to "repair" (Schegloff, Jefferson, and Sacks 1977). But the highly marked character of ritual speech works to disrupt the background assumptions of ordinary interaction. The quandaries for authoritative agency induced by its dependence on ancestral warrants arise from the play among the presence of representations, the absence of their imputed origins, and dependence on others to recognize their claims. In the scenes of encounter, these take the form of problems about where to attribute the authorship of words, the responsibility for acts, and the true sources of material goods. They may be registered in pervasive tensions, wary alertness, and especially in the aura of danger remarked on by many observers of ritual (on Sumba, for example, see Hoskins 1993b: 229). The recalcitrance of representations is one way that people experience the fact that they are embedded in a world of language, institutions, economic circumstances, and social others that are, historically and logically, already given before any particular intention to act. That the most public and consequential acts in Anakalangese society center on this very recalcitrance is of critical significance, for it entangles the intrinsic difficulties of representation with the hazards of politics.

To understand formal action, it is crucial to see what it actually excludes and how, implicitly, it constructs the alternatives, the failures and threats against which it poses itself. Precisely because ritual grounds the assertion of authority in representations—which imply a gap between representational form and represented substance—and insists on the consequentiality of correct forms and risk of bringing on misfortunes, it is haunted by "the possibility that something could go wrong" (Dirks [1992] 1994: 498). In Anakalang, this possibility is registered from the start in the emphatic self-reference by which formal action is framed and set apart from the rest of life, and the participants' attendant caution and alertness to error and misfire. By focusing on practice, I wish to preserve both the identity and the disjunction between representation and represented. For instance, when Anakalangese act like ancestors, they do not mistake themselves for them. Fostering this tension between identity and disjunction, like that between inside and outside the frame, formality *itself* lends a sense of vulnerability to the actions it undertakes.

This book argues that scenes of encounter as exercises of power are prone to certain hazards. These are functions, in part, of the vulnerability imposed by the need to interact with others. They also arise from the semiotic and pragmatic problems of coordinating several aspects of power and authority. This problem of coordination depends in turn on relations of cooperation (such as that between husbands and wives) and domination (such as that between masters and slaves) as well as on characteristics of representation itself. The challenge of coordinating power and authority folds the difficulties of ritual media back into the realm of practical politics. I want to keep the authority constructed in speech, the legitimacy founded in exchange, and the power of goods in play without reducing them all to a single dimension. It is important to hold in view the relative autonomy of knowledge, economic strength, and political skill. The most talented speaker cannot act effectively without exchange valuables. The wealthiest cattle owner cannot act legitimately without supporters. The highest-born nobleman cannot go into the public eye without productive ties to sisters and wives. In the constant effort to keep these several dimensions of power and authority working together lies the continuing dynamism of formal action in Anakalang, as it presents both a challenge to the ambitious and a resource for the weak.

At the extremes lie rupture, domination, or dissolution. Historical memory combines with ritual drama to make violence or dishonor possible outcomes of negotiation, at least in the imagination. To be sure, warfare is no longer likely, and actual violence uncommon. But scenes of encounter evoke the possibilities and threats in a form of play that can tread close to actuality. Nothing happens mechanically. In Anakalang, as in Algeria (Bourdieu [1972] 1977: 10), scenes of encounter are always "arousing mock quarrels that are always on the verge of becoming real ones," their art consisting in being "'carried along' by the game without being 'carried away' *beyond* the game, as happens when a mock fight gets the better of the fighters." But at times the mock fight *does* get the better of the fighters (Bateson ([1955] 1972), shattering the frame altogether, a possibility that is important to the very meaning of the frame.

Hostile rupture is one sort of frame-breaking outcome. Another is the possibility of total domination. Exchange is haunted by the ambiguity between threat and solidarity, and can transform a relation of cooperative alliance into one of domination.

The notion of hazard poses two claims against functionalism. One is that the articulation of ritual with political economy is not in terms of goals: rites do not function under directives from economic interests any more than they are the sole creators of those interests. But political economy forms one critical condition of possibility for people's most authoritative actions and for their vulnerability to circumstance. Moreover, although those actions cannot be reduced to being reflections or mystifications of political economy, economy is directly implicated in the very meaningfulness of actions through the causal logic of indexicality. Second, the smooth functioning of rites is not necessarily desirable. As a result, rites need to risk failure, the game must be capable of carrying away the players. The dramatization of risk provides a fundamental, but neither unique nor unchallengeable, component of the meaning of being rich, poor, affine, dependent, ancestor, or living descendant. The structure of performance seems to induce participants to imagine a number of alternatives and risks, one effect of which is to portray social interaction as a fundamentally risk-laden undertaking and a great achievement (see Lévi-Strauss [1949] 1969: 48).

In the end, hazard is not only an actual condition of interaction, or only an idiom by which Anakalangese can interpret hierarchy and domination, although it can be both. Through imagining the hazards of formal interaction, Anakalangese have a way of naming the apparent paradoxes that supposedly permanent ancestral identities require constant work to sustain and that self-assertion (whether of ambitious individuals or of entire clans) puts one in dependence on others. The element of risk, actual and imagined, should remind us not only of the limits that mediation imposes on the legitimate exercise of power but also of the importance of the unintended consequences of action. The representation of challenges is in part an effort to master contingency by portraying outcomes as accomplishments. But the same effort in practice exposes players to *actual* risks, not all of which can be subsumed under an account of their intended goals or self-awareness. These risks provide some of the fracture lines—such as those between wealth and rank, solidarity and domination, artistic performance and coercive force, commodity and ancestral valuable, textual tradition and verbal power— that may emerge in different historical circumstances. The fracture lines

open up a series of alternatives, as some Anakalangese discover liberation while others find marginality or oppression in the various forms of
"modernity" increasingly on offer. If we are to understand the shape
and effects of historical experience in places like Anakalang, we must
seek out the existing lines of tension they expose. If Anakalang is any
guide, the representation of power at once reflects and displaces the hazards to which agency is prone. The hazards of representation, in turn,
must be in question wherever we think we have found power on, and in,
display.

# CHAPTER TWO

# Geography, History, and Sociality

In 1987, I faced a delicate fieldwork situation, as a family with which I had good relations became embroiled in a rapidly escalating feud with their affines. Since there were times when I was the only participant who was on speaking terms with all parties, I began to feel a bit like the narrator of *The Great Gatsby*, privy to the secret griefs of wild, unknown men. Indeed, I was faced with the ultimate hermeneutic test, when people on each side would ask *me* to explain what the others could have meant by various moves. It is not false modesty to confess that my bewilderment exceeded theirs, since—my woefully inadequate cultural competence aside—I alone knew how little their respective accounts agreed on even simple matters of chronology. As in many quarrels, each side's narrative alone presented a coherence that the two together lacked.

Tensions were running high between Ama Koda and his wife's father, Ubu Elu, and the head of Ubu Elu's own principal *yera* (his wife's natal family), Ubu Tara. Nonetheless, they continued to fulfill their fundamental obligations to one another. Yera are owed respect by their *ngàba wini* (the groups into which their sisters and daughters have married). Ngàba wini are materially indebted to their yera, from whom their own wives and mothers have come, as the source of lifeblood that flows only through women. In structural terms, matters were quite clear: Ama Koda defers to Ubu Tara. In practice, matters are complicated by the cross-cutting dimension of wealth. As it happens, Ama Koda was richer than Ubu Tara, so much so that one of Ubu Tara's sons was Ama Koda's herdsman and thus virtually his dependent. One demand for deference was met by another, both exacerbated by the vigorous claims of all concerned to bear noble rank.

Ubu Tara knew he was dying (probably of witchcraft), and as the culminating effort in his assertions of status, he had carved a large stone tomb for himself. With expensive feasting and ritual, he had this tomb dragged from the quarry to his hilltop village. By convention, atop the stone were two bamboo poles from each of which hung a valuable textile known as the "banner," a gift from his own principal yera (see fig. 1). Ubu Tara's family had held a conference to make arrangements for the tomb dragging and accompanying exchanges. They had not invited Ama Koda, despite the fact—so Ama Koda claims—that they can't manage anything without his organizational ability and material support. He did attend, however, along with Ubu Elu, at the time of the dragging itself. But when they arrived in Ubu Tara's village, they were received no better than any other guest, with betel and then coffee, very politely—"as if we were strangers, in fact, as if they were thinking, 'I hope they're not here to ask us for something.' When they walked by us, it was with heads held high, like deer." Ama Koda and Ubu Elu were so offended that they left right after eating. As they did so, one of Ubu Tara's sons leaped up onto the tombstone and took the two banners there (which had been removed from the bamboo poles and neatly folded up) and handed one each to Ubu Elu and to Ama Koda. Arriving back home, Ama Koda opened his and discovered that he had only half a textile. (Textiles are woven as a pair of symmetrical pieces that are then stitched together along the long side.) On asking around, it turned out that during the tomb dragging, the banner had snagged on a tree branch, and someone had cut off the tangled half. Once folded in the village, this was no longer apparent. Now Ubu Elu threw Ama Koda's cloth to the floor and ordered a child to take it back to Ubu Tara's village with the message 'I'm not yet so poor that I need a bit of cloth to cover my loins!' The boy later returned with the message that Ubu Tara's sons would come the next day to make up for it. The story continued to unfold—at one point, it reached comical heights of absurdity as a boy was sent back and forth between two distant villages with a horse that neither party would accept from the other—until several months later an exchange of horses, pigs, and gold, mediated by ritual speakers, finally made peace between the two sides.

The first thing I want to observe about this incident is the question of

Figure 1. Dragging the top piece of a tomb from quarry to village. Two cloths raised on bamboo poles serve as "banners" (near Sotu, June 1986).

intentionality. When I suggested that Ubu Tara's son was certainly unaware that the cloth was ripped—to have given it knowingly would be both unmotivated and outrageous—Ama Koda rejected the suggestion out of hand. This was entirely characteristic on two grounds, first, the going assumption that there are no accidents and thus that the world is full of signs; and second, that others are so inscrutable and potentially hostile that plausibility—at least what I took to be plausibility—is not part of an argument.

The next thing I want to observe is the role of vicissitudes to which material signs are prone. Ama Koda correctly placed great semiotic weight on the physical condition of the cloth, but that physical condition was subject to nonsemiotic happenstances. Note as well the rapid series of roles through which the piece of cloth moved: by turns, yera's conventional obligation to ngàba wini, figurative banner, physical encumbrance tangled in a tree, token of regard meant to placate an irate guest, vehicle of insult, and, finally, metaphoric rag of poverty and rejected gift. In practical terms, this sequence of roles illuminates three things about objects as social media: that they are readily separated from the moment of the transaction, and with it, the words, gestures, and other critical aspects of context; that they are available for multiple interpretations; and that, however semiotically we may treat them, they remain material objects and thus vulnerable to all that can happen to things.

This would be so obvious as to go without saying were it not for a curious artifact of the polarization between symbolic and materialist approaches to society in the 1960s and 1970s, a tendency to reduce objects to being either economic and utilitarian goods or semiotic vehicles. In the following chapters I will suggest that both the value and the possible interpretations of objects are underdetermined. I am talking about underdetermination, not indeterminacy: objects are *not* open to any arbitrarily imposed set of meanings. Rather I want to stress two things.  First, meanings and values are not inherent in objects but are functions of practices of interpretation and exchange. This means they are neces-  sarily caught up in the uncertainties of social action. Second, the very materiality of objects means they are not fully arbitrary signs in any Saussurean sense. Their very materiality makes a difference both in the sources of their meanings and in their destinations, such that they are subject to shifting physical, economic, and semiotic contexts. This means that it matters how societies invest themselves in things—which in turn, I will argue below, requires an account of how they speak of and to themselves with words.

The variety of ways in which Anakalangese can see status, power, wealth, and the meaning of relations to be, at least in principle, mutually implicated suggests that the social power of exchange cannot be located fully in labor, use, or market value, or in iconism or conventional symbolism. To the extent that value, utility, and sign function are involved in practices and events, they are subject to the effects of economics, politics, and even disease and drought. They do not in themselves provide us with a fixed place outside of and secure from the dynamics of social action; nor do they provide omnipotent human agents with fully malleable media.

The power and value of exchange objects are to be sought at the intersection of their everyday uses, their character as signs, and their potential roles in a range of economic and performance contexts. Being underdetermined as media of value and meaning, they call for speech, interpretive practices, and political strategies. This means that objects, which can always take on what Grice (1957) calls "natural meaning" (signs based on causality, as a tear means the cloth was snagged in a tree), should be actively transformed into bearers of "non-natural meaning" (intentional signs, as a torn cloth means an insult): it prompts Anakalangese to view the physical world as overflowing with evidence of purposes. When Ama Koda received half a cloth, he privileged the semiotics of intentional meanings over the "natural" meanings of material happenstance and assumed the worst. In sending back the cloth, he demanded further signs to restore the honor that others would never acknowledge had been lost. As the tensions escalated, cloth alone ceased to serve to bind these wounds, and the ante rose, until gold had to enter the fray. When gold entered, it could travel only by way of full performance and the poetic speech of intermediaries. Once violence threatened, no one would dare rely on the capacity of things to speak for themselves.

## ORDER AND REPRESENTATION AS
## ETHNOGRAPHIC PROBLEMS

The feud between Ama Koda and Ubu Tara is exemplary in several respects. For one thing, it encapsulates the physical and semiotic mobility and the density of objects and hints at the critical role played by speech in the effort to control them. The story thus introduces topics that I will explore in much of the rest of this book. In addition, the conflict introduces the tension and occasional threat of violence that pervade Anakalangese life. As this not unusual story makes evident, the tension enters even into the ritualized solidarity between close affines bound by that most intimate of alliances, matrilateral cross-cousin marriage, the union between the children of a brother and sister. Yet this kind of marriage and affinal solidarity in general are celebrated by normative discourses in Anakalang as the ideal practical embodiment of the cosmological harmonies expressed in myth and ritual. This is evident in another story, equally characteristic of this part of Sumba, to which I want to juxtapose the feud of Ama Koda and Ubu Tara.

Lois Onvlee's ([1949] 1977) description of the ritual exchanges for building an irrigation conduit in Mangili, east Sumba, is a classic in the tradition of Durkheim and Mauss, analyzing an elegant system of paired terms of verbal and visual metaphors that align exchange, gender, marriage, cosmology, and agricultural production. In Mangili, two channels, one "male" and one "female," distribute a river's waters between two complexes of rice fields. The female channel requires two wooden conduits, which, following a recursive logic of oppositions, are in turn "female" and "male." When the female conduit has to be replaced, the group that owns the fields it serves must obtain the log from their wife givers. They do so by replicating the stages and exchanges of a marriage, and the new log is introduced into the irrigation system as a bride.

These exchanges involve gendered gifts of female ear pendants and male ornamental chains that represent the rice fields and the irrigation channels that nourish them. At the same time, the conduit is also an occasion to renew bonds between affines, for "these groups are determined to come together" ([1949] 1977: 161). All metaphorical levels are woven together, for marriage and the irrigation system are both "but reflections and manifestations of the cosmic forces which make all life possible. . . . So is life served" ([1949] 1977: 160).

Events like that described by Onvlee were probably not rare in east Sumba in the 1930s, and I witnessed very similar procedures in Anakalang in the 1990s. Such pervasive metaphorical links among cosmological beliefs, ritual activities, and structural order have made East Nusa Tenggara a rich source for scholarship in the tradition of Durkheim and Mauss (e.g., Forth 1981; Fox 1980; Geirnaert-Martin 1992a; Lewis 1988; Needham 1980; Traube 1986; van Wouden [1935] 1968). This tradition forms an essential background to any understanding of the region. But although the cosmological analysis of ritual is necessary, the story of Ama Koda and Ubu Tara suggests that it is not sufficient. I have begun by juxtaposing feud and ritual to suggest that nothing social happens automatically. If normative expectations and ceremonial behavior do not simply manifest an existing, underlying harmony or just work to control potential disruptions, then the existence of public representations cannot be taken for granted. Ama Koda's feud should suggest that even building the Mangili conduits doubtlessly required efforts whose outcomes were not foreordained.

It is, of course, not surprising to find that ritual and feud coexist, but anthropologists (at least) are often inclined to dwell on one at the expense of the other, situating the two at different levels of analysis: to see, for example, disorder as a contingent disruption, or attribute the appearance of order to political hegemony. But as I will argue over the next several chapters, the representation of order and the agonistic quality of social existence may not be joined only by happenstance. Indeed, the very media of order seem to to conjure up their own alternatives. In Sumba, present misfortunes are often attributed to ritual errors in the past. Thus each act in the present bears the potential for future misfortune: however much they may celebrate formality, Anakalangese remain aware of the sanctions for missteps. When their ventures do not fully succeed, this is not simply a matter of extrinsic politics, or inadequate fulfillment of a cultural mandate: the perception of alternative outcomes, of risks taken, can itself be part of the meaning and powers of action.

This dimension of collective representations becomes all the more important when shared *practices* unite people, such as Christian and non-Christian Sumbanese, whom historical circumstances have led to divergent *beliefs*.

In tandem with the problem of order is that of sociality. The picture of Mangili that Onvlee paints is one in which groups are driven by a desire to form social bonds. But why, if the desire is so strong, should forming bonds require so much effort, have "demanded people's constant attention" (Onvlee [1949] 1977: 151), and produced such metaphorical elaboration? In the formal scenes of encounter that I discuss in this book, affines such as Ama Koda and Ubu Tara face each other in highly public situations, and approach each other as if they were strangers who must traverse a vast social and semiotic distance before they can recognize one another. Their formality casts into relief a more general tone of caution that is common in Sumbanese views of sociality. Listening to other accounts of Sumba, we can hear rumors of similar suspicions and tensions. In east Sumba, for example, people see interaction as "difficult, demanding, and full of pitfalls" (Forth 1988: 134). So too, in west Sumba, a simple social call is likely to provoke the thoughts "what opportunities, and what threats, does this scene of quiet hospitality portend?" (Mitchell 1988: 64).

More pointedly still, Anakalangese often use metaphors of warfare when they talk about marriage negotiations and compare words to blows given and received (see chapter 6, note 9). Yet people who enter into these negotiations usually know each other well, are bound by a thick weave of ties, and may be neighbors or frequent visitors, and their social and kinship identities are well-established: little should appear to be problematic. If scenes of encounter seek to overcome a social, perhaps even an ontological, distance, it is often a distance that they have also constructed. Public actions in Anakalang are carried out as if people continually had to make peace with one another, and in fact the outcomes are not fully predictable. This is a familiar characteristic of formal exchange, in which, as Mauss ([1925] 1990: 81–82) puts it, "men approached one another in a curious frame of mind, one of fear and exaggerated hostility," for in "segmented" societies, "it is always with strangers that one 'deals,' even if allied to them."[1] But Anakalangese exchange conjoins two aspects of material transactions, predicated on two opposed social conditions, for alongside high formality exists a contradictory element of haggling. Formality presupposes social distance across which groups approach each other with wariness. In contrast,

Figure 2. Women dance the *negu* in the village plaza between stretches of oratory by men (Lakoka, October 1986).

bargaining presumes an underlying condition of political order, and negotiators therefore "feel free to risk the conflict inherent in barter without invoking all the danger, magic, prestige and hierarchy that go with ceremonial exchange" (Hart 1986: 648). Conjoining the two, Anakalangese often depict themselves as forming relations with people who, even when long-standing intimates, are at least potentially, and within the frame of performance, strangers. This does not mean that exchange functions in order to suppress a prior Hobbesian state of warfare: rather, the very act of dramatizing peace seems constructed as if to summon such alternatives to mind. As strangers communicating across a figurative distance, affines must tell each other who they are and what they are doing. The heightened *display* of their desire for union is both predicated on and suggestive of the possibility of its absence, and places great weight on mediating representations.

## GEOGRAPHY AND HISTORY

That in Anakalang social identities and relations, and even speech performances, are mediated by material things means that they are subject to the constraints and scarcity to which objects are prone. The production and consumption of objects have consequences for their social

and semiotic possibilities and call for a brief introduction to their geographic and historical context. In the context of Southeast Asia, the two
things most immediately striking about Sumba are its dryness and its
low population density. The visitor arriving from Bali at the port or air-
field in Waingapu, East Sumba, is likely to be stunned by the vast empty
landscape, the deeply eroded ravines, the sun-blasted grasses, the lone-
liness of the isolated hamlets in a landscape resembling parts of the
American West. The island lies in the rainshadow of Australia and is
one of the driest spots in the Indonesian archipelago. Especially forbid-
ding are the grasslands of the north coast and eastern half of the island,
amid which are scattered gardens of maize, cassava, taro, and other tubers. The limestone terrain soaks up unreliable rains and conceals underground rivers that mysteriously surface in some spots only to disappear again in others. To the west and south, the landscape grows lusher,
settlements larger and closer together. The most favored regions are able
to sustain wet rice crops, which, lacking riverine irrigation sources, are
vulnerable to drought. The resulting economic marginality is matched
by social isolation: Sumba, especially the interior, has been off the main
historical trade routes that follow the chain of islands to its north and
remains marginal to this day. Although in the late 1980s Sumba received several airplane flights a week, most of the island remained out of
reach of the national television network, radios were scarce, and news-
papers were not readily available (Corner 1989: 179).

At Anakalang's geographic, economic, and social heart lies a flat valley, about nine kilometers long, of rice fields and pastures, surrounded
by rolling grass and forest-covered hills.[2] Sparsely populated outlying regions stretch to the southern coast, providing access to important forest
and ocean resources (Witkamp 1912: 12–13). As a settlement frontier
(Reid 1988: 25–26), they also provide an escape valve, for by reputation
this is a zone of former slaves, horse thieves, and witches. Compared to
the denser regions of Indonesia, Anakalang feels little population pressure on the land, to which virtually no one lacks some access.[3] This has
two important consequences for contemporary forms of power. First,
until very recently there has been little out-migration (Corner 1989:
190). This means the labor of young men and women remains available
for local appropriation, and their marriage prospects are subject to exchange and the performance of ritual speech and thus to the powers
those activities grant their elders.

Second, because the principal means of subsistence remain in local
hands, Anakalang has weak ties to the cash economy. Although cattle and horses possess great potential monetary value, their role in

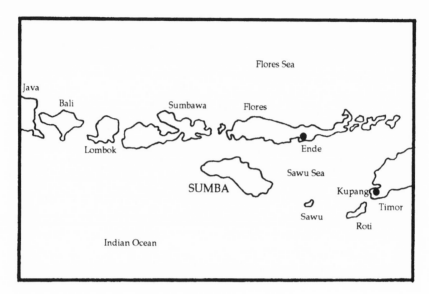

Map 1.  Sumba and the islands of East Nusa Tenggara.

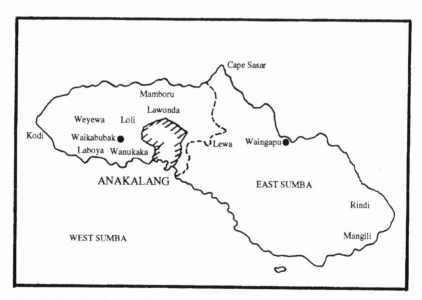

Map 2.  The island of Sumba.

exchange imposes serious barriers on sale.[4] There are few sources of wages, and most Anakalangese see the sale of labor as degrading.[5] The other main source of cash is small-scale production of coconuts, coffee, betel and areca, candlenut, chickens, eggs, vegetables, and clay pots. For trade in most of these goods, people rely on a semiweekly market that has been operating in central Anakalang since the 1950s, supplemented by a small cluster of shops owned by Indonesians identified as "Chinese" or "Muslims" (Riekerk 1934: 94; Versluys 1941: 438). Despite the appeal of the market as a place of gossip and novelty, Anakalangese tend to view trade with great ambivalence. In contrast to the dramatic encounters of ritual and exchange, the market is the realm of mundane necessity and calendrical regularity.[6] Above all, many men and women hold in aristocratic disdain the open display of self-interest inherent in buying and selling.

Given the obvious power exerted by colonial regimes, postcolonial states, spreading mass media, and the ongoing percolation of world markets, it has become common to describe "local" exercises of power in places like Anakalang as forms of resistance to external forces. To dwell exclusively on resistance, however, can become reductivistic: the state is only one of the things Anakalangese are likely to have on their minds. In particular, my concern with the conceptual and practical grounds of representation leads me to pay particular attention to the sources of powers and authority to which Anakalangese lay claim when they face *one another*. I will discuss their historical circumstances here primarily in reference to the current stakes in scenes of encounter. What makes the representational practices I observed in the 1980s and 1990s viable is not a state of isolation but a reconfiguration of the terms of power within which discourse and transactions operate. The powers of representation take their meaning *in part* by contrast to other powers, such as administration, finance, and violence, that remain prerogatives of the state. Nonetheless, representational practices are not simply empty symbols or survivals of a more authentic or self-contained past, remnants left after the real thing has been removed. They possess an enormous ability to mediate authority, power, and social identity within the spheres of action most available to Anakalangese.

Geographic and economic factors permit the relative self-sufficiency that shields many Anakalangese from the more direct effects of their articulation with a larger economic system. The political economy of cattle ownership, which I will describe below, also encourages cultural conservatism, especially but not exclusively, among the wealthiest Anakalangese. In much of Indonesia, the state is an overwhelming presence,

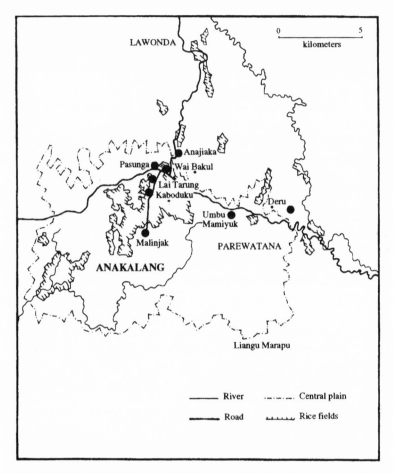

Map 3. Central Anakalang and Parewatana, showing sites mentioned in text. (Adapted from U.S. Army Map Service, 1943, "Netherlands East Indies, Southern Zone Grid, 75/XLVII," reproduced from a Dutch map dated 1937.)

but from local perspectives in Anakalang, it appears most prominently in the form of partially enforceable directives, less effective exhortations, and a trickle of development funds that flow as patronage through the hands of local officials. This allows many people to experience the state either as a distant, potentially benign patron or as a distinct language and discursive style (Indonesian and certain kinds of bureaucratic speech associated with it; see Keane in press). In addition, the heavily centralized structure of government contributes to the perceived autonomy of local politics. A cornerstone of the New Order regime has been the concept of the floating mass, according to which rural districts are to be kept away from the distractions and disruptions of politics in order to devote themselves to production (Hefner 1990: 243). Because local government serves primarily to transmit directives from the top down, it can seem to be more a sinecure than a field for independent action. Anakalangese eager to exert power are likely to direct their efforts into the local politics of exchange.

Because of its poor natural resources and distance from main trade routes, Sumba has undergone relatively little economic exploitation by outsiders in either colonial or postcolonial periods. As a result, to this day few Anakalangese have been forced to rely on the market as either producers or consumers, and therefore few are heavily dependent on government-supplied infrastructure and middlemen. Before this century, Sumba's main resources (primarily horses, a dwindling supply of sandalwood, and slaves) attracted only sporadic, if occasionally violent, intervention from the outside.[7] Until the Dutch suppressed the local interisland slave trade at the turn of the twentieth century, the northern coasts were especially vulnerable to periodic raids from neighboring islands. Seafaring Muslims from neighboring islands supplied markets in Bali, Java, and points beyond with slaves from Sumba (Needham 1983), and present-day Anakalangese remember hearing of the climate of fear during the dry season. The combination of slave trading and cattle raiding kept the fires of local warfare continually stoked.

Until the beginning of this century, the interior of Sumba was reputed to be a place of continual warfare, leading one early report to claim that "there is no other rule on Sumba than the rule of the strongest" (Roos 1872: 9). In addition to suffering slave raids by outsiders, precolonial Anakalangese themselves raided and took heads. Raids were spontaneous forays bent on taking cattle or gold or wreaking vengeance and seem to have involved more bluster than bloodshed. In contrast, headhunting, although also a form of revenge, operated within a ritual frame that was opened with formal oratory and concluded when the head was hung on an altar in the center of the village, a ritual incorporation similar to harvest rites (Kruyt 1922: 563–555; Wielenga 1923: 308–309; for Anakalang, see Keane 1990: 104–112). Because of the possibility of violence, early Dutch attempting to explore west Sumba failed to make it to Anakalang (Roos 1872: 92) and a generation later east Sumbanese guides were still afraid to enter (Witkamp 1912: 756; see also Wielenga 1911: 166 ff.). Direct Dutch intervention in Sumba came only in their final push to consolidate their colonial holdings to the margins of the archipelago. The first posts in interior west Sumba were established in 1908 (Groeneveld 1931: 10), although periodic flare-ups kept west Sumba under military rule until 1933 (Riekerk 1934: 51, 67–69; Waitz 1933: 9). Under the policy of indirect rule, around 1913 the Dutch began to set up a system of local rulers, known by present-day Sumbanese as "kings" (Indo. *raja*). In west Sumba, however, these rulers had almost no legitimacy (Groeneveld 1931: 13–14) and were little respected by the Dutch, at least at first (Lanze 1919: 55, Wielenga 1912: 149–150).

In Anakalang, the energetic and charismatic Umbu Sappy Pateduk (in office 1927–1953) took full advantage of his opportunities as raja. By means of numerous strategic marriages he built up a powerful set of affines. These affines provided him with enormous resources for exchange, which allowed him to dominate others who came to him for support in their own rituals and exchanges. Other people he subordinated through direct patronage and threats, until, it is said, he was able to demand a cut of every important marriage exchange in Anakalang. He also seems to have tried to endow his own position with ancestral aura by reinvigorating Anakalang's great biannual ritual, Descent to the Ratu Valley (see Keane 1990). This last move, however, an apparent usurpation of ritual authority by an ambiguously powerful government office, drew objections from Dutch observers (Riekerk [1941] n.d.: 6) and remained controversial after the last ritual was held in the early 1980s. For all their wealth and ties to governmental power, however, the members of Umbu Sappy's family never succeeded in establishing a political or ritual hegemony in Anakalang. Other Anakalangese are inclined to scoff at the pretensions of Umbu Sappy's "clan" (kabisu) to ancestral preeminence, insisting that kabisu are fundamentally autonomous, their dealings with one another being, in principle, encounters between equals.

Umbu Sappy was able to concretize his reputation in the form of a huge stone slab that remains the largest tomb on the island, forthrightly named "Most Macho" (Raisi Moni; see fig. 3). Unlike some other powerful men of that day, he was also able to perpetuate his standing into subsequent generations. He had several children educated in Dutch schools and passed on his office to a son. As the postcolonial state began its slow reorganization, the new position of regent (bupati) of West Sumba, an office directly under that of provincial governor in the state hierarchy, fell to this same son. In the 1980s and early 1990s, after several intervening officeholders, the post passed on to Umbu Sappy's grandson, whom family wealth had been able to send through the university system. This current regent, along with several other members of the family, is part of a small elite that has succeeded in the national sphere. A significant portion of this elite can trace its fortunes back to the Dutch education provided to promising children of nobility, and most are self-consciously modern. Some, especially those most actively involved with the church or least able to make frequent visits to the island, retain only slender attachments to Anakalang. Many, however, find it worthwhile to assure their continued presence in their villages of origin by building houses and tombs and sponsoring exchanges and feasts. Their involvement is not only a testimony to the continued moral demands of exchange, it also has a practical consequence. Forced to listen to their supporters and their exchange partners, they are reminded that there remain some limits to the financial and personal independence promised by modernity.

In comparison to many parts of the Dutch East Indies, Sumba seems to have felt the colonial period relatively lightly. The single generation of Dutch rule generated little violence, involved only a handful of personnel, and imposed few demands aside from a limited amount of corvée labor on the transisland road and a head tax (Versluys 1941). The two most powerful consequences of the Dutch presence were the removal of violence from local hands (and those of slave raiders) and the introduction of Christianity. Warfare was important in male self-image, and the threat of abduction and even raiding seems to have lurked behind some marriage negotiations. Headhunting ventures provided young men with a productive role in ritual practices otherwise dominated by elders and gave the latter in turn a way to appropriate the powerful but potentially disruptive energies of youth. In the 1990s, actual violence was rare, but threats were not. The way in which violence lives on in local imagination is suggestive. Young men are expected to be tough, hard to control, and prone to testing their mettle with the occasional horse theft: one might still hear words like those of an exasperated Dutch administrator, "The Sumbanese, you know, would be no Sumbanese had he not stolen some cattle at least once in his life. . . . The Sumbanese regards cattle theft as a sort of sport" (Waitz 1933: 54; see also Vel 1994: 65). But now the state holds a near-monopoly on violence and is seen by most Anakalangese as heir to the peace-keeping role once assigned to the Dutch.

At present, Anakalangese tend to distinguish between state and local

Figure 3. Raja Umbu Sappy Pateduk (seated at center, with dark jacket) and ratus, atop his tomb Most Macho (Raisi Moni) in Kaḅoduku, 1949. Umbu Sappy wears two gold mamuli pinned to his jacket and a round "sun" on his head. Ratu Ubu Marabi, the dancer in a dark jacket, wears a maraga on his chest. (Photograph A. Bühler. Courtesy of the Museum für Völkerkunde, Basel)

powers less as illegitimate or legitimate than by contrasting features: force of arms and technocratic rationality versus efficacious speech and the moral authority of ancestral procedures. This reflects a familiar way in which societies have responded to colonial and postcolonial distributions of power, by distinguishing between external power and internal spiritual authority (see, e.g., Chatterjee 1993: 6). In Southeast Asia and the Pacific, such distinctions often seem to build on local "diarchic" traditions that divide authority between two kinds of ritual or political office. Diarchies institutionalize contrasts between, for example, coercive or instrumental force and passive but morally superior authority, outside and inside, junior and senior, mobile and immobile (Bowen 1991; Fox 1977; Heine-Geldern 1956; Sahlins 1985; Schulte Nordholt [1966] 1971; Shore 1982; Traube 1986; classic discussions of European analogies are Bloch 1961 and Kantorowicz 1957).[8] In contemporary Anakalang, however, complementary offices are less evident than the *intrinsic* tensions between the authority and the hazards of ritualized action.

The second major effect of colonialism, Christianity, bore a more slowly burning but longer fuse.[9] The first missionary to Anakalang, from an orthodox sect of the Calvinist church (Gereformeerde Kerken), set up shop in 1933. After ten years, however, he could boast of only 180 converts out of a population of 22,000 (Luijendijk 1946). The pace of conversion only picked up after the failed coup of 1965, when, despite Sumba's distance from the violence that swept more politicized parts of Indonesia, people saw religious affiliation as protection against possible association with atheistic communism (Webb 1986). Still, Christianity only began to approach majority status in Anakalang at the end of the 1980s. By then, large numbers of children were receiving religious education in school, groups of young adults began aggressive conversion campaigns, and the tacit agreement that Catholics and Protestants not compete over turf began to crumble. A state made nervous by Islamic activism elsewhere began trying more actively to suppress paganism and to pressure civil servants into acquiring one of the five officially sanctioned religions. In a world disciplined by bureaucratic categories, all possibilities should be accounted for: as ratu Sulung tells it, the regent faced him, held up his hand, fingers spread wide, and, pointing to the space between two of them, said, "There are five religions—but where are you? You're nowhere, you're lost down here in between somewhere." Nonetheless, in the late 1980s, the regency government of West Sumba, contravening state policy, still accepted "marapu" (ancestral ritualist) as a religious identification on identity cards, and in 1993 at least one local official in Anakalang was an active ritual specialist.

Given the complexity of the processes and consequences of religious conversion (discussed in Keane 1995b, 1996), I can only note here their most direct consequences for the analysis of "scenes of encounter." Not surprisingly, ancestral rituals are decreasing as the number of practitioners dwindles. In the process, participants' (various) understandings of the nature of ritual action, such as the dominant views on how language works, seem to be changing (Keane 1995a). Presumably fewer Anakalangese now take into consideration the possible presence of the invisible listeners during the performance of ritual speech. Fewer as well are likely to view the chief power of ritual speech to be its effects on the world (although both perspectives were still quite common in the 1980s). This in itself is one argument for focusing on the *practices* of ritual rather than only on *beliefs* that practitioners might hold. In the previous chapter I mentioned the doubts that have been raised about efforts to explain cultural practices in terms of a fully shared set of

beliefs. Whatever the situation in the past, it has been several generations since it could be assumed that even all adult male Anakalangese
held the same explicit beliefs. Ritual practices, however, especially formal exchange, still bear a great deal of authority even for members of
different religions and in different relationships to the market economy,
something it is the aim of the succeeding chapters to explore.

For most people, Christianity is associated with the Dutch and, as a
legally recognized religion, the present Indonesian state. Anakalangese
memories of the Dutch are softened by comparison with both the current, more interventionist, New Order regime and the brutality of the
brief Japanese occupation (1942–1945) that effectively ended colonial
rule. During the occupation, cattle were seized, respectable people were
humiliated, and labor was aggressively extracted. This is emblematized
in the sharp memory of total deculturation: cloth disappeared and people went back to wearing barkcloth. After 1945, the Sumbanese found
themselves by turns under nominal Dutch rule again, then within the
Dutch-supported State of Eastern Indonesia (NIT), and finally as part
of the Republic of Indonesia (Doko 1981). Of the struggles by which
Indonesians gained independence, strengthened their sense of collective
achievement, and in some places toppled older ruling orders through social revolutions (Reid 1974), only rumors reached Anakalang. Although
I heard many vivid stories about the Japanese, when I asked people
about the period of independence they could find little to recall.[10] With
the central government distracted, distant, and poor, Sumba was largely
left on its own until the 1960s, and the system of kingships was only
abolished in 1962, long after similar vestiges had been eliminated elsewhere. By the 1970s, a strong oil-based economy allowed the state to
push its development policies more aggressively. In Anakalang, however, these are evident largely in the remains of failed, or partly successful, projects: a somnolent cooperative, abandoned plantations, and a
couple of settlements meant to draw people down from the hilltop villages to the roadside. More effective was the national school-building
program begun in 1973 (Warren 1992: 214–215), which in Sumba put
elementary schools within walking distance of much of the scattered
population. By the 1990s, efforts were under way to draw Sumba further into the national information network by gradually extending television transmission and electrical power into rural districts.

Besides the schools, the state is felt most directly through its ongoing—and not entirely successful—efforts to rationalize and make use of

local government. For Anakalangese, these efforts began to feel especially interventionist after the village law reform of 1979. The reform
was meant to bring the divergent systems across the country into uni-
formity: the province divided by turns into *kabupaten* (Sumba consisting of two), *kecamatan*, and *desa* (administrative "villages"). This challenged Anakalang's last vestiges of the colonial system of indirect rule by
subjecting long-term officeholders to election every eight years. Desa
heads are in the often delicate position of representing the state to the
village, while the state works to transfer power away from them to
the kecamatan, whose officials are felt to be less tied to tradition and
more beholden to central authorities (Warren 1992: 257). Having little
to gain from the government, when desa heads are faced with conflicts
between obligations as officeholders and as kabisu leaders, they are
likely to fulfill the latter. Among other things, to keep strong relations
with their neighbors requires effort, and aggressive implementation of
development policies is not necessarily the most successful way to retain their authority (see Keeler 1987). It is therefore not surprising that,
in most cases, desa heads remain men whose authority draws on their
kinship ties, wealth, ritual knowledge, and skills in exchange. People
often counter their frequent efforts to conflate these sources of authority with their status as government officials by trying to distinguish between what properly lies "in the duty of custom and in the duty of government" (*ta diha adat yeka ta diha pareta*), in which the purpose of
the disinction is to protect what autonomy they can claim for the former
against the demands of the latter.[11] In debating the proper role of the
government in local affairs, Anakalangese are often able to take advantage of its own rhetoric. Since the 1980s, desa officials and civil servants have been required to attend courses in the state ideology, Pancasila. This five-point doctrine has been kept intentionally vague, and
many Anakalangese have become adept at using it to back up their own
arguments against specific government initiatives. For example, one desa
head defends his refusal to convert to Christianity on the grounds that
Pancasila protects him against religious coercion. The story is not, however, simply one of local resistance against oppressive forces from outside. When people find themselves at a disadvantage in local terms, they
may try to make use of the alternative social identities and legal procedures introduced by the state (Vel 1992). In general, however, subsistence farmers provide the state with relatively little direct leverage.[12] This
limited hand allows Anakalangese, relative to many other Indonesians,

a fair amount of leeway to act in the ancestral name of social groups that the state challenges, the modernists decry, and the church suspects.

## KABISU AND BLOOD FELLOWS

When people in Anakalang talk about serious, authoritative action, the actors of whom they speak are more likely to bear the names of settlements, ancestral villages, houses, kabisu, ancestors, or ritual offices than those of living individual men and women. This way of speaking reflects an understanding of the nature of agency. In Anakalang, to act legitimately is to act like, on behalf of, or in the name of ancestors. Ancestral identities are fundamentally collective and extend beyond the limits of the present time. Ancestors and kabisu are mutually defining. Through the kabisu and its constituent houses, a person is identified with original ancestral couples, certain fixed places on the landscape, expectations of and ritual obligations to ancestors and places, and property rights.[13] The kabisu and house also define the line of transmission of the offices of ratu (priests or ritual specialists). Although the kabisu can be described in terms of patrilineal descent, in practice it is the rituals (which address ancestors not as males but as husband-wife pairs) and the property that give it an identity. A child's kabisu affiliation depends on the completion of the parents' marriage exchange. Although the ideal is for continuity from fathers to sons, as is characteristic of "house societies" (Boon 1990; Lévi-Strauss [1975, 1979] 1982), the actual composition of Anakalangese kabisu is subject to ongoing processes of affiliation and loss. At the heart of these processes are the scenes of encounter discussed below.

Kabisu identity is embodied in the most prominent human artifacts on the landscape, cultivated lands and the hilltop villages that tower over them. Despite the apparent concreteness of the objective signs of the kabisu, the actual social entity requires constant effort to sustain. Its visibility represents achievements won over vicissitude. Historical narratives frequently refer to branches of or entire kabisu that have disappeared, broken into fragments, or been absorbed into or even slaughtered by other kabisu, evident in numerous village sites where only overgrown tombs now remain. In addition, the existence of scattered marginal settlements of people whose kabisu affiliations are inactive or forgotten demonstrates that kabisu identity is neither a given nor an ineluctable necessity for economic survival.

Figure 4. A small Anakalangese hilltop village, showing the dancing plaza fringed with modest tombs. In the background are pastures and rice fields, in the dry season (Sotu, June 1986).

Each kaḅisu is, in principle, based in a "great village" (*paraingu ḅa-kul*) that is supposed to have been founded by the earliest ancestors. A great village contains the house sites (*yili uma*) that belong to the named segments of the kaḅisu, groups known as "houses" (*uma*). House sites are conceptual place markers, supposed to persist regardless of the presence or absence of physical structures. When standing, the house serves as dwelling, shelter for pigs and horses, meeting hall, storeroom for ancestral valuables, and site for house and kaḅisu ritual.[14] At the center of the village lie large stone tombs and at least one plaza (*talora*), used for ritual dances, great exchanges, and feasts (see fig. 4). The accumulated number of tombs testifies to the age of the village, and thus to the capacity of the kaḅisu to maintain itself in place. Their size indicates the wealth and power of the exchange relations by which particular people were able to command the labor to drag them from distant quarries.[15]

Lesser settlements and garden hamlets descend from, or are "branches" (*kajanga*) of, these great villages. The branching relations among villages are conceptualized in terms of descent, younger brothers and dispossessed or adventurous sons who hived off from their villages of origin. As people contemplate the relations among settlements, they perceive direct links between age and status and, ideally, degree of ritual completeness. The altars, ancestral valuables, and house sites of great villages embody their claims to represent the totality of the kabisu, which is manifest in practice during the largest rituals, for which members of even the most distant garden hamlets should return to the great village. Lower status is reflected in ritual dependence, historical recentness, and impermanence—for until tombs have accumulated, the hamlet is considered to be ephemeral. Great villages, situated at the tops of hills, display a relative distance from ordinary work that echoes their identification with ritual activities and other public representations of kabisu identity. Hamlets, in contrast, are associated with ordinary labor and social or geographic marginality, being situated either in the midst of fields or on settlement frontiers. In narratives of the ancestral trek, the ancestors are often said to have left behind a pair of dependents, husband and wife, in each garden settlement along the way. Today, to call someone a "garden person" (*tau ta oma*) is to accuse them of social nullity. By summoning scattered descendants back together, periodic rituals, funerals, and important exchanges momentarily rewind the threads of descent by which they have been disseminated across the landscape and reassert their links to the status of founding ancestors.[16] The varying degrees to which villages have achieved completeness are the outcomes of ongoing processes of schism, on the one hand, and accumulation, on the other. Ambitious leaders in branch villages concretize their exchange careers in material signs of their influence, on which subsequent generations may seek to base their assertions of ritual status and rank. The competing claims of declining ritual centers can be challenged by holders of material "proofs" to the contrary, which they may obtain either through pillage or usurpation, or simply by taking on responsibilities (such as guarding ancestral valuables) of which the great village is no longer capable. The media of representation in Anakalang have the effect of partially subjecting political agents to the vicissitudes of material objects.

Cutting across kabisu identity are relations of shared bodily substance with one's "birth fellows" (*oli ḍaḍi*). Anakalangese generally accept as relatives by "blood" (*re*) only persons who are linked through women, through unnamed matrilines known as "blossoms" (*wàla*).[17] People say it is blood that joins them to others in inherent relations of empathy. Blood-based identity is situated in bodies, local memories, and emotions and lacks public, objectified forms. In contrast to bonds of kabisu membership, which require ritual maintenance and can produce intense factional rivalries, and those of affines, which demand ongoing exchanges, unmediated relations of blood are created by nothing more than physical procreation. In conversations, people use the expression "birth fellow" to imply pure solidarity—sometimes as a rhetorical move when seeking assistance on otherwise shaky grounds. Relations of blood provide an alternative to the danger of pure otherness, on the one hand, and the burdens imposed by more formal relations, on the other. By tracing the links through females, people discover they have birth fellows in socially distant villages, a series of "places of origin" (*pinya pawali*). The passage of one's blood maps a series of points across the landscape, chains of villages, the sources of mothers and destinations of daughters. In referring to these stopping places in the journey of ancestral women, men and women rhetorically deemphasize the obligations of affiliation in favor of the claims of descent, speaking of themselves not as deferential and debt-bearing affines but as grandchildren who are to be protected. People's ability to swivel between these two rhetorical possibilities reflects the inherent tension that lies between affines, who are both others and extensions of oneself.

## THE VALUE AND CHALLENGE OF AFFINES

Uniting bodily substance and ritual identity, marriages create groups far larger than the individuals concerned, for the entire kabisu depends on sources of blood and is deeply concerned in turn with the destiny of its own descendants.[18] Since matrilines are not readily objectified, each kabisu treats its daughters as its own, and their blood as a resource that can potentially be recaptured by retaining their husbands. As in many systems of alliance the option of taking in husbands who are unable to complete their marriage payments is an important power resource for ambitious groups (Ortner 1981). The autonomy of kabisu identity and the mutual dependence among kabisu exist in a tension that comes to its fullest form in the negotiations between affines. Although normative claims emphasize the deep respect and sense of obligation between affines, this respect is crosscut by several sorts of ambivalence, including the potential desire of yera (the wife's people) either to absorb or to reject their ngàba wini (the husband's people), or of ngàba wini to abandon their yera in favor of more powerful affines. The rhetoric of alliance also displays ambivalence, as the two sides play off their solidarity against the otherness across which they face each other; united as partners, divided as negotiating parties. Sustained affinal relations depend on recurrent public acts of mutual recognition constructed in scenes of encounter (and, encompassed within these, scenes of hospitality).

Marriage in Anakalang is emphatically asymmetric.[19] One of the strongest existing prohibitions is on reversing the direction of marriages between two houses or kabisu.[20] People say that would be like trying to make the blood flow back upstream. Rather, women and their children move irreversibly, like "fish released into the lake, horses set loose in the pasture." When brides are taken off in marriage, their mothers and sisters weep at the loss: men and women experience marriage as the passage of women outward from their original homes. Conversely, since affines must be able to rely on one another, at least some man in each generation should add to the strength of the existing alliance by marrying a woman from a kabisu classed as yera to his own. Such marriages can be spoken of as uniting a woman's "father's sister's child" (*laleba ama*) and a man's "mother's brother's child" (*ana loka*). By repeating the father's marriage, the son returns to the source and renews the alliance with his mother's people. For the mother's people, such renewals are a powerful means of binding others to themselves and their projects. By staying with tried and true affines, each side also comes as close as permissible to endogamy (Boon 1977: 139). The male's perspective was put in very succinct terms by a conversation I overheard in 1993: Ama Rita was talking to his sister's eight-year-old son: 'When you are old enough to get married, come to me for a wife. After all, when you dig a well, you put it close to the house, don't you? You don't go to the other side of the hill to fetch water, do you?' Women, in turn, often say they favor asymmetric alliance because it provides them with companions and protectors in their husbands' villages, the sisters and fathers' sisters who have traveled there before them. One practical consequence of asymmetric alliance is that each group finds itself pivoting between affines as it draws on its ngàba wini for the goods demanded by its yera, and vice versa.

The exchanges that accompany asymmetric alliance in societies like those of Sumba, Timor, Maluku, highland Sumatra, and northern Burma have been described as a traffic in women by men (Lévi-Strauss [1949] 1969; see discussion in Butler 1990: 38–43 and Rubin 1975). But viewed from Anakalang, the notion of "traffic" should be qualified. First, some marriages result in the movement of the husband, not the wife. Second, marriage is only one element of (albeit a logical precondition for) a much wider set of transactions and ritual obligations lasting several generations. Third, neither bride nor groom is (at least normatively) supposed to have much agency in the matter, both being relatively passive objects of collective actions. Since mothers do speak up and have some control over the disposal of certain valuables, it is more accurate to say that senior men (and women) collaborate in a traffic in junior women (and men). Men have a greater say in the decisions, to be sure, and carry out the speech performances and the transactions. But part of the argument of this book is that the agencies at work in these events are not directly identifiable with the individuals who enter into them. As constructed in representational practices, the gender of these agents is not straightforward.

According to Marilyn Strathern, the critical structural difference between men and women in Mount Hagen (Papua New Guinea) is that, as wives, women "cannot unambiguously participate in the political confrontation of clans, for they represent the interpersonal links between them" (1972: 154). Anakalangese women likewise find themselves between; one woman told me that what most worried her when listening to her own marriage negotiations was that her father's pride would lead him to make demands that would impoverish her husband, for which *she* would then be blamed by other members of her husband's family. The role of Anakalangese men as transactors and speakers can be seen as a function of their position in interaction: located relatively unambiguously within a distinct single social identity, they face men whose identities are defined, at least within the parameters of the particular event, as other. In claiming a privileged relation to speech, men are at once distancing themselves from low forms of work and laying claim to agency that extends beyond their immediate surroundings and an identity grounded in the ancestral past. They speak and act on behalf of collectivities (kabisu, houses, the living and the dead). In doing so, however, they are no longer acting as male individuals but as figures of authority called "mother-father" (*ina-ama*; see chapter 6). So too, since ritual representations often stress gender complementarity, some male ratus take on "female" roles such as cooking or dancing as women (Keane 1990). But the "maleness" of the ratu's social and biological identity exists at a distinct logical and practical plane from the highly schematized and selective aspects of "femaleness" that he *performs* in ritual. As Strathern remarks (1981: 676) "the value put on womanness is not necessarily to be equated with the value put on women." The work of representation remains largely the work of men, but its outcome entails a certain abstraction from sex and mortal bodies.[21] The groups in whose name men act encompass the productive activities of pairs of husbands and wives. These groups do not so much possess genders themselves (kaḫisu, for instance, are identified with ancestral named couples, not single males) so much as wield representations of gender. These shift according to context, refracting and selecting among more mundane differences in work, bodies, and daily sociality.

Marriage should provide a woman or man with not just a spouse and children but with affines as well. It is above all affines who make a thriving economic and social existence possible, and much of the quality of a household's political life, even of domestic relations between husband and wife, depends on the generosity or stinginess, ease or stubbornness, of affines. By convention, yera are the source of life for their ngàba wini and thus should command great deference, reinforced in material terms by the debts fostered and renewed in recurrent exchange. In return, yera should foster and protect their affines.[22] Along with this protection goes the threat that it will be withheld: a yera's curse may cause the woman to be infertile or her children to be sickly. Expectations that yera will be protective are much greater in the case of old marriage alliances, in which the allies have in a sense proven that they are worthy of one another and reliable. An old alliance, a "smooth path, worn down trail" represents for ngàba wini a well-known and tested source of life; for yera, a guaranteed resource on which to call for exchange valuables and a secure haven for their blood descendants. To open a new alliance, "pile up soil for a dyke, clear a new garden," is difficult and risky, although, like a new garden, it may ultimately prove fruitful.

Two factors introduce structural tensions into the normative harmony between affines. First, the definition of cross-cousins is broad enough, the histories of former alliances complex enough, that even if several brothers all marry "mother's brother's children," their wives may each come from a different group. As a result, the brothers, who should be cooperating for all exchanges with each other's affines, may find themselves torn by conflicting loyalties and demands. Their collective identity may be fractured by individual marriages. Second, not all marriages renew alliances, and some marriages do not even result in the transfer of a bride: the husband may enter his wife's family instead. Such differences make it possible for Anakalangese to *evaluate* marriages relative to one another. As Susan McKinnon (1991) has argued for Tanimbar, in Maluku, the superior value of proper marriages is not simply a way of speaking about norms, from which reality occasion-

ally, but irrelevantly, deviates. The discursive construction of good marriages is reflected in practical terms: whereas a novel marriage is an idiosyncratic relationship between individuals, a marriage that follows an
existing pathway (*lara*) is by definition part of something larger than
itself. The latter contributes to the permanence of an alliance between
groups, something that takes concrete form in the wider causal effects of
the exchanges it sets into motion. Its value is therefore part of a broader
understanding of agency and identity and is measured against the alternatives, the plethora of less highly valued, conceptually short-term marriages. The value of matrilateral cross-cousin marriages reflects their
role in sequences of authoritative interactions that appear to transcend
the spatial and temporal dimensions of the present circumstances and
persons. They take their meaning, in part, against the background of
humbler outcomes and the possible futures they evoke.

As the story of Ama Koda and Ubu Tara shows, normative claims do
not tell the whole story. Here we see affines who are supposed to owe
one another respect and protection responding to one another with
mistrust and rivalry. Far from being idiosyncratic, the tensions between
the two groups illustrate a pervasive quality of contemporary Anakalangese life. Like most relations mediated by exchange, those with affines contain a deep ambivalence between identity and difference, solidarity and aggression. To give a valuable to an affine both affirms the
existence of a relationship and challenges the affine to respond. However much affines may seek to treat one another as collective extensions
of themselves, they also resist being treated this way. However much
they identify with one another, they must remain ambiguously foreign
to one another. Economic and even demographic vicissitudes contribute
to the political limits to their mutual trust, limits that make each marriage, at least potentially, a "venture" outward, fraught with risks (Lévi-
Strauss [1949] 1969: 48).

The kaḅisu's collective interest in repeating alliances along with the
normative deference owed by ngàba wini to yera are challenged by the
status rivalries, the value of autonomy, and changes in economic standing. Possession of wealth is a practical necessity for the operations that
maintain identity (rituals, exchanges, marriages), but those operations
are also crucial in translating a material condition (wealth) into a meaningful one (authority and status). The practical need for and high normative value placed on strong alliances exist in tension with the desire
to be free of excessive demands by others and to have a certain freedom

Figure 5. A kaḅisu faces the ancestors: Ratus of Parewatana lead one man and woman from each household to a sacred spring, where they seek signs from the spirits of how their prayers and oratory have been received (Liangu Marapu, December 1986).

of maneuver. The threats that one's affines present exist on several planes. One is that they will forget their allies and begin to act too independently. Thus people are very sensitive to evidence that their support has not been called on for some project or exchange, or that they have not been invited to a feast—that, unrecognized, they are being treated as "strangers" (*tau heka*). Another possibility is that one's affines will eventually come to dominate and even absorb one—the fate, for example, of impoverished nobles whose sons marry into their wives' kaḅisu. Yet another is that one's affines will decline demographically or economically, failing to produce offspring or sustain a lifelong exchange relationship. In addition to such practical chances, the very game of exchange and formal encounters requires a certain display of risks faced and overcome. As the chapters that follow will show, the complex character of these hazards can be seen in the great weight that people place on verbal and material signs and in the problems they raise. The social heart of this side of risk is the threat that one's affines will not recognize the identity one asserts or the rights one claims. The hazards of social life are at once practical and conceptual, preconditions and products, dimensions that cannot readily be disentangled.

## DEPENDENT, SLAVE, AND THE
## REPRESENTATION OF RANK

Kaḇisu and gender identities are crosscut by distinctions of economic power and rank. Although economic power and rank often map onto one another, they draw on distinct sources whose differences impart a crucial tension to local politics. Much of the economic politics of Anakalangese life hinges on control over cattle.[23] Garden land is plentiful enough to allow most people to feed themselves without entering into drastic relations of dependency on others (Vel 1994). But to maintain basic social relations with others, to sustain a decent reputation, and to avert the ire of ancestors one must have access to cattle and rice. Several decades of efforts by missionaries, development agencies, and officials to replace buffalo with the plow for preparing rice fields have had virtually no success in Sumba (Krul 1984). The planting system requires more people than any single household is likely to contain, and very few people possess large herds. This creates an often tense mutual dependence between cattle owners and those who work with them. Dependents expect assistance in everyday needs and support in large ritual and ceremonial exchanges. In turn, the enterprises of powerful and ambitious men, such as great feasts and the raising of tombstones, depend on their ability to get others to contribute labor and materials and, by joining their entourages, to display the strength and breadth of their influence. Even the most abject dependents may offer resistance, most effectively during the mobilization for exchanges, by which they remind the dominant of the mutuality of their relations.

Relations of domination and dependence do not necessarily involve differences of rank. Anakalang and east Sumba are, however, distinguished from west Sumba by the relative prominence of two marked categories, noble (*maràba*) and slave (*ata*).[24] Rank in Anakalang is far from straightforward, because of historical transformations, differences between ideals and actualities, the way the rivalrous and segmentary character of Anakalangese society makes direct comparison of groups and persons difficult, and the fact that people are very cautious about making explicit public claims about the status of others.[25] Contemporary talk about low rank is further obscured by several factors. First, slavery is outlawed in Indonesia, and everyone knows that this is the "age of independence" (Indo. *masa merdeka*). Second is the sense of delicacy or caution. Many people consider slaves likely to be witches as well, and to expose them invites retribution. In talking to me, some people loudly denied that slaves exist, others referred to them only in whispers or silently gestured to their little finger. At the same time, many Anakalangese proudly assert that they are more like the refined (*magutung*) and sharply hierarchical people to their east than their neighbors to the west, where rank is even more ambiguous or absent altogether.

Noble (*maràba*) and slave (*ata*) stand together in contrast to a residual, unmarked class of ordinary folk, "kabisu people" (*tau kabisu*), or "the many" (*tau ma dangu*). There seems to be no widely accepted explanation of where rank differences come from. In some stories, the ancestors seem already to have had slaves when they arrived on Sumba. Some people say slaves were ordinary people who were redeemed by or otherwise became economically dependent on wealthy kin; others say they were captured in war. Self-enslavement, either out of poverty or to pay off a heavy fine, seems to have occurred within living memory. Such explanations reflect what people imagine to be the consequences of economic failure, in particular, the ultimate hazards of exchange (see McKinnon 1991: 265). Dependents and slaves alike must rely on others to provide them with spouses or to bear their marriage payments for them. Even war capture can be seen as a function of economic weakness, because only captives whose kin would or could not ransom them actually became slaves.

Note that these accounts do not appeal to biological or genealogical essences. Rather, when people talk about nobles, they often talk about their wealth and by extension, their generosity and protectiveness—and their danger when angered. A noble who is not generous (*boraku*), who is stingy (*magohu*) or simply poor, lacks an essential quality of nobility. I will return to the meanings of wealth in chapter 7, but will here simply note that the activities that most distinguish a noble in practice—setting up great tombs, holding feasts, maintaining dependents, negotiating dynastic alliances, and sponsoring the marriages of others—require not only supporters but wealth as well. The failure of contemporary nobles to live up to expected standards of generosity is a frequent complaint of those who look back fondly on the past.

The wealth of nobles is necessary not only for attracting followers but also for their own social reproduction. People often attribute high rank to a house's ability over the generations to restrict marriage to others of their own rank. They also claim that the expense of marriage payments should be appropriate to the rank of the bride, and thus that continuation of a descent line's high standing requires the ability to pay the highest levels of bridewealth (see Kapita 1976a: 41). Although the level of marriage exchanges is a much more fluid and complex matter, it is true that wealthy nobles will be reluctant to recognize the status of potential affines who are not likely to be strong supporters in the future. Paying their own bridewealth permits them continually to return to the sources of their own noble blood by marriages in previous generations. If blood is not an essential bodily source of noble identity, its continuity at least indicates the ability to carry out successful noble *practices* of negotiation and exchange (see Beatty 1992: 271; Leach 1954: 149). In this case, nobility is in part a *product* of the ability to stage and conclude important "scenes of encounter," the subject of the next four chapters.

At the same time, people make clear that nobility should not be confused with wealth (a distinction parallel to that between slavery and dependency). This distinction often comes into play when people complain about someone whom they consider to be merely rich. One especially unpopular man of my acquaintance was also one of the wealthiest, a man whose industry—and, it is said, "economic" and stingy ways—allowed him to send his children to university, permitting them to rise to high levels of the provincial government. Yet it was well known that his mother was his father's slave, taken as a lover late in life. Lacking a sense of honor, this man had nothing to lose by refusing to act as a wealthy noble should. No one was surprised when he died suddenly, or when his funeral was filled with omens of disaster, and one son went temporarily mad.

By the 1980s, slavery was a very delicate topic to raise in conversation. I could identify very few people as being clearly of slave descent. One was Kuta. He was first pointed out to me as the source of another man's "name [which] emerges" (*ngara hunga*): in the name avoidance that marks everyday polite speech, the latter is known as "Kuta's Lord" (Ubu nai Kuta). A stout and boisterous man of middle age, Kuta lived just outside his master's village, by the side of the road, where he owned a small kiosk. People considered his participation in trade to indicate both his lack of a sense of honor and his inherent cleverness, an undignified skill at economic calculation. He was uninhibited by the demands of honor and exercised a fair amount of license, inviting himself to join people's meals and expressing himself loudly. But when his now-deceased master's son held a huge feast in 1993, Kuta still performed one defining service of the slave, as "the one who bears the betel pouch" (*na ma halili karera*). Embodying his master's hospitality, he wore a decorated and well-stocked betel pouch over his shoulder all day, and everyone was free to call him over and help themselves.

A more intimate relationship between former slave and master was that of Laiya and his half-brother, Ubu Neka. They shared the same father, Laiya's mother having been the slave whom Ubu Neka's mother brought along with her in marriage. Laiya and his wife lived in the same house with Ubu Neka and his wife. The relations between the two men closely resembled those between older and younger brother. Laiya depended on, showed deference to, and received commands from Ubu Neka. He worked his own field, however, in addition to the work he performed alongside Ubu Neka, and had his own horse.

Masters handle the marriages and funerals of former slaves. In 1993, one noble went all the way to Waingapu, a daylong bus ride away, to fetch the body of a former slave. Even though the man had left many years before to make a life there as a tobacco seller, when death came, his master felt obliged to go in person and bring him back. When I asked people why he bothered, they replied he would be ashamed not to: what would people say of him if he were unable to take care of the funeral of his own slave? Here the identification between and complementarity of master and slave appears clearly. The slave, who is marked by a lack of honor, is bound to the master by ties of material dependency. The master is bound in turn to the slave by honor. Even when the slave has in all practical terms eluded the control of the master, in the end, the meaning of the slave resides not in labor or services but as a manifestation of the master's sense of honor and self. In this we can begin to see the distinction between the slave and the ordinary dependent for the self-definition of the noble.

If Anakalangese slavery was a form of domination, this does not mean that domination defined slavery. For one thing, other forms of domination, along lines of wealth, age, gender, and generation, were much more common than, and sometimes more onerous than, slavery. Moreover, the ownership of a slave did not necessarily produce obvious material and social benefits. For example, although labor can be extracted from poor dependents, this was not always the case with slaves. Whatever the practical resemblances between dependency and slavery (see Reid 1983: 9–11), slave status in Anakalang was sharply distinguished in ritual and conceptual terms that were critical to the meaning of both slave and noble status. Anakalangese slavery seems to support those analyses that play down labor and emphasize the way in which the slave is "an extension of his master's power, . . . a human surrogate" (Patterson 1982: 4). What is critical is the peculiar social identity of the slave and his or her contribution to the status of the noble, rather than productive utility (Kopytoff 1982). When Kuta served as "the one who bears the betel pouch," he was performing a basic service on behalf of the host similar to that performed by younger brothers, sons, or poor relatives. But kin would never be called by this expression, which denotes a formally recognized category. Conversely, no nonnoble should receive guests with "the one who bears the betel pouch." When performed by a slave, the carrying of the betel pouch duplicates in highly formal terms and marks as a sumptuary privilege what is otherwise a commonplace form of etiquette. The formally recognized character of this privilege marks the noble as someone for whom, *in principle*, the status of betel pouch bearer properly exists—rather than someone who, *in practice*, happens to receive guests politely. By institutionalizing such practices, the role of slave implied that hospitality was part of the very definition of nobility. By displaying the capacity of the noble to act through others, the role of slave also characterized nobility as possessing an inherently expanded agency. The betel pouch carrier thus exemplifies several general features of representational practice, both verbal and material, to which I return in the chapters that follow.

The practices that defined Anakalangese slavery suggest that slaves and masters were identified with each other in ways that, deeper than mere contingency, are doubly representational. Not only did the slave serve on behalf of and symbolize the status of the master, he or she may even, at least figuratively, have replaced the master. This possibility underlies a number of ancestral stories, of which an excerpt from the ancestral history of Parewatana is characteristic. When Ubu Pabal sought the hand of Rabu Roru, her father refused to recognize him and set him a number of obstacles to overcome, with nearly fatal results. When Pabal persevered, the father finally pretended to give in, but in fact he attempted one last deception. He took Rabu Roru's slave and dressed her in fine cloth, gold, and ivory. Meanwhile he had Rabu Roru dress in rough cloth, covered her with ashes, and made her stay by the hearth. Despite this, Ubu Pabal's dogs immediately recognized the true noble and ran up to her, licking off the ashes and exposing the deceit.

Reconfigured as an institution, the deceptive substitution of slave for mistress becomes the exalted representation of mistress by slave. In the past, when a noble bride was transferred to her husband's household, she wore plain garments. It was her "brought slave" who bore the marks of nobility. Known as the "adorned child" (*ana moha*), she was heavily decorated with good cloth, gold ornaments, tortoiseshell comb, and ivory bracelets. As the betel bag carrier replaces the activity of the master, so the adorned child replaces the body of the mistress. The manifest representatives of master and mistress imply that the absent figures whom they index transcend their particular embodied forms.

The formal substitutability of slave for master reached its apotheosis in the institution (now lapsed in Anakalang, but still practiced in east Sumba) of death attendants, literally "those who are supported in walking" (*pahapagangu*) (Kapita 1976a: 64–65; Kruyt 1922: 530; Onvlee 1984: 400; see also Forth 1981: 199). This practice was restricted to the most important nobles. The attendants were one or more pairs of slaves, male and female, who stayed by the corpse during the wake. They wore the finest cloth and ornaments of gold and ivory. Some people say the mortuary gongs would send them into trance, a simulacrum of their master's condition in which they could actually communicate with the dead. Illustrating how closely they were identified with the noble, one man told me, 'We'd take care of those slaves like race horses. They did nothing but eat. If they didn't like the food, they'd sulk.'

If nobles were not defined by some bodily essence or by wealth, on what was their distinctiveness founded, and what does that tell us about legitimate wealth and authority in Anakalang? An important hint of the meaning of nobility is this: when people want to say that a family has *real* noble rank, not simply acquired wealth, they refer to them as *ubu nai* (lord of). The possessive particle *nai* is used only of relations between persons. The allusion is to the use of slave names to avoid uttering the name of the noble (see chapter 5): thus Kuta's master can be spoken of as Ubu nai Kuta. Kuta's name gives concrete form to the master's rank.

There is a broader implication to the institution of slave name, which associates rank with ancestral agency. In formal scenes of encounter, each kabisu addresses the other with a conventional name (*kaḍehang*) that is used only in ritual speech. To use this name helps contextualize the event within the ritual frame and identifies the participants as acting in the name of an entity that exceeds the particular time, place, and personnel. This address name is the slave name of the ancestor. More specifically, the slave in question is supposed to have been the man who went out in front in battle. He thus personifies the master's agency in its most masculine, assertive, and outward-facing forms. Through the use of these names, groups recognize each other's ancestral warrants.

By implication, the existence of the noble–slave relationship, and the extended agency it embodies, is an important verbal condition of possibility for the existence and activity of the kaḅisu.

The slave name suggests that the identity of the noble is embedded in a crucial form of displacement: the noble took his or her name from someone else from whose public deeds credit accrued to the noble. That other served as the living representative of the noble whose own name was suppressed. The formulation "Ubu nai X," however, does not simply suppress the name, but dramatically points to its absence. What slaves made possible, in part, was the public expression of the capacity of nobles to extend themselves through the bodies, words, and names of others. In this respect, the possession of a slave was the ultimate development of a wider logic of displacement. Nobility lacked any other strong essentializing ground, such as an ideology of blood. Without the slave, the noble was merely another possessor of wealth, at best. The possibility that wealth and rank, that power and legitimacy, may come unstuck never entirely disappears. Although slavery functioned in part to translate relations of economic domination into more substantial social claims, at the same time it was also linked to the threat of slippage that accompanied those claims. This threat is embodied in a host of persistent anxieties about former slaves: that they may turn out to be witches, that they deal in poisons and arson, that they populate distant settlements with thieving runaways, or, being both more clever and more ruthless than nobles, that it is they who will acquire the untamed powers of money.

## TOWARD MEDIATION

The steady work of men and women provides the materials that can, potentially, be transformed into momentary acts of representation with the potential to transcend the limits of their time, place, and individual agency. What the ability to represent can mean is suggested by the figure of the slave. This meaning includes action at a distance, the implication that one exceeds one's bodily limits. Recall the feud between Ama Koda and Ubu Tara, with which this chapter opened. Among other things, the feud exemplifies a series of tensions: between individual emotions and collective representations, fallible actions and ancestral order, accident and intention, economic power and affinal norms. In principle, these tensions are mediated by representations (horses and cloth, gold and speech) through which the relation between affines is objectified: it is depicted in metaphors and embodied in the flow of goods. As the mediation begins to crumble, Ama Koda's anger seeks out sources in the reading of signs, ranging from the deerlike posture of his affines to the torn banner. Torn, the materiality of the banner fails to serve: it remains a sign for Ama Koda, but one that has left its donor's intentions behind. No longer part of a representational action in which both Ubu Tara and Ama Koda participate, the piece of cloth exposes the rawness of the feelings between them. No longer the representative, the indexical presence, of a good affine, the cloth suggests to Ama Koda a humiliating alternative—that his yera are trying to transform a respectful demand for respect into arrogant subordination, that somehow they have forgotten who he is and would deny him the recognition a good ngàba wini and a wealthy ally deserves. To make peace, the two parties must raise the mediating representations to a higher level, mobilizing cattle, gold, and ritual speakers. All of these mediating elements are produced in the social and economic conditions that I have described in this chapter. But these conditions of production alone are insufficient to produce honor, authority, or agents that others will recognize. What I turn to now are the processes of transformation at work in the action of representation, beginning, in the next chapter, with the labor of bodies.

# CHAPTER THREE

# Things of Value

On the eve of Indonesia's Independence Day, August 1986, Ubu Sebu held a nightlong rite called a *yaiwo* to celebrate his baptism into the Dutch Calvinist church, to be held the following morning. Celebrations of conversion are not uncommon, but this one was especially important. Ubu Sebu, a close relative of Umbu Sappy, the last colonial "king" of Anakalang, had been an influential ratu. His sense of momentousness displayed itself not only in his choice of a baptismal date but also in the story of his conversion. In sharp contrast to the more mundane processes of persuasion, coercion, and opportunistic calculation to which most Anakalangese admit, Ubu Sebu recounted how he had been summoned, in a malarial vision, by the Divinity itself (see Keane 1995b). Now he had invited all the remaining active ratus, as well as his affines and kabisu fellows, to the village plaza next to Umbu Sappy's great stone tomb, to announce to the ancestors his conversion and to introduce his successor as ratu, Ubu Bura. It was an occasion for conviviality, competitive displays of ritual expertise, nostalgic reminiscences about a departing era, and a fair amount of behind-the-scenes politicking as some participants sought to dampen their mutual antagonism in time for the church service.

Yaiwo center on singing and dancing, punctuated by orations. After each speech, the singer resumes, picking up key phrases from the oration for his song. The relation of speaker to singer is one of transmission, as the singer passes the words on to their true addressees, the ancestral spirits. Such events provide not only displays of harmony but also a

stage for debate and contestation. After Ubu Sebu had spoken, Ubu
Bura took the floor and made his first complaint. Due to the Christian
circumstances, even though the oratory and singing were following the
proper forms and had been preceded by a feast of pork, no offering
prayers had been said before slaughtering the pigs. Not a single chicken
or piece of betel had been given to the ancestors.

> The spirits don't know how to respond to the language of the living. . . .
> There's nothing for them to receive, am I right? Just words for them to hear.
> But as for the prayer that says "Eat the rice, drink the water, receive this!" . . .
> Now *that's* the ancestral path that was passed down for us to follow. But
> this here *talk* is all we give them, all they hear—there's no *material* for them
> to listen with, for them to receive with.

The procedural complaint revealed more than orneriness and filibuster,
although it arose from one and served the other. Ubu Bura was pointing to something important, as many people later agreed. The problem
is neither a mere technicality nor an esoteric matter of interest only to
priests; it pervades not only rites for ancestors but all formal interactions in Anakalang. Ritual words, whether spoken to spirits or to affines, must rest on the "base" (*lata*) provided by material objects, lest,
people say, they fall through the cracks on the floor into the mud and pig
excrement below the house. Ubu Bura's words emphasized the pragmatic link between words and things in several ways. He named the
speech event of prayer by quoting the reflexive language with which
prayer opens, the giving of offerings. The offering is the medium for
speech, "material for them to listen with, for them to receive with."[1] It
is as if to speak without objects is to speak to deaf ears. The powers of
speech, to which I turn in the next chapter, are considerable. But what
Ubu Bura was pointing out was that speech alone *ought* to be ineffective
and that to treat it as sufficient in itself is an act of egocentric hubris. To
understand why this should seem obvious to him, we must look carefully at the lamination of value, identity, and signification embodied in
objects.

In Anakalang, the forcefulness of exchange objects is intimately bound
up with their signlike qualities, with which they are endowed in part by
ritual speech. The nature of this intertwining suggests that neither words
nor things should be assumed in advance to be the primary media of exchange and communication, or the unique loci of value. Objects are not
sign-vehicles alone, nor is their capacity to represent the giver or to bind
the recipient an infallible property (a constant lament of local traders
who unwisely extend credit). Conversely, ceremonial exchange exists

along with—and may slip over into—alternative kinds of transaction, such as sale, barter, or loan. The demand for words serves as a reminder of something occasionally overlooked in classic approaches to exchange: that the meaning of objects and their identification with persons are not necessarily self-evident (Merlan and Rumsey 1991: 228 ff.). In asking what, and in what way, objects "represent," we must also look at their production, the transformations they undergo, the vicissitudes to which they are prone, and the alternative trajectories against which representational practice seeks to confine them. Many writers have drawn on linguistic and semiotic models to explain the value and desirability of material objects (e.g., Barthes [1967] 1983; Baudrillard 1981; McCracken 1988; Rossi-Landi 1973). But a full account of the interrelations between words and things is not merely a matter of discovering a semantics of objects analogous to that of words. It requires looking at the multifunctionality of both speech performances and objects and their practical articulations. Any approach to Anakalangese exchange must take seriously the coexistence of the semiotic, physical, and economic character of objects.

## WORK, GENDER, AND TRANSFORMATION

Since Hegel and Marx, it has been common to see physical production as the objectification of human subjects. But if objects are truly components in the active self-constitution of humans, as I have argued in chapter 1, they are inseparable from the dialectics of interaction *between* humans. One implication of this argument is that they must be viewed not just in relation to production but over the entire course of their "biographies" (Kopytoff 1986). These biographies include possible "diversions" from their expected trajectories (Appadurai 1986) and the variety of ways in which they are consumed (Baudrillard 1975; Miller 1987). By "trajectory" I mean to stress two dimensions of motion, that by which objects circulate through people's activities and that by which activities produce objects, relations, or events that can enter into new orders of activity. This motion is generated in part by what Nancy Munn (1986; see also Munn 1983) calls "transformative action." This refers to the processes by which the outcomes of certain conventional acts create the potential for actors to expand their capacities and influence beyond the spatially and temporally restricted circuits of production and consumption. These pragmatic outcomes depend in part on the physical properties of the objects involved. What I wish to stress here is that the transformations are both expressive and causal. This means that to understand objects such as tombs and cloth as representations, they must be situated within (but not reduced to) the transformative processes of which they are the outcomes. In this section, I will outline some of the relations among different kinds of "economic" activity that form one dimension of the transformative actions within which representational practices take place.

Formal exchange in Anakalang extracts certain kinds of objects from the general economy of production, utility, and consumption and imposes constraints on how they can properly be handled. The act of exchange is a moment in their transformation into things that circulate and finally, in some cases, that can be held onto forever (see chapter 8). The transactors of valuables can hope that, eventually, the social agency that they construct through these transformations can be incorporated into ancestral identities that stand out above the risks to which ongoing activity is prone: concretized in tombs and villages, recalled in names and histories. Similar processes are widely attested. For example, Maurice Bloch and Jonathan Parry (1982: 32) argue that tombs can represent an eternal order that is created by repudiating exchange. Similarly, in discussing the competitive politics of (male) reputations in Kodi, west Sumba, Janet Hoskins says, "Death removes a person from the risks of exchange and begins the process of his transformation into an ancestor" (1993b: 140). This process includes the raising of stone tombs much like those in Anakalang. What I will stress here is the way in which these transformations are mediated by, and objectified through, representational practices. As they separate objects from consumption and utility, formal transactions cast their semiotic properties into the foreground. In the process, the social character of the transacting subject is also reconfigured. Formality, selectivity, and indirection effect a series of transformations that leads away from the mortal, laboring, gendered body and its corporeal needs. Through representational practices, people become (ambivalently) identified with past ancestors and the present collectivities who take their names. This identification underlies their claims to authoritative types of agency. As will become apparent, however, the effort to endow the living with the attributes of the dead poses inevitable dilemmas.

The preconditions for such transformations are everyday production, consumption, and casual sociability. The agencies in play at this level exist at a small scale; the individual who works and eats and the household that owns the garden of maize and tubers and cooks at a single cooking hearth. Household consumption is especially identified with the work of women, reflecting a general association between women and routine diligence.[2] Women care for children, tend pigs and chickens, and manage such tasks as cooking, washing, and fetching water. When people gather, women are responsible for the smooth flow of coffee, tobacco, and betel on which men say fruitful interactions depend. In a pattern common in Southeast Asia and the Pacific (Atkinson 1989; Lederman 1986; Rosaldo 1980; Tsing 1993), men's activities contrast with the ongoing but low-intensity work of women.[3] It is men who undertake the occasional, highly visible, and even dramatic tasks such as constructing houses and fences, or slaughtering and butchering cattle. Young men prepare rice fields for planting by driving buffalo over them and watch over the herds in pastures sometimes far from the house. More senior men often try to withdraw from labor as much as they can. Freed from much of the ongoing tasks of daily subsistence, they therefore also have more time for exchange, ritual, and political maneuvering (see Lederman 1986: 131). But the poorest men, who cannot maintain large households of helpers, may be unable to fulfill such masculine prerogatives and may even have to engage in women's work, becoming less distinctively "male."

Many men recognize that their efforts to acquire wealth and reputation are ultimately grounded in women's work, speaking, for example, of the gradual accumulation made possible by the wife who patiently raises pigs. Out of an economy of pigs eventually lies the promise of herds, and from herds, the exchange relations that produce gold and strong supporters. By the same token, people sometimes attribute other men's economic and social failures to trouble in the marriage. Men will speak of such a household from the perspective of the visitor: the coffee comes late, the betel runs out, the woman neglects to prepare food. Women experience their role as crucial but also, at times, oppressive. They complain that they are held responsible when the men run through the supplies without a thought.

In fact, men often work beside women in the gardens, and some women assert themselves strongly amid the deliberations of men. Ubu Dongu boasted to me that his wife is so good at ritual speech he can send her to handle minor affairs in his place. Rabu Bita rightly claimed to know more than her loud-mouthed husband, who must consult with her before going too far out on a limb. And Ina Seja was prone to laugh at her husband's conversations with me about ritual knowledge as a relatively harmless obsession, although she was also annoyed that it often keeps him away from the fields. But men, at least those with ambitions, portray themselves in terms of sitting and talking. Although very few men are able to escape labor altogether, some speak of themselves as if they can. One skilled ritual speaker, for example, told me that he lives by talking, not gardening, though I know he spends long hot hours in the fields.

Households can reproduce themselves physically with just maize and tubers. A stock of garden products can support the most casual forms of visiting among close neighbors and kin. The capacity of these foods to mediate more expansive relations, however, or to sustain memories and obligations—to engage with others and to extend this moment's activity into the future—is very limited. The next step in the expansive media-tion of social identities is embodied in betel and rice, which, as across Southeast Asia, are basic media of polite sociability. Both require access to resources that are both more scarce and more permanent than ordi-nary swidden gardens. Betel, when not bought in the market, comes from areca palms. These must be planted and take years to reach matu-rity. Thus they index ongoing control over a single plot of land and the present outcome of long-past intentions. Like tobacco, betel is a form of consumption that is not food, and as such, is a metonym for the world of luxuries beyond subsistence (see Onvlee [1933] 1973a: 27). The betel quid is also iconic of interaction. It combines two distinct elements, betel pepper (*kuta*) and areca nut (*winu*). When catalyzed by slaked lime, the two components produce a stimulant whose external mark, blood red saliva, resembles none of the original ingredients.[4] A minia-ture transformation of value, the resulting whole, a "chew" (*pamama*), is greater than the sum of its parts.

Betel marks the individual's basic potential for transforming con-sumption into sociability. When two people meet on the path, it is sim-ple good manners to stop, briefly exchange betel pouches, and have a chew. Moreover, the value of betel as a vehicle of recognition can be foregrounded by stylistic formality. Thus when receiving guests, one might graciously hand each visitor a separate dish of betel. Betel is pre-eminently social and a metonym for each individual's capacity to ex-tend hospitality to, and thus recognize the worth of, another.[5] But it is rice that enables people to enter into more serious and long-lasting interactions.

Rice requires access to wet rice fields, the claim to which, unlike household gardens, ultimately rests with kabisu, and demands the col-

lective labor of buffalo, men, and women—normally beyond the scale of
a single household—to work them.[6] Rice is the proper food to serve
guests, and a baseline requirement for any event that gathers together a
wide range of people, such as a funeral or meeting of kabisu fellows.
Unlike exchange goods, however, rice is not the stuff of formal debts.
Whatever informal tallying in fact goes on, it would be excessively "economically minded" (Indo. *ekonomis*) to be seen to calculate and balance out the giving and receiving of rice.[7] Nonetheless, rice is a condition of possibility for the creation of debts. It permits households to
engage in hospitality and cooperation with socially more distant others
than could be managed with garden produce. Thus a stock of rice helps
keep alive the ongoing baseline of sociability on which a household presumes when asking others for help in exchange. Even when a household
is not itself a host, by contributing rice to the feasts, funerals, and other
hospitable acts of others, it can claim to participate in the agency that
is constructed through such acts. Through everyday hospitality, maintained by women's diligence in keeping up the smooth flow of betel and
rice (and more recently, tobacco and coffee), people display their self-
respect and their respect for others. On this base, more momentous projects can be constructed, formal exchanges with the potential to transform the nature of a relationship from that between strangers, literally
"other people" (*tau heka*), into some form of the inclusive first person,
"us" (*duta*).

Household production can enter directly into exchange by way of
pigs, which are conventionally the responsibility of women. Women
who lack them can convert forest and garden products and chickens into
pigs through barter, sale, or borrowing. Pigs are labor intensive, because they are fed scraps that must be chopped up and are often cooked;
to have plenty of pigs testifies to everyday diligence in a way that a herd
of horses does not. Once a household has pigs, it has a component of
ceremonial exchange or a good that can be informally traded upward
(someone who needs a pig for an exchange may be forced to barter a
horse for one). The pig is a critical transition point: it is the most valuable animal normally recognized as the property of a woman. A man
who wishes to use a pig must obtain the permission of the woman who
raised it and (if it is not for a marriage exchange) compensate her with
a gold ornament (*mamuli*) to "cool the trough." In this act of recognition, the only formal exchange to take place *within* the household (which
normally acts as a unit), the formal transformation from women's labor

into representational practice is effected. Before turning to the representational dimensions of valuables, I will first show some of the alternatives against which formal exchange is constructed.

## REGIMES OF VALUE

The way in which Anakalangese see status, power, wealth, and the meaning of relations to be, at least in principle, mutually implicated, challenges any analytic attempt to maintain a straightforward distinction between utility and symbolic value. In practice, however, formal exchanges implicitly stress the semiotic dimension of objects, play down utility, and rigorously exclude money except as a symbolic piece of metal. Nonetheless, formal exchanges are embedded within a larger political economy of both social signs and usable things, and take some of their meaning from the way in which they differ from alternative "regimes of value."[8] Explicit talk about correct tradition (*pata*) is one of the ways in which the barriers between exchange and its alternatives are maintained. Anakalangese can point to the coexistence of exchange with markets, barter, usurious lending, and theft in order to insist on its distinctive moral value (see Thomas 1991). For example, when Ubu Kura tried to impress upon me the superior morality of exchange, he said that the same pig that would get you five buffalo and five horses in marriage exchange would be worth the price of only a middling buffalo and a small horse if sold. He found in market values a way to measure the heavy weight of the obligations imposed by proper exchange. Such comparisons are part of the background against which exchange has long been carried out. They simultaneously represent formal exchange as morally elevated by virtue of its supposed exemption from the calculation and rationality of other transactions and as a difficult burden.

When directing a marriage exchange, Ubu Neka once shouted at the men who were negotiating, 'Slow down! We're not buying and selling in the marketplace!' The point of explicit comparisons between formal exchange and alternative regimes of value is usually to affirm the status and compulsory nature of "real custom" (*na pata mema*; see chapter 7) as a discrete domain of social action, which Anakalangese often contrast to "politicized custom" (Indo. *adat politik*). The latter expresses local historical imagination in terminology that reflects contemporary national culture. The word *adat* reifies colonial and postcolonial concepts of primordial order, whereas *politik* has primarily negative connotations of dirty tricks and self-interested maneuvering. In reference to exchange, "politicized custom" denotes competition, calculation, and profit and confines these to the disorderly present. These are familiar themes in talk about capitalist relations (Hugh-Jones 1990; Parry and Bloch 1989; Taussig 1980). But I will argue that they also manifest more specific concerns about the potential detachment of objects from persons, concerns which are implicated in exchange itself.

The comparison of exchange and its alternatives often implies a claim about rank. Anakalangese frequently assert that market thinking is purely a recent and (usually) deplorable development, that in the past, no one calculated the value of what they gave you. But now we live in a selfish era whose slogan is "as long as I [get mine]" (*mali nyuwa*). As a way of expressing and historicizing the difference between formal exchange and its alternatives, people sometimes talk about the economic irrationality of the past. For example, one man told me that people used to trade like quantities for like, regardless of the actual substance: one sack of rice would go for one, much more expensive, sack of coffee. He was suggesting that the folly of his forebears consisted in being taken in by the very materiality of things. They were unable to perform the symbolic operations embodied in money: exchange value in those days was inseparable from the things themselves (see Keane 1996; Wielenga 1908). Part of the subtext here is a display of aristocratic disdain for haggling and calculation. The hierarchical implications of alternative regimes of value become explicit when some people observe that those Anakalangese who engage in trade are usually of low rank, because, they claim, such people are naturally more clever at calculation.

Calculation implies a play on the relations between the object as sign of something other than itself and as a source of value in itself, which is most evident at the boundaries between formal exchange and other kinds of transaction. The boundaries among kinds of transactions are permeable, if not conceptually then practically, for there are few exchange valuables that do not have some value in other contexts. For example, a horse received from Christian affines in marriage exchange can be sacrificed to "pagan" spirits, or sold for cash. This permeability is both a resource and a threat, insofar as a skillful, or simply powerful, player can take advantage of it, but the existence of alternative schemes of value bears the increasingly real potential for undermining the status claims of exchange, a threat at once logical, political, and economic.

Despite the traditionalist tendency to claim for the past the high values of ceremonial exchange, and confine less exalted alternatives to the present, all sorts of transactions have been available to Anakalangese, even before the introduction of markets and shops.[9] The social logic of the alternatives can be illustrated by two ways of compensating people for assistance rendered. *Kahewa* is given for some special skill, such as that of a ritual specialist or carpenter. A formal exchange of cloth, metal valuables, and living animals, it distinguishes skill from mere labor, which is sustained with cooked food, tobacco, betel, and coffee. The latter items are all consumed within the individual body of the worker, their objectual duration confined to the period of the work itself. In contrast, since the valuables given in kahewa are determined by the affinal statuses of the kabisu of recipient and donor, they presuppose collective identities, and, since they are eventually reciprocated, they entail future interactions.

In practice, boundaries among kinds of transactions can be problematic. This can be seen in *madara*, travel to other ecological zones on the island, bringing local products such as tobacco or salt to trade for food during times of hunger at home. Madara carries a potential for transformation into longer-term relations, but one that is highly contestable and unstable. For example, Markus's father's mercenary approach enabled him to exploit madara relationships to build up a considerable herd between the 1940s and 1960s. As the owner of several good rice fields he often attracted visitors from Mamboru on the dry north coast, from whom he could get a buffalo in return for four sacks of rice. In his eyes, these visitors from afar were mere strangers (tau heka), with whom any future ties were uncertain. But other people attempt to transform past madara into long-term relationships. For instance, when a young couple from previously unrelated kabisu decided to marry, the memory of former madara came into play. The man's kabisu approached the bride's people hoping for some recognition, saying 'We are birth fellows (oli dadi) in the rice bin' to allude to those visits. This was an acceptable approach. But later on, when negotiations became troubled, someone from the bride's group commented, scathingly, 'They only called us birth fellows because they were hungry.'

These examples illustrate the unstable relationship between madara and other forms of exchange. For Markus's father, the moment of exchange is clear and bounded, like sale and purchase. The suitors, in contrast, hope to awaken in past madara a potential for transformation into future affinal bonds. The complaint by the bride's kabisu, however, shows that this potential is subject to retrospective ratification or rejection: had the negotiations been more gratifying, they might have recognized a stronger foundation in those madara. Such alternatives display the possibility, in any given instance, that people may hold conflicting interpretations as to what kind of transaction they are, or had been, engaged in, and thus what potentials for future transactions now exist. Part of the work of formal procedures is to narrow the play of possibilities.

## METAL AND CLOTH

The most formal kinds of exchange impose the greatest constraints on potential interpretations. They do so in part by limiting the kinds of objects involved and by emphasizing the properties by which they serve as representations (signs) and representatives (of agents). This is done by treating them as material signs themselves and as interdependent with a distinct plane of verbal signs. Material objects contrast in several ways to the familiar Saussurean model of the arbitrary sign, which signifies only by virtue of a social convention, and whose phenomenal qualities (such as color or sound) are relevant only as marks of difference from other signs. Objects cannot be produced at will but must be sought from somewhere: they are subject to scarcity and are relatively easy to quantify. Moreover, even highly symbolic exchange valuables bear physical properties in excess of their purely conventional attributes, which contributes to their potential for diversion into use or to alternative kinds of transaction.[10] Finally, they have durability. Non-consumables persist over time, across multiple transactions, passing through the hands of many people and taking on a range of possible functions. The materiality of objects is a condition of possibility for their movement across social and semiotic domains. For example, the charisma of the Thai hermit monk, once objectified in the form of an amulet, is able to enter into the mundane realm of distinctly non-ascetic purposes, such as good luck in the lottery (Tambiah 1984: 336; for similar boundary crossing between sacred and secular in Europe, see Geary 1986 and Stallybrass 1996). The multiple uses, mobility, and durability of objects allow them to extend the agency of their producers and original transactors. But the same properties entail the possibility that they will become detached from their transactors altogether. Their powers are mutually implicated with certain dilemmas, something that, as I argue below, they share with ritual speech.

In Anakalang, the objects of exchange belong to a clearly delimited class, which helps protect their role as conventional symbols of intent. In this role, they are known as *dati*, the material objects conventionally required by a given transaction or ritual. As dati, valuables fall into two categories, goods given by ngàba wini and by yera. Ngàba wini's goods consist of items of gold or other metals, machetes, swords, spears, horses, and buffalo. Yera's are cloth, pigs, and (on a single occasion, the trans-fer of the bride) ivory bracelets. With a few marked exceptions, a gift from one category should be reciprocated only with a gift from the other, regardless of the context (be it marriage, land transaction, spirit ritual, peacemaking, or mortuary rite). Exchange valuables include both special goods and objects of everyday use. The latter include cloth and the often humble machete, commonplace items that flow easily between exchange and ordinary use. Other valuables, such as ceremonial spears and what are sometimes described in ethnographic literature as "orna-ments," lack any function outside of ritual and exchange. They can be of gold, silver, brass, or tin.[11] Of particular importance is the omega-shaped mamuli (fig. 6), the image of which is carved on tombs and woven in cloth and has even been reproduced in the giant form of a gateway outside a soccer field in the regency capital (Keane 1988).[12]

Whether commonplace or rare, in daily use or held in reserve, an im-portant part of the value of all Anakalangese inanimate exchange valu-ables is that they are not produced locally. The link between distance in space and time can be seen in how people talk about the origins of metal valuables. Metal valuables seem simply to exist and circulate. They do not come *from* anywhere within Anakalangese experience. When, for example, I asked people about the sources of mamuli, the first answer would be to locate their origins in the past. After I pressed Ubu Sebu about who makes mamuli today, he replied that *real* mamuli aren't made anymore. Those that are made today are just imitations.[13]

Although he is surely aware that gold can come from trade and that smiths still work it today, Ubu Sebu's characteristic insistence on the distinction between real and spurious valuables points to ancestral ori-gins as the true source of value. This is brought out by several myths of origin in which the materials for metal valuables are autochthonous, but their fashioning lies in foreign hands. Anakalangese identify the original metalworker, Ubu Tara Hawu and the kabisu often associated with him, Hawu, as coming from Sawu, the island east of Sumba (his-torically a source of many metalworkers). Ubu Tara Hawu passed on his specialty to the kabisu, whose members are said to own the original tools for smithing gold. But these are now kept hidden away as an-cestral valuables that no one knows how to use (see chapter 8). Signifi-cantly, many people draw a connection between their metalworking skill and relatively low mythic status: Hawu, as befits a kabisu whose very name identifies it as foreign, has no properly ancestral land. Unlike a fully legitimate kabisu, whose status is well established by first settle-ment or affinal gift, they are dubious latecomers, having merely bought

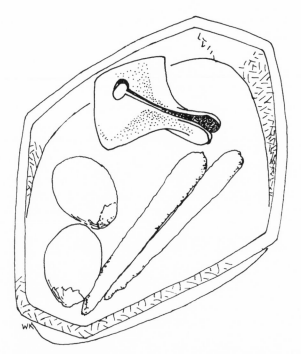

Figure 6. Mamuli with round areca nuts and long betel peppers in an offering dish. (Drawing by the author.)

their land in return for gold and silver ornaments. Thus the contrast between legitimate permanence, embodied in the kabisu's possessions, and the shifting ground of market relations is projected into the very origins of exchange itself.

The fashioners of metal are foreign, but the actual materials come from the earth. In one version, before arriving in Sumba the ancestors were traveling together across the seven levels of sea and eight levels of sky. They were in darkness until, at the fifth level, Sulphur Cave, Stone Hollow, they encountered the first glimmers of light. There they used lightning to shatter the stones that blocked their way. The glimmering stones turned out to be gold, from which Ubu Tara Hawu later fashioned the first valuables.[14]

Another story is revealing for the links it draws among gold, the earth, fertility, and exogamy. In the earliest days, when people were few, and ignorant of proper marriages, there were seven brothers and eight sisters. Each brother married a sister, leaving Rabu Màbal alone without a mate. There came a large fieldmouse seeking to marry her. In the words of ratu Ngongu of Lai Merang,

That night the mouse spoke with Rabu Màbal, whispering, "Your father just wants cattle, wants me to bring gold, pure gold, *madàka, tabelu, làba, maraga,* all of gold. What don't I have in my house!" So spoke the mouse. But it's true. Madàka come from that mouse, the price of Rabu Màbal. Tabelu come from that mouse, the price of Rabu Màbal, from the very beginning. From the beginning. Didn't use cattle for bridewealth. Didn't pay for her like that for Rabu Kareri earlier. It wasn't the same. Ubu Sebu, earlier, married because of his magical powers, Rabu Màbal because of the price. . . . It came from Grandfather Mouse (Boku Malawu). "So, just wait, tomorrow I'll bring it, first I'll go now." He left, he went, this Grandfather Mouse, he returned bringing two madàka: "Here, give this to your father." She said [to her father] "Here is what was brought by Lord Mouse." . . . He brought that which is hung here [at the ear], four of them, they're still around, when we Descend to the Valley [for ritual]. They're here too [as inalienable valuables], those which are stuck on the chest, they're here, they're here.

Having obtained Rabu Màbal, the mouse waited until she was pregnant before bringing her back to his home. But this was a hole in the ground and she could not squeeze through the entrance, until finally the mouse cut her into pieces. From these descend the various garden crops.

As in the previous story, gold arrives as an originary intervention into human society from the outside. The ambiguously disastrous consequences involved in the first case of exogamous marriage, dismemberment that leads to fertility, illustrate the well-attested tension underlying marriage alliance in both myth and practice, to which I will return. The introduction of gold as a medium, at least in ratu Ngongu's version, both facilitates the entrance of an outsider into an otherwise self-contained society and creates an alternative to more direct exercises of bodily powers that had been sufficient to effect the alliance. The story of the mouse represents gold as a lesser replacement for greater, direct forms of action. Like the story of the dog, it depicts metal as lying at the origins of properly social existence.

## THE EXCESS OF MEANINGS

The power and value of valuables in exchange are to be sought at the intersection of their everyday uses, character as signs, potential roles in other regimes of value, and functions in performance. The division of goods according to categories of affines, reflecting a twofold division of the social universe, invites us to seek this division in the symbolic nature of the goods themselves. In particular, it is tempting to see them as "male" and "female" valuables (Rodgers 1985; Weiner 1976, 1986). In many societies, such gendered goods are explicitly said to "replace" gendered bodies that have been lost through marriage or death (in eastern Indonesia, see Barraud 1979: 218; Geirnaert-Martin 1992a: 264; McKinnon 1991: 263). But an object does not replace *everything* about a living person; at best it does so selectively. As Strathern (1988) argues, such "replacements" must be understood with reference to male and female *qualities*, abstracted from the actual living persons who bear them. To understand how goods have, represent, transfer, or transmute gender requires a closer look at both their semiotic nature and their articulation with political economy.

As signs, valuables can be understood in terms of iconism (resemblance), indexicality (connection), and symbolism (arbitrary conventional attribution), although not necessarily in coordination. It has been common for anthropological exegesis, like earlier traditions of iconology, to concentrate on icon and symbol, which are more accessible to semantic interpretation. But it is important to look at indexicality as well. Indexical signs are linked to what they signify by existential connections: they show causal effects (as a scar indexes an earlier accident) or actual proximity (as an exit sign marks a certain door). Less overtly conventional than symbols, they can make signs seem inherently more plausible and thus help naturalize socially conventional signifieds, such as authority and status. By their very character, they also forge bonds between causal and logical meanings and thus can play an important role in the articulation of political economy with representations.

The cultural uses of material objects as signs can develop several different aspects of form at once. A good example of this is Gregory Forth's (1981: 126–127) discussion of the meaning of metal chips in Rindi ritual. He mentions in turn their hardness, durability, and shininess (all iconic properties) and their (indexical) associations with wealth, with life-givers, and with the earth. As his account makes clear, without further evidence there is in principle no reason to privilege any of these readings; indeed their multiplicity may contribute to ritually valuable polysemy. Moreover, ambiguity may be tactically advantageous, as suggested by Edgar Keller's (1992: 258) account of a rich, self-made Laboyan who favored an idiosyncratic style of tying his headcloth, with the ends hanging down. The man himself claimed this was a reminder of his humble origins, but others took the dangling ends to refer to *other* people, over whom he was asserting his dominance. His deployment is vulnerable to the underdetermination of iconism, something he may be

taking advantage of, allowing him both to boast and to deny the implications of doing so.

Even spears and swords, which come from ngàba wini, and whose
gendered character might seem relatively straightforward, can be semiotically complex. Indexically, swords and spears are associated with war
and hunting, aggressive activities of men. Iconically, they (along with
the horns of the buffalo they often accompany) might be phallic as well,
although I only heard one Anakalangese suggest so.[15] Explicit discourses,
such as kabisu histories, favor some aspects over others. In several, an
important spring is created when an ancestor strikes the ground with a
spear. One ancestor used his weapons to split the sea, making the settlement of Sumba possible. Such stories conjoin the life-threatening character of weapons with life-giving. The metaphors of ritual speech similarly depict weapons as instruments that create fruitful connections.
For example, ngàba wini brings to yera's funeral a machete to clear
away hindrances in the path of the deceased and a spear for the dead to
use as a walking staff. In some rites and marriage exchanges, the machete is said to "open the path," clearing away obstacles, and in a ritual
to restore the damage caused by incest, the spear is called "a snare pole"
to reach across the gap between offended parties. Such verbal conventions appear to discover iconism opportunistically, seeing in weapons
not just the ability to cut and pierce but also a length, shape, or manner
of grasping.

A similar range of possibilities runs through the uses of cloth, given
by yera. The cloth used in exchange and ritual also serves as ordinary
clothing.[16] Thus, like machetes, it can move directly from formal to daily
use. As clothing in motion, it seems to operate at the margins of the self
(Stallybrass 1995), at once identified with the wearer and transferable to
others. Ritual speech brings out other dimensions of cloth. In contrast
to the social and bodily state of undress, ritual preparedness is figured
as having one's "headcloth fitted for the head, waistcloth tightly wound
at the waist." A cloth given in the final stages of marriage exchange is
figured as shading the bride on her passage, "rain shelter, sun shade."
This same expression also denotes the protective qualities expected of
a mother's brother, who reminds his sister of this when bringing cloth
for the naming ceremonies of her children. Literalizing the metaphor, it is
the latter who should give the first layer of cloth to be wrapped around
the corpse before burial. Many other ritual practices also draw on clothing's enveloping function. For instance, sacred or "hot" objects and
activities (carving, pounding and cooking rice, washing sacralia) should

be wrapped in or hidden behind screens of cloth. This protects them from the gaze of spectators and protects passersby against danger.

These words and actions find the iconism of cloth in its properties as an opaque and unbroken surface. Other figures draw attention to its pliability, softness, and fragility. In many contexts, a gift of cloth is said to clean off the dirt of a journey or to wipe away the recipient's blood, sweat, mucus, or tears. Being soft and absorbent, cloth lends itself to interpretation as a medium of nurturing actions. But it is also less durable than metal.[17] This has led ethnographers elsewhere in eastern Indonesia to propose that the impermanence of cloth, in contrast to metal, replicates the contrast between the social mobility of women who marry across social boundaries and the ideally lasting identity of patrilines (McKinnon 1991; Traube 1986).[18]

But perhaps the most direct gender association of cloth is in the role of women as weavers. Many studies of cloth look to the production process as a source of value, meaning, and gender identity. As is common in many weaving traditions (Messick 1987; Weiner 1989), people in Sumbanese cloth weaving districts also draw analogies between the production process and female reproductivity (Forth 1981: 150, 369; Geirnaert-Martin 1992a: 94; Hoskins 1989). Such analogies combine indexical ties between the gender of weaver and the woven with iconic and symbolic aspects of the activity itself. Anakalang, however, has neither weavers nor an elaborated discourse of weaving.[19] Yet everyone in Anakalang knows that elsewhere cloth is woven by women. In fact, cloth's value for them may have all the more power precisely because local women do *not* weave. In Anakalangese experience, cloth is not the outcome of the actual labor of particular women. Detached from its origins in this way, yet still presupposing *some* women's labor somewhere, it is well suited as a *representation* of women in the abstract. Like metal valuables, cloth may take some of its value precisely from its distance from the site of production. Both cloth and metal enter the Anakalangese world already fashioned. By allowing their representational properties to come to the fore, this supports their potential to stand for the enduring *groups* that transact them, rather than the individual, gendered, and mortal *bodies* that produce them.

## SOCIAL ANIMALS

No exchange can take place without metal and cloth, but important transactions and offerings also require animals. Ngàba wini's gifts of metal travel along with horses and buffalo; yera's cloth accompanies pigs. Like metal and cloth, their value and significance draw on varied sources, but their uses and production also introduce a distinct set of problems. The small Sumbanese horses have some utility for riding, carrying light loads, and occasionally racing, but their numbers in Anakalang outstrip their functions. Pigs serve only as exchange goods, offerings, and meat. Among all exchange valuables, buffalo are unusual in their utility. Since they are used to trample rice fields before planting, they are important instruments of production. They therefore form a critical node at which economic power and authoritative transactions meet. Nonetheless, this position alone is insufficient to account for their value.[20]

One thing that buffalo, horses, and pigs share is a semiotic capacity for displaying their owners' wealth to the world at large. Living in corrals and pastures, horses and buffalo are highly visible to passersby and their numbers readily calculated. When brought to or from an exchange, rite, or feast, the buffalo and horses are led, the pigs carried in bamboo cases, accompanied by a boisterous procession of men and women. The gongs, cheers, songs, and ululations of the entourage draw the attention of everyone within earshot, which often reaches for several miles. Processions themselves are pragmatic icons of the extension of self, as the sound of the gongs (their distinctive tones capable of indexing the particular village that owns them) carries the group's reputation.[21] On arriving at its destination, which may be at the far reaches of Anakalang or even, with the help of rented trucks, distant parts of the island, the visiting party stands in the plaza in front of the house, dramatically presenting both the entourage and the gifts it has brought (fig. 7). This presentation can have a confrontational quality to it, as the amassed visitors challenge the recipient to accept the debt the gifts entail.

In most cases, the lifelong circulation of an animal comes to a climactic finale on the village plaza, when it is killed for a funeral, feast, or ritual. Buffalo provide the greatest spectacle.[22] Adults and children, women and men, all enthusiastically watch, cheer, and loudly comment as men lead a struggling animal out into the plaza, where one of them will slash the jugular. The spectators attentively seek divinatory signs in the death struggle: as Ama Pedi explained to me, part of the fascination lies in the dramatic possibility that something unexpected will happen. When a buffalo falls too quickly, so too will the standing, wealth, or health of the hosts. Pak Yos's uncanny midlife demise by choking,

Figure 7. Procession of yera stands in the plaza of ngàba wini's village and confronts them with pigs (on bamboo frames) and cloth (both displayed and carried in baskets). This photograph was taken during the exchanges occasioned by the completion of a new house by ngàba wini (Gàlu Rota, July 1987).

for instance, was given divinatory support at the time of his burial. One buffalo died with its legs rigidly up in the air, another with its horn stuck deeply in the ground. People took these to confirm the ominous purport of Pak Yos's death, that his wealth would never pass on to his children. The inherent possibility of misfire is implicated in the haruspices that accompany every non-Christian kill, from chick to buffalo. Chicken entrails and pig, buffalo, and horse livers are examined for signs that the gift has been rejected or gone astray.[23]

Once the slaughter is complete, the carcasses are distributed among the visiting parties, who butcher, cook, and consume them.[24] After the feast, the buffalo horns and pig jawbones are preserved. Horns are usually displayed on the exterior of the house, jawbones hanging along a cord inside.[25] Over the years, certain houses accumulate stacks of horns and rows of jawbones, animals and events transformed into a quantity of durable, nearly identical tokens. As the accumulation of horns and jawbones suggests, transactions involving animals are evaluated primarily in terms of category (yera or ngàba wini goods) and quantity. Except for the sex of the animal (steers and stallions are more valuable than mares and cows, sows are excluded from exchange), qualitative distinctions, such as color, are of little importance. The quantitative dimension of exchange valuables is a measure primarily of the status claimed by donors and the recognition accorded to recipients. The qualitative dimension functions performatively to construct the contextually relevant social gender of each party. Regardless of whether the exchange concerns an actual marriage alliance or some other relationship, the two parties define themselves through the objects they give, as being categorically yera and ngàba wini. Both the quantity and the size of the animals involved in any exchange are subject to intensive scrutiny, gossip, and speculation. Pigs are measured by the number of men it takes to carry them in a procession, horses by broader categories of age and sex.[26] The most finely graded scale speaks of buffalo horns in lengths measured against a person's outstretched arm, the speaker commonly pointing to the spot while mentioning it.[27]

Despite the pressures—from ancestors, exchange partners, and their own self-esteem—against selling animals on the market, people know that animals can be converted into cash.[28] But amid the constant discussion of animals given and received, people resist talking about them in monetary terms, preferring instead to use the conventional bodily measures.[29] The value of exchange is to be found in part in the way it stands out *against* this conversion as both a practical and a discursive reserve of value. It is only under translation into money that different kinds of animals can be measured directly against each other. Most exchange obscures any direct measure of reciprocity by which individual pigs and buffalo can be equated. Prestation and counterprestation are often separated in time, mingle actual animals with promises of varying certainty, and always include cloth and metal along with the animals. As I noted above, however, when people talk about exchange in normative terms, they may take *rhetorical* advantage of monetary measures to show the disparities between the two partners' prestations: since the animals given by ngàba wini are much more valuable, in market terms, than those given by yera, the remainder expresses the value of the gift of lifeblood provided by yera—as well as everyone's respect for tradition.

The tension between economic and semiotic dimensions of exchange can appear as a distinction between the abstract obligation to give and the concrete relations between persons. Sometimes people try to separate the two. For example, Ama Pedi's father's brother had no son, and over the years, Ama Pedi treated his father's brother's daughter's husband (*layewa*) as one of his own closest ngàba wini. Although this was appropriate, he had exploited the relationship to the point that when his father's brother died, the layewa tried to prevent their prestations from entering his herd. At the time of the burial, they brought a buffalo as was their obligation, but they insisted that it be included among the animals slaughtered on the plaza, saying the buffalo was for the deceased, not for Ama Pedi. In fact they had no right to determine where the prestation went once it had been given, and this demand failed. It seems, however, they then made a secret arrangement with another one of the parties at the funeral, one of Ama Pedi's yera, who then made off with the buffalo without permission. In this case, the act of giving (a duty to a deceased affine) is strongly separated from the economic value embedded in the object itself (an advantage accrued to Ama Pedi).

In contrast to cloth and metal, pigs, horses, and buffalo are produced through local efforts. By the convention that makes them the responsibility, respectively, of women and men, they can index gender. But, as the ubiquity and value in exchange of metal and cloth suggest, production alone may not be sufficient to bind objects to their transactors. What do the measures of value tell us? The size of buffalo horns and pig tusks (horses lack enduring signs of value) are measures of age. But what does age index? In Kodi, Hoskins argues, the value of animals' age is "the time spent raising them, and the 'biological' investment made by their owner" (1993b: 203). As Hoskins (1993b: 210) points out, however, the fact that pigs require more work than buffalo does not make them more valuable: a buffalo's age indicates how long a man has had his own household and thus tracks the progress of his own biography. To generalize her point, like Marx's labor value, this time measures, not raw effort expended, but time socially evaluated.

The less individualistic pattern of Anakalangese ownership and exchange and the important role of pigs, the products of women, bring out the importance of how "investment" articulates with representational practices. Animals are in constant circulation. Moreover, in important exchanges both moral and economic pressure force the principal transactors to use animals provided by their affines and kabisu fellows (see chapter 7). For both reasons, most of the animals exchanged or killed in any instance are unlikely to have been raised by the transactor. Where, in addition, labor itself is not highly valued, another thing that an animal's age measures is its relative longevity, socially understood: older animals have either circulated through longer chains of exchanges or been withheld longer against the pressure to kill them. To the extent that the donor or sacrificer is identified with the animal, it is as a transactor, not producer (perhaps this is why the divination reflects on the recipient, not the donor).

For animals, as well as metal and cloth, a crucial step intervenes between production and public evaluation. In principle, most valuable objects arrive into one's hands having already passed through previous exchanges. This has consequences for the gendered identity of buffalo and pigs. Detached from the site of production, displayed and passed on through scenes of encounter, they are transmuted into representations. They are given and received by groups who face each other as yera and ngàba wini, generic categories of affines. In their hands, valuables serve less as indexes of the gendered individuals who once produced them than as detachable representations of gendered qualities—not men and women, but selected conventional aspects of maleness and femaleness (see Strathern 1981, 1988). When people collectively face each other as affines, their prestations contribute to one another's most publicly visible and authoritative identities as kabisu and derive from their relations with other, absent kabisu as well. But to understand how these acting subjects are constructed requires a closer look at the forms of representational practice.

DOUBLED SIGNS

The boundaries between formal exchange and other kinds of transaction require a certain amount of policing against the fallibility of memory and the workings of deceit. One effect of the high formality of exchange events is to help separate signification and utility, emphasizing the semiotic character of objects that also bear use and market values, part of the ongoing effort it takes to keep gift and commodity distinct. This is reinforced by the ritual speech that often implies that neither party desires the objects in question but is only compelled by ancestral mandate. Acknowledging the possibility of misconstrual, people say that marriage is not like going to the market. They insist that they seek objects not for the value of the things themselves, as in purchase and sale, but as representations, expressions of each party's value for the other. Underlining this insistence is the great attention they pay to the proper forms of transaction.

Exchange is set apart from other transactions in part by the formal structure of a double movement, which works to confine and direct its semantic and pragmatic possibilities. Objects move at once *against* the countergifts to which they are by convention opposed (such as metal against cloth), and *in tandem* with counterparts. The former movement is one of counterposed categories of things that elicit one another, as the categories of givers, yera and ngàba wini, mutually define one another. It is called *pitaku*, the reciprocal relation between one move and its response, or the equivalent that covers (*tanga*) the debt.

Objects in formal exchange rarely travel alone, however, but are matched with other objects. Each animal (or unitary set of animals) is represented by its "partner" (*gàḅa*) or "tether" (*laiku*). This is a small valuable, cloth from yera, metal or occasionally its symbolic equivalent, paper money, from ngàba wini. If one's prestation or verbal statement is to be binding, efficacious, and serious, one must "place it in the basket's weave, place it in the offering dish." This refers to the giving of a token in an offering dish (*tanga liḍi*), along with a small amount of betel pepper and areca nut.[30] The objects given in the offering dish are called "Sawunese betel pepper" (*kuta Hawu*). This allusion to the proffered betel is a euphemistic displacement, modestly referring neither to the prestation nor even to its token, but only to the betel chew amid which, as it were, the cloth or metal token is silently discovered. In keeping with this trope, the offering dish is treated as if it were being used in the ordinary etiquette of receiving guests. Betel is always included with the tokens, the dish is then politely passed over to the recipient, and when it is eventually returned with a counterprestation, the old betel has been replaced with a fresh supply.

When the prestations are large, are meant to convey several distinct intentions, or are to be divided among several recipients, the offering dishes are carefully lined up in rows (fig. 8). In marriage exchange, they are set out in order of the quantities they represent, the largest to the donor's right, "up there" (*nai ḍeta*), the smallest to his left, "down there" (*nai wawa*). In speech, they are referred to in the same order, from "above" to "below," and the speaker usually points to the dish in question. With expectations of eventual fertility, like crops in the garden, they are "put all in rows, planted in a line." This phrase expresses how the row of dishes is itself an icon of the entire procedure, diagrammed as an orderly sequence of actions. Another couplet, "the singer's sequence, the column of dancers," refers to both dishes and sequence, evoking in turn other linear forms of order such as ritual dances and the succession of poetic couplets. The combined dish, betel, and token forms the "instrument for speaking" (*papanewi waingu*), grounding the words

Figure 8. Ngàba wini meet to discuss their resources and sort out the mamuli, chains, machetes, and other tokens that will go in the offering dishes at one stage of negotiation (Lai Bodi, May 1986).

that direct the intended recipient and pragmatic force of the gifts, dwelling on the question raised by any prestation: "Where does it strike?" (*beya na pinya pawànanya?*), "Where is its path?" (*beya na larana?*).

Built into this are two temporal features, for neither the objects that move *against* each other nor the objects that move *along with* each other are ever exactly co-present. Each is a physical token of a promise made, or a commitment fulfilled. The relation is asymmetrical, for tokens in the dish appear prior to what they represent: although normally many of the animals are only promised for sometimes quite distant or vague future delivery (one gives their "shadow" [*mawu*] or "name" [*ngara*]), the tokens *must* be present and change hands for the exchange to occur.

Depending on the category of donor, either cloth or metal can be used as "Sawunese betel pepper." This use of tokens to mark intentions and situate the act within a larger project is echoed in the use of the offering dish in other transactions and recalls how visitors are received each with an individual dish of betel. One reason for the use of the offering dish is to formalize the act of giving. As Ubu Logi put it, 'I give an offering dish to a visitor so when I serve him/her chicken, s/he doesn't just think it happened to die of disease.' The token is a form of "proof" (Indo. *bukti*), a mark or sign (*tada*) of words and intentions that remain after the moment of speaking and giving.[31]

The insistent attentiveness given to tokens and dishes implies a latent alternative. As Ubu Logi's remark suggests, people are aware of the possibility that the gift will become detached from the giver and the intent. Objects require the reflexive capacity of language if they are to serve as fully efficacious media of social relations. One pig, horse, or piece of cloth is pretty much like another of its kind: it is words that specify what kind of action is being performed, and from whom the prestations come, to whom they are directed, and what kind of act they perform.[32] If the transactors do not formally state the name, purpose, donor, or recipient of the gift, it remains "in the dark" (*ta kapatang*). The recipients can know only "what came out" (*na ma lauhung*). One not unusual incident illustrates both the importance of the token and the sheer difficulty imposed by the formality of exchange. After negotiating a marriage all night, two kabisu had reached the stage of relaxed socializing after ritual speech was no longer necessary and members of each party could come into the same room, share betel and tobacco, and talk to one another directly. The leaders and their speakers were totaling up the animals given and promised by ngàba wini over the course of the

night, using areca nuts as counters. Ngàba wini came up with thirty,
whereas yera figured thirty-nine. At this, yera reached into their baskets
and counted out the chains, mamuli, and machetes they had received.
This took several recounts, as ngàba wini progressively acknowledged
thirty-two, thirty-four, then thirty-five, while yera persisted in thirty-six
head. Finally someone remembered that ngàba wini had forgotten to
count the cow that had been killed to feed the visiting yera, and everyone broke into relieved laughter. Since twelve head had already physically passed hands, this left ngàba wini with a debt of twenty-four. Suddenly one of the leaders of ngàba wini objected that this total should
be only twenty-two, since it included two horses whose "destinations"
(as prestations named "riding horse" and "cotton") had not been mentioned during the final count. Angrily yera replied, 'How could that be?
That would mean you owe us twenty-four! Where's the proof that you
ever gave us those two?' Without denying the fact that two *animals* had
in fact changed hands, in the heat of the moment they challenged the
claim that those particular named *prestations* had ever been given, because ngàba wini had spoken of them but inadvertently had not given
anything in the offering dish. This meant that if some means of cooling
tempers and soothing the insulted were not found, yera could make off
with two head as a free gift.

The doubling of exchange tokens is also, in part, simply a matter
of increasing the highly formal character of the event. Like the use of
poetic language, it frames the event as ceremonial and, by elaborating
each action, enhances the perception of consequentiality and difficulty.
Like an elevated register of speech, it frames the act as one instance of a
highly marked type of action. It embodies general properties of both
verbal and material signs in Anakalangese exchange, one referent of the
couplet "shadows on the dry land, reflections on the water" (for another, see chapter 7). What is visible in the dish is a token of something
that is larger and usually economically more expensive, spoken of in
words but physically absent. This relation of representation operates
along two dimensions, for the present and absent objects move in tandem with present and absent persons, namely, the spokesman and the
party on whose behalf he speaks. The reduplicated forms of exchange
here, by linking physically manifest persons and tokens to nonmanifest
agents and goods, support the more general attribution of efficacy to an
invisible realm, the spirits of the dead and their contribution to the
charisma of the living.

## AMBIGUOUS ATTACHMENTS

Such apparent minutiae as the manipulation of tokens and dishes reflect an Anakalangese understanding of action, that formality guarantees purposefulness and helps identify the agent. Underlying this emphasis on formality is another supposition about social interaction, that nothing can be taken for granted and that the circulation of an object is itself insufficient to define the character of the act or actor. Effective action requires signs that enable the isolated act to be understood in reference to a larger project. As a result, the capacity of objects to serve semiotically as representations and economically as representatives of persons is unstable and requires constant effort to sustain. Recall again the quarrel between Ama Koda and Ubu Tara over the torn banner, described at the beginning of chapter 2. On the one hand, the conventional meanings that material signs convey are vulnerable to the accidents to which objects are prone. On the other hand, so strong is the general expectation that objects will signify, that Ama Koda resists interpreting anything as accidental. The respect accorded to a ngàba wini (Ama Koda) by his yera (Ubu Tara) through the gift of a "banner" is readily transformed into the insult of torn cloth. This is made possible in part by the way in which material signs expose semantics to objective circumstances and in part by the way in which people's manipulation of objects constantly works to transform natural qualities into signs of persons. If a cloth really represents its transactors, how could a torn cloth fail to do so as well? If objects are parts of larger projects, could the giving of a torn cloth be only an isolated incident?

The use of the offering dish rests on the assumptions that people are fundamentally inscrutable yet the world is full of interpretable signs. Exchange works at the intersection of these two conditions, with the result that both the temporal extension of particular acts into effective projects and the identification of persons with things require ongoing effort. If a prestation elicits a counterprestation, part of the value of that completed round of exchange lies in the possibility that it might *not* have done so.[33] If a round of exchanges constructs the identities of the transactors, and serves each to recognize the other, slippage represents the possibility of denial and shame. Conversely, success is conceptualized not in the orderly or mechanical workings of reciprocity but in gambles won.

The social and cosmological powers of exchange cannot be located

*fully* in labor, use, or market values, or iconism, or conventional symbolism, or even an a priori bond between person and possession like the
Maori *hau* of the gift (Mauss [1925] 1990). The potential for expansive
agency that exchange possesses is not found in the objects alone but
in the repeated events wherein they are transacted, in the links forged
among sequences of events, and in the words spoken as the objects
move. The ongoing effort that Anakalangese must put into exchange
seems to respond to something to which the Maussian view of exchange has given short shrift. Mauss's great insight was to challenge the
Cartesian obviousness of the distinction between possessing subject and
possessed object. But the very workings of exchange depend on the fact
that the identity between the two (however they are characterized in a
given locality) is not seamless: their relation has a double character. For
objects to be able to exteriorize and represent their possessors in circulation, they also must in some way be detachable from them. One Anakalangese view of this ambiguous autonomy, and its implications for
the displacement of agency, is shown in a story Ubu Laiya told me. As a
wild young man, he stole and even murdered, aided by a stone that endowed him with invulnerability. Eventually, when he came to realize
that this stone was also interfering with his wife's fertility, he decided to
get rid of it. 'But you can't do this on purpose. You have to lose it by accident. So you put it loosely in the fold of your waistcloth and go on a
long trip. At some point you cross a river and it loses itself.' An object
that is fully separate from oneself should be easily disposable, but one
that is fully attached would not be subject to loss this way.[34]

In Simmel's ([1907] 1990: 66–67) terms, the desirability of objects
lies in our perception that they are separate from us and resist our efforts to encompass them. But this separation is only one side of a (historically and culturally specific) relationship, of which the other is that
possessions are extensions of the self: in acquiring property, like procreation, "the sphere of the individual extends beyond its original limits, and extends *into another self* which, however, is still 'his'" ([1907]
1990: 323; emphasis mine). This capacity for "extension" only exists to
the extent that the object is *not* fully identified with the subject. It follows from this double character of objects that the subject must engage
actively with them, that possession is a form of action ([1907] 1990:
302–305). And, at least in Anakalang, that action is implicated with the
actions of others.

The relentless work—and the formality, the politics, the talk, the attentiveness—demanded by Anakalangese exchange seems to be one way

of responding to these circumstances. Exteriorization and objectification work hand in hand with detachability and mobility. Herein lies both the promise and the risk posed by things, as vehicles of representation. Sent into circulation, they can extend the identity and agency of their transactors. By the same token, they may become lost to those whom they would serve. The capacity of the prestation to stand for its owner over the course of its travels is not an inherent property of objects themselves, but requires human activities and interactions to sustain. These activities include the work of speech, which at once constrains the threat that things will escape those who hold them, yet whose representational forms threaten speakers with distinct kinds of loss.

# CHAPTER FOUR

# Loaded Terms

Is this a baptism? No,—say the ablest canonists; inasmuch as
the radix of each word is thereby torn up. . . . But in the case
cited, continued *Kysacrius*, where *patrim* is out for *patris*,
*filia* for *filij*, and so on—as it is a fault only in the declension,
and the roots of the words continue untouch'd . . . [this] does
not in any sort hinder the baptism.

> Sterne, *The Life and Opinions of
> Tristram Shandy, Gent.* IV

Recognizing the problematic character of material objects as representational media, Anakalangese are quite explicit about the need to bind them to words. Animals killed undirected by proper speech will die "startled" (*katatak*), their spirits going astray; gifts for which the path (lara) has not been spoken are essentially lost to the giver as debts and representatives. Like material objects, to be efficacious these words must be formally constrained and elevated above the condition of everyday circulation: they must be "loaded onto a boat, mounted onto a horse" (*pahailu ngidi tenangu, pawuatu ngidi jarangu*). I know of only one occasion when someone tried to negotiate a marriage without using ritual speech, but the sense of squalor and hostility it produced is instructive. The groom was a Timorese orphan who had been raised in an Anakalangese family, the bride a woman whose deceased father had been a policeman from Flores and whose mother was from another part of west Sumba. Nonetheless, in 1987 the two parties met and attempted to carry out a scaled-down negotiation. The speaker for the woman's family was a minor official who prided himself on his knowledge of customary procedures (Indo. *adat*). This knowledge turned out to be all theory and no practice as he quickly floundered. Attempting to save the day, he suggested that they switch to the "*adat* of Christianity" (an adat whose existence no one else would acknowledge) and began speaking in Indonesian. Ngàba wini protested vehemently at the shift in both register and language, but eventually the negotiation stumbled on to a conclusion.[1] Humiliated, yera's speaker disappeared even before the women had finished cooking the concluding meal. When I returned in 1993, ngàba wini was still referring to the event with resentment and deeply offended self-esteem, saying that they had been treated not as "humans" (*tau rara*) but like blocks of wood. It is not clear what kinds of relations they will have with their affines over the years, but certainly yera's ability to call on the moral obligations of ngàba wini is seriously impaired. Cattle, cloth, pigs, and gold have passed between the two parties, but they entail little more than tokens detached from their donors, wealth with no strings attached.

A growing body of research on poetics, performance, and linguistic pragmatics has shown with great subtlety the multiple powers of formal speech. What the approach to Anakalangese ritual speech that I undertake here adds is a sense of how ritual speech can also render problematic the efforts of speakers to find in it a fully stable and unchallengeable ground for their actions. Viewed in relation to material objects, ritual speech functions to complete their passage from one party to *bracketing* another, to delimit their meanings, to direct their effects, to assure their identification with their possessors, and to cast their transmission within an ancestral frame of action. As a component of representational practice, ritual speech is critical to what I have called "recognition," and thus to constructing the agency and authority of those who wield it. It works to assure that what might be but a momentary happening is in fact a repeatable instance of a general kind of act—not the fortuitous demise of a chicken, for instance, but the hospitable offer of a meal. It does so by weaving around actions a rich metaphorical text, through less salient effects of its formal properties and in the dynamics of performance. In the process, ritual speech mingles the voices of living individuals with those attributable to the ancestral collectivity in whose name they try to speak. Many of the problems that ritual speech poses are effects of this implicit heteroglossia: no matter how authoritative the forms of speech, they never fully succeed in transcending the speakers and the moment in which they speak. Although ritual speech provides speakers with a medium of authority—one that establishes a hierarchical relation among not only genres of speech but kinds of speakers— it also limits their powers. Although it serves as a source of ancestral meanings, it also locates its speakers within a diminished present. In the process of endowing groups with agency, it also limits their ability to control or take responsibility for the outcomes of their actions. As it proclaims order, it implies slippage and the risks of failure.

When people in Anakalang talk about ritual speech, they usually focus on its most prominent feature, the canon of couplets that has been handed down from the ancestors. Although they may stress the unchanging nature of these couplets, in practice much of the effectiveness of ritual speech lies in the ability of speakers to use them innovatively. Performance thus bears an ambivalent relationship to its context. It should simultaneously elevate specific actors and their actions to a plane that transcends the immediate context while at the same time remaining strategically responsive to the particular circumstances of the event. This dual character, reflecting the problems of performativity raised by Austin and Derrida that I discussed in chapter 1, draws on several functions of language that make it possible to cite, quote, and use "ancestral" forms of speech. I argue that the authority and difficulties of ritual speech arise in part from its mediating position between ancestral order and actual events. This mediation is dialectical insofar as it does not simply attempt to fit actual events into a preexisting template but also works to *construct* in concrete forms the very ancestral order that it appears to *reproduce*. Correlatively, it mediates the actions of individuals and the agency of larger groups. Ritual speech—elaborating on certain common properties of language—works both to locate itself within a *presupposable* social context and to *create* a social context around the moment of utterance. This is the verbal aspect of the dialectic of recognition, the construction of given actions and actors as recognizable types. Through this double process, speakers help objectify the identities of the groups on whose behalf they speak and those that they face. Mutually constructing each other as social subjects, they also mutually challenge one another to recognize them and be recognized. Such constructions are subject both to the slippages to which mediations are prone and to the politics inherent to interaction. Each party's claims to ancestral authority are, potentially, subject to misconstrual or denial by the other.

The high formality with which these challenges take place thus should not obscure the fact that their outcomes are not foregone conclusions. A ritual speaker does not only take on an ancestral voice, he or she also indexes the fact of *not* speaking colloquially. As a strategy of avoidance, ritual speech suggests that interaction is often a difficult and agonistic as well as a cooperative and dialogic enterprise. Successful interaction can be socially creative, but slippage and pragmatic misfire point to failures that can produce political and economic consequences.

This element of risk, as both positive challenge and negative threat, is already implicit in the treatment of exchange valuables, a particular construction of more general properties of social action. The chapters that follow will ask what is being avoided and explore the nature of this risk. In this chapter, however, I will first describe the formal resources that at once constrain and construct it.

## LANGUAGE IDEOLOGY

It is impossible to overlook the extraordinary position of ritual speech in Sumbanese society. The words of the ancestors (*li marapu*) are crucial not only to formal interactions but also to how people talk about the distinctive identity and value of being Sumbanese within the contemporary Indonesian world.[2] From early in the colonial period, written accounts of Sumba have been laden with quoted couplets, and even a casual visitor in the 1990s was likely to be impressed with the ubiquity and prestige of ritual speech. Even if the visitor does not attend a ritual or negotiation, she is likely at least to hear people identify their villages by their couplet names. Ritual speech rivals cattle and kinship as a popular topic of daily conversation. While the actual performance is more restricted, many—perhaps most—adult men and women pride themselves in being able to sprinkle couplets in their speech with the ease and aesthetic pleasure with which educated English speakers once quoted Shakespeare and Cicero. Like such speakers, Anaklangese men and women tend to assume that ritual embodies what is most important in cultural knowledge and thus to insist that it ought to be the primary concern of the ethnographer. Nonetheless, the salience and value of speech must be examined critically and the temptation to mine ritual speech for its contents alone must be weighed with this question in mind (Irvine 1979: 779). In this chapter I will stress a second problem as well: although ritual speech is often analyzed as a source of authority, in Anakalang it is also implicated in the limits and paradoxes of authority as well.

To approach the value and defining characteristics of ritual speech, it is useful to begin—although not to end—with Anakalangese language ideology. By this I mean speakers' own assumptions and understandings about "the nature of language in the world" (Rumsey 1990: 346; see Woolard 1992). Such assumptions affect both how people perceive language and how they use it. At its most apparent, language ideology often dwells on differences among languages and speech styles, providing explanations for the perceived superiority of one over another, reflecting and justifying social hierarchies. Language ideologies may operate in less apparent ways as well, however. For example, although language functions at many levels simultaneously, speakers will tend to focus on some functions over others. Thus it has been argued that, for cultural, historical, and linguistic reasons, English speakers are inclined to see the default or unmarked function of language to serve as a vehicle for making propositions, true or false statements about the world (Silverstein 1979). In contrast, Ilongot, for example, see language first in terms of directives, as a means of getting people to do things (Rosaldo 1973, 1982). How people understand their language to function can both reflect their concepts of person and agency and in turn help shape how they act. Thus the uses of language and the forms that are most valued in a given society can provide special insight into the powers that speakers are trying to draw on. Language ideology, however, is only partly captured in what people *say* about language. People's talk about language is likely to be less nuanced than their practical but tacit understandings that are embedded in how they actually *use* language.

Anakalangese ritual speech has many sorts of value. It can be seen, for instance, as an index of undying tradition, an emblem of local identity, a high art, or a metaphor-laden "dictionary of culture" (Kapita 1987). For many Anakalangese, however, what is most important is its efficacy. To speak effectively is to "shake the leaves from the tree, make the vines echo," to make things happen. One's own speech can cause others to loosen their grip on valuables that one desires, or can soften the demands of stern affines. Some forms of speech have direct physical effects. People say that when the raja Umbu Sappy Pateduk dragged his enormous stone tomb, "Most Macho," it would not budge until the great ratu Umbu Marabi's chanting induced it to move (a similar feat was supposed to have been accomplished just a couple of years before I arrived). Ubu Dongu told me his father's war oratory caused horses to rear up, the ground to shake, and the water to spill from the jugs. When ratus and experts in marriage negotiation boast of their skills, they often contrast their words to physical labor. Ratu Joka told me that he never goes to his gardens, because his voice works for him. He claims that every piece of cloth he owns has been given to him for his services.

Having visited ratu Joka at work in his garden many times, I know he exaggerates, but his way of boasting echoes the claims people make for the ancestors, whose extraordinary powers testify to their superior command of speech. When one man was explaining to me the meaning of "bitter" (*paita*) in its sense of "being tabooed, filled with superhuman power," he summarized the point by saying, 'It's like the marapu: when they say something, it happens.' For instance, when on their original trek across the seven seas and eight skies the ancestors were blocked by a wall of gold, one of them cried out to summon the lightning and whirlwind that shattered it. When Ubu Pabal sought the hand of Rabu Robu in marriage, her father set up a series of obstacles for him to overcome. These obstacles required him to tame the wild, which he accomplished with his voice alone: when he called the wild pig and the forest hen, they obeyed. Such deeds exemplify what the living might hope for from speech. No one now seriously expects to shatter walls by voice alone, but the stories suggest the desirability of being able to do so. Such stories identify ancestral speech with agency that will never fail. Its powers can overcome any obstacle raised by the material world, any challenge posed by social others. The agency embodied in ancestral speech, at the limits, is self-sufficient, requires no cooperation with others and no bodily activity other than the action of the voice alone. In such a world, the constraints imposed by contemporary social interaction can be surpassed: true ancestral speech may even obviate the need for material exchange. Thus Ubu Sebu obtained Rabu Kareri as his wife through his ability to summon rain with his voice. People shake their heads with envy when they add, he didn't have to use gold to get her. What sets the ancestors apart from the living is that for them, there was no gap between word and world. Their descendants aspire to master at least some of this potency through the use of ritual speech, which iconically reproduces ancestral words and indexically proclaims the speaker's links to ancestral powers.

Ancestral stories suggest that when Anakalangese imagine what it would be like to escape the constraints of everyday sociability and its politics, they often focus on formal speech (even though some, as I have noted, identify this speech *with* politics). But since in everyday life people palpably lack ancestral powers, they must look to other than everyday varieties of language for powerful speech. Just as formal exchange takes some of its meaning by contrast to other kinds of transaction, so ritual speech stands out against the background of everyday ways of talking. Anakalangese sometimes also say that "in truth" (*bakalanga*) all Sumbanese speak a single language; it just happens that everyday speech hides this unity. When people use "in truth" like this, they are often pointing away from the actual conditions of things and toward the fully authoritative forms from which they have lapsed (thus a village may "in truth" have twelve houses, although only two are now standing). As some people put it, at the time of Babel, we all spoke a single tongue. Ritual speech is all that remains of that original unity. To support this assertion, they can point to the fact that Anakalangese ritual speech makes use of words from other Sumbanese languages. As a result, people say, a good ritual speaker should in principle be able to function anywhere on the island—that this does not work out in practice must be due to the fact that no one now alive knows ritual speech as well as the ancestors did. This aspect of language ideology correlates the powers of ritual speech with spatial extension, social unity, and antiquity. It contrasts ritual speech to everyday speech, associating the latter with the general contemporary condition of spatial constriction (dialects distributed among small localities), conflict, and recentness. It posits an originary state of unity, the possible return to which is implied, but never entirely achieved, in actual moments of ritual speaking. To appropriate Bakhtin's description of relations between standard and nonstandard languages, "A unitary language is not something given but is always in essence posited—and at every moment of its linguistic life it is opposed to the realities of heteroglossia" (1981: 270).

Since differences among local languages are ideally subsumed under the unity granted by ritual speech, the most salient feature of Anakalangese language ideology is the distinction between ritual and nonritual speech. Although in practice there is a continuum between them, the two poles form a conceptual contrast. Ritual speech (*teda, loloku*, or synecdochically, *kajiàla*, negotiation speech) was created by the ancestors. It is the canonical vehicle of formal and effective spoken communication, "the customary words of negotiation, the line of words of speech" (*pata li kajiàla, lola li panewi*), an icon of ancestral order.[3] Nonritual speech is essentially the residual category, an unmarked term, unadorned *panewi*.[4] Their differences correlate with those among occasions, places, times, and kinds of speakers. "Worthless talk" (*panewi onga*) and gossipy "wind talk" (*panewi ngilu*) are associated with the heat of day, impermanent garden hamlets, and women and young men, or other people unlikely or unable to engage in public expressions of authority. In contrast, the most important ritual speech should occur in the cool of the night (appropriate for blessing) and is associated with

ancestral villages and the acts of male elders. Unlike ritual speech, colloquial speech is not restricted to specified locations. It occurs in market,
hamlet, and garden, takes unregulated forms, and is unaccompanied by
material gifts or offerings.[5]

Colloquial speech, in this view, represents some of the threats against
which ritual speech must protect itself. This can be seen in the prayers
and offerings that must be made at the close of a night of orations. They
raise the orators' words up into the house, lest they go astray and fail to
reach their destination, remaining exposed in the plaza. Material offerings and accompanying prayer seek to assure that those words "not be
chilled in the rain, idle in the sun," and thereby bring on misfortune. Such
figures treat speech as potentially mobile, detachable from its speaker
and those on whose behalf he or she speaks.

Ritual speech also differs from colloquial speech in its proper speakers. Unlike members of more rigidly sex-segregated societies, Anakalangese do not make a point of insisting that women must not perform
ritual speech. Rather, they tacitly understand that it is not quite appropriate for them to do so, more a matter of contingency than rule (see
Tsing 1990).[6] Young people are also inappropriate as speakers of most
genres of ritual speech, since they lack both biographical experience
and generational proximity to forebears. Certain demanding tasks, however, such as marriage negotiation, are best handled by vigorous men in
midcareer. Rank is a somewhat more complicated matter, for although
ritual speech is associated with the values supposedly exemplified by nobility, nobles tend (with many exceptions) to delegate speech to others.
For all the value attributed to ritual *speech*, the act of using it does not
endow its *speaker* with high status. As will become apparent in chapter
6, possession of a speaking voice is not itself the best evidence for the
locus of agency.

## PARALLELISM

In Anakalang, as across Sumba, the compositional heart of ritual
speech is a large canon of couplets; a compilation from east Sumba contains 3,187 such couplets (Kapita 1987). These couplets are said to
have been created by the first ancestors and to have been passed down
to the living unaltered, except for the inevitable losses due to forgetting.
Most people assert that no one ever invents or adds to the existing body
of couplets, that prerogative being confined to the earliest origins of

Figure 9.  Ratu Umbu Kana Dapa Namung performs oratory at the edge of the village plaza (Ḍeru, December 1986).

cultural things.[7] In doing so, they associate invention with other forms of indiscretion, in which the speaker asserts his agency to the point of usurpation.

Sumbanese couplets are organized by a strong version of the parallelism that marks a wide range of ritual and poetic traditions, from the biblical Psalms to Mayan prayers (see the survey in Fox 1971). In Anakalang both lines of a couplet normally have the same syntax, and with varying degrees of strictness, the second line matches the first semantically. The most straightforward way couplets form this matching is through repetition, treating the line as a frame in which one word can vary:

| na ma kayisa ḍa ḍaitu | the one who receives the shoulder burdens |
| na ma kayisa ḍa kaliangu | the one who receives the head burdens |

More common is a sort of paraphrase, in which the second line repeats the sense of the first in different words:

| na pawolu tau kawunga | promised by the first people |
| na parawi tau madaingu | committed by ancient people |

Paraphrase, however, is only one of a wide range of ways in which the couplets form equivalents between their components. For example, words may be paired according to semantic analogy (boat–horse), indexical links to a shared referent (dog–horse: conventional hunting companions of males), antonymy (ascend–descend), and hyponymy (body–teeth).

Many terms are paired simply by their membership in the same semantic set, such as color terms and place-names. Such terms are sometimes optional, and are important for allowing speakers to improvise with the materials available. For example, the couplet

| lara li | followed path |
| ada pala | crossing trail |

can be expanded to become

| lara liya | followed path there |
|   pali waingu jaraya |   for horses to follow |
|     ta pali Laboya |     going the Laboyan way |
| ada palaya | crossing trail there |
|   papala waingu tauya |   for people to cross |
|     ta papala Wanukaka |     crossing the Wanukakan way |

In such couplets, the place-names, like color terms, appear to serve a largely prosodic function, with perhaps the additional effect of suggesting the encompassing power of the register by explicitly denoting spatial distances.

Although the vast bulk of couplets preserve syntactic as well as semantic parallelism, some lack either. This is especially evident in place-names, such as the formal name of the sacred village Lai Tarung, Black Topknot, Stone Pillar (Metungu Kawuku, Kaḅaringu Watu). This couplet has two revealing properties. First, what primarily unite the two lines are their links to a shared referent, in this case, to one unusual house in the center of the village. The first line is itself a metaphor for its roof thatching, comparing it to a ratu's hairstyle. The second line refers to the stone pillars that make this house unique. The second property this couplet illustrates is that the parallelisms between individual words (black–stone, topknot–pillar) are not found elsewhere in the canon and show no evidence of significant underlying semantic relations evident in other contexts. It is the lines, not words, that form pairs, which, as I will argue, has further implications for the meaning of parallelism in Anakalang.

Does the power of ritual speech lie in its metaphorical richness? After all, parallelism has been interesting to anthropologists and linguists in part because it seems to promise a key to the central metaphors of a culture. To ask this question requires a closer look at how pairing works. In Sumba, although parallel couplets set up equivalents among words, discrete pairs of words are not themselves the working units of ritual speech, and they rarely occur in isolation. Instead, entire lines pair with entire lines. As a result, in Anakalangese ritual speech, parallelism of individual words is shaped by co-occurrence conventions. That is, ancestral mandate binds words not only to their equivalents in other lines but also to the rest of the words in the same line: in the couplet

jara ma padewa               horse of the spirit
asu ma pa-ura                dog of fate

it is not sufficient to observe that "horse" pairs with "dog," "spirit" with "fate" (a paradigmatic relation). It is also important to maintain the link between "horse" and "spirit," "dog" and "fate." Syntagmatic conventions link "horse" with "spirit" as well as with "dog": to switch "spirit" and "fate" would be a solecism. But it is not primarily the semantic structure of the couplet that guides the listener. The listener can usually distinguish which lines pair with which by sound (prosody, breath groups, and intonation) or syntax. In practice, moreover, Anakalangese listeners are likely already to know the couplets being used, because the most common speech events tend to be structured around a limited range of conventional choices.

Normally each line is syntactically self-contained: in those cases in which it does not form a canonically complete sentence, the second line adds nothing to make it so. In addition, the syntactic structure of each line of a couplet is identical to that with which it is paired—but not necessarily any other adjacent lines. As a result of these two conditions, the second line contributes nothing further to the linguistic structure of the whole couplet. The *formal* self-containment of each line is at once reflected and overridden by performance style. On the one hand, a speaker will often accentuate the boundary between the two lines with a pronounced pause: "to the opened mat—[pause]—to the proffered pillow" (*ta tapu na pawalahu—ta nula pakacorungu*). On the other hand, speakers and listeners clearly share a strong sense that a single line is not complete until the second line is spoken. This is reflected in two ways. The intonation of the first line often rises to a final peak, creating a sense of incompleteness that requires the descending profile of the second line to complete it. To leave the second line unspoken would also leave the intonation profile of the couplet hanging, as it were, in midair. As if to forestall this possibility, listeners sometimes pronounce the second line, especially if the speaker pauses too long or stumbles over it. So tightly associated are the two lines that citation of one is sufficient to evoke the other. In casual conversation, I have often heard one person mention one line of a couplet only to have a second fill in the next line, as one might complete a friend's half-expressed thought.

That Anakalangese emphasize the couplet (rather than either individual pairs of words or longer units) can be seen in the way in which they refer to specific ritual acts, by citing a crucial couplet, which they do not decompose into constituents. Often it is sufficient to mention only the first line of the pair, since one line evokes the other. For example, part of a marriage negotiation is framed by the formal act of feeding the guests, which can be referred to in ordinary speech by the first line of the couplet summarizing the often lengthy invitation, to "eat the rice, drink the water." In Anakalangese talk about talk, or metalanguage, one line is the "partner" or "fellow traveler" (gàba) of the other. This term focuses on the fact that two lines occur in a sequence and are both present in a single stretch of discourse (rather than, say,

existing in paradigmatic alternation, as "complements" or "replacements," as *hèpa* of one another, which would stress the fact that where
one is present, the other is absent).

I stress this point because it has implications for how we move from
couplet to society and culture. It is tempting to identify pairs of terms
with other pairing phenomena in society, such as the pairing up of ratus
in major rituals (Keane 1990: 95–102). This identification was encouraged by the Dutch tradition of interest in dual structures in the region—
recall Onvlee's description of the Mangili conduit in chapter 2 (see Forth
1988: 130; Needham 1980; van Wouden [1935] 1968). Indeed, it is
abundantly clear that in Anakalangese cosmological aesthetics, to have
authority and completeness, things typically must be in pairs. It is less
clear, however, what can be learned of a cultural order from the couplet. Couplets manifest a strong formal preference for pair formation,
but this does not necessarily mean that the results—the particular pairs—
can be identified directly with the process itself. Furthermore, if we devote our greatest attention to the most salient bearer of semantic meaning,
the lexeme, it may lead us to lay too much weight on the apparently
context-free semantic content, at the expense of the other dimensions
of the contexts in which couplets appear, such as their position within
larger texts, the place of those texts within performances, and the articulation of spoken performance with the circulation of objects.

## INTERPRETING COUPLETS

Parallelistic couplets have attracted much scholarly interest for the
potential insights they offer into questions both universal and local in
scope. The first approach is closely identified with the work of Roman
Jakobson (1960), who sees parallelism, very broadly defined, as the core
principle of poetics that underlies the rhetorical efficacy even of simple
slogans such as "I like Ike." Parallelism is not restricted to semantics (as
in juxtaposed words), phonology (as in rhyme schemes), or prosody (as
in meter) but can occur at all linguistic levels: thus even the micro rhetoric of the slogan "I like Ike" draws both on phonological structure
(the series of identical vowels and the pair of identical consonants) and
the subliminal semantics which playfully embeds the subject "I" within
the object of its fondness, "Ike," and "Ike" in turn within the verb "like."

Jakobson's enthusiasm has been criticized for having too powerful
an explanatory force. If one can find sets of symmetries and equivalents
in apparently endless proliferation, it becomes difficult to establish what

poetic structures are pertinent in any given instance. Analysis must be guided by some sort of constraint. One such guide can be attention to poetic functions (Silverstein 1976) or effects (Culler 1975). As Jakobson's critics point out, language provides an embarrassing richness of possible equivalents. In practice, parallelism selects those equivalents that are *relevant* and *powerful*, those that are latent within speakers' knowledge of their own language and that draw on matters of particular value or interest. Thus, for the speaker, parallelism can often make a message especially convincing through the somatic force of repeated sound structures that create equivalences that subliminally appeal to what everyone already knows. For the outsider, parallelism can provide some insight into what the poets and their audiences themselves intuitively consider to be the most interesting equivalents.

Because the poetic traditions of eastern Nusa Tenggara are so highly valued and rely so heavily on parallelism, this latter approach has promised a special key to local worldviews. James Fox (1974, 1975), following Jakobson, analyzes canonical parallelism as a way of discovering semantic networks. He describes the ritual speech of Roti (an island east of Sumba, near Timor) as resting on the foundation of a basic lexicon of terms whose pairings with other terms form a stable semantic network. The terms do not simply form pairs haphazardly but exist in a hierarchy: primary symbols, such as "tree," organize more peripheral ones, such as "stone," "lontar palm," "east," by virtue of the fact that each of the latter can pair with the former (Fox 1975: 119).[8] In a further extrapolation from couplet to performance context, Fox argues that the lexical pairings represent a premise of the rituals in which they occur. In Roti, then, the problem posed by Jonathan Culler is apparently resolved by the cultural ontology that determines the hierarchy among symbols. Conversely, the analysis of poetic *form* (parallel couplets) leads us to underlying *semantic* relations, which are evidence in turn of a basic cultural ordering of the world.[9] In ritual speech, the privileged form these relations take is that of metaphor.[10]

Fox's insight, in developing Jakobson, was to emphasize how the very *form* of the couplet creates meaningful tropes. The matching up of terms (for instance, their placement in the same position in successive lines of a couplet) implies a semantic comparison between them. Thus many of the pairings mentioned suggest analogies between two terms (boat with horse) or relate both to an implicit third term (men are exemplified by their relations to dogs and horses). Like other metaphors, those formed by pairings foreground selected aspects of a term over

others: when "pig" is paired with "chicken," it is in terms of its place in
a domestic economy associated with women's work; when paired with
"shrimp," as something netted or trapped; when paired with "monkey," as a wild animal that leaves tracks that can be difficult (for men)
to follow. In addition, the fact that Anakalangese couplets conventionally form links not only *between* lines but *within* each line as well adds
another dimension of possible metaphor. Such conventions may or may
not embody semantic and cosmological principles, but a couplet like
"horse of the spirit, dog of the soul" forms a secondary trope (horses
have or are like spirits) in addition to the primary one (horses are like
dogs).

Although many couplets are composed of individual lines that themselves are metaphors ("white horse finish line"), in other cases the figurative character only becomes apparent in the conjunction of the two
lines and other evidence of formality. For example, formal reception of
visitors is referred to with otherwise quite ordinary phrases, "drink water, eat cooked rice." Looking, then, from the constituent units of the
couplet to the resulting whole, we can see another aspect of its tropes.
Unlike many everyday metaphors, in the juxtapositions created by parallelism each line can serve as figure and ground by turn. The couplet as
a whole, then, appears to be a metaphor for a third term, that which
might otherwise be denoted in colloquial speech. Thus one might denote "going to visit yera" (*laupa lai yera*) with the couplet "arrive at the
horse's face, come to the dog's snout" (*tàka ta haga jara, toma ta ora
ahu*). Here horse's muzzle and dog's snout each *symmetrically* figures
the other, while at the same time, as a pair, they *asymmetrically* figure
the colloquial phrase.[11]

The metaphor-creating character of couplets has two general effects
on ritual speech as a register. One is that it compounds the strangeness
of ritual speech imparted by noncanonical syntax and some esoteric vocabulary.[12] Even experienced ritual speakers comment on the difficulty
of figurative language, some claiming that this proves that the ancestors, who used it all the time, were more able and intelligent than the
present generation. A second effect is that the entire register seems to
bear a metatrope in its own right. If there is any overriding principle
organizing the semantic field of Anakalangese ritual speech, it is that
powerful or valuable matters tend to be figured in terms of humble components of everyday life (seagulls, tree stumps, hearthstones, pillows).
This pattern can be read as itself a reigning trope of deference: the very

greatness of the matters spoken of is implied by the exaggerated humility of the terms in which they are put.

The value and meaning of couplets, however, is not a matter of metaphor alone. For one thing, a large portion of the pairings made in ritual speech do not create significant metaphors. For example, paraphrases often draw on straightforward synonymy (pairing, for example, *taka* with *toma*, both meaning "to arrive") or closely related terms from the same semantic field ("master," *mauri*, and "owner," *mangu*). Some couplets are formed by taking equivalents from other Sumbanese languages, such as the Anakalangese and Lolinese words for "dog" (*ahu* and *bongga*).[13] The couplet "veil the flint, smoke secretly" (*tàkul ma regi, bubat kaḅuni*) uses words that Anakalangese identify as coming from both Weyewa (*tàkul*) and Laboya (*bubat*). Although this may accentuate the esoteric or encompassing claims of the *register*, such synonymy-through-translation does not in itself seem to produce *semantic* effects. Furthermore, in many cases the metaphors seem to be so obvious as to be semantically trivial. Sometimes the couplet simply elaborates on an existing expression in colloquial speech. For example, to denote "tomorrow," literally "daybreak" (*na wehangu*), one may use the couplet "at daybreak on the land, at the sun's rising" (*na wehangu na tana, na hunga na hadei*). Yet another aspect of couplets that militates against a strongly metaphorical interpretation is the ceremonial form of proper nouns. Any place and person that might be referred to in ritual speech has both an everyday and an elevated form, the latter being a couplet. Typically, but not exclusively, the first line is the colloquial name, often extended with a modifier: Ratu Valley is formally Ratu Cave Valley, Monkey Lake Hollow. The couplet form of personal names is made by joining the husband's name to that of his (principal) wife. In the case of place-names such as Black Topknot, Stone Pillar (cited above), it is the formal *fact of being in a pair* that seems to be most important, as semantic and syntactic parallelism can be dispensed with. The poetic opportunism displayed by the wide range of techniques for creating couplets suggests that the formation of pairs is more important than a single cultural semantics.

It is a commonplace in Sumba that it is impossible to "translate" ritual speech. But what does that mean? Not, I take it, that there is no possible word-by-word equivalence to be found in the vocabulary of Indonesian. Nor does it mean that there exists no Anakalangese metalanguage by which a stretch of speech can be glossed. Something else seems to be at issue. There is no normal situation in which one might find oneself interested directly with the semantics of couplets. Provoked by my own labors, Anakalangese relished admonishing me with an anecdote—well worn by the time of my departure—that suggests how the exegetical context is not local but arises in contact with outsiders. It concerns a Dutch student who had done research there about fifteen years before. Inquiring into ritual speech, he would first seek literal translations. For example, he elicited the fact that the couplet *jelineka na jara pakaletigu, laijuneka na ahu papawujiagu*, an expression that refers to one's act of oratory, meant "my riding horse leaps, my summoned dog jumps." With this, to my initial bewilderment, the anecdote would end, with chuckles all around. Eventually I concluded that the humor, so obvious as not to require stating, is that it expresses a faux pas: the Dutchman, normally associated with cosmopolitan knowledge, great wealth, and power, reveals his vulgarity by focusing on the obvious, misdirecting his attention from the real import of the expression. What is lost in the translation of a ritual text? People's response to the anecdote (and their occasional reluctance to provide me with glasses) suggests that a single-minded concern with semantics alone misses out on crucial pragmatic functions of speech: for example, how poetic style indexes a high register, how the iconic form of the couplet supports the association with ancestral completeness, how performance displays the authority of the speaker, how the right choice of words defines a context and brings results. Literal rendition is to translate everything but what counts.

If ritual speech generates metaphors, it does not do so productively. Sumbanese couplets are supposed to come from a fixed set. By the time most people have reached adulthood, they have heard the vast majority of couplets hundreds, perhaps thousands, of times. Couplets are neither newly created nor newly to be understood: they do not have a "hidden meaning" to be worked out on the basis of information fully present at the moment of utterance. Anakalangese listeners are not in the position of the ethnographer who approaches the poetry of ritual language with a fresh ear and finds in its metaphors new meanings. In contrast to the work of the ethnographer, that of the typical listener does not force confrontation of couplets as revelatory and requiring exegesis. The role of the ethnographer who seeks in the couplet a direct representation of a cultural code is a unique one in this regard and encounters ritual speech in an unprecedented interpretive situation. This certainly does not disqualify semantic discoveries, but it does suggest that they should be situated in relation to the formal and pragmatic dimensions of speech.

One aspect of ritual speech that is lost in translation is the way in which formality—the fact of following an overt rule and the associated notion of completeness—gives meaning to the couplets. In the case of names, for example, the canonical form is directed not by metaphor or some other referential capacity. Rather, the canonical name is shaped by the requirement that it exist as a double and that it thereby fit into, that is, be capable of serving as a unit in, formal speech. This, of course, accords with the prominence and importance of dyadic forms in general throughout East Nusa Tenggara. There may be a more specific aspect to this as well. The paired form of the couplet may serve as an icon of successful social difference-with-conjunction, coexisting with the ideals of encounter and exchange that characterize most formal speech events in Anakalang. For the line only "means," both as metaphor and as poetic unit, when conjoined with its appropriate partner. It is important to recognize the difference in analytical levels here: it is not likely that one can read directly from the content of such representations into cultural ontology.

## CANON AND CONTEXT

Although canonical couplets form the compositional heart of Anakalangese ritual speech, performance is almost never the repetition of a fixed text. As in many traditions of formulaic oral performance, speakers improvise by drawing on and interweaving a preexisting set of elements. In Anakalang, the most salient (but not the only) elements are couplets. When used, however, the core couplet can be expanded or productively articulated with other couplets. For example, the couplet A (comprising lines A1 and A2) can be expanded with the supplements X1 and X2 to produce A1 + (A1 + X1) / A2 + (A2 + X2). Thus

| | | |
|---|---|---|
| malunguka na laḍu | already evening the sun | A1 |
| malungu waingu wikinaka na laḍu | already evening by itself the sun | A1 + X1 |
| na wesanguka na riḍung | already daylight the night | A2 |
| wesangu waingu wikina na riḍung | already daylight by itself the night | A2 + X2 |

A couplet can also be interwoven with other couplets. Take, for example, the following sequence from an oration (*taungu li*) during one genre of oratorical event (*yaiwo*).

| | | |
|---|---|---|
| abu mu urung ḅamu rangu | don't hear poorly | A1 |
| ḅamu tuwu li panewinya | when you connect the words of | |

|  |  |  |
|---|---|---|
|  | speech | B1 |
| na talora ina-ama | the mother-father plaza | C1 |
| ḅamu dedinya na kawedu | when you erect the veranda | D1 |
| abu mu yabaru ḅamu elu | don't see unclearly | A2 |
| ḅamu kayi li kajiàlanya | when you receive the kajiàla words | B2 |
| na pàba watu | the aligned stones | C2 |
| ḅamu sapanya na talora | when you bind the plaza | D2 |

This is an intercalated set of lines that can be disassembled back into the core couplets of which it is composed, the eight lines A1 + B1 + C1 + D1 / A2 + B2 + C2 + D2, being the product of the four couplets A (1 + 2), B (1 + 2), C (1 + 2), and D (1 + 2). Each couplet is syntactically distinct and can be used or quoted by itself. In actual use, such couplets are often linked to one another as parts of longer sequences that have their own coherence. In this passage, the orator addresses the yaiwo singer, who will be quoting this oration on taking up his song (which is addressed to the spirits) after the orator has finished. With couplets A and B, the orator adjures the singer not to misunderstand his words when passing them along. Often these couplets are sufficient, but in this case the speaker elaborates, naming another addressee and specifying the type of the speech event. Couplet C refers to the spirits, who are the real audience to whom the singer will convey the orator's words, and couplet D denotes the fact that this is an instance of oratory in the plaza (and not, for example, a prayer). The entire passage, therefore, has its own syntax, with a core performative (the appeal to the singer) and the qualifying additions. Much of the improvisational art of ritual speaking comes from the way the couplets allow speakers to construct long and variable sequences.

Another critical component of performance and its efficacy lies in linguistic features that are independent of, and for listeners much less salient than, the canonical couplet. These are grammatical details that vary from event to event and within a single event, from speaker to speaker and moment to moment. Couplets can be modified by affixes, highly indexical elements of language, such as pronouns, deictics, aspect markers, and modals, that locate it in relation to the speakers and the speech context.[14] Such modifications are crucial to the flexibility and the effectiveness of ritual speech practices. In particular, they mean that ritual speaking is rarely a matter of rote recitation or simple quotation of a self-contained unit of text; it is not like quoting a passage from the Bible, repeating the Lord's Prayer, or uttering a proverb (although any given stretch of ritual speech or ordinary conversation can contain quotations embedded within it). Instead, the couplet is grammatically woven into both the emerging text of the speech event and the surrounding context of participants, activities, material transactions, and spatial setting.

The same core couplet can be run through a virtual conjugation of possible modifiers over the course of a speech event. The following examples come from a single oratorical event (I have kept the verb stem aligned so that the variation can be seen more clearly).

| | |
|---|---|
| *jeli*neka na jara pakaletigu | my riding horse now leaps |
| tauna ḍina *jeli* na jara pakaletigu | thus is it that my riding horse leaps |
| kaḍa peku *jeli* ḍa jara pakaleti | may it be that their riding horses be able to leap |
| *jeli* na jara pakaletigu yaiyu | my riding horse leaps here |
| kana peku *jeli*jialakaka na jarana | that his horse might also leap as well |
| *jeli*neka na jaragu | my horse now leaps |
| ḅana *jeli* na jarana | when his horse leaped |

By convention, the core couplet whose first line is *jeli na jara pakaleti* denotes a turn of talk in a ritual speech event. The modifications allow the speaker to refer to his own words, and to those of others, framing quotations or soliciting others to speak up. They situate the present stretch of speech in time with reference to other turns of talk and in social space with reference to other speakers. This allows speakers a certain amount of flexibility. In addition, such small grammatical variations help make presupposable the encompassing activity, an implicit dialogue, to which the present moment is only one contribution.

For listeners, however, the grammatical inflection of couplets is insignificant compared to the salience of the canonical core. This can be seen in the way people quote couplets that have been used in performance. Whether they are recalling ritual speech in a casual conversation or repeating another's words in the midst of a ritual dialogue, they often drop those grammatical components that they consider to be irrelevant or accidental. Only the canonical core survives (see Forth 1988: 146). All of the lines given above, which I recorded in actual performance, would probably be cited after the fact simply as *jeli na jara pakaleti*. The tendency to drop the grammatical inflections reflects both Anakalangese language ideology and the actual structure of ritual performance. As language ideology, the omission of deixis expresses the underlying assumption that couplets derive their power from their permanence and the fact that they transcend the limits of the present context. To the extent that deixis situates them in the present, its removal restores them to their proper ancestral state.

Ritual performances are likewise shaped by speakers' practical intuitions about what is important and efficacious in ritual speech. As in many ritual and liturgical speech traditions, Sumbanese ritual speech tends to omit many of the common indexical devices found in ordinary speech.[15] In Sumba, the role of linguistic variation in establishing ritual authority in Weyewa (where the basic principles of ritual speech do not differ significantly from Anakalang) has been shown in detail by Joel Kuipers (1990). Kuipers has persuasively argued that over the course of certain kinds of ritual events, speakers increasingly drop those linguistic markers that refer to the actual speech event, denying the situatedness and particularity of both persons and circumstances. These include lexical and grammatical reference to the speaker, other participants, and the present time and place. This process works in tandem with poetic formality, which makes salient those aspects of speech that allow it to be treated as an object that transcends particular circumstances or speakers. Much of the authority of ritual speech and some of the sense of hazard that attends it lie in the inevitable tension between the effort to treat language as a text or a code and the need for particular people to use it within particular contexts.

# CHAPTER FIVE

# Text, Context, and Displacement

Much of the previous chapter was about how the formal qualities of ritual speech emphasize the "textual" dimensions of language. In this way, ritual speech contributes to the sense that it embodies an unchanging ancestral heritage that transcends the here and now. But if living people are to benefit from this heritage and the authority it promises, they must speak. Moreover, they must speak to others, construed as in some sense present. The presence of the addressee and the nature of dialogue are critical to ritual speech as action. They also pose a host of difficulties and hazards for those who would speak.

The tension between textual and contextual dimensions of ritual speech has already been suggested in the difference between couplets and their indexical inflections. This tension is also registered in the role played by certain lines that do not enter into couplets. In ritual speech, each turn of speech opens and closes with conventional phrases that are not parts of canonical couplets. Like the optional grammatical forms, these unpaired lines play an important role in articulating couplets with their context, in this case, that of other speech and other speakers. They frame turns of talk, create clear dialogue roles, and index what speech genre or type of speech is taking place. In marriage negotiation, for example, each speaker begins with the cry "Listen to this!" (*Tana-wudo!*) and concludes by saying "I stow it" (*Bijalugi*). Prayers typically open with a conventional attention-getting cry, "Well!" or "Come on!" (*Màla!*), followed by an injunction to accept the offering, such as "Spirit, receive the chicken!" (*Kayi na manu marapu!*). In most ritual speech genres, similar cries punctuate the speech at fairly regular intervals. These are conventional forms of address. In some genres, such as oratory and negotiation (kajiàla), the address terms must elicit an immediate response from another speaker. For example, in a yaiwo event, the orator periodically shouts out "Oh yaiwo singer!" (*O ma yaiwo!*), and a third person (a proxy for the singer) shouts back "Come on—come!" (*Maiye mai!*). In prayers, the addressees are invisible spirits, who themselves remain mute. Nonetheless, what all these cases have in common is that they dramatically portray ritual speech as interactive: it is overtly addressed to someone else. In fact, so effective are these cries that during one ritual I was attending, when a well-known madman stood up to orate in couplets the respondent chimed right in. The flow of cry and response went smoothly, unaffected by the fact that *what* the man said was, everyone agreed, incoherent. As long as the formal structure was successful, the respondent carried out his role without hesitating.

The presence of the other, implied by the very forms of ritual speech, is also found in another kind of nonpairing line, that which frames reported speech. A great deal of Anakalangese ritual speech consists of quoting the words of other speakers. This is due in part to the structure of the speech events, in which speakers either reply to what their interlocutors have said or pass on messages from one speaker to another (see chapter 6). Reported speech, however, is also a means by which particular moments of speaking are linked to the effects and entailments of previous and subsequent speech acts. In particular, it is the locus of much of the explicitly performative work of ritual—making, confirming, reporting on, and fulfilling promises, "that which was promised, that which was committed." In the process, it also implies that the fact that the significant action in question (even during exchange) is, to a large extent, a form of speech.

Anakalangese conventions for reporting speech and even their own thoughts give them the surface form of exact quotation. That is, the embedded words are presented as being icons of someone else's words. This tends to emphasize the "autonomy" that reported speech has within the speaker's discourse (Vološinov [1930] 1973: 115–117), which can be a way of stressing the public character of the reporter's knowledge (Besnier 1992: 167; see also Lucy 1993). In Anakalang, it is a form of deference, playing down the individuality of the speaker's intervention while lending to it the authority of conveying that which, in theory, everyone should already know. In Anakalang, this modesty is carried further by a preference for the simple verb of quotation, "to say" (*wi-* plus pronominal suffix). The person who does the quoting thereby refrains from going on record as interpreting what might be the force of the words being reported. That is, unlike English, Anakalangese quotation does not take forms like "she ordered," "he implied," and so forth. The most canonical way to report another's words is a stretch of direct quotation followed by a verb of saying. In ritual, this sort of embedding of reported speech can be carried quite far, as when a diviner quotes the words he desires the spirit to say: " "" 'come to take it' I say" you (should) say' I say" ( """ *mai pateki' wigu" wimu' wigu*"). As this example shows, the verbs of quotation (*wigu* and *wimu*) juxtapose references to several changes of speaker or speaking part. Such juxtapositions are common, especially in marriage negotiation. As will become apparent in the next chapter, each speaker must often quote whole sets of previous statements made by other people, thereby iconically portraying the very act of transferring or delegating the message, as it distances the speaker from it.[1]

Extensive use of reported speech has another important property as well: it makes salient the repeatability of the spoken text. This was brought home to me very forcefully as I observed the arrangements for a large funeral. A dozen or so men had spent several days going to many far-flung villages to convey the formal invitation to the burial. Now the messengers gathered again at the home of the deceased to report the results. Although the chairman of the meeting repeatedly told them to be brief, each messenger recited in full the stereotyped exchange that had transpired in each village, despite the fact that everything except the final reply had been identical in each case. Such repetition, like other decontextualizing features of ritual speech, seems to insist that what is happening is not a direct expression of the individual interests and agencies of the speakers. Anakalangese place great value on this effect of ritual form: it at once manifests the authority of people who claim to act like, or on behalf of, ancestors or other authorities and displays the deferential behavior of those who know how to do things correctly and how not to act willfully. But by stressing the "iterability" of language, it also hints at how the signs in play are, at least in principle, never fully under the control of those who use them.

## BOUNDARIES AND CONTEXT

Anakalangese tend to see ritual speech as clearly and distinctively bounded off from everyday speech, but in practice the different registers form a continuum (see also Kuipers 1990). Casual speech may show emergent poetic properties, or bits of formal speech may appear in its midst. This is especially evident in Anakalang during conferences (*ba-tang*), in which the participants are conversing in colloquial speech about matters of great importance. Periodically, speakers, especially men who expect to be taken seriously, are likely to shift into a more authoritative "key" (Goffman 1974), a recognized and systematic reframing of how their actions are to be taken (for instance, as serious or playful). They begin to repeat certain phrases and accentuate their intonation. Their speech starts to take on more regular prosodic qualities and repetition gives even noncanonical phrases the structure of couplets. As they get closer to a full "breakthrough into performance" (Hymes [1975] 1981), they may introduce more and more couplets into their speech.[2] The other participants will usually recognize the shift and begin to yield the floor, letting the speaker continue without the usual interruptions. As this happens, one of the listeners is likely to start calling out formal back-channel cues, such as "Yes, this is true indeed!" The speaker in turn may start to use a formal address cry. In the following excerpt from a recording of a conference (Lakoka, Oct. 1986), Ubu Dongu has been speaking in a fairly colloquial manner. Now he cries out the ritual name (Dedungara) of the kabisu to which everyone present belongs. For clarity, I have italicized the couplets:

| | |
|---|---|
| Hanina Dedungara | Besides that, Dedungara |
| (Jiaḍi!) | (responder: Yes!) |
| Ma, ḅa jara ḅa ganak ḍuda ya, | Well, since we are all complete horses |
| b·a dukanaka na inada jiaka | here, all our mothers and fathers, |
| na amada, tentu, | certainly, |
| *jara ganak dàḅade,* | *we are all complete horses,* |
| *tu màtu dàḅade. . . .* | *we are all full people. . . .* |
| Taka jiakayaya "aaa da papemaḍa" | But if we were to say again "eh, they |
| jiaka wedaka na walu | don't know that," |
| tentu panewideka | certainly we speak |
| *tutu na paraka papeda* | *according to however much we know* |
| atau *tutu na paraka pa-itada* nu | or *according to however much we see* |
| ḍumu Dedungara. (Jiaḍi!) | Oh Dedungara. (Yes!) |
| Jiaka da ningukaka umada, | If we didn't have a house, |
| giḍadaka ḅata kaḅuangu ningu? | where would we gather? |
| Giḍadaka ḅata panewi ningu? | Where would we speak? |
| Giḍadaka ḅata ḅatang ningu? | Where would we confer? |
| (Ai malangu tàkakaka ḍuna.) | (Yeah, this is true indeed.) |
| Giḍadaka ḅata lori ningu, ei? | Where would we exist, huh? |

The first line after the address cry (*ḅa jara ḅa ganak ḍuda ya*) is the citation form, the first line, of a conventional couplet. Shortly thereafter,

Ubu Dongu uses a complete, canonical couplet (it means that the meeting has a quorum). It is as if to say, since empirically it happens that we are all here, then, speaking now with illocutionary force, let us performatively "be all here." This move from mention to use suggests that the situation is to be interpreted—perhaps retrospectively—as a token of a type. In addition, he comes out with a repetitive series of rhetorical questions ("where would we . . . ?"). These are not canonical couplets, but the parallelisms they create add to the formality of his intervention. At this point, the role of conference participant is verging on that of a ritual speaker.

When Anakalangese speak in couplets, they present their words as iconic of ancestral types. The fuller the performance, the more they are casting the context in which they speak as an authoritative event. In addition, various conventions assure that the particular type of event is identified in various ways. Some are quite explicit. Event types can be denoted by referring either to the speech or to the material objects they require. Recall ratu Bura's complaint, at the beginning of chapter 3. He speaks of missing offerings by citing the opening lines of the prayers: "First you stick a pig, then you 'receive this here, for eating rice, for drinking water.'" In doing so, he implicitly characterizes that action as essentially a form of speech.

A more esoteric way of indexing the type of event is provided by genre conventions: certain couplets should be confined to certain sorts of events. For example, when a marriage negotiator used the expression "crossing the sea, leaning on a spear" to express the distance that his party had traveled to meet the other, his listeners compelled him to pay a fine, since the term should be restricted to peace making after a fight.[3] Like sumptuary regulations, such restrictions help assure that the use of certain forms will index the activity in which they are used as being an instance of a certain type of event.[4] The typification to which self-reference contributes also works to frame any given performance as being essentially a repetition of an ancestral way of acting. In providing the performers with a source of authority, this also entails a disclaimer, that 'these are not willful acts, nor am I their principal agent.'

In discussing couplets, people tend to be very alert to pragmatic errors: when I visited one ratu in 1993, he interrupted our conversation, on some unrelated topic, to correct a mistake—a wrong pairing of lines—that he claimed another ratu had made during a rite I attended in 1987. When I asked speakers about the couplets they had used, my questions were redirected toward, not 'what' the metaphors denote ("what does it say?" *gana wena?*), but how to use them. Unlike the Dutchman mentioned in chapter 4, one should ask of a couplet "where does it strike?"—just as one asks of an offering or a gift (see chapter 3). When one man told me the story of Babel, he characterized it in terms of performative failure: after the confusion of tongues, 'you'd ask for water, they'd bring you salt.' What is of interest to Anakalangese most often is what bearing words have on a given situation, their potential outcomes, and how they define the context in which they occur (see Vološinov [1930] 1973: 68). It is *this* that is locally subject to puzzling out and interpretation. When I would go over transcriptions with people and ask them to interpret an obscure couplet, they tended to reply by specifying the circumstances in which you speak it, sometimes giving as an example some previous occasion when they had heard it used. So, too, it appears that when Anakalangese worry about mistakes, what is at issue is not failed denotation as much as it is practical incapacity or procedural error.

## THE WORK OF REFLECTION

Although ritual speech strives to have the effect of pure repetition of ancestral words, it would not work if it were no more than that. Even in the most restricted of forms, certain prayers, ritual speech is not merely a fixed or liturgical text, for it must speak in the name of particular identities and have context-specific effects. The way in which ritual speech speaks of its context can be seen in three short examples, drawn from oration (*taungu li*), offering speech (*palaikungu*), and prayer (*nyàba*). Here are the opening lines of an oration in a yaiwo event.[5]

| | | |
|---|---|---|
| O: O ma yaiwo! | O yaiwo singer! | 1 |
| R: Maiye mai! | Come on—come! | |
| O: Ma yaiwo! | Yaiwo singer! | |
| R: Maiye mai! | Come on—come! | |
| | | |
| O: Jelineka na jara pakaletigu | My riding horse now leaps | 5 |
| mauri tena | boat master | |
| ta Walu Kerung | at Eight Bases | |
| laijuneka na asu papawujiagu | my summoned dog now jumps | |
| mangu jara | horse owner | |
| ta Walu Adung | at Eight Altars | 10 |
| | | |
| Ma yaiwo! | Yaiwo singer! | |
| R: Maiye mai! | Come on—come! | |
| | | |
| O: Yekaḍiwa nyuwa | It is I | |
| ma sailuya na soka | who switches the water spout | |

| | | |
|---|---|---|
| na ma sòduya | the one who binds the | 15 |
| na kaka ratu | cockatoo ratus | |
| ta Walu Kerung | at Eight Bases | |
| yekaḍiwaka yaiyu | It is I here | |
| na ma ḅorunya | the one who dons | |
| na ḅisi tara | the iron spur | |
| ta Walu Adung | at Eight Altars | |

| | | |
|---|---|---|
| Waiga ḍuku kayisa | Earlier I received the pot-rests | 20 |
| ḍa kaliangu ta katikuna | from his head | |
| jara ma padewa | horse of the spirit | |
| waiga ḍuku kayisa ḍa ḍaitu | earlier I received the burdens | |
| ta kaḅakina | from her shoulder | |
| asu ma pa-ura | dog of fate | |

| | | |
|---|---|---|
| Yaiwo! | Yaiwo! | |
| R: Maiye mai! | Come on—come! | 25 |

It opens with the conventional framing address to the singer of the yaiwo song, to which a third man, the ratifier ("he who answers," *na ma hima*—identified here as R) responds. The first three sets of couplets (5–10, 14–19, 20–23) are full of framing devices. The first set announces the fact of orating ("my riding horse now leaps") and identifies the speaker as the host ("boat master"), associating himself and the site of the event with his kaḅisu (one of whose epithets is Eight Bases, Eight Altars). The next set boldly and anaphorically identifies the speaker by first-person pronoun (13). The topic focus in "It is I" implies that the discourse (here, the frame set by the song) has already raised the question of identity; in this context, the statement implies a prior, implicit, question: 'who has set the gongs playing and the singer singing?' The identification is then filled out with a claim to authority (already implicit in the marked use of the pronoun) based on priestly leadership, as one who initiates ratus (which, it turns out, is one of the central issues in this event). This authority is grounded in turn in succession: he had received his office from his "horse of the spirit," which by convention refers to the most important members of his immediately preceding deceased generations—in this case, his father's brother.

Compare this to an offering speech (palaikungu) with the two prayers (nyàba) that follow it.[6] Two ratus sit on a mat, facing each other. Set between then is an offering dish, containing betel and a scraping of metal. The ratifier sits at the side and a small boy holds the chick that will be sacrificed. Speaking first, the senior man's offering speech directs the younger "praying ratu" in composing his prayer:

| | | |
|---|---|---|
| "Loḍu goru | "Neck sing | 1 |
| reja wici | feet dance | |
| kana ḍetanguka uma | in order to go up (into the) house | |
| kana hayinguka kahali. | in order to rise (to the) benches. | |
| Kaku walahuna nula | So I open the offered pillow | 5 |
| pakacorungu | | |
| hadàka ḅakuluna | great all together | |
| hawalu wojuluna | one more turning | |
| kaku taka tomana | so I arriving come | |
| kaku juaru ḍahina. | so I fall all in place. | |
| Ka jiajiàleya | May it be set | 10 |
| ḅana kabucuku na reja wici | when the dancing feet in step | |
| ka jiajiàleya | may it be set | |
| ḅana kadiawuku na loḍu goru | when the singing throat whispers | |
| ka pawolu tu kawungaya | established by the first men | |
| ka parawi tu madainguya | committed by the ancient men | 15 |
| na manu hangiwu | the one chicken | |
| na kawaḍaku hawàla | the one sliver of metal | |
| gugulu kanawi | sea cucumber tentacle | |
| laruhu mawita" | octopus legs" | |
| wenaka, | let him say,[7] | 20 |
| na ma tana totu | he who guards the land | |
| ta tàpu na pawàlahu | at the opened mat | |
| na ma ḍaiya nucu | she who watches now | |
| ta nùla pakacorungu. | at the offered pillow. | |
| Jiaka ḅa wemu nucu | If you say now | 25 |
| ḅamu nungaya ta leku | when you utter at the rope | |
| ḅaku 'inagu' | if I [address you] 'my mother'[8] | |
| ḅamu kayiya ta yea | when you receive it at the wood | |
| ḅamu kayi li panewi | when you receive words of speech | |
| kayi li kajiàla! | receive words of negotiation! | 30 |
| R: Malangu | True | |

Unlike the oration (and, as will be seen in the next chapter, negotiation speech), the offering speech is not broken up by declamatory cries. At the end, it is merely acknowledged by the ratifier (R). The first half of the speech is dominated by optatives (*ka-* forms), which denote the gen-

eral purpose of the offering and refer back to the previous event. The
second half, dominated by reported speech, is concerned with the attribution of agency and with successful delegation of speech to the praying ratu.

The offering speech opens by naming the very type of event in which
it occurs (1–2), in which a man sings in the genre called *lodu* as women
perform the line dance (*reja*). It then states the desired immediate outcome of the offering, that the words spoken will be sheltered in the
house (3–4), that is, arrive at their destined addressee. The speaker explicitly claims for this event the authority of actions that are grounded
in ritual forms, that is, the very form testifies to the fulfillment of commitments made by and to the ancestors (14–15). He then names the
offering (16–17) and provides it with an epithet (18–19). The optatives
are then framed by the verbs of quotation (20, 25), representing everything that has just been said as being the content of the message to be
delivered by the *other* speaker, the praying ratu, to whom the final sets
of couplets formally delegate the speaking part.

Immediately following this speech, the younger ratu says the prayer
over the offering dish, which holds the offerings that accompany the
chicken yet to come. In striking contrast to the soft, almost confidential
tone with which the offering speech was made, this ratu speaks in a
very rapid, chantlike monotone, beginning with the sharp two-syllable
declamation.

| | | |
|---|---|---|
| Màla! | Come on! | 1 |
| Hapa bìlihaka da pahapa | Just chew the betel-quids | |
| dumu angu | oh friend[9] | |
| kau tèkiha da kuta Hawu | may you take the Sawu betels | |
| wacihaka ta tanga woli | snatch them at the offering dish | 5 |
| dumu angu | oh friend | |
| wenaka ba tomane na rahi jara | he says when he arrives at | |
| | the horse race finish line | |
| [line unclear] | | |
| wenaka duna hama tuna duna | he says just like him | |
| bana tomana na ina | when the mother [spirit] arrives | 10 |
| jiaka bana takana na ama | and when the father [spirit] comes | |
| dumu angu. | oh friend. | |

Tomane na dungu rahi hapa          Arrived, the year for chewing
jiaka na wula rahi ngangu          and the month for eating

jiakaḍiyaka ḍumu angu              that's why, oh friend          15
[line unclear]

ḍumu angu                          oh friend

yayina hama tunaka                 just like this here

ḍumu angu                          oh friend

na ma totuya na lubu               he who watches over the underside[10]   20
  na ma nùla kacorungu               who is an offered pillow
na ma jiawa mawu ḍuna              she who guards the shadow
  na tapu na pawàlahu                the opened mat

ḍumu angu.                         oh friend.

Na woluyaka na gugulu kanawi       He made this sea cucumber tentacle   25
na rawiya na laruhu mawita         she forms this octopus leg

ḍumu angu                          oh friend

na manu hangiwu ḍuna               the one chicken
jiaka na kawaḍaku hawàla           and the one metal flake

ḍumu angu.                         oh friend.                       30

Kana hayika ḍuna                   To raise it up
  ta tapu na pawalahu                to the opened mat
kana ḍetaka                        that it go up
  ta nula pakacorungu                to the offered pillow

ḍumu angu.                         oh friend.

Dangu abi na lagoḍu ta urangu      In order that it not be chilled in the rain
abi na hawenangu ta laḍu           lest it be idle in the sun            35

ḍumu angu.                         oh friend.

Dangu ta hadaka ḅakulu             In order to once again be great
ta hawali wojulu                   to turn again

ḍumu angu.                         oh friend.

Dangu ka magoli paḍahingu          In order to be lying altogether       40
pataka patomana jiàlana            arriving come too

ḍumu angu.                         oh friend.

Dangu ka peku kadiawuku jiàlana    In order that it may whisper too
  na loḍu goru                       the neck song

| | | |
|---|---|---|
| dangu ka peku kabucuku jiàlana na reja wici | in order that it may be in step too the feet dance | 45 |
| dangu kamu pa-inunguka ta ura kamu pamawunguka ta laḍu. | in order that you shelter it from rain that you shade it from sun. | |
| Nukaḍiyaka na aluaku wewi pihunguna ḍumu angu nukaḍiyaka na pangali wewi kojianguna ḍumu angu | Right there it is the tracks of planting in holes oh friend right there it is the tracks poked with dibble stick oh friend | 50 |
| na manu na hangiwu jiaka na kawaḍaku hawàla. | the one chicken and the one metal flake. | 55 |
| Dangu kana ukaḍika: ma dowi ma daha | In order that it be given: the true the good | |
| pakoku pakaḍingi ta ati pakaraigu | begging throat my requesting liver | 60 |
| kayi wena lima hima wena àḅa | receive with hand answer with mouth | |
| kamu kayiya ta tanga woli kau waciha ḍa kuta Hawu Ubo! | may you receive it at the offering dish snatch at the Sawu betels Lord! | 65 |

This prayer opens with the conventional injunction to receive and is regularly punctuated with direct address to the spirit. In contrast to oration, negotiation, and some longer forms of offering speech, the prayer does not receive back-channel cues or response cries. Instead, like song and divination, it addresses the spirits directly. It identifies the event type and then follows with a string of optatives. Deictics, such as "this here" (18, 49, 52), verbally point to the offering as something really present to both speaker and addressee. The figure of "tracks" (50–53) identifies this offering as the objective material that completes the words previously spoken in offering speech and prayer. An epithet identifies the speaker (60–61), and the prayer closes with a further injunction to receive. The praying ratu then continues with a prayer over the chick, which the boy now holds out toward him.

| | |
|---|---|
| Màla! | Come on! |
| Kayiḍuya na manu! | Receive indeed the chicken! |
| Kayiya na manu, | Receive the chicken, |

baku woliya duku                                when I make it
    na uhu tutu ngangu                              the rice for eating
    na wai tutu inu                                 the water for drinking

[line unclear]

Dangu kana hangiya dumu                         So you can eat it
    ta nula pakacorungu                             at the offered pillow
na hayiya                                       raise it
    ta tapu papawalahu.                             at the opened mat.

Nuya                                            Here it is
    na aluaku wewi pihungu                          the planted hole track
    pangali wewi kojiang.                           dibble stick stabbed track.

Mu kayi wena lima                               You receive with hands
mu hima wena àba                                you answer with mouth

mu kayiya na manu                               you receive this chicken
    Ubo!                                            Lord!

The three speeches are pragmatically linked as the stages in the conveying of a single message. The links among them, however, do not take the form of exact repetition. The first prayer is much longer than the second. The offering speech names the event type with a single epithet (in short and long forms: 1–2, 11–13), whereas the first prayer elaborates, announcing itself to be part of an obligatory calendrical rite, the fulfillment of an obligation: "horse race finish line" (8), "when the mother arrives" (10), and "year for chewing" (13). The first prayer repeats and embellishes the proximal outcome (31–35, 40–41, 47–48) provided in the offering speech (3–4, 5, 8–9). It adds the reflexive request for blessings on the singer of the lodu (57–61). In contrast to the first prayer, which expands on the offering speech, the second prayer is a bare-bones performative. Presupposing and citing all that has already been said in the first prayer, it says only enough to point out that the offering in question is now a chicken and that there really is a chicken present.

The reported words within the offering speech are represented as the words of another: only the prayers directly address the spirit, but the use of reported speech also distances the speaker from what is said. Only the second prayer lacks any reported speech at all, but it is also the most decontextualized, iterable, and simple expression of giving and asking. Its form as a basic prayer is manifest in the high proportion of injunctions to receive relative to the lines that refer to the desired outcome—three single lines and one couplet directly saying "receive" and two additional couplets directing to eat, out of a mere seventeen lines. Only the prayers point directly to the offering with deictics ("there it is"); the offering speech only names them ("the one chicken, the one sliver of metal"), placing less emphasis on the copresence of speaker, listener, and object. Furthermore, only the prayers give instructions to receive offerings; the offering speech gives instructions to receive words. The prayers, then, especially the second one, contrast with the offering speech in their license to address the spirit directly, a license that seems to derive from their form as the most canonical, depersonalized, and decontextualized of speech forms and from their speaker's remove from the responsible party, those on whose behalf the sacrifice is made. The mutual relations among these three speeches take the forms of reported, cited, and presupposed speech. But there is no clear origin to this cited speech: although the two prayers quote or cite the previous offering speech, that which they quote has *already* been framed by verbs of quotation. That is, they are quoting words that, originally given as instructions on what to say, *themselves* anticipate their subsequent quotation.

## ICONISM AND HIDDEN NAMES

Although ritual speech seems to invite special efforts at interpretation, many of its most common features, such as a highlighting of poetic form, excessive redundancy, the weakness of some metaphors, the elevated forms of proper nouns, or even sheer obviousness, suggest that there is more at stake than a coded set of propositions. As I suggested in the previous chapter, the formation of tropes is an important aspect of the function of ritual couplets but does not alone suffice to explain their status and power. It does not account in cultural terms for why a metaphor should be more powerful than a nonmetaphor. Moreover, by focusing on denotation, this approach scants the fact that couplets are used to achieve consequences: they are not merely profound, they are efficacious. The existence of couplets in which neither metaphor nor cosmological duality seems to be significant (such as many place-names) suggests that this *formal* quality, being a pair, has a value in its own right.

I will argue that the form of couplets is *itself* a form of deferral and provides a reflexive icon of the relations between spirit world and the very performances in which they occur. This is most apparent in the figurative nature of poetic speech. The register of ritual speech in Anakalang is a way of saying the (semantically or referentially) "same thing" in "different words." Moreover, at the same time that the couplet as a *totality* forms a trope, the fact of being a pair also provides an *internal* model of its *external* relations. That is, the relationship of couplet to colloquial expression is (partially) mirrored in the relationship between the two lines of the couplet itself. Each line serves as a figure for the other: the couplet displays *in itself* the same possibility of saying "the same thing" in two "different" ways held by ritual speech as a register. This is most apparent when elements of the colloquial expression are embedded in the first line of the couplet, such as "daybreak" in the couplet "at daybreak on the land, at the rising of the sun," or in the ritual versions of many place-names. I propose that there is an implicit cosmological principle at work here. An approach that emphasizes denotation would treat the second line as a supplement to the embedded colloquialism contained within the first line. The structure of deferral, however, reverses these relations. Because the ancestral is supposed to be the more fundamental of the two, Ankalangese often see the relation of couplet to colloquial as one of completeness to diminishment. In this perspective, the colloquial is a lesser version, a falling away from the more complete forms identified with the ancestors. This relation of diminishment reflects the general sense Anakalangese often express, that the historical passage of time itself involves an ongoing falling away from completeness. The colloquial version of a place-name, then, serves as the citation form or title of the full couplet. The relation of diminishment between colloquial and formal versions treats the everyday as if it were only a reflection of the more complete (ancestral) reality expressed by ritual. The very *forms* of poetic speech thus convey a powerful vision of the nature of lived experience that is not directly coded as a proposition in either explicit statements or metaphors. In fact, this vision is likely to be all the more compelling precisely to the extent that, experienced as the aesthetic rightness of poetic form, it is subliminal knowledge.

I am proposing that the couplet exemplifies and brings to the fore a more general pattern of displacement in Anakalangese representational practices, which underlies both cultural assumptions about the nature of reality and the forms that agency and authority can or should take. In Anakalangese language ideology, ritual speech at once supplements and suppresses the speech of everyday life. But this is not simply because everyone in Anakalang obediently accepts a shared cultural text. It is due, in part, to the effects of linguistic form. Ritual speech is superordinate to the language of everyday activities, and yet it remains a diminished sign of the true speech of ancestors. Thus it at once indexes the value of its context while simultaneously reminding its users of a certain loss. By highlighting the fact of avoidance, ritual speech epitomizes ways of construing the nature, powers, and dangers of representation found in everyday practices.

The importance of avoidance and displacement is made apparent by their pervasiveness in the everyday practices around personal names. Anakalangese naming practices are organized around a principle of displacement that can be recursively applied. Everyone has an "original name" (*ngara mema*) or a "good name" (*ngara piyana*) of which most other people are ignorant, and those who know should avoid using it in either address or reference. This contrasts with what is normally used, the "name that is uttered" (*ngara patiki*) or the "name that is called" (*ngara pa-aungu*). Moreover, people tend to avoid even the latter, especially in situations demanding special delicacy, referring instead to status, place, or kinship. For example, when Pak Niko, who had once worked for the Forest Service, was first approached by a spokesman seeking to open marriage negotiations for his sister, the latter addressed him as "the lord Forest Service." Similarly, when special politeness was called for, people sometimes referred to me by the name of the place where I lived, "the lord Monkey Banana" (*na maràba* Kalowu Kauki). In more casual or intimate conversation, people favor nicknames. Like word pairs, no single semantic principle is at work. Sources include physical characteristics ("Wispy," referring to the tangled appearance a child's hair had when she was born), personality ("Standing Tongue," for a woman who cried constantly as a child), clothing style ("Upright Headcloth," for a man who ties his headcloth in a distinctive way), idiosyncratic behavior ("Reflection," for a woman who is always looking at herself in the mirror), place of origins ("Gena," for a woman from east Sumba, home of the dialect known as "magena"), the date of birth ("June"), or events at the time of birth ("Bill Clinton," for a child born in November 1992).[11] Not all nicknames are unique, but all index contingency and entail avoidance.

Most common of all, however, is teknonymy, by which parents are addressed and referred to with the name of their eldest child, regardless of sex. The parents of Bani are "Mother of Bani" (Ina Bani) and "Father of Bani" (Ama Bani). The teknonym "Mother of Bani" is a product of recursive displacement, because it avoids the child's real name (which is Kaledi) and appropriates instead the child's uttered name (Bani). This uttered name in turn involves still another set of displacements, since

Kaledi takes his uttered name from another man, his "namesake" (*tamu*). This older man named Kaledi has a "horse name" (*ngara jara*), "Valiant Male" (Moni Bani), the abbreviated form of which becomes young Kaledi's uttered name. The horse name, taken from one's best riding horse, is a common source of uttered names for men of standing.[12] In actual use, even the horse name is allusive, since it is usually only an abbreviation of the horse's full name. Thus we arrive at the teknonym "Mother of Bani" through a series of steps away from her "real name": from parent to child, from child's real to uttered name, from self to namesake to horse, and, finally, from full to abbreviated horse name. Most horse names involve yet further displacement, since they derive from (and thus allude *back* to) the owner who takes their name: they permit a man, in effect, to speak of *himself* as if he were speaking of a horse.

Both horse name and namesake illustrate a second principle of naming, linkage to another referent or representative. Substitute names are not simply negations of the real name but often point *toward* something else as well. Horse names forge a link between man and horse, the horse providing a vehicle for statements about the man. As a form of representation, the horse stands for, while remaining subordinate to, the man. Namesakes are also closely, although less asymmetrically, linked. The elder namesake should show a special interest in the affairs and well-being of the younger, and each namesake usually addresses the other simply as "namesake." A man and woman whose respective namesakes were husband and wife are also likely to address each other as "namesake." Ama Riti told me that he is unable to scold his own grandson, because he is named after Ama Riti's father; even without using the name in question, it would still be like scolding his own father. Although all the forms of displaced naming to some extent highlight the codelike character of language, this is most evident in the use of the word "namesake" as a form of address. An epitome of reflexive speech, this term *instantiates* a speech practice (the mutual avoidance of namesake names) by *naming* it (the existence of a shared namesake). It is as if to allude to the very existence of the code were already sufficient to carry out the deference that the code enjoins.

Strategies of displacement highlight the fact of avoidance, pointing to the existence of something that is suppressed. People are always aware of the existence of the real name, whether or not they know what it is. Without revealing the substance of his real name, Ubu Elu, for example, prominently displays its existence, in the form of initials tattooed on his forearm. Although most nicknames bear no connection to the real name, the most common forms of "uttered name" are predicated on the understood existence of this silent name. Thus Bani receives his horse name, and possibly his very character, from the "real name" that links him to an older man. Likewise, to use the word "namesake" as a term of address is to display the fact of not saying the suppressed name. The "real name" is again subject to a sort of virtual use at the end of life. Every name is conventionally paired with another, a "keening name" (*ngara hau*), by which the deceased is addressed in the songs of mourners during the wake over the corpse. The name itself remains unspoken, but since the links are public conventions, its existence and even content are indexed the moment its substitute is uttered.

The value of this sort of displacement can be seen at both extremes of the spectrum of possible status. At one end, the slave can be addressed directly by name with impunity. Moreover, as I mentioned in chapter 2, the slave's name (*ngara ata*) can itself serve as the displaced name of the master. The kaḍehang, the name by which a kabisu is addressed in ancestral rituals and marriage negotiations, is the ancestor's slave name. This is not esoteric knowledge: I once heard a man speak derogatorily of a neighbor, clinching the matter by observing that his real name is the kaḍehang of a certain kabisu. The slave name is also called the "name (which) comes out, emerges." This term suggests that the relationship between real and uttered name is at once one of suppression and hierarchical extension of the self: the slave, who represents the master, emerges in place of that which is veiled and superordinate. In addition, people refer to the category of truly high nobles as "Lord of." Like "namesake," the expression "Lord of" is reflexive, the code speaking of the code itself. This expression implies that the very essence of nobility is the ability to displace naming, to master self-representation in terms of a general, ancestral code. A parallel relationship between displacement and status can be seen in the way non-Christians commonly accuse Christians of hubris for daring to speak the name of God. Non-Christians, by contrast, refer to the highest spirits metalinguistically, that is, by reference to the very suppression of the act of naming: "unuttered namesake, the unspoken name."[13]

What is at stake in these practices? One possible answer is simply deferential indirection. Naming rites, however, may provide further illumination. First a false naming must be prevented, then divination must establish the correct namesake. The first operation occurs the moment the newborn cries, when it is given a temporary generic place holder, Ngongu for boys, Tiala for girls. If the parents do not act immediately, the demonic Owner of the Land will name the child, who will later suffer disease or some other misfortune. Three or six days later, if someone has not already asked to be the child's namesake, one is chosen through divination: the mother offers her breast to the infant, while someone else recites names from within the kabisu. The child signals the correct name by beginning to suck when it is spoken. The need to give a generic name suggests that the child is appropriated for humanity only through active intervention. Unlike that intentional but generic action, the second rite narrows the name down to an individual link to a specific other person and displaces the agency away from the parents, onto the child, or perhaps the ancestor acting through the child. In contrast to the names that emerge in everyday talk, which permit all sorts of playfulness, novelty, and individuality, the underlying "good" names must be iterable types.[14]

The "good name" is one whose only true link to the person is through an original act, a baptism that forges an existential tie between person and name. Although such names may have semantically transparent meanings, and the divinatory process through which they are bestowed suggests there is a real connection between namesake and new bearer, they are bound to the (unique) person in the world. To speak them is a highly indexical act, bearing all the intersubjective abruptness of a brute act of pointing. Anakalangese treat their utterance as the verbal equivalent of startling someone, a challenge to one's composure that threatens one's self-possession and esteem in the eyes of others. In contrast, titles identify the referent as one of a class of things in the world (Errington 1988: 111–112). Like the ritual couplet, deferential address at once avoids the directness and intimacy of the index and constructs that of which it speaks as being an instance of something more general. The person who can be named through such avoidance terms is one who can lay claim to an identity that transcends the context of here and now, one who is not confined by the limits of the particular body.

But names are not simple possessions of their bearers, they are predicated on the dialectic of recognition. My name is most often spoken by others, and it is in *their* use of my name that *my* identity is publicly recognized. To the extent that "good names" are secret, to utter them is to place oneself in an intimate—and, more important, an authoritative—relation to its bearer, like that of a parent who was present at the moment of naming. As the philosopher Hilary Putnam (1975) argues, language's ability to refer to things in the world by name is ultimately

grounded not in a semantics of underlying descriptions but through indexical links to "baptismal events," original acts of naming. This entails a "linguistic division of labor": some speakers have more authority than others.[15] Unlike "namesake," which focuses on the code, or a
nickname, which has something of the character of a proposition, or
a slave name, which focuses on a social relation, the "good name" is
grounded in an originary act of authority exerted by someone else over
the person. The moment in which this act occurs is shrouded in protective devices, which are reinforced by the subsequent practices of displacement. All this displacement points back to what is not being spoken, as if it were necessary continually to construct the very center that
is apparently being presupposed.

## DISPLACEMENT, AUTHORITY, AND DANGER

Displacement serves two functions, extension and avoidance. The
noble's identity, for example, is at once extended outward by, and hidden behind, that of the slave. Representation, as a form of displacement, is a matter both of potentials created and dangers averted. Potential for ancestral authority and avoidance of self-exposure are both
evident in the importance of the canonical core of the couplet. The emphasis on this core, in perception and in practice, stresses those properties of language that are least linked to the speech context or to speakers' intentions. It is an instance of a more general process that has been
called "entextualization" (Bauman and Briggs 1990). Entextualization
stresses the context-free dimensions of language at the expense of its links
to particular speech events. It seeks to produce something like a timeless
text, whose linguistic forms imply that its sources and meanings lie beyond the realm of particular speakers, circumstances, and interests. By
emphasizing the "monologic" dimensions of language (Bakhtin 1981),
decontextualization provides an important source of authority for ritual speech and other "officializing strategies" (Bourdieu [1972] 1977).
In Anakalang, by foregrounding the ancestral couplet at the expense of
the particularity of context, ritual speech implicitly portrays the particular event and participants as instances of general types. The ancestral
character of those types is demonstrated by the iconic form of the couplet, discussed in the previous chapter.

Yet monologic forms of language pose a dilemma: they must bear
*some* connection to those who speak them if they are to invest speakers
with authority. In Anakalang, the actual use of ritual speech should

index the presupposable existence of links to the ancestors. That is, in the absence of other sources of legitimate knowledge (such as invention, inspiration, or possession), to speak with ritual couplets, in full performance, displays that the speaker has received them by way of transmission along a "chain of authentication" (Putnam 1975) from their originators. On the basis of this indexically *presupposed* link to its origins, ritual speech thereby conveys an ancestral warrant to the present actors and actions. This conveyance is a form of indexical *entailment*; that is, if the forms are correct, it follows that the actions are authoritative.[16]

Part of what makes it possible for speakers to take on the mantle of ritual speech's authority, however, is its susceptibility to grammatical inflection and rhetorical choices. Because the words are grammatically responsive to the context, the act of speaking inserts itself into its environment, and the words—to a certain extent—are identified with the speaker's persona. The limited amount of inflection permitted in ritual speech constructs what Bakhtin (1981) calls a dialogic relationship between the identity of the speaker and the voice of the ancestors. The living speaker partially enters the world of ancestors, while at the same time the words of the ancestors enter into the activities of the living. This ambiguity of voice exposes speech events to slippage, the possibility that either the uniqueness of the speaker or the relatively empty ancestral frame will expel the other. In Derrida's terms, the quality of iterability haunts particular speakers' assertions of agency. By the same token, their assertions of agency threaten to undermine the authority they seek through the use of iterable, ancestral forms.[17]

The power of the couplet in this particular cultural context, then, lies in part in its ability to serve as an icon of the mediated relations of deferral that make of any given set of actions and actors a shadow of their fuller, invisible and silent selves. The couplet provides a means to take on ancestral powers at the same time that it implicitly points to what is missing. Anakalangese are quite insistent that no actual performance can ever be perfect, given the fact that the present is always in a state of diminished knowledge, wealth, and power compared to the past, "shadows on the dry land, reflections on the water." Any actualization of the ancestral is only a deferral of a full performance.

In stressing displacement, I am drawing attention to formal and pragmatic qualities of speech, rather than concentrating only on the semantic effects, such as cultural metaphors. Use of the couplet, speech that is "loaded onto a boat, mounted upon a horse," indexes the fact of

speaking in an elevated register, the couplet itself forming an icon of figurative speech. Ritual speech displays the fact of substitution for the
colloquial, that one could "say the same thing" in more than one way,
different ways having different social values. Such a juxtaposition of
styles, although a general feature of language variation, is heavily exploited by ritual speech and promotes in the listener a kind of "rela-
tivized consciousness," an awareness of movement among alternatives
(Bakhtin 1981: 295–296, 323–324).[18] The high formality of ritual speech
makes evident its distance not only from alternative styles but also
from the everyday speaking subject and speech event. It portrays serious
and effective interaction as due to the command of representations. The
iconism of ritual speech form, semantics of metaphor, indexical functions, and (as will become apparent in the next chapter) the pragmatic
structure of performance all help to constitute the participants, speaking
and nonspeaking, as representatives of social entities that exist beyond
the time and space of the momentary context. *Semiotic* representation
here functions as *social-political* representation.

At the same time, representational practices both respond to and
evoke an atmosphere of danger and risk. Anakalangese describe the need
for mediated representations not only in terms of deference but also in
terms of danger. The metaphor and indirection of ritual speech in Rindi
are called "screen" or "shield" (Forth 1988: 135), one form of the hedg-
ing common to encounters, for example, with spirits (see Metcalf 1989:
63). In Anakalang, people say that without ritualized negotiation marriages would inevitably result in war. In interactive terms, the danger is
posed both by visible and invisible others. As I have noted above, the
pervasive sense that social others put one at risk has been well stated
by ethnographers of both east and west Sumba. When Ama Koda interpreted the gift of a torn cloth as a sign of otherwise opaque intentions,
as recounted in chapter 2, he was doing something that came naturally.
The most ordinary interactions require attentiveness to possible signs,
such as a stumble, choking on coffee, tying one's headcloth in an unusual way. Even relations to the very spirits in terms of whom one's own
most fundamental social identities are established, in kabisu and house,
are tenuous.

The risks of speech are nowhere more evident than in the words that
maintain the ties between living speakers and the dead from whom they
have received them. The ratu who must speak these words is said to be
"one who clears the tangled vines, who enters the snake-ridden forest,
who crosses the crocodile-filled river." A characteristic example of the

risks is the case of ratu Kadi, who was in charge of the prayers during a ritual in 1987. After several nights with little sleep, and amid the growing tension as the climactic segments of the rites approached, ratu Kadi, a man in his thirties, collapsed. A few days later I visited him as he sat by his hearth, still pale and apprehensive, and he shared with me his musings.

> My father died because he added [improvised] words when singing the rite. As for me, this [fainting] is the first time anything like this has ever happened to me. There were two chickens and a pig, but I put the second one first. First of all, I didn't pray when they first gathered, because they did the leaf divination at that time, and that's not my portion. In addition, it's actually ratu Boru who should pray here, not me. Now when the diviner said he wasn't able to do it, the job was given to me, because it was already night and we couldn't go hunting for Boru. Really I wanted to refuse, but they told me it was only for tonight. So I agreed. . . . After roasting the chicken [sacrifice] . . . I felt my body grow hot in the chest and the belly. I said, "This thing is hot, better offer to Boru to handle." But they didn't go look for him. So I made them look—they hunted all the way from Prai Rara to Lai Ḍeta, while I was going up to the village to invite the marapu to attend. Arriving back here, after I had drunk [coffee] in the Great House, I went to my own house to bathe and change my shirt. There I saw the person who was supposed to be searching for Boru, who said he hadn't had a chance to go. So I sent two people to the village to fetch him. Meanwhile I waited in the Great House. They returned and I started the event, offering the task back to Boru. Boru answered "Eh, indeed, I can't now," because he hadn't followed right from the start, also it's already near the time, "it doesn't feel right." Again I said I can't continue. . . . So, like it or not, I had to accept. I had already spoken out front, what could I do, well, you witness yourselves what will happen. Because I felt it in my body. So I began to pray. Began clumsily. Suddenly all was dark. I didn't know anything further.

The following week, a rite was held to restore ratu Kadi. Another ratu told me that they have to beat the gongs when they do this, which means sacrificing two pigs. He emphasized this is because it's not simply as if ratu Kadi had spoken in error, it's as if he were actually dead. Indeed, ratu Kadi got off easy. When I visited another ratu in 1993, he was mourning the death of his teenaged daughter, which people said had been brought about by a speech error he had made not long before.

A certain possibility of error or of failed recognition is a semiotic problem even in ordinary Anakalangese life. It is accentuated in formal encounters, for, as the following chapters will show, establishing the nature of the event and the agents is a collaborative achievement and has consequences for reputation and good fortune. A person's interlocutor might be incapable of granting the recognition he demands, or demand what he cannot give. He might speak in error, or his addressee might fail to apprehend his speech. His interlocutor might not accept the event as being of the desired type, or himself as the type of agent that he proposes to be. More significant, encounters run the risk of failure even in the face of mutual interest of either party, due to misunderstanding and confusion, often promoted by the complexity of ritual encounter. The sense of danger is thus also a recognition that interaction escapes the intentions of its participants. Anakalangese tend to assimilate this opacity of others to the pragmatic and semantic underdetermination of ritual signs. This attitude is summed up in the couplet: "sound of the hawk, the rustle of the duck [wings]." As one man explained it to me, the hawk is too high overhead to see, but it always gives a warning before snatching a chick. In the dark of the night we can hear the wings of invisible ducks passing overhead. In practice, the couplet can be used to refer both to the uncertainty and obscurity of the knowledge that the living have received from distant ancestors and to the muffled sounds that one party hears coming from behind the wall where another party discusses what to tell them before sending over their spokesman. It may also refer to the compulsion upon the living of ritual obligations formed by previous generations. What the situations share is the juxtaposition of necessity, expectation, serious consequences, and the inscrutability of signs. But failure is not always merely a danger to be avoided. One master trope of ritual performance lies in a sense that ritual speech is an encounter with and a victory over certain dangers. Ritual speech must create an arena in which the play of encounter seems to entail risk, if the outcomes are to be of value. The next chapter turns to the scene of encounter to examine some of the challenges and risks of interaction.

CHAPTER SIX

# Voices, Agents, and Interlocutors

Among the ancients, that celebrated Delphic inscription, Recognise Yourself . . . was as much to say, divide yourself, or be two.

Shaftsbury, *Characteristics of Men, Manners, Opinions, Times*

As media of representation, words and things work both to displace and to extend the agency of those who put them into play. To do so, however, they cannot remain in the virtual realm of the ancestors but must enter into concrete practices. In particular, they mediate interactions that themselves involve displacement, delegation, and representation. These interactions require performances that might be called "scenes of encounter." That is, they are highly stylized and take place on a public stage, involving varying sorts of participation and spectatorship. They portray serious action as a confrontation, between two (and usually no more than two) groups. They thus embody a model of how action works and how people (and spirits) ought to accord each other recognition, and they define the legitimate range of possible agents. The structure of the scene of encounter thus exemplifies Anakalangese concepts of authority and at the same time bears within it some of the dilemmas and constraints that haunt them. With the sweeping rubric "scenes of encounter" I wish to draw out the features common to a wide range of events. These range from everyday sociability up to rites involving several kabisu. The participants include both the living and the dead. This chapter, however, focuses on one kind of encounter, *horung*, the negotiation of marriage exchanges between kabisu, which is equally valued by Christians and non-Christians and is the most common, expensive, and political of formal interactions in contemporary Anakalang.[1]

Just as ritual speech brings to the fore certain properties of ordinary language, so too scenes of encounter formalize and emphasize certain aspects of ordinary interaction. In particular, ritualized encounters distinguish among several different participant roles and elaborately separate various aspects of "voice" and "agency." They are vital to how groups of individuals act as kaḅisu, with all the authority and agency of an entity that transcends the particulars of time, place, and living bodies. Scenes of encounter also implicitly display how those identities depend on interaction, active self-portrayal, and recognition elicited from others. Yet, as I have argued above, the formality and authority of Anakalangese ceremonial encounter operate in a complex relationship to order and risk. If the scene of encounter is a form of real action, it must entail the prospect of failing. What is more, the forms of speech and speech event do not only constrain the possibility of failure, they also contribute to how it is imaginable.

## VOICE AND AGENCY

The performance structure of Anakalangese ritual events highlights the participant roles inherent in everyday talk. It separates them and distributes them among discrete actors in a stylization of ordinary dialogue. In doing so, it elaborates on what Goffman ([1979] 1981) identifies as the animator, who actually voices the words, the author, who determines which words are to be said, and the principal, to whom the words are attributed or who is held responsible for them. An example familiar to Americans is the division among press secretary, speech writer, and president. Although participants in everyday conversations rarely need to attend to these distinctions, the scene of encounter brings them to the fore and can throw them into question. In doing so, it iconically represents social action as a form of dialogue between a pair of speakers, writ large.

Anakalangese performance forms a striking contrast to the individualistic assumptions that underlie many of the contemporary arguments about "voice" and "agency" in Western social science and literature (see the critique in Scott 1991). Negotiations, for example, separate "voice" and "agency" and performatively attribute both to suprapersonal subjects. By "voice" here, I mean simply the acts of formulating and delivering speech. The person who speaks does so by virtue of having been "girt at the waist, given a staff in the hand" by a principal, an act of formal delegation known as "taking on the shoulders, carrying on the head." The performance structure groups together the persons in whose name the event takes place along with others who benefit from it, who direct it, or whose intentionality it manifests; in distinction to the bearers of "voice," these persons share "agency," a capacity to motivate, respond to, and resolve authoritative, recognizable actions and events.

In its everyday forms, this separation of voice and agency includes the simple display of deference by way of indirection. Thus to avoid the presumption of direct address is a pragmatic equivalent to avoiding a person's "good name" by using a title or "horse name." The separation of voice and agency is also a familiar means of "saving face." It allows participants different ways of evading responsibility for error or offense by implying "this is not really me speaking" (what Du Bois 1986: 319 calls a "personal volition disclaimer"; see Brown and Levinson 1978). But to appeal to such universals as "face" does not tell us why face should be at issue in any particular instance, and why it takes the forms it does. The separation of voice and agency effected in the scene of encounter takes place against a background of Anakalangese notions of risk, whether from the violence of spirits or the shaming ire of humans. People may even speak, somewhat hyperbolically, of an alleged threat of warfare that lies behind the formality of negotiation. For some Anakalangese, the agonistic quality of kajiàla is a form of displaced combat, which one man described to me as a "war of brains" (Indo. *perang otak*). One ritual speaker, telling me about the need to choose one's words carefully, said 'This language is like shooting: if I say "eye," I'd better hit the eye. I can't hit the foot or you'll get stirred up and become more dangerous.' The trope of warfare thus has a dual relationship to the scene of encounter, for it at once characterizes the dialogue *form* as iconic of combat and represents speech as an *alternative* to (thus indexing potential for) violence. The two meet in the ambiguous border between play and fight, as in one couplet that compares dialogue to the often heated ritual spear fights (*pasola*) elsewhere in west Sumba: "We throw spears at each other like Laboyans, we toss wood at each other as in the sea worm rites."

The agonistic quality of scenes of encounter points to an almost Hobbesian dimension to Anakalangese views of the underlying nature of social relations. I once asked one experienced master of exchange what would happen if one did not marry with the mediation of ritual speech and speakers. He replied, as if it were obvious, 'Why, then we'd have war.' This is a far from idiosyncratic view. In 1993, a skilled negotiator was telling me about the gifts he had received for his services. As he put it, 'We give things to the *wunang* [ritual speaker] because it's like we're going to war—he's the head of the war party. One false sentence and he's had it.' Others say that the fact that failed negotiations today do not cause wars is simply proof of the present government's power to keep the peace. The ease with which warfare comes to mind is illustrated as well in one incident (mentioned in chapter 4) that resembles a Freudian slip. Seeking to emphasize the arduousness of his party's efforts to forge an alliance with their interlocutors, a wunang spoke of the two groups as coming together from afar, "leaning on a spear, crossing the sea." The leaders of the other party immediately objected and fined him, for, as he surely knew, the proper context for the couplet is in peace negotiations. He had unwittingly assimilated the making of marriage to the ending of warfare.

The trope of warfare refers in part to historical memory as well as to a common view of marriage, which many Anakalangese assert was carried out by capture in ancient times.[2] Even today, the threat of actual violence is not altogether absent, even within a single party. I was once attending a funeral when a panting messenger arrived to summon the desa head to another village. As they hurried off, I learned that a fight had broken out among the members of one party to a marriage negotiation and men were threatening each other with their machetes. It took the intervention of three desa heads to prevent a fight. Nonetheless, although the trope of violence draws on the concreteness of memories and living tensions, it cannot be fully reduced to them.[3] Scenes of encounter do more than prevent violence or loss of face. When affines negotiate marriage or enemies make peace, they do so by means of performance roles and rhetoric that alike represent them as coming together across great social and spatial distance. Speakers call out to each other as if from afar and are figured in tropes of a journey over rough terrain. The fictiveness of this drama is most evident in formal encounters between groups that have been allied for generations, existing in warm, daily contact. Here the perception of threat can be understood not just as a hedge against failure but as a way of publicly displaying the *value* of the relationship that is renewed through negotiations, implicitly portraying renewal as a difficult achievement.[4] I will argue that the perceived threat is associated, in part, with the general power that formal encounters have to shape social relations, with consequences for the economic standing, rank, and honor of those who enter into them. The power is real, and thus the outcomes are both uncertain and potentially dire. As in many societies in which exchange is central (Mauss

[1925] 1990; Sahlins 1972), Anakalangese figuratively depict warfare
to be the limiting case of a general threat that lies behind the scene of
negotiation. In contrast to ritualized speech events in which the consequential action occurs elsewhere, Anakalangese marriage negotiation
can be the site of real contest. It requires confrontation between two—
and only two—sides. The two parties usually have a common stake in
the successful outcome of their encounter, for an expensive transaction
adds to the reputation of both sides. At the same time they often bear
opposed interests, since too great a payment by ngàba wini may be ru-
inous. In negotiating prestation and counterprestation, each party must
find its way between the competing demands of honor and economy.
The tension between these two demands is complicated by the fact that
each of the two parties to the exchange is composed of many persons
whose own interests may not coincide: for example, the collective reputation of the *group* may do little to compensate the costs incurred by
their *supporters* even in the long run. Furthermore, the outcome, a mutual achievement of both sides, is out of the hands of any single set of actors. If, as I argued at the end of the last chapter, Anakalangese assimilate the inscrutability of signs to that of persons, violence may be one
way in which they imagine the consequences for themselves of that
inscrutability.

In addition to overcoming implicit threats, the separation of voice and
agency, and their distribution among several distinct roles, have other
effects, as representational practices. First, in common with other ritual
and political forms of action, they permit principals to remain offstage
but implicitly and authoritatively present. Second, they implicate the
participants in a scale of action beyond that of everyday sociability, involving an agency that transcends that of individual persons. Role structure and textual properties of ritual speech help index the group as an
entity that in itself possesses agency. Finally, performance draws attention reflexively to the acts of both speaking and exchanging goods. In
doing so, it emphasizes both that agents are exerting highly conscious
control over representations and that these representations derive from
ancestral knowledge that everyone ought to respect. Each party thereby
also shows that it recognizes the other party as an agent that, like itself, knows the proper ways of doing things and is able to act on that
knowledge.

The scene of encounter is the locus for identifying and ratifying social
ties that are always in the process of shifting, growing or diminishing. In

negotiating alliances, the link between winning recognition and marrying is delineated in several myths about the first ancestors. Although the first marriages came about through superhuman feats rather than negotiation, they contain elements that still inhere in the drama of negotiation, challenge and recognition. For example, in the founding myth of Parewatana (see chapter 2), Ubu Pabal's own mother's brother refused to recognize him and denied him his right to his mother's brother's daughter, Rabu Robu, until he earned this recognition (and even afterward, tried to foist off on him a slave). His structural status as sister's son was not sufficient to make him into an affine. This story exaggerates and exemplifies the tension between affines. So, too, the pragmatic structure of present-day negotiations stylizes and dramatizes the challenges each affine poses to the other, that yera will not recognize ngàba wini as a rightful ally and that ngàba wini will in turn not recognize the true value of the relationship that results.

The challenges of authoritative action arise not only between groups but also within them. In the negotiation of exchange, each party is normally composed of disparate elements. In addition to kabisu fellows and their affines, they might also include neighbors, various exchange partners, debtors, and other ad hoc supporters (who on occasion are not even Sumbanese). Within the frame of the performance—that is, when one group faces another—these internal differences are momentarily suppressed, since formally only two sides can meet. Regardless of their actual composition, the parties that negotiate exchange meet each other as kabisu. Whether the exchange is for marriage or some other purpose, such as peacemaking, these two parties are performatively constituted as ngàba wini and yera. This occurs the moment the two sides begin to represent themselves with words and objects. Speakers must use complementary forms of address and give complementary prestations: even if the negotiation eventually fails and the two parties never become affines, they must speak as affines for the duration of the encounter. Their categorical identities form a background that is presupposed by everything else that takes place: as Elinor Keenan (1974: 134) notes, to the extent people focus on some aspects of what is going on—here the objects being exchanged and the proper forms of speech—other aspects (in this case, their respective identities as yera and ngàba wini) are being taken as given. One consequence of *unsuccessful* performance, then, is to bring into question that which should be taken for granted.

Formality of text and performance are familiar aspects of ritual speech. By "formality" here, I refer to several of the features described by Irvine (1979), namely, the use of highly structured and consistent code, the invoking of positional (rather than more personal or contingent) identities, and a restricted focus on one situation. It is common, in discussing formality of speech, to give particular attention to the existence of strong constraints on code. One line of argument interprets these constraints as primarily coercive or conservative in function (Bloch 1975). Such approaches emphasize one feature of ritual, that of seemingly rigid formality, and sometimes lend themselves as well to taking at face value local assertions about the unchanging nature of tradition. As Irvine (1979) has made clear, however, "formality" is a complex notion, the properties and effects of which are not immediately self-evident. Thus ritual speech can serve ends other than conservative, stabilizing, or didactic ones. Among these ends, it has been argued, is that of maintaining the arena in which political contention might come about (Brenneis and Myers 1984: 11; Hill and Irvine 1992). Indeed, insofar as formality (in its various kinds) makes salient what might otherwise have remained quietly in the background, it may open up possibilities as much as foreclose them (Bauman 1977; Irvine 1979: 785; Merlan and Rumsey 1991). So it should not be surprising if, in certain cases, it is the most public events that are most likely to be the locus of transformations. Much will depend on what is at stake in a given type of speech event. When the central issue is defining and affirming group identities and relations, or asserting their value, speech performance may be not merely a means to, but itself a part of, the outcome.

Formalized encounter such as the negotiation of marriage payments is an important locus not only for solidary action and acts of exchange but also for the display of the group as such, as it is physically assembled and represented as a united front to face the affine. It is also the preeminent site for naming relations, identifying actors, and specifying the nature of the relationships in play—many of which cannot be assumed concretely to preexist the scene of encounter. Indeed, despite people's normative protestations to the contrary, the well-known fact that alliances are not always reliable suggests their value and continuity are not self-evident (Strathern 1984). Repeated cumulative scenes of encounter and exchange serve to give the alliance and its constituent parties a palpable form. The iterability of kajiàla and the compulsions of material debt work to raise them beyond the disparate moments of ceremonial encounter. In using kajiàla, each party shows itself as master of an authoritative voice able to engage in dialogue with an equally authoritative interlocutor. At the same time, in these moments social relations come to be objects of consciousness, and thereby subject to vicissitudes: they may be not only confirmed but also challenged.

## ḄATANG: GATHERING TOGETHER

The fully onstage negotiation emerges out of a vast sea of background discussions that culminate in full-scale conferences called "ḄA-tang." During each important step of the negotiation itself, the two parties undergo often protracted internal consultations before sending their speakers to face each other. In principle, a consensus among all participants within each party is necessary. In meetings, many people are often quite unrestrained about expressing their opinions about proper procedures, prestations, and the relative statuses of participating groups. One rationale for the openness of the meeting and the need for consensus is the general ideal of the solidarity among kaḅisu fellows and between them and those on whom they have called for support: the entire group should be made responsible for decisions. More specifically, those present are being asked to make contributions to the exchange and so have a material as well as a moral stake in the outcome. The ḅatang is thus a public stage on which the kaḅisu is present to itself and on which subordinate members have some opportunity to resist the desires of the leading figures.

The loose organization and often contentious manner of the conference reflect a process of constructing an elevated mutual interest out of the devalued condition of a willful and disparate membership. Ḅatang lie midway in the continuum of formality between everyday and fully ritualized interactions. They take place in the front room of the house, men sitting in a row along the benches, women at the sides or near the hearth. Women can participate, although rarely in the most authoritative styles of speech or commanding the floor for long. Their interventions often take the form of teasing, ironic, or chiding asides and sometimes storms of rage or weeping. Occasionally they take center stage, especially women of great personal authority or those with a special interest in the case, such as the mother of a bride or groom. These women can even prevent the negotiation from continuing altogether, as when a Catholic mother induced her kaḅisu to reject a Protestant suitor.

Unlike full ritual performance, there is no formal order of speaking, and topic focus is difficult to maintain: men lacking in influence can attempt to take the floor in a sort of filibuster to draw attention to grievances or stray into unrelated matters.[5] Although etiquette tends to permit long uninterrupted speeches by participants, when things heat up three or four men may all be fighting for the floor, as women join in from the sidelines. As Ubu Janga, a young man who attends many ḅatang but usually reserves his comments for private conversations, put it,

> That's why we all travel in a big group to the negotiation. It's not just so we can all eat meat, or so we can impress them with a big crowd. It's so we can confer and consult. Hence the couplet "turn the turning eyes, swivel with swiveling neck."

Just as exchange demands collective participation, so, too, negotiation must arise out of collective discussion. Speakers must go on record "in front of horses." With this expression, Anakalangese refer to speech addressed to a forum, the presence of the audience ("horses") implying that the speaker is fully committed to his or her words.

The ḅatang is distinguished from both ordinary conversation and full-fledged performance by the norm that everyone in attendance should speak up. Anakalangese insist that no one should speak or act alone—but this means as well that no one should, in the event, dissent. The leaders usually remain unobtrusive until they sense that everyone has had his or her say, or that the meeting must be brought to a resolution. By holding back, leaders spare themselves the embarrassment of making proposals that have no chance of being accepted. But there are further implications for how Anakalangese understand the relations of leaders to the gathering. There are two basic views—that leaders should not act against the collective wishes or that the group should not object to the actions of leaders. Which interpretation emerges is very much a matter of perspective: as Pak Migu complained to me, since people often are afraid to disagree with big men (the second perspective), big men can take their acquiescence at face value, as simply confirming that they are always right (the first perspective).

Despite the sometimes freewheeling quality of ḅatang, certain norms of deference should constrain the participants. When Ubu Remu was giving me his views on government one day, he compared it to a conference.

> When I was in Waingapu, I saw the DPR (national legislature) on television and realized it's just like a ḅatang, 'big conference, joint discussion.' That is, I can't be rowdy, even if I'm attacked by another speaker. I wait until it's my turn to speak, then I begin, "That's true oh sir"—only then do I lay into him.

Disputes over proper procedure break out frequently, and some negotiations have been delayed or even collapsed because of internal fighting. A man who claims high standing for himself often expresses this by saying that if he does not move, no one else dares to. This formula summarizes a core notion of leadership: if one is truly essential to an action, one can control events not by direct intervention but simply by holding back from action. At that point, all others will recognize that one is essential: the fact that nothing goes forward is sufficient testimony to one's own powers, expressed through the responses of others. When Markus's younger brother tried to enlist his support in acquiring a second wife, Markus, a Protestant, refused. He pointedly made his absence visible, sitting in front of his house by the side of the road, as the procession of yera passed. Seeing the eldest brother was not in attendance, yera suspected all was not right within this brother's group. These doubts were soon confirmed, for when the major supporters saw that the person most appropriate to be the sponsoring mother-father (ina-ama) was missing, they began to have doubts that eventually led to the collapse of negotiations. To hold back altogether, however, is drastic. More usually, leading men are defined by the timing and effectiveness of their interventions. Waiting until others have had their say, their words should at least seem to carry the day; as one man told me, 'All dogs bark, but only some track their prey to the kill.'

When Ubu Janga commented on the need for consultation, he was thinking about a recent event that exemplifies the consequences of acting without mediators. His kabisu (N) had already brought betel to kabisu K, constituting a formal agreement to go ahead with a marriage negotiation, and they were now at the second step. They met as they had before, at a house just outside the ancestral village proper, but now the site became a point of contestation. When N's procession arrived, bearing five animals, they were challenged by the ritual negotiator (wunang), speaking for Ubu Hami, leader of the most powerful family in K: 'Is N. accustomed to taking women from [the garden hamlets] outside their village?' Although everyone knows that negotiations often take place outside ancestral villages, to reply "Yes" would have implied that they were "small." And here they were, left standing in the field, having not even been given welcoming dishes of betel. Ubu Hami, they discovered, wasn't even in the house, but remained behind in the main part of the village.

At this point, the matter began to get out of hand. Instead of consulting with his party and going through his own ritual speaker, kabisu

N's leader, Ubu Kaledi, jumped directly into the fray and demanded to know 'Is there an ancestral house up there in the village?' By this he was issuing a counterchallenge, implying that the existence of a proper house in which to meet has not been significant enough for N to notice (something extremely implausible, since the two villages are only two kilometers apart and are bound by long-standing ties of marriage).

Now Ubu Kaledi withdrew to a neighboring house and waited while the members of K's party began to fight among themselves over what to do. After several hours, Ubu Kaledi—still without consulting his own party—strode over to K's house and announced that N was going home and would leave the cattle behind (at once a sign of disdain and a way to avoid the embarrassment of bringing home animals that had already left the village in a public procession). K was in an uproar, insisting they were about ready to start negotiating and pleading with Ubu Kaledi to be patient. But Ubu Kaledi led his party off, and they returned home late at night, empty-handed, hungry, and angry. Many of them had concluded that the only solution was to force K's hand by kidnapping ("snatching in the field") the girl in question.

Ubu Janga told me this to exemplify what happens when egoists clash. The problem was on both sides, since there was no one on either side who could rein in their leaders, as a result of which, neither leader was willing to back down. Ubu Kaledi should never have spoken directly, without consulting with the rest of his party and without going through his wunang. And now people like Ubu Janga were ashamed to go back to K, which will make each subsequent step more difficult and probably more expensive. Ubu Janga's story draws together two aspects of negotiation, the use of the speaker and the conference, under a single function, the avoidance of clashes of egos and face-saving. But this is not the only thing going on.

One of the major causes of failed negotiations is discord within a single side. The practical unity of a single party is produced by the goal of constructing good relations with an affine. Cutting across this are the potentially divisive interests of individual supporters in obtaining reciprocity for their material contributions. A common way in which this tension plays itself out is in debates over procedures, for there is rarely full consensus over either procedures or the authority of other people's knowledge thereof. As a result, people can claim that others have made "mistakes," which they often attribute to the self-interest of participants in the baṭang. For example, when the kaḅisu P was negotiating a daughter's marriage with L, they included a demand for a prestation normally given only after one or two children have been born of the marriage. A man from L, in telling me about this, attributed it to two factors: that P's leaders lacked confidence in their knowledge of exchange and, as a result, that they were swayed by the advice of supporters who were more interested in raising the amount of prestations than in preserving a good connection between affines. Sometimes failure in negotiations is attributed to the machinations of a single man, for reasons of envy or a simple perverse desire to make others fail—a claim that captures well the general suspicion with which people in Anakalang tend to view the actions of others. This suspicion reflects the unstable unity achieved by each party to the negotiation, as multiple contributing interests are momentarily suppressed by the presence of the others whom they face. Despite its conceptual autonomy, the practical coherence of one kabisu is thus predicated on interaction with another. What both the suspicion and the actual event bring out is the way in which both the economics of exchange and the demands of the speech event force people, sometimes unhappily, into relations of mutual dependence. As Markus put it, despite a bad exchange, if there is goodwill, the immediate kin of the married couple can always work out a compromise in private. The problem is the *public* forum, both because it places so much pressure on people's pride and reputation and because it gives so many people a say in what transpires. Relations between a self and another are problematic enough. The ratifying and evaluating gaze of the third party, the public (both within and outside one's own kabisu), which allows them no opportunity quietly to forge a separate peace, makes matters all the more difficult.

## HORUNG: FACING THE OTHER

The major scene of negotiation is the formal encounter known as "horung." A horung, which takes place after a series of smaller but equally formal initial encounters, brings together two parties, one of (potential) yera, one of (potential) ngàba wini. In composition the two parties are symmetrical, consisting of all male heads of household who contribute goods to, or simply accompany, the principals, along with their wives and other members of their households in great numbers. The two parties should be roughly commensurate in scale. In part this is required by the ongoing internal conferring that requires consensus among participants and in part by logistics: there are prestations to be transported, betel to be distributed, coffee and food to be prepared. More

important, it would be shameful to appear with an inadequate following and equally shameful to be met with insufficient numbers by the opposite party.

Ideally the setting of the horung is the chief ancestral village of the
host lineage.[6] When the visitor's procession arrives, its members are
seated in a house or specially constructed shelter separate from the house
in which the host has congregated, and the betel and coffee of hospitality are distributed. There the two parties remain, spatially segregated.
Both parties can face last-minute shifts of support or material strength,
as supporters desert or new ones are recruited. Thus the size of the entourage is a rough index of the power of the group, the influence of the
leader, the quantity of the prestations, and the importance of the event.
In contrast to the scale of the party itself, the number of speaking participants in the formal negotiation is quite limited: most of those present serve as audience and witnesses (as a significant number do not even
hear the actual negotiation). The horung effectively expands what Goffman ([1979] 1981: 84) calls the "social situation," the physical area
within which people encounter one another "face to face," to include
people who are not physically present.

The structure of the interaction helps construct as agents social entities that are larger than the individual persons concerned. Within each
party there are a few named roles. The parents of the groom and bride,
the "boat master, horse owner" (*mauri tena, mangu jara*), are not normally leaders or even significant speakers in the group. Direction should
be in the hands of other men with authority in the kabisu. The latter are
known by the generic term for all sorts of leadership, "mother-father"
(ina-ama). By this expression (which is never used of actual "parents"),
a biological male is represented, in his authority as the personification of
a larger group, as dual-gendered.[7] Implicit within the formal expression
of agency is a temporal dimension. Early in a negotiation, yera asks the
visitors to identify themselves in reference to the mother-father: "Who
packages the betel? Who wraps the areca?" His presence in the background is supposed to guarantee the collective commitment of the kabisu
to stand by its obligations. This person stands metonymically for the
temporal extension presupposed in the scene of negotiation, by which
the present action is binding on the future.

Principals do not speak on their own behalf within the frame set by
ritual speech, but remain in the background, figuratively brooding, like
a "chicken which can't go down (from its roost), pig which can't go

out." They remain immobile, situated in the interior of the group (both physically and metaphorically), avoiding direct contact with the other group, while the speakers are on the periphery. Anakalangese also construe the nature of this collective authority in terms of deferential communication. As one man put it, the role of ritual speakers is like the bureaucratic chain of command of the Indonesian state: 'After all, you don't address the president directly do you? You go to the desa head, he goes to the district head, who goes to the regent, and so forth.' In a horung the principals should not directly present themselves to each other; the forms of interaction construct them as nonmanifest but presupposed presences. Typically, however, they gradually emerge into the foreground over the course of the negotiation as it approaches resolution.[8]

The negotiators and spokesmen are known as wunang, literally, "weaving heddles" (Adams 1980: 214). Unlike ratus (priests), who hold permanent ascribed offices, negotiators or spokesmen are chosen on an occasional basis and on the grounds of personal skill. As the occasion decreases in importance, so too does the degree of skill required of the person serving as wunang. One result is that the best wunangs also serve the greatest number of parties, whereas men of more ordinary abilities and knowledge represent only local interests, in relatively minor events. Degree of ritual knowledge, extensiveness of social and spatial range, and weightiness of event tend, then, to be mutually iconic.

In full-fledged negotiation, however, the leaders often do not even address their own representatives directly, for the hosts, at least, should have two pairs of ritual speakers. In each pair, one is the wunang, the other a respondent. The hosts must have one wunang "who sits the speech" (ma madidung na panewi), the man who actually voices the consensus of the party in full kajiàla, the ritual speech of negotiation. It is his task to formulate and present this consensus to the second wunang. The latter, "the one who travels" (na ma halaku), receives this message and conveys it to the "traveling" wunang of the opposite party. Neither wunang, however, normally participates in forming the actual consensus: their concern is with the forms of speech, in a division of responsibilites reflecting that between voice and agency.

Sitting next to each wunang is a respondent known as ma kadehang ("the one who serves as the kadehang") or ma hima ("the one who answers"). Furthermore, in terms of the performance, a wunang addresses not the wunang who faces him but rather this respondent at the latter's side—in formal terms, the wunang only overhears his opposite number.

The speech of kajiàla takes the form of a dialogue between these two speaking parts. The wunang periodically punctuates his speech to exclaim the kaḍehang of the opposite party, to which the respondent answers "Go on!" (*Màlo!*).[9] In addition to responding to the kaḍehang, the respondent periodically interjects stylized back-channel cues: "That's it!" "True indeed!" "Right!" Other than that he remains silent, and his only other action is to assist the speaker in carrying offering dishes or the betel pouch. Every kaḅisu possesses at least one kaḍehang, a name by which it is addressed in ritual dialogues. In keeping with more general Anakalangese norms of name avoidance, when using ritual speech the kaḅisu is never directly addressed by its everyday name but by this kaḍehang, which itself is usually an avoidance name for an ancestor, usually that of a slave. Underlying this use is a pragmatic trope of warfare, for the name is shouted out as if from afar, and the slave in question is said to be the one who went foremost in times of war.[10] The image of the slave also figures the division of speech roles: some say that a noble should have two slaves, the "person who is first" who speaks and "the person who is later" who receives the speech of others.

At length the leader gives the "sitting" wunang the message to be delivered. At this point, the actual couplets in which the message is to be conveyed may still be sketchy. The "sitting" wunang responds by delivering a brief summary to the leader by way of confirmation and then turns to the "traveling" wunang to repeat the message in its entirety (even though his listener has heard the entire message from first delivery and in summation). Having received the message from the "sitting" wunang, the "traveling" one recites it back to him and then walks over to face the wunang of the other side, who remains seated throughout this time in front of the visiting party (see fig. 10). The latter repeats it back to him to confirm that he has understood and then turns to the "sitting" wunang of his own party to pass it on. The sitting wunang then confirms reception and passes it on in turn to the leaders of the group (who were witness to the very first presentation of the message).

This process of verbatim repetition and prolongation of chains of communication through linked dialogue pairs is an important feature of kajiàla. This repetition seems to have both practical and stylistic effects. It helps the messengers remember the detailed message they are to convey, and it serves as a highly public confirmation of the message within the context of the gathering: no one should be able to claim later that they didn't know what was going on. Furthermore, some people add, it makes sure that the ancestors in the house are aware of what

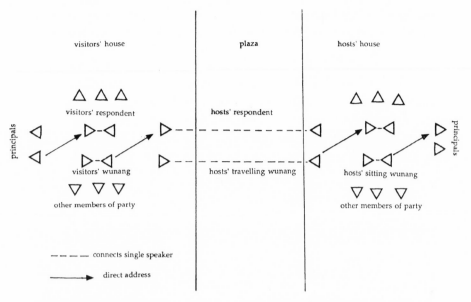

Figure 10. Schematic diagram to show disposition of the major participants in horung (not to scale).

is going on. But in addition, as I have argued in the previous chapter, repetition is itself a formal value. Repetition constructs a form of parallelism that has the effect of foregrounding the iterable quality of language and its detachability from the context and adds layers of mediating words between principals and authors, the animators, and the ultimate addressees. In the process, it forms a pragmatic icon of the distance that is to be progressively overcome through the course of the negotiation.

The figure of wunang is somewhat ambiguous. Serving at the request of more powerful persons, and mediating between potentially hostile parties, they can be self-effacing and soft-spoken (see fig. 12).[11] Their lot, like that of ratus, is often depicted as one of suffering, because they take on the worries and risks of others. In an oratorical lament, one wunang depicted himself as "tired with fishing, weary with hunting." Another couplet, "I am a single horse, I am an only child," uses conventional images of pathetic social isolation to stress the wunang's relative independence of the group he serves. Like women, they form connections between affines, joint weavers of consensus who "await the water spider, spin the cotton thread." After a tense moment during one ḅatang I recorded, a wunang turned to the mother-father of his party, saying,

> Yes, that's right Ubu. Because the two of us are the ones in the middle, right? We don't take sides between the two. Only, as you said earlier, my Ubu, indeed, that's right, I'm certain. Only, it's just that, oh Ubu, the good, it's good [to] "unify the seed in the garden, divide the water among the rice fields."

Wunang should restrain the excesses and tempers of their principals. Ubu Remu described one encounter between Ubu Dongu and a group of yera who had offended him in their previous encounter. When yera showed up in front of the house bearing prestations for a new round of exchange, as Ubu Remu prepared to address them, Ubu Dongu stood behind him the whole time whispering to him 'Chase them away! Chase them away!' Ubu Remu told me, 'We would have been within our rights to do so—but if I make peace between them, later both sides profit: Ubu Dongu can go to his yera any time he wants and ask them for cloth and pigs. Not that they give *me* anything—*he's* the one who gains.' As the last remark makes clear, wunang can take great pride in their disinterestedness. One of the most eloquent wunangs I knew, Ama Delu, insisted that the wunang's chief aim and greatest pleasure is to discover the path by which both sides can arrive at mutual happiness.

In keeping with their stature as figurative war leaders, however, many wunang are unusually self-confident and aggressive men, standing straighter and speaking more loudly than others (see fig. 11). A man skilled in ritual speaking is a "knowledgable male" (*moni pengu*) and a good wunang is said to be a "fierce tongue" (*tara bani làma*), while one who is uncertain or lacks fluency is *dumuru*, like the stumbling of a lame or frightened horse. Wunangs are somewhat exempt from ordinary social mores. One wunang, after a nightlong negotiating session at a stranger's house, made off with several coffee tree seedlings without asking. People suggested he was testing the strength of his spirit (*dewa*; see chapter 8): having built up his forcefulness through performance, he was pushing things to see how far his dewa could carry him. Were he to get away with it, his dewa would grow that much stronger.

Like ratus, wunang say they never actively learn their skills. Rather, the knowledge just comes to them. When I knew Ubu Laiya, for instance, he was about fifty, an extremely vigorous man who could be away from home for weeks on end, serving in negotiations all over Anakalang. Although his father had been an important player in exchange, he had not followed him but spent his teenage and early adult years gambling and stealing. Eventually, however, marriage led him to settle down

Figure 11. Strong speech: After several previous encounters ended badly, ngàba wini's wunang faces yera as they present a round of prestations in the plaza. The father of the groom stands behind the wunang, near the doorway (Manu Kaka, August 1986).

and his aging father began to send him to take his place in negotiation and prayer.

> But I never studied, it would be useless to try, tomorrow you'd forget.[12] You get it from dreams or visions. Like one night you'll dream the whole path of the dead [a long list of place-names in couplet form recited in mortuary rites], maybe next week you'll dream marriage negotiations. Nowadays I'm constantly dreaming *adat*, dealing with problems, like my mind is working while I sleep. I'm always on call, every week I'm needed somewhere. (WK: Weren't you nervous at first?) No, I was never nervous. In fact, I was eager for the other wunang to stop talking so I could start. If there are only a few people listening, I don't feel up for it—I really like it if there are more than a hundred people on each side.

Because wunang are men who are summoned and sent, it is inappropriate for a man of too high a standing to serve. Because they are mediators, it is also inappropriate for someone with too close an interest in the negotiation to serve. The position of wunang as one who is at once respected and defined, at least for purposes of the event in question, as an outsider, is shown in the formality of the material recognition he receives. Like payments to a ratu, as a kind of kahewa (see chapter 3) it is

distinguished both from payments for labor and from the free services
provided by close kin. It consists of cloth or metal, determined by the
category of the relationship between wunang and principals. The payment should not be too large, lest it define the wunang as a "stranger"
to those for whom he speaks.[13] Wunang usually stress the fact that their
efforts greatly outstrip any payment they receive. Ama Delu told me
that were a wunang to accept too large a payment, his very life would
be at risk. In this way, he stressed the relative autonomy of the wunang.[14]


## KAJIÀLA: THE SPEECH OF NEGOTIATION

Participant roles and performance structure make salient the act of
speaking and the structure of dialogue. The central act is that of giving and, even more salient, that of reciprocating, to "reply by tongue,
match by mouth," a figure for material exchange that identifies the giving of things with the structure of spoken conversation. The spoken text
is likewise permeated with self-reference, and sometimes with the implication that speech may fail. The first formal stage of negotiations occurs when potential ngàba wini appear at the woman's village. The scene
is enacted as if between strangers, and the visitors are formally asked to
identify themselves and their purpose.

| | |
|---|---|
| Beya na kurangu pawuku | Where is the intending shrimp |
| yeka na kaboku pamanyerang | and the searching fish? |
| | |
| na kabu jara | the horse's belly |
| yeka na kuru ahu | and the dog's throat? |

The scene of negotiation plays out an encounter in which nothing is
known except that which has been presented formally, on center stage,
within the spatial and temporal frame of the event.

Below is a transcription of the final stage of negotiation, beginning
with the opening segment of a speech made by the wunang of a party of
yera to his counterpart. The two wunang had met a month previously in
a smaller consultation to set the stage for the present horung. The speaker
opens the present encounter by using reported speech to confirm the
events of the previous meeting. Quoting the yera, he lists the prestations
(lines 10–13) made at that time to formally open the encounter by welcoming the guests with a meal. He then quotes the words with which he
had received the message brought by his interlocutor and had promised
to transmit it to his own party (lines 23–37). Finally he confirms that he
has delivered the message as promised (lines 42–47). The opening cry

(*tanawudo*) is a frame-setting formula that opens a single turn at speech. Pàda Pari (PP) is the kaḍehang used to address the ngàba wini, Palajangu (PL) is that of the yera.[15]

PL: Tanawudo, Pàda Pari!  Listen to this, Pàda Pari!  1
PP: Màlo!  Go on!

PL: Wimuḍipa nutu waiga:  You were saying just now:
"Laiju ḅamu keri  "Leap when you follow[16]
na tuwu li panewimi Palajangu  Palajangu connects your words  5
  of speech

pala ḅamu toma  cross over when you arrive
na kayi li kajiàlamu Palajangu  Palajangu receives your words of kajiàla"

Pàda Pari!  Pàda Pari!
PP: Màlo!  Go on!
PL: "Ta lolu na hawalangu  "By the one strand of chain  10
ta jara haingi  by one horse[17]

ta mamuli na hapapa  by one pendant
ta hapi haingi,  by one cow,

lau kana anyaka na auhu  go so he can eat the rice[18]
  ḅana tàka ta hadoka pena pari    when he arrives at the granary  15
    daku pawatu ngodu doku      I don't merely sit dumb as stone
lau kana inunyaka na wai  go so he can drink the water
  ḅana toma ta halibaru palolu"    when he has come to the benches"

Pàda Pari!  Pàda Pari!
PP: Màlo!  Go on!  20
PL: Higulna, Pàda Pari!  Another thing, Pàda Pari!
PP: Màlo!  Go on!

PL: "Na gapi paki Palajangu  "Palajangu clenches it

na tuwu li panewimi  he connects your spoken words
  kataku lima jara    takes in horse hands  25
na kayi li kajiàlami  he receives your words of kajiàla
  hoḅa ngidu ahu.    snaps up in dog's teeth.

Kaku pajìngipagi  First let me turn
ta pajìngi mata (PP: Màla)  my turning eyes (Go on)
  ta maurina na tena    to the ship master  30
    ta madiḍi oli pera      to the sitting parrot companions
      ta ḅoku mamu ḍumu        to your grandfather
kaku pabailipagi  first let me swivel
  ta pabaili goru    with swiveling neck
    ta ngoḍu oli lihina      to the seated flank companions  35
  ta manguna na jara    to the horse owner
    ta apu mamu ḍumu"        to your grandmother"
winaḍipa nutu waigana  he said just now

| ḅana pakayi koḅa kurangu | when passing back and forth the shrimp's skin[19] | |
|---|---|---|
| Palajangu. | (said) Palajangu. | 40 |
| Pàda Pari! | Pàda Pari! | |
| PP: Màlo! | Go on! | |
| PL: Ḍina pabailigi | So I swiveled | |
| ta pabaili goru | the swiveling neck | |
|   ḍa ḅoku mamu ḍumu | (as) your own grandfathers | |
| ḍina pajìngigi | so I turned | 45 |
| ta pajìngi mata | the turning eye | |
|   ḍa apu mamu ḍumu. | (as) your own grandmothers. | |

I will stress two points here. The first is the self-referential emphasis in this text on speech itself. The second is the degree to which participant roles in general and speech roles more specifically are named and characterized. The opening invocation is not to receive but to listen. This is followed by a locutive that names the other (the kaḍehang of the opposed kaḅisu) and then a recapitulation of speech in the previous encounter. This recapitulation itself consists in turn of a reference to the act of speaking (lines 24–27) and the use of the speaker's own kaḍehang (line 23), the address form used by the other to address him. The speaker then quotes his *own* speech as reported of a third person, implicating the principals on whose behalf he speaks (line 37). In addition, the self-reference of the speakers emphasizes the formal structure of the scene of negotiation: "so I swiveled the swiveling neck . . . " (lines 42 and 44) graphically depicts the act of turning about to face the party that one represents when conveying the message from the other side.

The passage confirms the exchanges made at the previous meeting, along with the formal name that metonymically specifies the type of event in question ("eat the rice, drink the water," already mentioned in lines 14 and 17, refer to the first stage in which visitors are formally received). Such self-reference has the performative effect of affirming the ongoing nature of the commitments in question and signaling that both sides agree on what they are doing. In the process it embeds the present within a longer series of events, forming a single project and, ideally, implicating the participants in a teleology to which there ought to be only one outcome, a successful union.

Reflexive moments are not always affirmative, however. Reported speech can be used to remind people of previous commitments from which they have strayed. Thus ngàba wini might claim to be fully prepared to give the core part of the marriage payment, the "tabooed cattle" (baḍa biha), without needing to negotiate, with the words

| Ku jara bani ngaru | I am a brave-mouthed horse |
| ku ahu tara ngidu | I am a fierce-toothed dog |
| | |
| koku pakaraiya na bokugu | begging neck my grandfather |
| ati pakadìngu na apugu | requesting liver my grandmother |

meaning 'I dare to ask for this woman.' If subsequently they turn out not to have everything that yera expects, yera can challenge them for having used these words:

| Waiga ta kawunga jeli jara | Earlier at the first horse jump |
| yeka ta kawunga laiju ahu | and at the first dog leap |
| | |
| mu "Koku pakaraiya na boku" | you (said) "Begging neck the grandfather" |
| mu "Ati pakaḍingiya na apu" | you (said) "Requesting liver the grandmother" |
| | |
| Jie ba nimi | But now |
| | |
| karera paparàkaga na bokumu | satisfy your grandfather's betel pouch |
| mu kàpu papatùḍanya na apumu | fulfill your grandmother's purse |

Quotation here has the effect of invoking words that had been said earlier as fully performative commitments.

Returning to the previous example, the lines that follow (lines 28 ff.) denote the act of referring the offer back to the party represented by the wunang: only now are the other participants mentioned. They are named in the roles relevant to the context established by the speech itself: the pair "ship master, horse owner" (lines 30 and 36) denotes the father of the girl, and the pair "parrot companions, flank companions" (lines 31 and 35) are the members of his party. The terms "grandfather" and "grandmother" (which here refer to yera as one pole in a structural relationship, but which can have the general sense of "ancestors") rhetorically play on the ideal of ongoing alliance to focus on the transformation of potentially unstable asymmetries between affines into more established status differences based on generation, such as mother's brother and sister's son. Having reported the gist of both his interlocutor's and his own speech, the wunang now reports that his task, promised in the previous meeting, has been accomplished. The compelling power of the promise is reinforced by echoing the very words in which it had been made. With this, he now makes the offer.

Having set the frame and named the relevant roles, the speaker brings the point of reference to the present. He lists item by item the prestations that his party has given, along with the counterprestations they now request. His speech frames these requests as reported speech emanating from various structural positions within yera. The naming of discrete components of bridewealth also serves to articulate the process of negotiation. It provides a series of distinct moments at which the ngàba wini can balk at the demands of the yera and the latter in turn show disappointment at the counteroffers made to them (see the similar structure in Keenan 1975). Ideally these moments of resistance exist in order to be overcome, thus accentuating the sense—even in secure, close alliances—that successfully concluded negotiation is an achievement. In practice, they can become the foci of serious contention.

This passage concludes with self-referential words that explicitly denote the successful transmission of speech, and thus, by convention, mark the end of one turn of talk:

| | |
|---|---|
| PL: Kaku loli waingu li | I convey the words |
| ngidi waingu peka. | bring the message. |
| | |
| Pàda Pari! Ḅijàlugi! | Pàda Pari! I stow it here! |
| | |
| PP: Jièdi! | Yes! |

Ngàba wini's wunang responds conventionally, by quoting his interlocutor's report of having to go back to his party. Continuing the focus on the act of speaking and manifesting the recurrent concern with words gone astray, he then confirms both the procedural correctness of the quoted lines and the situational correctness of the message that was conveyed:

| | |
|---|---|
| PP: Ada palaya | Crossing trail there |
|   papala waingu jaraya |   for crossing by horse there |
|     ta papala Wanukaka |     at the Wanukakan crossing |
| lara liya | followed path there |
|   pali waingu tauya |   for men to follow there |
|     ta pali Laboya. |     at the Laboyan way. |
| | |
| Da sagatu kalalakaḍimi | You didn't step on thorns |
|   uru tau ma dainguya |   steps of men of old there |
| da leti ta kadapukaḍimi | you didn't tread on rotten wood |
|   wewi tau memangu. |   track of ancient men.[20] |

He then goes on to refer to the most immediate stretch of speech, namely, the initial set of requests. He frames this reference with a couplet that denotes the act of making a formal statement (lines 1–4) and then, within the reported speech, names his own party as the object of address within the quotation (lines 5–8):

| | | |
|---|---|---|
| PP: Napaka jèli ḅalineka | So now he leaps again | 1 |
| na jara pakaletimu | your riding horse | |
| napaka laiju ḅalineka | so now he jumps again | |
| na ahu papawujiemu | your favored dog | |
| | | |
| "Kana tanawuwaka Pàda Pari | "So that Pàda Pari may listen to me | 5 |
| ḅaku talaru panaingu | when I put all in rows | |
| kana tanawuwaka Pàda Pari | so that Pàda Pari may listen to me | |
| ḅaku ḅajaru pamulangu." | when I plant in a line." | |

Lines 6 and 8 are doubly reflexive, referring to both the correct order of speaking and the straight row of dishes containing tokens of prestations. By associating poetic speech with the visible setup, these couplets stress the jointly iconic quality of both words and things, that they are diagrammatically faithful to ancestral procedures. Pàda Pari's wunang confirms that he will convey the message without alteration or mistake:

| | |
|---|---|
| Dana duhama ta mawu | Not rejected in the shadows |
| ugukaguhaka ta ugu lima | I grasp them in grasping fist |
| dana lèḅama ta lara | not discarded on the road |
| ḅàgikaguhaka ta ḅàgi kabu. | I gird them at girt waist. |
| | |
| Daku lagoru pakasilumanya | I don't damp the bells |
| ta lagoru koku jara | bells at horse's neck |
| daku paji pakaborumanya | I don't wrap up the banner |
| ta paji keri teku. | banner at pole's base. |

He will bring the message back to his own principal, who is identified as

| | |
|---|---|
| ma paḅorunya ta ḅoru ḅàgi | he who belts him at the waist |
| ta dutu jara mamu ḍumu | your own following horse |
| ma patakunya na taku lima | he who puts the staff in his hand |
| ta keri ahu mamu ḍumu | your own trailing dog |

The latter two couplets identify the principal as an established ngàba wini (conventionally referred to as "following horse, trailing dog"), thereby one who is indebted as well as someone who should be protected. They also identify the principal member(s) of ngàba wini as the unitary authorizing agency that lies behind the words of the wunang: it is this agent who gives the wunang his belt and walking stick, equipping him for the journey, figuratively across a long distance (that same figurative distance across which the kaḍehang is shouted), to face the opposite party. With the focus on the agency of the principal, it is common for the wunang to refer to himself in the third person as here.

In responding, the other wunang confirms the correctness of each item in turn, affirming that the offer will be passed on to his own party. Each item in the request receives its counteroffer, followed by qualifying lines that stress the perduring nature of the relationship between the two sides, as in this image connoting the generations of women who have already passed from the yera to occupy the hearth benches in the home of the ngàba wini:

| | |
|---|---|
| PP: Màli bìnukaḍiya na laḍu ḍeta | As long as the upper bench is full |
| màli màtukaḍiya na laḍu wawa | as long as the lower bench is crowded |

Since even the smoothest negotiation must move in stages of enacted resistance to the putatively weighty demands of the yera, additional hedges are necessary, ones that also play on the speech event character of the action. They express a firm commitment to the relationship; the ngàba wini will remember the debt and the promise that are brought about in this encounter:

| | |
|---|---|
| PP: Ḅada nungaha newimàdi | Even if not firmly uttered |
| katikugu ma tìdungu | my head will carry them |
| ḅada toraja tìkimàdi | even if not dyed and spoken |
| kabàkigu ma ḍaituha | my shoulder will bear them |

The yera's wunang will then receive the counteroffer and repeat it, again offering assurances that he will not misrepresent it. After reporting back to his own party, he will meet his counterpart again. Often these intermediate stages involve no further traveling between sides, for the wunang of the visiting party only need swivel about and face his own party, while his counterpart awaits the response. This passage back and forth between the two sides, enormously drawn out by the conventions of repetition and layering of speakers, slowly whittles away at the difference between the amounts demanded and offered. In addition to the prolongation that is built into the forms of communication, the negotiation is also protracted by a tendency on both sides to resist too rapid a resolution. Although this is in part conventional, a matter of honor and challenge, it can become quite earnest as well and develop into serious ruptures both between and within parties. Often a single nightlong session is not sufficient to bring the matter to an end. Eventually, however, most negotiations reach some sort of accommodation.

As the concluding passages approach, the wunang increasingly tend to break the frame of kajiàla, reverting to colloquial speech to count up the prestations agreed upon to that point, and the principals often take an increasingly active role. The latter emerge from their initial prescriptive absence in the first small meetings between the two sides to the point at which agreement has been reached and they finally come face to face. When the ngàba wini have reached the limit of what they are willing to give, they may throw themselves on the pity and understanding of the yera. In the example given here, the wunang adopts the "voice" of the bride or her mother (implied through the use of female speaker kin terms in lines 3, 6, and 8):

| | | |
|---|---|---|
| PP: Gàrikiwalinaka? | What else can be done? | 1 |
| Malangu nai boku<br>malangu nai ana moni. | Grandfather is right<br>brother is right. | |
| Gàrikiwalinaka? | What else can be done? | |
| Malangu nai apu<br>malangu nai rina moni | Grandmother is right<br>brother's wife is right. | 5 |
| Ba ai tàkakajaka<br>ku wo tàkakadinaha ana moni | If there really were (those items)<br>truly I would give them to brother | |
| laiku da ma betahu<br>ai da ma bata | (we are like) unparting rope<br>(we are like) unbreaking wood | 10 |

The reversal of gender may underline the subordination of ngàba wini to yera. It also represents the exchange as transacted not between men, across lineage boundaries, but as a gift from sister to brother. The last couplet here asks for recognition that a perduring debt has been established which need not be foreclosed at the present. At this point the direct, unnegotiated exchange between the wunang themselves closes the frame of the formal scene of negotiation. Now, at the point where *direct* participation in exchange by men who have until then spoken only as *intermediaries* to the exchanges of others closes the frame, the principals who have remained in the *background* can speak directly to each other. This meeting usually consists of some small talk and mutual assurances that the accounting of prestations on each side is in agreement and that the animals promised on credit will eventually be forthcoming.

## THE SLIPPAGE OF WORDS

I have summarized a case of negotiation that runs smoothly. But it is important to realize that in Anakalang, kajiàla is not a ceremonial event the outcome of which has been determined in advance, or becomes inevitable once the machinery is set into play. The insistence on correct form, the repetitive naming and delegating of roles, and the assurances that words will not go astray all operate against the background awareness that they could fail. Even wunangs nod. At such times, others, even the mother-father may have to intervene. This happened, for instance, in August 1993, when kaḅisu B, as ngàba wini, went to kaḅisu W for the second stage of exchange, to bind them to an engagement, after having already brought betel to initiate the negotiations. Since this was a relatively easy step, and the alliance was well worn, B relied on a close relative of marginal competence. W had just formally presented their guests with a meal and a prestation, called "orating neck," to ask their intention. Now B's wunang was conveying his principals' response. Nervously, he merely named ngàba wini's counterprestation, "mate of tracks," and the prestation from yera to which this was responding:

| | |
|---|---|
| Kayigaha | Receive them |
| hapapa ruku | a mate of tracks |
| hagàḅa kaḍu | a half-pair of horns |
| goru wara | orating neck |
| wihi laiju | leaping feet |
| ḅa winaga na ḅoku | so grandfather tells you |

This rather bald speech permitted yera to act confused about ngàba wini's full intention, and they sent over a cloth to ask whether their visitors meant to go directly on to the next, very heavy, stage of negotiations that same night. In more troubled circumstances, this might have led to an expensive turn of talk and exchange to clarify matters. As it was, the reply cost ngàba wini a mamuli, and some embarrassment as their mother-father stepped in to address yera's wunang directly, in colloquial speech. Later, this mother-father told me what their wunang should have said.

| | | |
|---|---|---|
| Agika na auhu | I eat the rice | 1 |
| inugika na wai. | I drink the water. | |
| Higulna: | Another thing: | |
| "Goru wara | "Orating neck | |
| wihi laiju" | leaping feet" | 5 |
| ḅa winaga na ḅokugu, na apugu, | as my grandfather, grandmother tells you, | |
| malanguna. | it's true. | |
| Nau wali namu: | So here then: | |

Figure 12. Deferential speech: Ngàba wini's wunang (left of center, leaning forward) speaks softly as he receives cloth (in front of him on the floor) during the initial visit to "bring betel" to prospective yera (Pasunga, August 1993).

| | | |
|---|---|---|
| "Kaku papane ta ngaru | "That I match with mouth | |
| lìbaru ta làma | reply by tongue | 10 |
| | | |
| kayigaha: | receive them: | |
| | | |
| na hapapa ruku | the mate of tracks | |
| ḍa hagàḅa kaḍu | the half-pair of horns | |
| | | |
| pakanguka mangu rauguha | together with their leaves | |
| pakanguka mangu loluguha | together with their vines | 15 |
| | | |
| ta ḅokugu | at my grandfather | |
| ta apugu. | at my grandmother. | |
| | | |
| Daku wolumaja padauḍa | I don't make their sites | |
| daku rawimaja panyieḍa. | I don't fashion their places. | |
| | | |
| Jiekaḍikiha | These are they | 20 |
| | | |
| ḍa paletigu ta wihi | what my feet tread | |
| ḍa pa-ugugu ta lima." | what my hands grasp." | |
| | | |
| wina | says | |
| | | |
| laiku logi | tied hair | |
| pinu ḅàgi | full waist | 25 |

| ḅana panewi pamagolingu | when he reclining speaks | |
| ḅana panewi pamanyobangu. | when he lying down speaks. | |
| | | |
| Higulna: | Another thing: | |
| | | |
| abi ḍa pàla binu wai | let them not cross on water | |
| ḍa halaku binu mapu | walk on grass[21] | 30 |
| | | |
| ku woluḍaha | I make them | |
| | | |
| palu ta kaḍena | hit on the back | |
| ràbahu kamodu | strike on the butt | |
| | | |
| kayigaha | receive them | |
| | | |
| hapang, hapang, hawàla, hapapa | a stick, a stick, a sheet, a mate[22] | 35 |
| | | |
| ḅaku toma ḅalija | as I come back again | |
| | | |
| ḍa kaboru kuta | the betel wraps | |
| ḍa kakoba winu | the areca packages[23] | |

This fuller and more nuanced speech has a more specific performative and communicative effect than the bare presentation of gifts. It opens by reflexively naming the acts being performed. One formally accepts the meal (lines 1–2), the other acknowledges and affirms the correctness of yera's other prestation (lines 4–5). It then names the counterprestation (lines 12–13). It immediately qualifies this, however, by declaring (lines 14–15, 18–19) that they give the requisite five animals as a group, without specifying their individual destinations. The implication is that the animals are too humble to stand up to public scrutiny through acts of individuating reference. In conjunction with the self-lowering couplet that modifies the verb of locution (lines 26–27), this prepares yera for subsequent requests not to press their ngàba wini too hard. It frames the supplicant as one who asks pity and deserves to receive it on the basis of previous ties (since only a long-established ally has the right to say "together with their leaves").

The concluding couplets strengthen the performative specificity of the act. As always, the animals are accompanied by tokens in the offering dish. The wunang should take care to name them, however, usually pointing to each in turn as he does so, to be sure that they are fully bound to both the animals they represent and the act they carry out. In this case, they are named both as a collectivity (lines 31–32) and one by one (line 35). Finally, this gift is linked to the previous encounter between the two groups (lines 36–38), when B brought the betel. By specifying this, he affirms the fact that the present carries through the momentum initiated and fulfills the commitments forged in the past. The fuller statement is thus at once more artful, more formal, performatively more secure, and communicatively more specific.

## CHALLENGES

The facts of memory and temporal depth, all those things that are most vulnerable to challenge in the heat of the moment, are most likely to be at issue in questions of appropriateness to context, because it is here that the use or omission of couplets can have constitutive effects. Thus another case concerns how speakers identify the type of relationship in which they are involved. As Ubu Hudi recollected his own marriage (which opened a new alliance), his wunang, Ubu Laiya, addressed yera saying

| | |
|---|---|
| kapapungu patàdung | planted beans |
| kamata papamula | planted sweet potato |
| | |
| wàla wai hawurutung | flecks of gurgling water |
| tada ai tanyalang | flakes of bark |

Since these couplets are properly employed only for old allies, using them gives yera an opportunity to criticize. In this case, for example, they objected:

| | | |
|---|---|---|
| Gàrikina ḍumu loku hàbi? | Why are you a paused-at river? | 1 |
| gàrikina ḍumu tana loliya? | why are you a stopped-by land? | |
| | | |
| Ḅakalanga | In fact | |
| | | |
| da dutu jara daimaka | not an old following horse | |
| da keri ahu memamaka. | not an original trailing dog. | 5 |
| | | |
| Ku kurung ḅaku rangu | I heard poorly | |
| ku yàbar ḅaku elang. | I saw unclearly. | |
| | | |
| Paḍuangu jeli jaramu | Let your horse leap a second time | |
| paḍuangu laiju ahumu. | let your dog jump a second time. | |
| | | |
| Ḅakalangu naumu: | In fact, it's this way: | 10 |
| | | |
| ma pakayiya na kana pipi | ones with connected cheeks | |
| ma pa-eriya na wuku mata | ones with matching eyebrows | |
| | | |
| tana tuwu | connected land | |
| watu lihi | adjacent stone | |

With these words, the offended wunang protested, suggesting (lines 1–2) that the speaker had strayed from the path (the opposite of the affirmative "crossing trail, followed path"). He then challenged the imputation that the two parties had a long-standing affinal relationship by repeating the claim by using a more common couplet (lines 4–5) in order to deny it. Reflexively addressing the question of speech, the wunang denied he has even received the message and displaced the problem to a confusion of the senses, asking for a rephrasing. At the same time, he softened his challenge by acknowledging the existence of a relationship, albeit one of shared descent through women (lines 11–14).

The offender retracted with these lines:

| Nau namu | So here | 1 |
|---|---|---|
| lauka daku jalakaka | that I not go too wrong | |
| lauka daku dokukaka | that I not go too mistakenly | |
| nau namu | so here | |
| kayigeya mamuli na hapapa | receive this one mamuli | 5 |
| kayigeya jaragu hangiu | receive this my one horse | |

Taking up the face-saving claim of some relationship, he limits the error (lines 1–3) and pays a fine (lines 5–6). The fine was reciprocated with one cloth, and the negotiations continued. Ubu Hudi explained to me that really only powerful nobles should make this sort of challenge: the yera in this case was led by two of the wealthiest and most influential men of the day. Only the wealthy have the resources to back up the exchanges and only the nobles have such a stake in getting things right that they can risk holding up the affair for such matters. Others might overlook errors, because their chief interest is that the negotiation goes smoothly. This distinction is significant. It is a good example of how wealth can be a practical precondition for "correct" action (see chapter 7).

Although the wunang are supposed to be dispassionate and disinterested, they are also often fiercely competitive and see in negotiation a chance to defeat an opponent. Ubu Remu, for example, told me of an event when his counterpart took what he considered to be an egregious departure from the correct procedure. When Ubu Remu replied with the conventional couplets that affirm the truth of what had been said, he embellished them with these lines:

| jia tàkawuka moni pengu paku | truly you are a male (who) knows the nail |
|---|---|
| ma pakuya na ngora tena | who nails the boat's prow |

| jia tàkawuka moni pengu halugu | truly you are a male (who) knows the load |
| ma halugu lima jara | who loads the horse's limbs |

This, he explained, was strategic: it is simple politeness to affirm the truth, but to add an unnecessary supplement to a conventional reply has the effect of flattery. The flattery forms a challenge. Either the other wunang will realize that he has been caught out in his error, in which case he will become embarrassed and stumble, or he will take the compliment at face value and become rash. In the latter case, he will be prone to further error and Ubu Remu may force his side to relinquish some of their demands. When Ubu Kuala told me of a similar situation, in which he bested his counterpart, he said, 'Their wunang's voice grew smaller and smaller, until you almost couldn't hear it.' The body registers the speaker's defeat.

## QUESTIONS OF IDENTITY

When Ubu Kura told me about the wunang who invented the lines "like thermos water, like short rice" (see chapter 4), he added that his counterpart should have challenged him, saying he acts the "same as a Bimanese, just like a Javanese," foreigners who wander around with no fixed place. More pointedly, he added, this implies that the erring wunang insults the addressee, 'you consider me not to be your match.' That Ubu Kura draws insult out of error is telling and underlines the interactive dimensions of the scene of encounter. Formal and correct behavior imply respect for and recognition of one's interlocutor. Mistakes can be taken to reflect, not the incapacity of the speaker, but his lack of respect for the listener. An unfocused or ill-prepared wunang is like someone scavenging rice in another's field after the harvest, his meanderings a function of his low status. But, as Ubu Kura put it, this can imply that the speaker 'is not taking *me* seriously, he treats me as not fitting for his opponent, as not his equal.' When his father found himself in such a situation, he challenged his counterpart: 'Do you say to me (I'm) "Not a cover for the basket"? Do you say to me (I'm) "Not a pair with the plate"?' According to this figure, two wunang should fit as a tight lid on a basket, or as a plate of rice should be paired with a plate of meat: one is incomplete without the other.

The challenge is thus that one accuses one's interlocutor of making mistakes because he does not consider you his match—not as *affine* but as *wunang*. In the case of Ubu Kura's father, the error was acknowledged with the fine of a horse. But the offense may be irreparable. This was the case, for example, when Ubu Kauwa faced a series of dubious maneuvers by his counterpart, Ubu Reku. Finally Ubu Kauwa became convinced that Ubu Reku and his party considered him to have so poor a command of kajiàla that they could get away with their tricks. As a result, he felt he had been treated "as a dog, as a pig" and now was unable to face them. On another occasion, a wunang fell into conflict with his own principal. Ubu Siwa apparently did not fully trust Ubu Bewa, so he sent along his own mother's brother to sit next to Ubu Bewa while he spoke. Moreover, the mother's brother kept intervening, until finally Ubu Bewa quit in humiliation. In both cases, the locus of honor and agency threatens to shift from principal to delegate. The necessary *delegation* of voice threatens to become full *detachment*. Not only the wunang but also those on whose behalf they speak may suffer the consequences. Troubles between wunang and his own party may, for example, anger the bride's ancestors and cause her to be infertile.

A peculiar case illustrates some of the ambiguity of displaced agency. When Kadi, a ratu of slave descent, was to be married, it was a noble who served him as wunang. One factor that permitted this apparent role reversal, which I found very puzzling, seems to be that masters should arrange the essential life-cycle rites for their slaves. Nonetheless, the master found a way to reverse the valence of the relations of displacement. Here is how he recounted the event to me about a week afterward:

> It's all finished, but it was nearly first cock's crow before they stuck the pig [for the concluding meal]. They didn't want to, said there had to be a horse. Five times I went over and back [between the two sides]. If I hadn't been there, there's no way they'd have made peace. They began to rage, wanted to put down that woman, machetes rose—I said 'Now it's not Kadi whom you're facing, but me. Go ahead and cut my throat.' Then I really got mad: 'I'm stupid, I don't know how to talk! You have to put words in the offering dish before they're true!' So they paid me a fine of one cloth because I'd gotten angry. . . . Because if later this case goes before the desa government [for mediation], it won't be Kadi anymore, but *me* who talks. So they gave me the cloth to surrender themselves to my discretion.

As the last comment makes clear, the wunang in this case is not serving as a representative of a higher-ranking principal but rather is a patron whose ultimate authority supersedes that of either principal or wunang himself. In this case, the fact that the higher-ranking man is in the foreground suggests a *lack* of representation and thus indexes the fact that no serious status is being constructed. The noble's threat points to the potential for displacement to collapse—in this case, implying that a more potent force, which has until now been concealed, will emerge to the foreground.

Marriage negotiations *do* break down, and indeed can provide the ground for wider hostilities. Just as the scene of encounter helps constitute both relations between groups and their internal unity, so too breakdown can occur not only between the two parties but within a single one as well. In addition to determining the relevant identities of participants, the successful performance of ritual speech specifies the nature of the event itself, the context of action. As a formal register it indexes the event as of a certain type and the present situation as reproducing one of a limited number of stock situations. The use of ritual speech helps delineate which features of the empirical situation will be taken to be pertinent, suppressing particularities in favor of authoritative types. But the scene of encounter can become problematic. In the following examples participants disagree over the definition of the event or of specific moments within it, or the distinction between voice and agency becomes confused.

The first case concerns a failure of the entire ritual speech frame itself, when, as I recounted at the beginning of chapter 4, an incompetent wunang lapsed into colloquial Indonesian. The offended ngàba wini complained that they no longer knew whom they were addressing, nor did they know who they were themselves, and that, as such they could no longer dare to speak as representatives of the boy. Here performance was unable successfully to index and denote acceptable positional roles: its failure was not merely one of reference but a challenge to the roles, and their durability, themselves. It threatened to dissolve a potential alliance between groups into a mere union between a pair of individuals, a matter with little social significance or temporal extensiveness and assuring no future exchange relations for the other participants.

A second case concerns the definition of an event within the frame of ritual encounter. A horung nearly came to grief over how the presence of the girl in the ngàba wini's village was to be typified. After earlier talks had stalled, the girl had run off to the village of the boy, where her action was understood to be of the type "following the mother" (*keri bai*), that is, taking a shortcut to renew an established alliance path. At the horung, however, her lineage came with prestations identified as those brought for pursuing a woman who had been "snatched in the field" by the man. It redefined the nature of the parties, since by attributing the agency to the boy's family and implying that connubial relations had begun it meant the couple was taken as an established entity (and the capacity of the ngàba wini to threaten withdrawal—as they had been doing—thereby severely limited).

Moves by one party can challenge the participation roles internal to the other: one encounter ran into trouble when the yera's wunang offered their prestations directly to the assembled hosts immediately upon arriving at the village, in an oration of formal conveyance (*papalangu*). This speech genre required a direct response on the part of the ngàba wini, meaning their wunang himself had to speak without consulting his party. In collapsing the distinction between the voice represented by the host wunang and the agency of the party he represented, the event also threatened to provoke schisms within his party, prompting him to make an offer that other participants might not back up. Here is an example of how solidarity *internal* to each party is maintained in part by the interaction *between* them. In this case, so great was the anger of the offended party that the wunang of the yera was in the end compelled to surrender the structural advantage afforded by the fact that the visiting party had the initiative in exchange. He did not specify what counter-prestations were being demanded, leaving it up to the ngàba wini to decide what to offer in return.

The outcome of this episode illustrates another consequence of the separation of voice and agency, that it works against the reversibility inherent in dialogue. In formal terms a given speaker never becomes an addressee, but is at most an overhearer, while the "swiveling about" of a wunang, as he delivers the other's message to his own party, in a sense appropriates the speaking part of his interlocutor. Yet in Anakalang the shifting and agonistic nature of relations suggests that positions might be reversed (and in terms of micropolitics, some supporters of one party may have links as well to the other, their loyalties and structural positions never fully assured). Thus although a formal reversal of roles between two sides is not possible, a change in relative material and strategic resources is. This was a threat partially activated in the case noted above, for the ngàba wini were able to take the initiative. At the moment of acquiescence, the yera's wunang went so far as to spell out the role reversal—significantly, putting it in terms of forms of address:

| | | |
|---|---|---|
| màli ma penguḍiya | as long as there is one who understands | 1 |
|   li lawi |   the way of marrying men | |
| màli ma penguḍiya | as long as there is one who understands | |
|   li mangoma |   the way of marrying women | |
| | | |
| ma ka-inama wimakaka na | so we call "mother" our following horse | 5 |
| dutu jarama | | |

| magu dutu jarakanagaka | although you are my "following horse" |
| amangu wimakaka na keri | we call "father" our trailing dog |
| ahuma | |
| magu keri ahukanagama | though you are my "trailing dog" |

The speaker, using the exclusive first person, here bows to the ngàba wini's superior command of kajiàla (lines 1–4) and in doing so transforms them figuratively from ngàba wini ("following horse") to "mother-father" (lines 5–8). The ngàba wini, conventionally humble, have been transformed into figures of authority, which in Anakalangese terms is a contradiction. The reversal cited here is extreme. It represents the limiting case, the reversal of parts inherent to dialogue, a possibility that is performatively denied by separating the speaker (wunang) and the addressee (kaḍehang).

Ritualized forms of negotiation are not, however, merely defenses against failure. They represent even well-established alliances in the idiom of distance. The very forms of encounter may provide conditions for disruption, for confusion of agency and voice.[24] This is what happened when Ubu Kauwa felt insulted by his interlocutor and Ubu Bewa mistrusted by his principal. In each case, the wunang was rendered unable to serve as the voice of another. In the first case the wunang's own agency was challenged and thereby brought into play, when it should have been subordinated to that of the principals. The second case was a reversal of the first: the wunang's ability to serve as a voice was challenged by incomplete delegation on the part of the principals.[25] Both problems resulted from insufficient practical differentiation among participant roles.

## SELF-REPRESENTATION AND SOCIAL ACTION

If a major outcome of the scene of negotiation is not simply the transfer of goods or brides, but the defining, redefining, and stressing of the value of relationships (Comaroff 1980; Merlan and Rumsey 1991; Strathern 1984), this outcome must be understood in terms of the means by which the value is expressed and risked. Kajiàla speaks of structural roles and relations, but it does not act simply by naming. The elevated register and distribution of roles pragmatically convey messages. To speak as an ancestor involves a double displacement, of language and of performers. If, as I argued in the previous chapter, the couplet serves as its own model of the relation between ritual and nonritual speech, it likewise models relations between participants within ritual as well as relations between ideal and actual performance, and even, perhaps, that between the ritual sphere of action and that which lies outside it. The parallel between registers and performance roles is expressed in the couplet "loaded upon a boat, mounted upon a horse," which denotes representation in two senses, not only the move into ritual words (as discussed in chapter 4) but also the delegation of the principal's voice to a ritual speaker.

The delegation of voice and hearing distinguishes utterance from agency. Implicitly, it depicts the agent as that which lies behind, that non-speaking subject implicated by the presence of subordinates and their use of kajiàla. More specifically, it treats interaction as a matter of command of representations and their mediators and of cooperative transmission of speech across great distance. The separation of participant roles constructs a site of interaction distinct from physically present speakers. If negotiation is structured as a dialogue, it is not a dialogue that occurs between the individuals who utter words. It is also not a dialogue that occurs within the limits of a single pair of interlocutors, involving instead a chain of redundant pairs. It is as if the speaking subject of everyday encounter, an individual who may be animator, author, principal, and addressee all in one, has been taken apart and reassembled at a scale above that of the individual. Only at the level of the entire party, and only insofar as it speaks in the name of ancestors, is there a unified speaking subject. Even when the interests and motives of a single prominent person direct the entire event (not always the case), the style and structure of the speech events all portray him as a dual-gendered personification of an entire kabisu. He speaks recognizably neither in terms of a more partisan interest nor in a voice located in the moment of speaking.

The performative linkage of leadership with the agency of the group is echoed in the evocation of ancestors. The negotiating parties, as in all Anakalangese ritual dialogues, are addressed by their respective kadehang, the terms of address for their ancestors. If lineage ancestors are themselves metonyms for the groups that take their names, the use of speech from the ancestors is also that most appropriate for—even a condition of possibility for—large-scale public endeavors. It is, after all, the ancestors who give their name to the lineage and ground its identity in the kabisu village. It is they who provide the speech through which the living can act in society and engage in collective endeavors. By implication, it is the group that has agency, which rises above the contending interests of its constituent members. The alternative, failed speech, is the threat and challenge that is always represented—even in harmonious gatherings—as the background against which these speech events occur. Indeed, as has often been observed (e.g., Hill and Irvine 1992: 21; Shore 1982: 247) and recounted (think of John Alden or Cyrano de Bergerac), to delegate speech is to risk losing grip on the action altogether. Furthermore, to act means to risk unforeseen consequences. If successful use of kajiàla puts into action a group speaking in a single voice, the speech event also alludes to and implies a potential for disintegration and the polyphony of particular interests. Such a disintegration, which has immediate consequences for material exchange, can threaten not only the particular alliance at stake but also the practical existence of the group itself as a social agent. But overcoming the perceived threat is not simply a functional requirement in the face of some sort of Hobbesian state of nature. It appears to be part of how the scene of encounter constructs an imaginable alternative, and thus contributes to the value implicit in negotiated relations.

Crucial as material exchange is, authoritative power in Anakalang also requires mastery of ancestral speech. But it is a mastery that can only come alive as a resource of a group, pragmatically implicated as the effective agent. Foregrounded as speech, the scene of encounter displays interaction as balanced in a model of two-party dialogue. But it also sets conditions for failure. Ritual interaction in Anakalang is not merely coercive, nor does it serve only to reproduce tradition pedagogically. Crucial to the formation and evaluation of relations, it offers by the same token a site for their disruption. I suggest that in Anakalang, scrupulous concern with formality may in fact serve as a tacit reminder of the risks of interaction, portraying the value—even providing a test— of successful relations. At the same time that their *words* speak in an idiom of perduring alliances and ancient kabisu, the *forms* of ritualized encounter pragmatically highlight the fact that active group identities and allegedly stable alliances are interactively and recurrently achieved. The sense of risk contributes to the perceived value of successful negotiation, in which self-knowledge and mastery of representations are necessary conditions for action to be social and thereby fruitful. At the same time, to the extent that the sense of risk inherent in the mutual *logical* dependence among speakers of kajiàla is inseparable from *practical* risks imposed by the tensions among cooperation and competition, it means that mastery is never fully stable.

# CHAPTER SEVEN

# Formality and the Economy of Signs

Incompetent performance exposes the vulnerability of the ties among words, things, and persons. This vulnerability can be glimpsed in the tumultuous conclusion of Ubu Ledi's funeral. As usual for a long-lived and well-connected man or woman, the wake lasted about a week. Each night a party of affines or other allies would bring a large pig or a buffalo to feed the scores of mourners. Eventually all these donations would have to be reciprocated. The entombment incurred further obligations, as each of the thirty or forty attending groups, each containing one to three dozen people, brought an animal that either closed or created a debt. Even the animals that closed debts had to be acknowledged with at least a counterprestation of cloth or metal. Since all the guests also had to be fed, a large proportion of these animals were slaughtered in the village plaza. Predictably, Ubu Ledi's kabisu found itself short of materials with which to reciprocate everything that had been brought in. The usual way to deal with this situation is through a long sequence of dyadic transactions, as ritual speakers representing the host bring small prestations of either cloth or metal to each party in turn, as assurances of their respect and tokens of their debt. For whatever reason (some said arrogance, though it may have been the inexperience and exhaustion of the relatively young men in charge), the kabisu did not take the trouble to do this. Instead, one of Ubu Ledi's sons stood atop the tomb in the center of the plaza and made a general announcement inviting them all to reassemble in eight days to discuss the reciprocity. This was so unsatisfying that it led to a humiliating scramble, as people grabbed what they could of the animals that were present. One group of ngàba wini managed to appropriate three pigs by sheer force: they had men sit on the bamboo carrying cases in which they had arrived, preventing anyone else from taking them. Later, at the appointed conference, two of Ubu Ledi's most important ngàba wini chose not to attend, rather than risk the mutual embarrassment of an unsatisfactory response. In support of his decision, one of them told me that of the eighty cloths that had been brought to the wake, there had not even been enough left to distribute among the affines as tokens of their debt.

The unseemly scramble seems to reduce the objects in question from their status as morally loaded representations that mediate social relations to being mere economic goods. Why the scramble, if—as theorists of exchange from Mauss to Anakalangese themselves insist—debt is so highly respected? In later conversations, people made it clear to me that one reason was anger and doubt inspired by the way the matter was handled. A general announcement, such as that made by Ubu Ledi's son, does not recognize particular statuses, and no material tokens are left to mark those words. It raises the possibility that in any given instance no debt had in fact been established. Strategically, it also meant that replies to each group could not be fashioned according to the specific circumstances, and so Ubu Ledi's sons' intentions remained uncertain even in formal terms. Finally, the prospect of a general, rather than dyadic, discussion of reciprocity must have been troubling, since everyone would have been watching what everyone else received. Formal encounters do not take place in isolation but are deeply implicated in other exchanges and events. They are subject to the scrutiny and evaluation of a wider public, whose attention to the play of power and reputation means being ever watchful for signs of respect, marked in reference to the fulfillment of or lapses from the forms mandated by the ancestors.

In the face of such possible disruption, ritual speech insists repeatedly that the speaker will follow the ancestral "horses' spoor, dogs' tracks" and will convey his interlocutor's message:

| | |
|---|---|
| ku loligu na limu | I convey your words |
| daku pakàpa ta ma ḍalumaya | I don't hide them away inside |
| ku ngidigu na pekamu | I bring your message |
| daku madiḍi wulu mataḍinya | I don't sit (covering up the waistcloth's) fringe |

Although highly conventional, and at times rhetorically disingenuous, these figures of lost words and misdirected things both reflect and reinforce a real sense of grave consequences. They express an omnipresent concern in Anakalang with the social force of signs, control over that force, and the slippage inherent in their passage. The concern with slippage appears to be, in part, a way of interpreting the temporal dimension that separates gift and countergift and thus the uncertainty of the politics with which exchange is invested. It also points to the dialectic of social recognition played out in formal encounters. The horung constructs a moment of crisis in which alliance faces either reaffirmation or disruption, the conceptually ever-present possibility that "the speech be torn" (*na matarina na panewi*).

But the notion of slippage involves not just practical, perhaps contingent, consequences for particular actors. It also refers to the way in which formal means of acting implicate their alternatives: the limits, dilemmas, and instabilities of the effort to bind together speech and wealth, authority and power. Speech performance is crucial to how the two parties demand and grant recognition of each other as partners worthy of the status each seeks to assert, something that requires a delicate interplay of challenge and acquiescence. Anakalangese concern with slippage of signs thus links the possibility that signs will not fully represent their transactors, the passage of time that separates moments of exchange, and the social distance that threatens to arise in the midst of each relationship. The scenes that display order do not thereby merely impose order on the world by mimetic action, but indirectly point to the fact that outcomes are interactively produced, out of the hands of either party, and, moreover, they derive some of their value from that perception. In addition, the scene of encounter is not only a form of communication or display, and it does not simply express, or even legitimize, power. It is a critical point of *practical* articulation between signification and political economy as well.

The articulation of speech acts and political economy within the frame of ritual action and their public evaluation are functions of two features of formality: the tight restrictions on verbal and material media and the requirement that words and things be transacted together. We should not take for granted that Anakalangese conceive of the boundaries among persons, words, and things in the same ways that, say, the post-Cartesian West has been inclined to. Indeed, for scholars like Mauss, societies like Anakalang have been interesting precisely for the challenges they seem to pose to Western and modernist understandings of the human subject and its relation to the material world. In the 1980s and 1990s, pressed by the state's strong emphasis on economic development, Sumbanese themselves are wrestling with similar challenges.[1] But the insistence that in all serious interactions the words and things must be transacted together is evidence that some sort of distinction between them is significant. That neither words nor things are efficacious on their own demonstrates their practical complementarity: each makes up for a lack in the other. In this chapter, I will discuss how a discourse of "rules" surrounds and constrains formal encounters and some of the practical implications for the economy of persons and things.

## THE RULE OF ACTION

In Anakalang, as elsewhere, public, formal action is neither spontaneous nor the mechanical enactment of cultural imperatives. At every stage, people discuss and debate how things ought to be done. These debates involve not only strategic calculations but also constant reference to a realm of ancestral procedural rules, pata. Thus, for example, a conference (batang) typically starts with one of the sponsors posing a problem to be resolved. In November 1986, Ubu Saingu spoke of a series of deaths that had plagued his village.

> Thus it is that I gather you now, all of you, my mother-fathers, as revealed in my heart, as arisen in my liver, that would be the reason why the people died, the cattle died, the dogs died, the chickens died, I say. So we should search our pata here, indeed, oh father of Tabung.

This way of talking presupposes that pata is something that already exists apart from the moment of speaking and that it can be searched before deciding how to act. It is maintained by reflexive discourse, collective talk about how things should be, are being, and have been done. But, I will argue, this does not mean that we best describe these actions by reference to an autonomous set of rules.

At its most general, *pata* denotes a repeatable, patterned way of doing things, whose ancestral authority is emphasized with the expression "the ancient rules" (*na pata mema*).[2] This word is often glossed by Anakalangese with the Indonesian *adat*, whose semantic range includes "tradition," "proper manners," and "customary law." The gloss is at once significant and misleading. On the one hand, this identification entangles the specific pragmatic effects of the Anakalangese discourse of rules with the complex history of political manipulation and reification that lies behind the Indonesian term *adat*.[3] On the other hand, it identifies pata with the highly articulate local discourses about traditional order familiar throughout Indonesian ethnography. My primary concern in this context is with the *practical* relationship between reflexive discourse and action. Talk about pata is about—but not identical with—the responsibility of the living to the ancestors, of one kabisu to another, and of the performer to the audience (Bauman 1977).

Ritual speech is full of conventional references to the fact that those rules are in question at the very moment of speaking. For example, before one wunang replies to the other, he first affirms the procedural correctness of the latter's words and transactions (even if he will then criticize them) with the couplet "followed path, trail for crossing" (*lara li, ada pala*). The common Austronesian image of the path (Parmentier 1987: 108–111) has several rhetorical implications. In this couplet, the emphasis is on repeatability. Moreover, there is a moral injunction to repeat, since the path becomes deeper and more distinct the more it is followed: an old marriage alliance is spoken of as a well-worn path traced by the repeated passage of women from one village to the other. Another implication is that those who follow behind are subordinate to the trailblazers who went ahead (see Keane 1995b). The image of the path conflates the authority of original actions and that of generational seniority: for example, in rituals, ratus "pursue the traces of grass flattened by prior offspring, follow the stone overturned by subsequent children."

But we should not misconstrue the character of reflexive discourse. Invoking pata is not necessarily the same as "following" it, either as a legal code or as a set of instructions. We may not best understand even the most ritualized forms of action in Anakalang by reducing them to a set of rules. As Wittgenstein (1953) famously argues, to explain actions in terms of rules invites infinite regress, for how could one know when and how to apply a given rule except by appeal to yet another rule? In Wittgenstein's view, our capacity to apply a rule rests with *practical knowledge*, what Gilbert Ryle (1946) calls "knowing-how," that cannot adequately be retranscribed as a proposition, some kind of "knowing-that."

Nonetheless, social interaction includes a strong component of talk about action that sounds a great deal like a knowing-that. Bourdieu ([1972] 1977) has rightly criticized certain kinds of anthropology for taking this kind of talk too much at face value. But he in turn risks overemphasizing the propositional function of this kind of discourse: to see local talk about rules as a form of mystification is still to judge it in terms of whether or not it is an accurate *portrayal of* real activity, rather than an internal *component within* it, an objectifying moment within a larger process (see Keane 1995a). It is not uncommon for social contests in many societies to focus on the very rules of encounter themselves. In the ritualized councils of Samoa, for example, political strategy includes choices about what steps to include or omit, the effectiveness of which depends on reference to an objectifiable—but never fully realized—model (Duranti 1994: 90). More overtly agonistic encounters in Malagasy (Keenan 1975) and Nias (Beatty 1992: 236) often include heated debates about proper procedures. The fact that such debates are expected parts of the interaction suggests not only that ritualized encounters do not simply instantiate a set of Platonic cultural forms but also that there *must* be room for disagreement.[4] As John Comaroff and Simon Roberts (1981) point out, in discussing Tswana legal cases, people have particular reasons to appeal to abstract rules, and only do so under certain circumstances. To know when and how to appeal to rules is itself a *practical* skill. To be permitted to appeal to rules is often a function of power relations (for a Foucaultian approach to this in Oceania, see Lindstrom 1992). Furthermore, the appeal to rules is directed at *other participants* and thus involves the rhetoric of persuasion. At the same time, the fact that both sides agree to debate displays the fact that they share a more fundamental assumption, that, whatever their specific content, ancestral rules *do* in fact exist, and they matter. Such debate, then, both overtly (as a contest of explicit claims about rules) and implicitly (as the shared assumption underwriting the contest of claims) is a form of reflexivity sometimes called "metapragmatics" (Lucy 1993; Silverstein 1976, 1993). Metapragmatics focus not on the content or formal structure of representations, but on the actions they perform, and within which they are embedded.[5] In a successful exchange, not only has each party succeeded in giving words and things to the other, they have also displayed their agreement about what those words and things *do*.

In Anakalang, talk about pata, when it is not simply invoking the general authority of ancestors, concerns immediate and practical decisions in reference to ideal actions and actors. By focusing on explicit talk about (presumably) shared rules, speakers are tacitly acknowledging two features of formal interaction. One is that each party seeks the other's recognition as acting legitimately. The other is that recognition is predicated ultimately on an encompassing third party, the ancestors who

provide the warrant for legitimate action and their descendants, the social contemporaries who evaluate it. This presupposed third party sub-
sumes both parties to the interaction: no longer my action or yours, to
act according to pata is something that *we do together*. In addition, the
act is no longer something we do at a particular moment, but a recurring
instance arising out of a *general disposition*: proper action thus says
something about the very character of the actors. Ritual action's claim
to iconicity serves in part to *index* the actors' actual links to the ancestors and their deference both to the idea of rules and to their present
interlocutors, as people for whom rulelike acts are appropriate. Debate
is in part a jockeying for position within those assumptions, a contest
of authority that also affirms the bounds within which that contest will
take place. But it is also something more: pata provides a way of talking about how participants are to evaluate each other's actions. When
people search for the right way to go about doing a ritual or setting up
an exchange, they are in part anticipating the regard of those others
whom they will face, spirits or affines who have the ability and the right
to judge the offerings or prestations inadequate and the speech incor-
rect. Thus, to the extent that planners act as if they are going to "follow" a rule, they are not only acting in reference to a presupposed past
but also anticipating a retrospective moment of moral evaluation in the
future.

Part of the work of the highly reflexive speech of negotiation is to
make the existence of these rules presupposable. People may, and often
do, disagree about the details. Common sources of disagreement include misconstruals of the situation in question, conflicting interpretations of the situation due to differing interests, and the existence of a
host of microregional variations (see note 4). Memory is both fallible
and political, and thus an action that had been permitted in a previous
generation as an exception might be remembered later as a precedent.
Moreover, performances remain open to subsequent reinterpretation, especially since present misfortunes are attributed to past procedural errors, compelling people to search their recollections, dreams, and divinations for evidence of mistakes. But participants' shared effort to act
with proper forms points emphatically to their underlying agreement
that they *should* be following ancestral rules for action (see Fox 1989).
The poetic and pragmatic work of formal interaction thus does not
only construct particular political alignments, status claims, and economic configurations. It also makes presupposable the ongoing, but
virtual, existence of an ancestral realm of directives.

At the same time, the metaphors that refer to pata also imply a variety of difficulties and sources of error. As Austin ([1956–1957] 1979) observes, to understand the socially defined character of an action, we must be alert to the specific ways in which it can fail. The activities spoken of in the discourse of pata can fail in a wide assortment of ways, with differing consequences. All these kinds of infelicity exist in reference to—indeed, help construct—the concept of pata. Disclaimers figuratively commingle three ways of failing: forgetting or losing the trail, going astray (following false or incomplete knowledge, or mistaking the situation), and falling short (for example, due to insufficient provisions). Images like "paths" and "traces of Lord's tracks in the twigs, traces of Lady's cutting-marks on the stump" imply the absence of those who made them. The repeatability provided by the path and the difficulty imposed by absence are combined in the figure of the uncertain hunt after wild prey: ratus are "they who follow the monkey tracks, they who trace the boar tracks." Such expressions *explicitly* deny the very authority that performance is *implicitly* asserting by other means. They form a constant reminder of the discrepancy between the virtual order of rules and their imperfect realization, something to which people refer explicitly. The living speak with self-humbling expressions, as mere children, "we (who are) new lips and we (who are) new eyes, dried shrimp, fish out of water, replacement priests, successor ratus," whose knowledge is but "a single strand, a single stone." Much of the content of meetings (batang) concerns proper procedures. Modesty combines with real anxieties, expressed by the speakers assembled by Ubu Saingu:

> If we really look at this problem, it's heavy, heavy. But let us not be heavy-livered. . . . Only the trouble is, Oh father of Tabung [Right!]. . . . Who will we rely on? Who will we rely on? There are no longer they who truly knew the, uh, the zigzags from the past, the rules for doing it. . . . There's no Mother who reveals, who raises the throat. There's no Father who informs, who opens the eyes.

As Ubu Saingu's request that the meeting "search out pata" suggests, the correct response is not simply given but requires investigation and discussion. Deference to ancestors and caution about being seen to exert individual agency mean that a collective voice must be constructed during the meeting, in the name of pata.

> Later, outside (the village), in going down (from the village) not yet far from the plaza, or on arriving at our houses, uh, in gathering over here, uh, or gathering up there, let's not talk further behind (the scenes) (saying) 'Actually, according to me, it should be like this I say. According to me myself, friends.'

That's my opinion, oh father of Tabung. [Right.] Now each of us should put out what we know. Be it right, put it out. Be it not right, put it out. For later on, the language of each, that's what will be completed (by the rest).

The typical resolution is framed as a compromise with contingency. As one man put it, during a meeting to plan a ritual,

Yeah, if we say 'there are no longer any (who really know the rites),' as we here offspring and children put it, well, it just means we just have to put out whatever we might know. . . . Even though the split wood is insufficient, even though the drawn water isn't full.

The metaphors suggest the infelicities to which ritual actions are prone, as straying from the path, forgetting, or incompleteness. In addition, critics of ritual speakers insist that one may *subtract* from, but must not *add* to, the received canon of couplets and rules for their use. This view manifests both an assumption that time entails loss, a falling away from ancestral plentitude, and a disclaimer, that one properly portrays oneself not as the real agent but as someone who is merely following ancestral mandates. Most of the exchanges and rituals that actually transpire, in this view, never achieve the full form, but remain only "shadows on the dry land, reflections on the water" of the ancestral models (compare Forth 1981: 375).[6]

The continual explicit reference to these possibilities does several things at once. On the one hand, it is a way of exhibiting deferential and cautious demeanor. To assert otherwise would be an act of hubris inviting both ancestral retribution and the resentment of other people. But deference mingles with an awareness of the afflictions that error can bring—illness, death, drought, fire, lightning strikes, or simple social humiliation—and people take their incapacities very seriously. Etiquette and anxiety meet in the displacement of agency onto the ancestors. To refer explicitly to the fact that one is following pata is also to declare one's own lack of willfulness. It is to insist that one is only doing what one must, fulfilling an original obligation as in this couplet (whose inclusive pronouns unite speaker and addressee): "We don't forget our grandfathers' promise, we don't forget our grandmothers' commitment." This both displays the speaker's respectful humility and reminds all listeners that failed actions are also breached promises, which are enforced by vigilant if invisible listeners.

Shared talk about pata gives principled grounds for evaluating formal actions. In itself, however, such reflexive discourse is not sufficient to coordinate the performative and causal dimensions of action. In practice, it is the distinctive properties of words and things, working in tandem, that make evaluation both plausible and effective. For example, the capacity of material objects to endure is an important element of the way in which scenes of encounter forge links between past and future events. Persisting after words have fallen silent, objects can enter into new exchanges or remain as marks left by previous ones. The play of words and things articulates that of presence and absence: by formally creating debt, words spoken now assure that objects, which are presently lacking, will be given at a future time. At that time, those objects will later remind their recipient of the words being spoken now. Present and future, word and thing are bound by successful performances.

This pragmatic relation between past and future transactions is iconically portrayed by pata as a sequence of steps, embedded within a larger project. As Ubu Roru told the assembly called by Ubu Saingu to "search out pata," "This [pata], it's like this bamboo—there's the joint, right? There are the internodes, right? This adat is just the same. There's its joint, there's its internode." In performative terms, each step should imply the successful completion of previous steps. The perspective that can encompass at a glance the multiple discrete components of action, what Bourdieu calls a "privilege of totalization" that "makes it possible to apprehend at a glance . . . meanings which are produced and used polythetically, that is to say, not only one after another, but one by one, step by step" (1977: 106–107), is not, in contrast to Bourdieu's assertion, restricted to the ethnographic outsider.

Ritual speech reflexively grounds the performative force of the object with reference to this sequence (see chapter 1, note 13), both by representing the gift as a token of a type ("here is The Mother's Brother's Portion") and placing it within a larger temporal sequence ("here is the fulfillment of my earlier promise").[7] Both effects presuppose the existence of discrete units of action within the encompassing schema of pata. Prestations give material form to a conceptual sequence by which relations between people are formed and maintained. The words with which they are transacted provide them with names that distinguish their place in relation to possible prior and subsequent prestations.[8] Sequences are built by both logical and causal implication. This can be seen in the negotiation between kabisu P and W. At the end of their second major encounter, "going up into the house," P, as yera, had provided their ngàba wini with a pig known as the "smell of roasted fat." The meat of this pig is to be distributed when they summon their allies to request their support in the next encounter with P. As a named prestation, the gift serves as a conventional performative that initiates the next step. But as meat, it is also a practical condition for W's ability to assemble itself into a single agent. At the next meeting, however, ngàba wini threw themselves on the mercy of their yera by saying that they had insufficient means to complete the payment yera expected and asked that they be permitted to transfer the bride informally (without gong playing), leaving the exchanges temporarily incomplete. Such a transfer is embarrassing for yera, for it suggests to the public at large that they do not respect themselves or the bride enough to demand fuller prestations. This demand should have been made in the previous meeting, to forestall the giving of the roasted fat pig. Having accepted it, they are now committed to going ahead into a fuller exchange. To do otherwise would be to suggest that yera had been unable to provide a foundation sufficient for ngàba wini to assemble their supporters, or that the two sides are so unbalanced as to be unable to honor one another. But notice the foresight this requires—ngàba wini is not supposed to wait until they see the outcome of the "roasted fat" distribution before they decide the next step. Although nothing is nonnegotiable, this requirement places them at the mercy of their yera. As it happened, yera took offense, reading ngàba wini's material inadequacy as evidence of disrespect. This is an example of how pata, by providing a model sequence, makes it possible to evaluate in semiotic—and thus *moral* terms—the *practical* consequences of participants' material resources and performance skills. It helps give meaning to the outcomes of exchange by attributing them to the character of the participants and their relations to ancestors.

## THE IDEA OF PATA AND THE VALUE OF OUTCOMES

The sequence of steps portrayed by pata condenses the power of formal action to link momentary acts together in reference to a larger trajectory. But each step in the process also poses the possibility of disruption. Thus the very model of the sequence implies that any successful completion has occurred in the face of the possibility that it might not have. In part, this possibility is a simple political fact, reflecting the need to obtain the cooperation of people who may have conflicting interests (for the strategic manipulation of ritual timing and sequence in Kodi, see Hoskins 1993b: 222 ff.). But the possibility of disruption

Figure 13. Stylized sociability: Women from yera and ngàba wini exchange betel pouches on the front veranda before formally "going up into the house" for further negotiations (Pasunga, August 1993).

is not only a contingent matter, external politics impinging on or expressed in the separate, and pliant, materials of culture. It is also implicit in the very structure of pata, rendered visible at the moments of transition from unit to unit, which do not run in a seamless flow so much as in an interruptable ratcheting. This was best expressed to me by a Christian, Ubu Siwa, recalling his long lapsed ritual role.

> If I don't move, no one else can. They all gather, but I'm not there yet. After all are there, only then am I called from my house. I can say I'm not ready yet and they have to wait. They summon me several times. First I say I'm not ready, then that I'm getting ready, then I'm dressed, then that I'm leaving. They wait for me from morning to evening, from when they begin to pound the rice until it's already cooked and placed on the plates and already gone down to the village plaza.

Underlying Ubu Siwa's boast is a claim that his acts are the critical precondition for collective projects (at least one ritual, in fact, *requires* a ratu to hold out until summoned several times). The structure of ritual sequences makes practical interdependence a condition for outcomes of differing values. This is evident not only in the dangers that attend ritual but also in the status implications of marriage.

Anakalangese marriage exchanges should follow a series of named steps that enact a stylized narrative by which the supplicant wooers identify themselves to the bride's surprised household and gradually overcome their resistance to releasing their daughter. They form a process of separation from one kabisu and incorporation into another, culminating in the exchanges made after the birth of children, which securely establish their kabisu affiliation "lest (the child) be an egg (laid) in the twigs, lest (the mother) give birth in the rubbish" (see table 1). Children born before the completion of the sequence affiliate to the mother's kabisu, a matter of political and economic importance.[9] This narrative is divided among a series of discrete units, each of which must be completed, a shortcut negotiated, or an alternative sequence embarked on (as when the couple elope midway through the process) before passing on to the next. As a result of this structure, any given prestation or offering, in theory, presupposes the successful completion of those that come before it in the sequence. The material outcome of a negotiation registers in objectual form—in goods received or not received—the relative completeness of the speech event. Recall that the metaphors for pata imply a whole series of possible kinds of deviation from correct procedure. Given that most horung (as indeed most rituals) *will* fall short of the full model in some way, how that shortcoming is to be interpreted is subject to negotiation. It is a political outcome, for example, not a preordained rule, that determines whether a shortfall in ngàba wini's marriage prestations represents a serious debt, a lenient yera, or a shamefully inadequate ngàba wini.[10]

Talk about pata provides a means of evaluating action and its outcomes. As noted above, the discourse of pata tends to identify the "truest" rules with their most "complete" version, just as it treats the more elaborate rites as more efficacious (and, as described in chapter 2, more "complete" villages as superior). In part because practices may subtract but not add to this version, it is seldom, if ever, achieved.[11] Marriage exchanges have consequences for the affiliation of the couple and their offspring and the status of the groups who negotiate over them. Matrilateral cross-cousin marriage exists in contrast to a range of alternative outcomes to negotiation, registering as social effects the potentials for domination or rupture inherent to the moment of giving (Boon 1977: 122). At one extreme, "marrying in" (*lalai tama*), a groom who is unable to make a minimal prestation is absorbed into the bride's kabisu. Lost to his own kabisu, he—and more important, his children—become subordinate members of his wife's kabisu.[12] Kabisu will usually struggle

TABLE I    THE PATA OF MARRIAGE EXCHANGE:
SOME COMMON OPTIONS

---

[1] First meeting: "bringing betel" (*ngidi pamama*)
Purpose: to initiate negotiations
Sequence of main components:

   a.  "betel pepper wrapping, areca nut sheath" (*kaboru kuta, kakoḅa winu*) commits both parties to undertake further negotiations

   b.  "make the time, set the date" (*wolu rahi, rawi nalu*) sets a date for the next meeting

[2] Second meeting: "cover the betel" (*pitaku pamama*)
Purpose: commits the parties to forego negotiations with other parties without penalties
Sequence of main components:

   a.  "open gate, clear path" (*waiha ḅina, bowa lara*) for new alliances, to allow ngàba wini to enter yera's village

   b.  "challengingly ask, firmly inquire" (*tuturu katana, daliru karai*) yera demands their visitors identify themselves

   c.  "go up into the house" (*ḍeta ta uma*) having until this point met on the veranda, this permits ngàba wini to enter the house

   d.  "unroll the mat, offer the pillow" (*palekaru tapu, kahorung nulang*) welcomes the guests

   e.  "eat rice, drink water" (*angu auhu, inu wai*) hosts feed the guests

   f.  "lock chest, nail ship" (*uhi pati, paku tena*) formal commitment: includes the "smell of roasted fat" pig (*wawi hihuk*) that ngàba wini will use later to feed its own supporters whom it will ask for help in the next set of exchanges

   g.  "make the time, set the date" (*wolu rahi, rawi nalu*) sets a date for the next meeting

[3] Third meeting: "pass over the woman" (*papalang mawini*)
Purpose: formally transfers bride to husband's household
Sequence of main components:

   a.  "eat rice, drink water" (*angu auhu, inu wai*) hosts feed the guests

   b.  transferral (*palebarung*)

      b1.  "pass the benches, cross the partition" (*lebaru ta laḍu, palaku ta hàda*)

      b2.  "plant wood, stow rock" (*tehukungu ai, ḅijalungu watu*)

      b3.  "tabooed cattle" (*ḅaḍa ḅiha*), a fixed set of items includes a mamuli, "back scars" (*kapila kaḍenga*) for the bride's mother, for lying with her back to the fire after childbirth

      b4.  "mother's brother's portion" (*tagu loka*), for the bride's mother's brother

      b5.  "guards the underside, protects the shade" (*totu lubu, jawa mawu*), for the resident of the bride's ancestral house

TABLE I    THE PATA OF MARRIAGE EXCHANGE:
SOME COMMON OPTIONS (continued)

---

   b6. "mother who rules the land, father who governs the river" (*ina pareta tana, ama kuwaha loku*), for local government official, if participating

   b7. "mother who goes out in the morning, father who enters in the evening" (*ina ma palauhung barubaru, ama ma patamangu bana malung*), for the mother-father of the bride's mother's marriage

   b8. "mother hen, father pig" (*ina manu, ama wawi*): for mother-father of the bride's party

  c. "advise, inform" (*panau, papekang*): pair of cloths given directly to the couple by the bride's mother's brother without negotiation

  d. "struck dog, stuck pig" (*ahu papalu, wawi pakojia*): a closing meal, each side providing the meat for the other

  e. "*jangi*-wood staff, grass horse" (*taku jangi, jara witu*): direct exchange between the wunangs

---

hard to prevent this from happening to their men, but they may be economically unable, or politically unwilling, to support the individual. Here is a case in which the outcome of exchange is directly registered in status: the low level of exchange is mirrored in the low status for the individual and the losses to the kabisu that result.

At the opposite extreme is the marriage of a noble woman to a wealthy man of very low rank. While supposedly very rare, the possibility of such unions seems to have great conceptual importance, given how often people mentioned it to me. It seems to represent a tantalizingly illicit opening for social mobility and for romantic or at least sexual motives. When the noble family cannot prevent the marriage, especially when the man of low rank is also rich, they will force an exchange called "throw the stone in the lake, break the string," in which they demand a huge prestation, to be paid in full. This move intentionally transmutes a possible alliance into nothing more than the single moment of a unique encounter. It effects this transmutation by sheer excessiveness of scale, overwhelming the ngàba wini with a demand so great that no further debt can be conceived of between the two. The purpose is to break off any continuation of affinal relations. There is no performance, no step-by-step negotiation, no construction of a temporal project that acknowledges and strengthens the value of each party for the other. Instead, like purchase and sale in the marketplace, it is a closed transaction that repeats nothing from the past and has no bearing on the future: relations between the two groups begin and end there.

In between the extremes of absorbing the husband and expelling the wife lies a range of possibilities and ambiguities. Here is where the semantic functions of speech can have a critical performative function, by naming just what is going on, when steps are taken to be *omitted* rather than *elided*. Since the sequence of exchanges enacts the increasing separation of the woman from her parents' household and her incorporation into that of her husband, any incompleteness leaves these identities and this process only partially fulfilled. The institutional outcome is a function of the transformation of quantities of goods into qualitative differences of meaning.

The schematic model of pata imposes a discursive measure by which people can evaluate particular exchanges and the alliances they mediate. Since acts of ritual speech require goods, greater wealth permits longer and more elaborate speech. Thus, all other things being equal, the "fullness" of speech performances should be both iconic of wealth and indexical of the quality of ancestral authority. In particular, the role of material goods in formal practices tacitly links the very meaning of nobility to the concept of ancestral rules: nobles are implicitly those who are best able to fulfill the proper cultural norms by which everyone is evaluated. At the same time, this role places any particular claim to noble status at risk, insofar as that claim is predicated on practices that require both political and material backing to accomplish. Wealth is not sufficient to provide one with authority, but the evaluation of authority according to the "completeness" of exchanges makes it difficult to maintain noble status without wealth.[13] The fact that authoritative practices demand political influence and economic clout makes for tension between rank and wealth to which I return below. Impoverished nobles and commoners can look very much alike, and many Anakalangese nobles wish for a world in which pata would tell you all you need to know about their status. Since hierarchy is partially objectified in the form of "complete" exchanges, however, it is vulnerable to the aspirations of new riches.[14] Yet, constrained by the forms of representational practice and the demands of interaction, the meaning and value of exchange objects is never reducible to the resources they index. Goods alone cannot transform economic power into ancestral authority.

## OBJECTS AND OTHER PEOPLE

The fact that before entering into exchange material goods must come from somewhere, and after the exchange they perdure somewhere else, introduces a causal logic into the interaction of social subjects. Once I have given someone a buffalo, it enters into their own heightened powers of exchange. Conversely, valuables are like a minor form of charisma as their owners find themselves the focus of other people's efforts to obtain them. But the discourse of pata imposes a further constraint, that goods of opposed categories travel in opposed directions. It is not the semiotic features of the goods as much as the practical constraint imposed by pata that permits the gift to represent the giver. The metal, horses, and buffalo that I, as a male yera, receive from ngàba wini do not so much "replace" a lost sister or daughter, or "stand for" her husband, as they make it possible for me to pursue relations with yera of my own. My power to give to yera is predicated on my having earlier received gifts from ngàba wini: my yera in turn should recognize in me a source of their own powers to exchange buffalo with others. The contribution this buffalo makes to their powers is the *economic* reflection of our *moral* articulation with each other. Since people need cloth, metal, and animals not only for marriages and funerals but also for relations with ancestors, they often view marriage as a function of the demands of exchange: goods are simultaneously means and ends. When I asked Ubu Joka why one should marry one's cross-cousin, he replied as if it were obvious, 'So that I'm strong, because I have two sides. So I can go to one for buffalo, one for pigs. If I didn't have two sides, where would I go to ask (for buffalo and pigs)?'

The semiotic classification of goods, as yera's or ngàba wini's, supports their role in representing exchange partners to one another. The poetics and pragmatics of ritual speech permit one speech event to appear, in part, as repeating an ancestral original. But it is the indexical properties of objects—functions, in part, of their material durability and scarcity—that permit the outcomes of one event to be registered in the potentials fulfilled in the next. Their objective persistence from one event to the next helps those who handle them to construct their actions as ongoing "projects" that transcend the contingencies of the particular moment and expand beyond the immediate circle of participants. Mediated by material objects, temporal and social expansiveness work in tandem: past exchanges live on in the potential for future exchanges, and my role as one group's yera makes possible my role as another's ngàba wini.

This expansiveness has another dimension as well. The projects of any given set of individuals tend (both normatively and practically) to be inextricable from the agency of larger groups, up to the kabisu, with

whose resources and in whose names they act. Most important exchanges involve quantities far in excess of what any single household
commands. Even if one could afford to act alone, it would be both an
act of hubris and politically unsound to do so. Here is how wealthy
Ubu Dongu explained to me why he provided only five of the thirty-one
animals given for his son's marriage:

> Even if you can pay all by yourself, you wouldn't do so. . . . If you've offered
> to help someone, like with their marriage payments, and you're turned
> down, you'll never want to attend again, you'll just think to yourself (if in-
> vited), 'Ok then, if you want to stand alone—go ahead!'

What Ubu Dongu omits is that these ties of cooperation also create and
reproduce hierarchical relations of dependency and support. As a man
on the patronage-dispensing end, he would be both unwise not to build
those ties and impolitic to describe them as such. His statement then
contains—but is not reducible to—a sense of strategic advantage masked
by what Bourdieu ([1972] 1977) calls "euphemism." For young men to
refuse his assistance is also to refuse Ubu Dongu the chance in the future
to make claims on them, in the name not just of patronage but also of
the kabisu, as the collective agency in whose name they all are compelled
to act. But Ubu Dongu's words do accurately reflect both the explicit
norm of cooperation and the strategies and resentments that go along
with it: if an affine has been overlooked when someone holds a large exchange, they may resent the implication that they are no longer considered adequate or trustworthy partners. The overlooked partner may try
to force an exchange, as Ama Jon discovered when he held a feast to
celebrate the completion of his new house. One uninvited ngàba wini
showed up and gave him a horse. This not only put Ama Jon in debt, it
also compelled him to pay restitution for the insult of leaving him out.

As is common in exchange systems, most goods in Anakalang have
been obtained in prior transactions, and any given exchange usually im-
plicates participants in debts incurred in other exchanges, which are in
turn implicated in still others.[15] For example, when Ama Pedi's brother
was under pressure to give his yera a horse, Ama Pedi took one from
the herd of Ubu Siwa, his own ngàba wini. In principle he had the right
to do so, since Ubu Siwa still owed him several horses. But Ubu Siwa
had already promised that horse to one of his own kabisu fellows for a
negotiation to be held only days later. Thus, in effect, a demand by his
yera's brother's yera ended up putting *him* in the humiliating position of
reneging on a public commitment, and may weaken his kabisu fellow's

position in turn. Such commonplace situations—what people call a "leaky corral" (*bowa gàlu*)—make evident that the displays of self-esteem and of respect for others are not matters of communicative intention alone. Externalized in material forms, the capacity for representation manifests and is constrained by economic possibilities. In such ways, the causal logic of *material* constraints helps constitute a totality that extends beyond the reach of any specific *moral* bond that might directly link the people at either end of the chain of debts.

The mutual dependence of exchange partners is both material and verbal. Each group depends on the other for the goods with which it can then enter into other transactions. Each likewise depends on an interlocutor to address it with its own kabisu name, the kaḍehang. That both dimensions of interaction work together is in turn an effect of the collective discourse of pata. They combine verbal recognition with material capacities, which depend on interactions whose outcomes escape the intentions of particular actors. They also manifest a tension between challenge and cooperation: mutual dependence entails mutual threat. As I have discussed in previous chapters, scenes of encounter dramatize the agonism implicit to exchange. The materiality of exchange goods makes it difficult to separate political and moral challenges from economic circumstances (or vice versa). Ritual speech explicitly acknowledges their mutual implication. For instance, one couplet expresses disappointment that others have not reciprocated one's gift, as if they were intimidated by one's own power and wealth, figured in images of dangerous creatures, "like an unseen python, like an invisible crocodile." A wunang glossed this as meaning, 'When we see these animals we run away. If I'm not met with counterprestations, I'll go home thinking maybe they take me for a crocodile or a snake.' Although the iterative quality of scenes of encounter gives to alliances the appearance of durability, their agonistic structure engages the participants in challenges by which each demands the other recognize its capacity to act with authority, embodied in proper speech and appropriate goods. At the heart of negotiation lies mutually constructed acknowledgment—and potential defeat—of each party's capacity to act effectively and to receive and grant due measures of respect. Anyone who enters into exchange runs the risk of, for example, giving prestations too great to be reciprocated or failing before the demands of an exchange partner.

Recall again Ama Koda's feud over the torn cloth given to him by his yera, described at the beginning of chapter 2. It exemplifies the interdependence among pride, recognition, and everyday semiotics. Under-standing the ambiguity of formal etiquette, Ama Koda rejects the polite reception he receives when he is in his yera's village. He takes their treat-ment of him to be constructing him as an outsider. As such, it denies him the recognition he expects as someone whose agency is critical to that of his affines (without him 'how many times would they have ended up in a mess'). The theme of agency underlies Ubu Elu's conclud-ing threat as well ('at the funeral, don't form your own procession, join my entourage'). Should the problem not be resolved, Ama Koda will not in fact act as an independent agent, but only as a subordinate to a man who is required to attend by nothing less than the strongest demands of mortuary obligations. Notice as well the way Ama Koda phrases his sense of being rejected, in terms of the perennial anxiety about exchange, debt, and dependence: they treat him as if he were a suppliant come to ask them for goods. His insult is saturated with scorn: as if *he*, on whose wealth they depend, were to seek help from *them*. Underlying these individual rivalries are the operations by which col-lective agents are constructed. Ama Koda knows that his yera's ability to act like a kabisu depends on their economic relations with people like him.

The complex nature of the outcomes is reflected in a tension between the practical need for actual valuables and the reputation sustained through debt. This tension can break out into a more exposed show of interests, as in the scramble for goods after Ubu Ledi's funeral described at the beginning of this chapter. The political economy of exchange means that a group without good relations with strong affines lacks not only *semiotic* tokens of *existing* spiritual power and social standing but also the *economic* capacity to forge *future* relations.

## THE MARKS LEFT BY WORDS

If the formal constraints described by pata hold, then objects mark enduring relationships by indexing particular acts of giving. Objects therefore serve as anchors for memory and proofs of words spoken, un-derwriting the performative efficacy of present actions on the future.[16] This can be seen in the act of peacemaking, which should in principle be binding into an unlimited future. When Ubu Ngailu and his brother made up after feuding for years, they engaged in a symmetrical exchange, each giving a cloth and a pig to the other and making a small speech. In his speech, Ubu Ngailu publicly declared the cloth he had just received to be out of circulation, saying 'I will never let go of this. It will remain with me so I remember this event.'

Ubu Ngailu's cloth, however, is not only a reminder of a momentary event. The act of holding it back is itself a highly marked and continuous exertion of will (one whose implications will become more apparent in the next chapter). It extends the effects of the singular act of peacemaking into the future as the manifestation of the enduring authority of its possessor. In a context in which valuables continuously circulate, and in which everyone is under constant pressure to exchange or to support others in exchange, declaring even a piece of cloth off-limits without alienating other people is in itself a strong act. When I returned to Anakalang after an absence of six years, Ubu Pàda showed me that he still held onto the cloth I had given him, despite what must have been countless opportunities to give it away. When his son wrote to tell me of Ubu Pàda's death several months later, he made sure to let me know that they had buried the cloth with him. The cloth at once served as a memory of me and of the act of giving; to withdraw it from exchange both memorialized and supplemented that original act—in this way, I too was honored. By such acts one brings to a halt the flow of goods that had led from ultimately unknown sources to oneself: the buck, as it were, stops here.

When Ubu Ngailu holds onto the cloth he received from his brother, the act is endowed with meaning both because it registers the outcome of a speech event and because of the way the cloth is embedded within a larger economy of circulating things. The subsequent presence of the cloth among Ubu Ngailu's possessions indexically presupposes prior acts of speaking. The time may come when Ubu Ngailu will need to decide whether to deny the reasonable request of one of his own kin or affines or to not enter into a subsequent exchange himself, rather than release that cloth back into circulation again. But withholding it from further circulation only makes semiotic sense to the extent that cloth, as a material substance, has a certain scarcity as unique existent—a different cloth with iconically identical qualities (such as having the same color or design) would not serve the same indexical purpose.

The logical-causal structure of the scene of encounter is part of what makes it possible for one event to have effects in the future. If all else holds, then the presence of the pig under the house, the horse in the corral, or the metal chain in the room, *presupposes* the prior exchange of authoritative speech with which each was transacted and grounds the *next* set of exchanges into which each is brought. The distinctive properties of words and things (identity over repetitions versus physical durability, reflexive acts of naming versus semantically underdetermined presence) also indicate the power of their conjunction: valid speech performance places the speaker in a continuous lineage linking past to future, while successful exchange of objects makes one a node in a continuous chain of contemporaneous partners. Both dimensions of social being depend on the invocation of absent others, namely, dead ancestors and living allies who are not participating directly. The conjunction of words and things fosters, renews, and concretizes the imagined community within which living people work to situate themselves. The strongest agents are those who are best able to display to the world at large their ability to link these two dimensions of social identity. Their success further enhances their chances of future success, by virtue both of the possession of objects available for use in exchange (an "economic" dimension) and of the reputation for having used the forms of speech that are presupposably indexed by those exchangeables (a "symbolic" dimension). Ritualized encounters, by articulating words and things, work to make these two dimensions inseparable. The speech in which the objects of exchange are enveloped invests them with this capacity to forge links between past and future actions, as well as between the value of things and the value of acts, and in the process displays their relationship to the threat of slippage and dissipated force. The resulting goods are signs of successful speech, while speech in turn acquires some of the practical efficacy with which goods are endowed by their physical and economic properties.

Although words are not inherently subject to scarcity in the same way that objects are, the requirement that each turn of talk rest on the "base" of goods ensures that words will have their cost. This is both a causal effect and an icon of the relations between the invisible realm of the dead and the material circumstances of the living. As long as these norms are maintained—something that the demands of one's interlocutors, one's public reputation, and, perhaps, the attentive gaze of ancestors make difficult to avoid—any exchange valuable in one's possession indexes a *presupposable* previous transaction.[17] Thus, if the rules of transaction have been followed, virtually all my metal and cloth goods, many or most of my horses and buffalo, and at least some of my pigs presuppose the previous speech events of which they are the material outcomes. Indeed, the formality that links things to words, and constrains the kinds of things that count, functions in part to make that presupposition valid. If the boundaries separating exchange from other kinds of transaction fail, so too will the presupposing indexicality that makes objects traces of former events fail as well.

In addition, however, formality involves a second sort of indexicality, that which *entails*, making explicit or transforming, the circumstances it indexes. There are several ways in which entailing indexicality works in Anakalangese exchange. One is the framing of a given event as being an instance of an ancestral type of action. Another is the casting of the agents in the event in typical roles, associated with ancestral identities: wunang, ratu, and mother-father, yera and ngàba wini, all situated in reference to kabisu. These are familiar aspects of how ritualized forms of action in many societies help participants construct their claims to authority and the recognition of others. But in Anakalang there is another aspect as well, for entering into highly formal and wary interaction with another indexes social distance—even where the two groups are normally on warm and easy terms with each other. This sense of distance, however, is focused on the difficulty of using formal words and things. The allusiveness and indirection characteristic of ritual speech make it vulnerable to misinterpretation. Its ancestral sources expose living speakers to error. Restricted to an oral medium, any given verbal performance endures only in fallible and contestible memories. Exchange valuables alone are both relatively underdetermined and not in themselves sufficient to establish clear denotations or unambiguous performative acts. The relative autonomy of ancestral words, and of material things, therefore, is simultaneously a source of their authority and a threat to those who use them. The fact that interaction hinges on their use gives concrete form to the hazards each party poses to the other. It is to this, in part, that Anakalangese seem to be responding when they insist that they have only inadequate knowledge of the real pata.

# CHAPTER EIGHT

# Subjects and the Vicissitudes of Objects

One evening in December 1986 the leading men and several prominent women of kabisu P gathered to confer in their unfinished Great House. A month earlier, the senior man of the senior lineage had died. During the funeral, it became apparent that a gold mamuli that was supposed to be kept in this house, which was his lineage's responsibility to safeguard, was missing. The mamuli was the kabisu's ancestor's portion (*tagu marapu*), called R, the slave name of the kabisu's founder. Over the course of that evening's debate, it came out that the deceased man's brother had pawned the mamuli to another member of the kabisu, Ubu Wolu, for one buffalo and Rp 500. Ubu Wolu claimed he had no idea what happened to the mamuli, but it is widely assumed he sold it long ago to a Chinese trader. At any rate, no one recalled having seen it since they stopped "feeding it" with offerings after the majority of the kabisu entered the church in 1966.

This was far more than a simple case of theft, opportunism, or even confusion. The weight of the matter was summarized by one man:

> I don't know if this (R) is supernatural, none of us (incl.) know. Who knows whether it's of true copper, (as for) the ancestors when they stored it, we ourselves can't know this thing. . . . We don't really know, all we know is that it's a sign of unity (*tada pakahaingungu*), from a single grandfather, that's all we know.[1] It's a true betel pepper, it's already a sign of unity, a sign of the ongoing pata. Another of us dies, then our grandchildren die, then we die again, (then) our grandchildren, that (mamuli) there is for unifying on

and on. That's the thing, oh brothers, so if we talk about R, it's given its gift every year, each month our grandfathers, up to four years, eh, this guy, it's not just something recent, this talk of R, that's the talk.

Despite his deferential disclaimers of ignorance, he made several things evident. The gold object was "stored (or laid down)" (ḅijalu) by the ancestors, it receives offerings, and it is not used for marriages. It bears a representational relationship to pata, to continuity over time, and to present social unity. Furthermore, no one can say "it's my own gold" because it is "a common (collective) thing" (Indo. barang umumu). Now several possibilities were raised. One was that the five "grandfathers," that is, the commonly recognized segments of the kaḅisu, should split up and go their separate ways, each taking back the contribution it had made to the rebuilding of the Great House, and that they should work out a system of rotation to continue working the rice field belonging to that house. The argument was that since the function of the house had vanished, there is no longer any purpose in remaining together as a kaḅisu. To avoid this, they met a second time, so that, as one man put it during the debate,

> We can openly together discuss 'What would be the best way?' in order to take the best resolution, 'lest the land be torn, lest the stone be split' in that circle (of kin) there in one Great House.

In the end, the group decided that the son of the man who pawned it would give a buffalo to Ubu Wolu and the latter would find a gold mamuli to replace R. Assuming that Ubu Wolu ever does come up with a mamuli, it would then, somehow, have to be inducted into the house—although the prospect of this coming to pass is far from assured.

It is unlikely anyone really took the threat of breaking up the kaḅisu seriously, but the proposed outcomes are revealing nonetheless. P is nearly entirely Christian and maintains neither the rites for R nor, by and large, the beliefs to which they refer. Furthermore, this religion is not a superficial imposition; P was one of the first kaḅisu to achieve a Christian majority, and many adults had been raised from the start in Christian households. Their main settlements are close to the main road and marketplace. Drawing on the vocabulary of national development, they compare themselves favorably to the "backward" (Indo. terbelakang) "village folk" (Indo. orang kampung) of other kaḅisu. The members of this meeting have little doubt of the antiquity of their shared valuable, but they are not overly impressed with its sacred qualities, nor do they much fear ancestral wrath. They do, however, insist on R's importance. To do so, they use the language of functionalism and representation: R is a "sign of unity." This interests me especially because they are willing to entertain the possibility, however rhetorical, of serious social rupture, even though they seem to have rejected the overt cosmological model that would explain it. It is in part because of such incidents that I have stressed practices here, rather than attempting to rest my observations, finally and entirely, on an account of Anakalangese "beliefs." Having sat through several meetings in P, I am inclined to say that the kabisu members accept widely differing explanations, from those who really do fear ancestral wrath to those who would treat the mamuli as a "merely symbolic" instrument for political ends, something that can be replaced. Probably most men and women in P are not sure *what* to believe. Yet few are willing, at least publicly, to suggest that R does not matter.

How inalienable ancestral valuables like R matter is in part a function of their relation to both the reality of kabisu and the flow of *other* objects through the lives of kabisu members. Their importance provides an insight into what is at stake in the play and the hazards of encounter. Inalienable valuables form one response to the challenge that political economy poses for iterable order and that the demands of authority impose on action. Like similar objects in many societies, they offer a partial exemption from the risks of interaction. Furthermore, they form a third step in the transformations by which Anakalangese construct themselves as agents that transcend the present time and place, and the gendered, mortal persons to be found there. As exchange involves objects that have been elevated beyond the immediacy of bodily labor and consumption, so inalienable valuables form objects that have been elevated beyond the flow of exchange and the division between affines. They suggest that something can be reserved from and accumulated out of the ongoing activities of persons, by which living individuals can be finally and definitively identified with dual-gendered ancestral powers and immortal kabisu.

I will begin, however, by discussing a pervasive component of Anakalangese identities, the spirit (dewa). If inalienable valuables condense both the promise and the difficulty of objectification at the level of collectivities, both promise and difficulty are also at issue in the ongoing life of each person's dewa. The concept of dewa condenses much of contemporary Anakalangese understandings about the relations between speaker and speech, possessor and possessions, action and its outcomes. The strength and well-being of one's dewa are what is most immediately at stake in interaction. Then I will turn to the efforts to escape or transcend the uncertainties and instabilities of a social existence that demands interaction with others, mediated by words and things. These include the elusive notions of gain from sources outside of society and value without the hazards of interaction with others.

## ATTRACTING THE FLOW OF THINGS:
## THE CONCEPT OF DEWA

The scene of encounter is the focus of sociability at its most public and most diagrammatically agonistic. It provides the occasion at which skills are tested, reputations challenged, economic and political powers put into play. Gifts bear the potential for creating relations of dependency, and so social standing, autonomy, and, ultimately, identity stand or fall in the verbal mastery of claims and responses. Not all exchanges are equally authoritative. Incompetent performance, for example, can end up setting into motion objects only partially able to represent their donors, their power over the recipient diffused, the resulting ties between participants ambiguous. Such weak transactions are unable to link one moment of exchange to others in the future and threaten to turn into barter—or to form asymmetric bonds of dependency. This may also mean that the exchange does not contribute to the participants' capacities to engage with *other* groups, thus failing to situate a given dyadic transaction productively in outward-expanding lines of further transactions.

The outcomes of exchange are commonly expressed by Anakalangese in terms of the strengthening or weakening of the transactors' dewa, or spirit. Dewa is not only a principle of life but also the basis of people's innate relationship to objects, of successful interactions, and, one might say, their charismatic ability to attract or otherwise move others. Dewa can be variously glossed as (a) spirit, (the) soul, fortune, fate, life force, or reproductive potential.[2] Onvlee ([1957] 1973b: 211–212) interprets the term as "that in a man through which he is as he is, . . . his character and to an important degree, also his appointed fate," and that which differentiates one person from others.[3] The latter remark is especially insightful, for dewa seems to characterize the conjunction between material circumstances, the trajectory taken by men's and women's lives over time, and the distinguishing features of their identities. It has often been remarked of societies in which exchange is important that people are prone to narrate their biographies as a series of objects received and given (e.g., Thomas 1991: 30). This is certainly true of Anakalang. But such narratives are more than sequences of discrete instances; they are stories with a direction, the growing triumph or failure of the person's dewa.

People's accounts of the nuances of dewa vary greatly, ritual specialists usually providing the most detailed and esoteric versions.[4] My interest lies more in the everyday discourse of dewa. In particular, I wish to show what light the concept of dewa casts on the stakes of exchange and on concerns that are shared even by the many Anakalangese Christians who do not accept, or even know, much about the spirit world. The discourse of dewa is often a way of talking about that which connects subjects and objects, persons and possessions. There is a strong interactive dimension to this, for the state of a person's dewa is the most reasonable explanation of the actions of other persons toward him or her. As a prayer says quite explicity, one's dewa (or that of one's ancestors) should cause others to

| jiaka boru regi | pour out men's cloth |
| jiaka boru lawu | pour out sarongs |
| | |
| jiaka raba kawu | pour forth buffalo |
| jiaka raba jara | pour forth horses |

As Ubu Joka put it to me when discussing how mortuary prayers appeal to the dewa of the recently deceased, 'Just as we drive the fish out from their hiding place under the rock, so the dewa of the dead person goes and moves the hearts of others so that even if they don't want to give anything, they come anyway, their things come to us.' Similarly, it is a forebear's dewa, "who has debts afar, who has debts nearby" (*na ma wuta ma marau, na ma wuta ma marani*), that goes along when you try to collect debts from others. Your success is due to its power. These examples express the common perception that the generosity of one's partners and the ease with which one enters into exchanges with them are effects of one's *own*, or a closely affiliated, dewa. As expressing a desire to resist others' autonomy, this perception seems to find an echo in Emerson's remark, "We can receive anything from love, for that is a way of receiving it *from ourselves*" ([1844] 1983: 94; emphasis mine). In Anakalang, that incoming goods manifest the strength of one's dewa was the complaint of one man who told me why his kiosk had failed: 'If you give people credit, they'll just feel honored, and won't feel any need to repay the debt.'

An important aspect of dewa is its role in mediating between the labor and wealth of the living and their relations to the dead. Perhaps somewhat like Polynesian *mana* (Keesing 1984), the dewa represents the intervention by some external force that is needed if individual efforts, such as reproduction, are to be fruitful. Attempts to control the flow of valuables and part of their meaning hinge on the way Anakalangese understand the relationship between wealth and human subjects. Central to this understanding is the basic assumption that people's control of resources is more than economic happenstance. While everyone understands the need for intelligent strategy and hard work, actual outcomes depend as well on a wide range of contingencies, from the fertility of marriages and the plentitude of the rains to the temperaments of exchange partners. Underlying the success and failure of strategy and work are more fundamental resources. Mortuary rites, for example, work to restore the dewa of the deceased to the house, to remain close to the living.[5] The two main, and conceptually intertwined, effects of this proximity are wealth and fertility. The dewa of the most recently deceased generation are based in the sleeping chamber, where the living conceive children. Similarly, the ordinary work of individual bodies is unlikely to produce greater results (wealth and strong alliances, for instance) unassisted. The dewa of recent ancestors are responsible for the wealth-producing outcome of labor and in this function bear the epithet "dewa of riches, dewa of making" (*dewa poti, dewa wolu*). They are beseeched in ritual, "in order that the buffalo corrals, the horse corrals, the basket (of cloth), be cool." Effort is necessary as well, Anakalangese realize, but experience shows that it is not sufficient to assure worldly success.

In contrast to functionalist explanations, however, these accounts of dewa do not serve simply as, for example, rationalizations of that which cannot be controlled. By making wealth meaningful, they help explain why it should harmonize with status, greatness, and personal influence over other people. Wealth or its absence should not be simple economic happenstance but part of one's place in a greater world, both cosmological and political. Any increase or decrease in people's powers of exchange is evidence of the relative strength of their dewa. One of the most common ways in which people talk about dewa is as it registers the effects of material interaction on the person. By way of example, Ubu Dongu told me,

> To not be given betel, that's like killing the child's dewa. If I go to a feast and my child isn't given an offering dish as well as me, there should be sanctions. This goes for betel, coffee, meat, everything.

He went on to explain the effects of objects on dewa this way:

> If we push away good fortune (*yularu kanyuru*), in the end, it'll just keep on like that, until we're old. There'll no longer be any good fortune. Like if I refuse a colt because I want a bigger horse, then the giver won't want to give anymore. Whatever there is, we have to receive it. But if the dewa is fitting, even my ailing horse will thrive. It's not because of us, but because its place is good. If we push away good fortune, it's not a fellow human whom we push away, but God. So He withdraws (his support). We have to foster (our good fortune).

The condition of bad dewa becomes self-perpetuating. According to Ubu Sebu,

> If your dewa always rejects good fortune, good fortune wants to enter, but it doesn't because the dewa isn't fitting. Not because of anything I do on purpose. People want to enter, bring valuables, but our hair whorls aren't matching, maybe the husband's is fitting but not that of the wife, so that person doesn't come in, bring those valuables. So that, as long as you remain in that household, you're between life and death. . . . If my wife's hair whorl (*kawuluru*) isn't good, then whatever I receive won't stop by in the house, it goes straight out again. Not only will we not be able to keep hold of the animals we receive in exchange, but even the animals we already have will go, like they might die on us . . . (but if they are fitting, *pahama kawuluru*), if my wife gives to me so I'm strong to go out, like if I'm invited somewhere, before I go, I eat my wife's rice, then I will be given things. . . . The signs of this condition are that you always have good fortune when you go out, you never have dreams, these are signs that husband and wife are fitting. Like me. If I'm angry, my wife is silent. If my wife is angry, I'm silent.

Such talk about matching dewa of husband and wife is among the most direct ways in which I have heard people in Anakalang acknowledge the role of household production in the creation and transmission of value. The concrete form by which Ubu Sebu and others exemplify the condition of matching dewa refers to the wife's role in the household fortune. 'For instance, if I am fitting with my wife, then she's good at raising pigs and so forth, then we will receive horses and they won't go out (i.e., into other people's corrals) any longer.' This comment reveals two assumptions. One is that it collapses the distinction between production (raising pigs) and the outcomes of exchange (the circulation of horses). The other is that it treats the successful household as a single unit. To stress a distinction between male and female would display fissions in the light of failure. The relationship between husband and wife should be "horses of matching dewa, dogs of matching fate-lines." Significantly, it locates the source of value, not in the work of individual, sexually differentiated bodies, but in the immaterial character of a dual-gendered married couple. Working together, this pair can face other households, each constructed in the context of exchange as a single agent, whose "gender" (e.g., as yera or ngàba wini) takes the forms of representations: products, circulating goods, and spoken couplets.

## DEWA AND VICISSITUDE

Acting on the principle "don't push away good fortune," ratu Bura, one of the two men I knew who didn't smoke, would always accept a cigarette if offered and park it behind his ear. In simple terms, to reject good fortune is insulting to the donor, and people often warned me never to turn down food, coffee, betel, or tobacco. But it also has consequences for oneself, which will be manifest in stingy partners, the obstacles they pose, and the feelings of shame to which these give rise, all evidence that one's own dewa is weak. Failure in exchange may also be a function of the relation between the dewa of husband and wife. One man put it to me this way: people want to give you things, but your dewa refuses them, this is "hindered dewa" (*patipang dewa*). That is, the concept of dewa expresses the charismatic principle by which the actions of *others* are assimilated to *oneself*—and thus both the negative and positive outcomes of risk.

But dewa does not exist in the abstract. It is both manifest in and causally bound up with the media, speech and objects, by which persons are represented to and recognized by others. Powerful speakers possess powerful dewa. When, as described in chapter 5, ratu Kadi collapsed while performing a ritual, he showed the weakness of his dewa, as well as a lack of support from his father's dewa, which did not accompany him as he spoke the prayers. As in other forms of objectified charisma, the relationship between material interaction and dewa is circular, because the state of the dewa that results has further consequences. One who is affronted comes away with the feeling of a "small dewa" (*meduku dewa*). As Ubu Rebu put it,

> When we gather, such a person walks timidly, doesn't speak up, like if he comes to our house, he doesn't directly climb up on the veranda where we sit and stick out his hand, but creeps along to the far end and sits there. . . . If the regent visits the desa office, such a person goes behind everyone and slips into the rear of the group, rather than entering in front and going up to him, offering his hand, and saying hello. Or if he makes a conveyance oration, his enunciation isn't right. Or his clothing isn't suitable.

Such a person lacks self-respect, doesn't know his or her "own value" (*wili wikina*). Gifts strengthen the dewa. For example, during a wake, Rabu Riti, a visiting mourner, stumbled as she was stepping down out of the house. The host immediately jumped up, grabbed a cloth from the pile of cloths brought by visitors, and placed it on her shoulder, saying it was "for wiping up the blood." This move was meant to "raise her dewa" and prevent it from being "startled" into flight.[6]

Dewa is thus a way of conceptualizing not only one's relations to others and to material possessions but also one's own self-possession. A lost dewa leads one to be inattentive or to faint, or more seriously, lose one's sense of propriety or one's good fortune. The concept of dewa thus expresses the role that others play in one's own sense of self. To be embarrassed, startled, or insulted is to lose some of one's dewa.[7] Like insult, embarrassment is a product of interaction gone wrong, a denial of recognition that displays the effects that *others* have on one's *own* self-possession. The weakening of dewa *because* of interaction may in turn *produce* further affronts in the future. When Ubu Kabàlu was roughed up and spoken to harshly by a government cattle inspector, for example, he sponsored a large feast to "make the spirit return" (*pahalungu hamangu*). This meant inviting affines and kaḅisu fellows, so that the flow of prestations into the village—and the display of his supporters' regard for him—would restore him to himself. If a weakened dewa brings about weakened material well-being, increasing the flow of goods through one's hands should strengthen one's dewa.

The concept of dewa condenses ideas about identity, self-respect and public esteem, life, the efficaciousness of effort, and material wealth. It is not simply that a strong dewa brings wealth or that wealth is merely the expression of a distinct principle of charisma. Wealth and dewa are both resources and products, both simultaneously displayed and generated in interactions. The concept of dewa, then, may serve to represent a wider set of concerns that underlie the significance and power of interaction in Anakalang. Dewa seems to provide a way of talking about the claims that persons (as possessors) have on things and that things (as prestations and ancestral valuables) have on persons.[8] Moreover, it expresses the capacity of a person or a group to have agency or act as a social subject, to have differential identity, to possess self-respect, reputation, and effectiveness in relations to social others and to the material world. The dewa links that capacity both to the actions of other living persons and to one's own relations with the dead—and thus to the ways in which individuals and their actions extend both across social

space and back through time. Lying behind the elaboration of ceremonial encounters and the significance of exchange valuables is the fact that
scenes of encounter with others, human and spirit, generate, and are in
turn affected by, the growing or declining powers of dewa. If discussions of "the gift" often stress the animation of the object, the circularity I am describing should bring out as well the objectualization of the
animate.

## BEYOND RISK

In conceptual terms, the discourse of dewa provides a partial explanation for why wealth, cosmological power, and rank should covary.
In practical terms, the regulatory effects of pata work to assure that
the flow of valuables, the possession of power, and the legitimacy of ancestral actions correlate with one another. In principle, wealth is a simple function of rank, since both manifest powerful dewa. The problems
arise in practice: the display of wealth (stacks of horns, great herds,
large stone tombs) is available to anyone who can accumulate property,
and high birth in itself does not necessarily provide one with sufficient
means to display all the signs of wealth. Thus rank's conventional objective forms expose it to the risk that what wealth indexes will not be
rank. To some extent, for example, rank is vulnerable to the assaults of
the newly rich, a consequence of objectification itself (as one wunang
said to me with scorn, 'Nowadays even garden people want to demand
one hundred head of cattle in marriage'). Numerous sumptuary regulations and beliefs, such as the claim that bridewealth in excess of that
appropriate for the bride's rank will be dangerously "hot," seek to control this risk.[9] Nonetheless, such efforts to control the relationship between wealth and rank cannot be fully successful. To the extent that
hierarchy is embodied in its objectifications, it is affected by the vicissitudes to which objects are prone. These include vagaries of material circumstance such as infertility, disease, and crop failure, as well as shifting political and economic fortunes. The concept of dewa means that
misfortune may lead people retrospectively to reevaluate others' claims
to ancestral authority.

The most prominent hazards to which the dewa is prone are effects
of interaction. They reflect the threat implicit in each participant's dependence on recognition by others. Indeed, since drought, disease, and
other such misfortunes are likely to be attributed to ancestral anger, they
too can be understood interactively. Bound up with representational

acts, the hazards registered by dewa also express the possibility that words and things either will not affect their recipient as desired or will fail adequately to represent the person who wields them (for instance, as misunderstood speech or as unreciprocated or lost goods). Anakalangese often see this in agonistic terms: one person's or group's dewa can humiliate (*pawawa*) or beat (*talu*) another's in contests (largely male) of speaking skill, prowess, or exchange. The challenge that affines pose to one another can be spoken of in these terms as well. A man might attribute his success in obtaining another's daughter to the strength of his dewa, which bests that of the parents' putative desire to hold onto her.

This agonistic view of social interaction reveals something fundamental about the dewa. Talk about dewa appears to be a way of simultaneously acknowledging and overcoming the mutual dependence between persons. By attributing the generosity of others to one's own dewa, one is able to claim *their* acts as attributes of *oneself*. At the same time, such claims face practical limits. As I have noted above, many Anakalangese complain about the pressures of exchange, as people relentlessly come asking them for support, while at the same time they find themselves in constant need to sway still others for assistance. Such complaints bring out a common ambivalence about the continual flow of valuables. No matter how much Anakalangese may celebrate the Maussian obligations to give, to receive, and to reciprocate, the idea of an escape from exchange may carry a subversive appeal even for those most invested in its values. This is one variation on the dream that Lévi-Strauss ([1949] 1969: 497) describes, "that the law of exchange could be evaded, that one could gain without losing, enjoy without sharing." This fantasy need not be understood only in the parsimonious terms of a shopkeeper out of Balzac or other distinctively "modern" or "Western" individuals. In Anakalang, it expresses something intrinsic to the way in which representational practices constitute social subjects that extend beyond the particularities of the moment. An important dimension of the Anakalangese sense of nobility is captured by Aristotle's description of the great-souled man as

> one who will possess beautiful and profitless things rather than profitable and useful ones; for this is more proper to a character that suffices to itself. Further, a slow step is thought proper to the proud man, a deep voice, and a level utterance; for the man who takes few things seriously is not likely to be hurried, nor the man who thinks nothing great to be excited, while a shrill voice and a rapid gait are the results of hurry and excitement. (*Nichomachean Ethics* 1125a 11–16)

Aristotle's view of a great soul is predicated not only on the display of distance from necessity but also on self-containment and the denial of interaction with others. The bodily correlatives of this, the slow step and level utterance, are ones with which most Anakalangese nobles (and aristocrats in many other societies; Bourdieu [1979] 1984; Irvine 1974) would also concur: they are marks of a person who is free of unfulfilled desire. In Anakalang, however, the status of such great persons cannot ultimately be grounded in an abstract realm separate from material embodiments. Part of what is at stake is suggested by Simmel ([1907] 1990: 102) as he imagines the linkage between the autonomy of subjects and that of objects:

> Just as we think that we can find within ourselves . . . a final authority which is independent of the outside world; and just as we distinguish this being from the existence and character of our thoughts, experiences and development which are real and confirmable only through relations with others—so we seek in the world substances, entities, and forces whose being and significance rest exclusively within them . . . (and seek) what is steadfast and reliable behind ephemeral appearances and the flux of events; and to advance from mutual dependence to self-sufficiency.

Note that Simmel conjoins here a temporal dimension (the flux of events) and a social dimension (mutual dependence). In this view, it is interaction with others that exposes both subjects and objects to the hazards of flux. In Anakalang, the autonomy of objects is more than an analogy to that of persons. Great dewa and great rank must bear objective forms, and therein lies the rub. Although possessions promise to stabilize the claims of their owners, as material objects they also multiply the hazards of social and economic life by exposing those claims to mere physical contingency such as loss and destruction.

However much the concept of dewa appropriates the actions of others to oneself, it still leaves the subject open to the hazards of social interaction. The rest of this chapter considers two alternatives to exchange. The first, the ancestral valuable, embodies the possibility of holding something back from exchange altogether. The second, the demonic spirit familiar, represents the possibility of obtaining wealth from sources outside the world of human relations. The first focuses on potent subjects that transcend the fates of individuals, the second on individuals at their starkest and most asocial. The first is legitimating but often burdensome, the second attractive and illicit. Both involve some element of danger.

## ANCESTRAL VALUABLES

The most important and most legitimate exemption from exchange is found in the existence of inalienable objects, the "marapu's portion" (*tagu marapu*), which I will call "ancestral valuables." These are enduring, concrete manifestations of the ancestors.[10] Identified with the kabisu who own them, their singularity is marked by personal names. These names are usually either those of the ancestors themselves or those of ancestral slaves. Like the latter, they both embody and substitute for a less visible master, the ancestral couple. Nearly all ancestral valuables are carefully stored in the leading houses of the kabisu's ancestral village or, if the house no longer stands, in a neighboring house. They are kept in boxes, in baskets, or, in a few cases, inside a sacred drum, either in the inner sleeping room or in the attic.[11] In most cases, they should never be seen except under special ritual precautions. Anakalangese sometimes speak of them as the true inhabitants of the ancestral houses and justify the houses' need for continuity in terms of the ongoing care that valuables require. Even house sites fall empty, but their virtual persistence is embedded in the continued existence of their valuables under other roofs. As one ratu put it to me, 'Caves seem empty, but every cave has its swallows.' The valuables demand attention, and numerous misfortunes are attributed to their neglect.[12]

The virtual persistence and potential danger of valuables are exemplified in a ritual I attended in June 1986. The hilltop village of K had been uninhabited since before the Second World War, by which time the entire population had moved down to be closer to sources of water, their fields, or the roadside. Nonetheless, the ancestral valuables remained, in the form of gold that had been stored in existing dwellings and lightning stones left behind in a case inside a crevice at the village site. Through the years members of K occasionally felt that the valuables were appealing to their owners to restore them to their true residence. As usual, this appeal took the form of misfortunes—cattle struck by lightning, children constantly ill, recurrent droughts—until finally the owners, with some prodding by dreams, responded to the appeal. A divination rite established the source of the misfortunes, and several conferences hammered out a plan of action, despite the participants' repeated insistence on their ignorance of true pata, that they were but "new lips and new eyes." Summoning their main affines for support, they built a temporary shelter for the ritualists on the site of their senior house. There then ensued several weeks of ritual activity. Like other

major rituals in Anakalang, most of the time, effort, and expense were
devoted to public performances. Every night dancers filled the plaza,
while a crowd of kabisu fellows, affines, and neighbors watched from
the edges. The dance was punctuated by oratory contributed by members of the kabisu and representatives of yera and ngàba wini. The oratory consisted of highly allusive accounts of ancestral history and the
misfortunes behind the present rite: that they had suffered from "the
one who slashes with his horn, who strikes with his tail." From the visiting orators came general expressions of support for the kabisu and respect for pata. Day and night, a long sequence of prayers and offerings
accompanied each step as the valuables were informed of what was happening and why and a new shelter was constructed for them. Although
more esoteric than the dances, these rites were held openly in the front
room of the house. But the culminating, critical moment was hidden
from all but a small number of ratus. The latter were required to undertake the dangerous task of removing the valuables from their dark
storage place. Shielded behind cloth screens and immersed in waves of
sound from gongs and singers, the ratus washed them in ritually "cool"
water, anointed them with coconut oil, as one told me, "like bodies,"
then "fed" them offerings. (So dangerous are these valuables that on
another occasion I could see that the ratu who had to handle them was
shaking with fright.) At last, themselves shrouded in cloth, the ratus in-
stalled the valuables in their new home. Finally, a row of pigs was sacrificed to send the gathered spirits away. It may be a lifetime before
these valuables emerge again, and even when they do so, few people
will ever see them. Nonetheless, everyone is fully aware of their continuous power-filled presence in the dark.

The materiality of ancestral valuables has both temporal and spatial
features. It links the present day, in which they persist, with the past,
from which they have come. It also makes spatially distant origins
physically (if usually invisibly) present. And it permits ancestral power
to inhabit distinct spatial locations from which some places (e.g., hamlets
and pastures) are more distant than others (great villages).[13] In everyday
talk, ancestral valuables are often mentioned at the end of narratives as
a clinching remark. For example, the youngest of the three founding
brothers of Anakalang, Ubu Kawolu, was thrown by his older brothers
into a cave and left for dead, but his mother tossed a knife down after
him to help him survive. When people tell this story, they characteristi-
cally conclude by pointing out that his descendants still hold that knife
to this day. Another kabisu, Doku Watu (Shoulders Stone), claims to

have wielded the lightning that shattered the stone bridge by which the ancestors had crossed the sea to Sumba. A piece of the stone bridge, people add, remains in that village. Such objects often testify to superior but now lost ancestral powers: a spear that could strike open the ground to create springs, another that was used to cross the ocean, an ax that cut an enormous tree and cleared the village site. A few legitimate more contemporary assertions. For example, Makatakeri holds a miniature headhunting altar (*adung*) of iron, complete with tiny heads, as iconic support of its claim to mastery over the lapsed headhunting ritual for the cluster of kabisu associated with Lai Tarung. But all that is known of many ancestral valuables, such as Ubu Pabal's "banner," a small, tattered piece of foreign cloth, is that they were carried by the ancestor on the collective trek across the seven levels of sea and eight levels of sky, finally coming to rest deep within the house. And the bulk of these are otherwise ordinary gold ornaments.

Since ancestral valuables come from distant, unknown, or uncanny origins, they exaggerate a property common to cloth and iron valuables, their distance from (or their extraordinary power to supplement) local, bodily labor. The positive insistence that the present holders of ancestral valuables have received them in an unbroken chain from the time of origins implies a negative aspect as well. Ancestral valuables, like tombs, index a significant absence. For example, the spear kept in Lai Tarung is the "shadow," a synecdoche and diminished representative of Ubu Dangu, its original owner and the founder of the village. More than that, it indexes as well the missing sheath, which Dangu left behind in Tarung, a village in Loli, where he had previously stopped on his ancestral trek. The importance of absence to which such valuables point lies in one of the dilemmas of power already evident in the tension between textual and contextual dimensions of ritual speech. The remnant testifies to an originating event, yet its present immobility results from the lack of further events—at least of the same kind.

Ancestral valuables provide metonymic ties to nonrepeatable events that lie at the origin of a social identity that should, nonetheless, extend into the future. As metonyms, these objects represent the continued presence of the past, but they also imply its absence as well: they are, as people sometimes say, substitutes or replacements (*na hepanya*) for ancestral bodies, and people insist, "It wasn't *we* who made them." Like slaves, tokens in the offering dish, and ritual speakers, they are representatives, signs (tada), that imply the existence of something whose value or power is evident in the very fact that it is not immediately manifest. By replacing the ancestral body (which they do not even resemble), they also elevate it by a kind of disembodiment, transforming it into an undying and unmoving representation. In contrast to exchange valuables, which, as bonds and debts, presume a future in which they will remind people of the present event, ancestral valuables remind people in the present of past events.[14]

When Anakalangese speak of objects as the basis for a kabisu's identity and the efficient cause of its ritual actions, this may involve an element of deferential dissimulation, similar to the insistence that they only act in order to fulfill ancestral mandates. But to the extent that they attribute serious misfortune to the neglect of these objects and work hard to keep guardians in the houses that hold them, their words cannot be dismissed as only rhetorical. In fact, even many Christians who are skeptical about the spirits worry about their ancestral valuables. What might the pragmatics and semiotics of objects tell us about what is at stake in them for kabisu? Annette Weiner (1992: 33) writes, "What makes a possession inalienable is its exclusive and cumulative identity with a particular series of owners through time." A "particular series of owners" seems to presuppose as given the existence of some social identity. But recall that membership in Anakalangese kabisu is not defined in terms of biological reproduction, which is largely in the hands of yera. The transmission of the line depends on a number of factors, notably, but not exclusively, the outcome of marriage exchanges. Some sons leave to enter their wives' families, and other people's sons are incorporated through in-marriage, adoption, and adrogation. What, then, counts as a series and consolidates the identity over time of the successive owners by which the inalienability of the valuable is determined? How does that sequence of owners differ from other chains of ownership, such as those mediated by gift, theft, or purchase? In Anakalang, the objects themselves play an important role in constructing the continuity of social identities. As the debate over the loss of the mamuli R at the beginning of this chapter suggests, the very existence of the kabisu is predicated in part on the existence of its valuables.[15] As one man said, during a conference to plan a ritual in Parewatana,

> (As for) the Great House, if there is that, what's-it-called (i.e., the ancestral valuable) that we use to watch over the house, it means that's what makes us stand (strong). The village land dewa, the river mouth dewa (i.e., the dewa of the village), if we put the contents of the house there (the ancestral valuable), it means that's what we use to guard the house, that's what makes our food firm, makes our betel firm, makes our standing firm, makes our clothing firm, that's what it's about.

The house is built in order to shelter them and provide a site for their rituals. Priestly offices are maintained in part to provide them with offerings in rituals, and when young men are incorporated from outside, it is so that someone will inherit the valuables and take over their rites. Except where Christianity has become dominant, the major rites gather together the kabisu's scattered households even more extensively than marriage exchanges or funerals.

Ancestral valuables provide an enduring, objectified core to kabisu identity, but they also bear an important conceptual relationship to the ongoing activities of encounter and exchange. Exchange valuables display the extent and wealth of their current holders' alliances, as chains of active, contemporaneous relationships that follow female bloodlines outward through society. In contrast, inalienable valuables, like house sites, land claims, and tombs, ideally testify to the enduring temporal depth of the group that holds them, through series of husband-wife pairs, socially located in one place, that extend backward to a founding moment. Unlike a kabisu's house sites, rice fields, and tombs, however, it is a material property of ancestral valuables to be potentially mobile. Moreover, few ancestral valuables are physically distinguishable from objects that do circulate. Rather, what pragmatically sets them apart from circulating objects is their hidden, immobile state and the periodic rituals that sustain their ties to the living. These, along with the knowledge that some valuables have in fact been lost or set back into motion, through destruction in fire, capture in war, theft, or overwhelming exchanges (Geirnaert-Martin 1989: 460), give forceful meaning to their continued possession.

Objects whose circulation has been brought to a halt form an important conceptual counterpoint to consumption, the marketplace, and exchange. As demonstrated when Ubu Pàda held onto the cloth I gave him and when Ubu Ngailu promised to keep the cloth his brother had given him when making peace, to hold back an object is to exert control over the flow of things, demonstrating a capacity to divert some items from circulation. A similar test of the unassailability of a man's status is the ability to declare a certain possession out of bounds for exchange by dedicating it to the ancestors. Even a staunch Christian like old Pak Cornelis declared his favorite stallion to be a "marapu horse" (*jara marapu*), to be reserved until killed for his funeral feast. When Pak Cornelis speaks of "marapu" in this context, he appeals less to a realm of spiritual agents than to a notion of transcendence, the possibility of superseding the immediate demands of social interaction. The presence of the ancestral valuable in the house indexes a similar, presupposable, moment at which someone was able to arrest its motion. In displaying halted motion as a sign of power, ancestral valuables manifest a principle of kabisu autonomy. The ancestral valuable seems to offer a source of authority that exists independent of the never-ending encounter with affines and the hazards of exchange by which lifeblood and reputation are acquired.[16] The assimilation of valuable objects to transcendent sources of authority is reinforced by their invisibility. Ancestral valuables, unlike exchange goods, are hidden from the appreciative, desiring, or calculating eyes of others. Because they are known but not experienced, they are appropriate media for identities that transcend phenomenal experience, the kabisu identities that persist across space and time.

Ancestral valuables imply not simply stasis and lack of interaction but also the never-realized potential for complete self-sufficiency. The basket in which the ancestral valuables are kept is called "the warm basket, the warm room." The same term applies to the sleeping chamber in which the basket is often kept. The usual explanation is that the sleeping chamber is where the sexual acts of generations of forebears have taken place: as such, it is the site of biological reproduction and, more specifically, of that biological reproduction that counts socially, the regeneration of the house itself. Self-reproduction is, of course, impossible. As everyone in Anakalang knows, blood must be obtained in marriages that require encounters with others, outside the kabisu. Affines are inescapable. But at least, through their occasional participation in the ritual bathing of ancestral valuables, they can be momentarily subordinated to the persistence and distinctiveness claimed by the kabisu. By associating ancestral valuables with reproduction, the kabisu seems to be using a logic similar to that of dewa, discursively appropriating for itself the outcomes of interactions with others.

In the process, ancestral valuables assert the agency of the kabisu in its own reproduction in the face of its ongoing debt to yera as the true source of blood and, by metonymy, life. The objects hidden in the sleeping chamber speak of an alternative: just as the concept of dewa seeks to appropriate for the subject the outcomes of interactions with others, so, too, the ancestral valuables covertly locate the wellsprings of kabisu continuity at home, apart from external alliances. These valuables are identified with the risks of interaction successfully run and transformed into the power to retain objects against the flow and hazards of exchange. Such powers manifest the transcendance promised by kabisu. In exchanges, kabisu act as either yera or ngàba wini. As represented by their valuables, they exist as representations of ancestral married couples, their powers detached from the sexual dimorphism, work, and mortality of bodily individuals.

## RENEWAL AND RECOGNITION

Ancestral valuables substantiate the existence and persistent effects of nonrepeatable events. They do so by proving that something has endured from the past. The proof works not in the legal sense of a document, or in the genealogical sense of a bloodline, or, entirely, in the historical sense of evidence. Rather, the present possession of the valuable indexes not just a prior event but also the continuity of some social body that has been able to hold onto it in the face of the vagaries of political, economic, and demographic fortune. Although inalienable valuables represent the kabisu's claims to ancestral identity and power, these claims display a tension similar to that between transcendent texts and contextual actions implicit in the use of ritual speech. In both cases, living persons simultaneously claim to participate in that ancestral agency and situate it apart from themselves. As the discussion of dewa suggests, possession is a problematic relationship. By lying apart from persons, ancestral valuables require constant effort to keep them bound to the living people to whom they belong—or, perhaps, who belong to them.

Ancestral valuables thus exemplify the terms of the Hegelian dialectic that underlie the concept of interaction I discussed in chapter 1. The process of self-objectification involves two moments. The moment of externalization requires a second moment, that of sublation, by which the object is reappropriated by the subject. If the ancestral valuable serves as an indexical link that mediates between the living and the dead, it can only do so by virtue of recurrent activities by which the living assert their relationship to these valuables. These activities are rituals, icons of original ways of speaking and doing that were created by the ancestors to whom they are addressed. These acts thereby index the claims of the living to be legitimate heirs and vulnerable "descendants" (*susu-ana*) who deserve the protection and fostering of those whom they address. The living represent themselves, through ritual performances defined in reference to pata, as merely repeating rulelike actions, actions that can be repeated yet again in the future. In this way, their acts imply that it is not by mere happenstance that they hold these valuables. Rather, by treating the valuables in ritualized ways, with reference to the iterability of their acts, they assert their authority to hold them. As people who know how to follow pata, they claim the valuables because of who they are, true members of their kaḅisu, proper followers of ancestral footsteps—a quality that transcends any given moment, particular event, or individual actors. It is these activities, not just the facts of biological descent or even physical control of kaḅisu property, that work to make presupposable a relationship between living and dead. If all goes well, the valuables will remain quiet, as silent guarantors of reputation, successful exchanges, good crops, plenty of children. If, however, their living guardians fail to keep up their end of the relationship, the valuables will remind them of their potential separateness. Rather than, as it were, standing by their side, the valuables will confront their owners. Some valuables are known to have moved around by themselves. For example, there was a kaḅisu that had been forced by overwhelming debt to give one of its valuables to another. But the valuable continuously banged around in the box where the new owners stored it, finally frightening them into returning it to its rightful owners. Like the workings of dewa, such agency testifies to the legitimacy of the links between persons and possessions (see also Hoskins 1993b: 135–136). Most commonly, however, it is by assailing the living with misfortunes that valuables remind them that they have an agency of their own.

Ancestral valuables are more than simply one legal category of property among others. It is the *overlay* of their several dimensions—as traces, reminders, legitimating documents, distinguishing marks, and objects withheld from circulation—that makes ancestral valuables so powerful. This multifaceted character is brought out in Weiner's (1992) discussion of inalienable possessions, which, she argues, embody a response to universal problems of social existence introduced by historical change and biological realities of loss. In the face of these, inalienable valuables do a number of things: they hold memories, authenticate claims to ancestral powers, mark social difference, attract circulating valuables, disguise impermanence, symbolize female productive and reproductive powers, and facilitate the development of hierarchy by permitting accumulation. Since holding onto them requires work, skill, and sometimes even danger (Weiner 1992: 39), we can add to the list that their mere possession already indexes an achievement. To hold onto an object is an achievement, however, not simply because time exposes all human endeavors to loss. There is a more specifically social dimension to this achievement as well. Objects mediate interactions with others. In Anakalang, exchange partners form a constant pressure on the capacity of each person, household, or kaḅisu to retain its possessions. This pressure exists not only as an external fact of political economy and self-interested strategies. It is also intrinsic to the construction of social identities, which forces people, through acts of mutual recognition, into dependence on one another. In Anakalangese scenes of encounter, people's capacity to act with authority is a function of their ability to objectify themselves *for others*. But these self-constituting activities require that words and things be separated from their transactors and put into play, at the risk of loss.

Ancestral valuables institutionalize and foreground one particular aspect of the relationship between subject and object, the fact of possession. For Simmel ([1907] 1990: 240), the relationship of ownership reaches its strongest form with collectors and misers, for whom "it is not the quality of the object that is the genuine bearer of value; rather, however much quality is indispensable and determines the measure of the value, the true motivation is the fact of its being possessed, the form of the relationship in which the subject stands to the object." Simmel uses the example of medieval attitudes toward landed property, which he describes as entailing a certain "dignity" over and above utility. Like Aristotle, he asserts that the greatest dignity inheres in the display of independence from (apparent) necessity and desire, thus, from the demands of utility. Anakalangese inalienable valuables display in concrete form a comparable property of self-sufficiency, like that I have already discussed in relation to dewa: lacking either immediate utility or exchange value, they situate at the very heart of social identity an uncertain sign of autonomy.

## DEMONIC VALUE

Like dewa, ancestral valuables represent the effort to both appropriate the outcome of the risks of interaction and imply the limits to that appropriation. There are alternative sources of value, however, which suggest a real avenue of escape, but at a cost few are willing to pay. Since the promise and the risk of demonic familiars (*yora*) have several features in common with those presented by market, money, and government development projects, it is worth juxtaposing them, briefly, to the values of exchange and ancestors. Yora are demonic spirits that individuals encounter, usually in wild places like the forest or pasturelands. The yora will make a pact with this person, promising personal wealth. The person must seal the bargain by making some idiosyncratic commitment, such as taking on a certain food taboo or promising small offerings. The real trade-off, however, can be much more harsh—the death of one's first child, for example. In addition, it is generally assumed that the wealth one obtains from yora cannot be passed on to one's children. Yora not only represent the possibility of wealth from beyond society but also dramatize the threat of loss, and there are many stories about fortunes that have evaporated and predictions of others that will.

It makes sense that such wealth be ephemeral, since it often manifests individual willfulness. Usually people associate yora with men who are especially brazen or ambitious, and who can be expected to be willing to seek them out. The story one young man told me of his own encounter with a yora, however, suggests that wealth has an agency that lies beyond the volition of persons and emphasizes the risks of rejecting good fortune when it is offered to you. It took place in the isolated farmstead where he lived before moving to town to take up a position as a schoolteacher.

> One night I dreamed that three beautiful women came to offer me good fortune. I wanted to refuse. But the next morning, when I went out to relieve myself, I went to my usual spot, but nothing would come out. I went to another, but still nothing would come out. I kept trying new spots, and in this way I circled the corral until I was beside the rock at the center of the hill. There I saw something like the mouth of a snake opening and closing. It turned out to be a big gold chain. I wrapped it in cloth and took it into the house. It writhed in the cloth like a snake. I wrapped it in red cloth and put it in a chest. Soon afterward, a large buffalo cow walked into my corral. It was so tame, it would take salt right out of my hand. So I had my younger brother brand it. Not long after that, my brother died. This was because we hadn't prayed [to spirits] because of this good fortune. Later when Ubu Sima was buried, I buried that gold chain with him (as a mortuary prestation). Then I fled to Waikabubak, because I didn't want to go back to that house. I'd rejected good fortune and now I'm afraid. I told my father not to give away that buffalo cow, but he did anyway. I swore there would be dangerous consequences, and sure enough there were.

Eventually his two brothers went mad because they rejected the offering of the yora.

Yora are at once attractive and illicit because they provide an alternative to the claims of exchange partners. Anakalangese usually also assume that wealth obtained from yora is sterile and will not devolve onto the next generation. Yora thus also represent the possibility, attractive to some, threatening to others, that wealth may be independent of both exchange and inheritance and thus may subvert its coordination with rank. The asocial logic of yora-derived wealth shapes contemporary ideas about government development projects, usually referred to as *proyek*, another source of wealth outside of society. One of the first things I learned in Anakalang was not to describe my work as a "project." The primary connotation of "project" is personal access to apparently unlimited sources of money, given for no evident purpose.[17] Like yora, the "project" is distinguished by the inexplicable entry of money from no comprehensible or stable source. The fact that this wealth is ultimately sterile parallels its lack of indexical grounding in the ongoing scenes of encounter by which more lasting entities are constructed: its lack of legitimate origins is reflected by the lack of a reproductive future.

This is a story of yora, as told to me late one night by Ubu Dewa Damaràka.[18]

> Ubu Nyali Malar had the first egg. Ubu Nyali Malar was going to retrieve a buffalo someone owed him, when he came to the mouth of a cave, where he encountered two snakes fighting. Seeing this, he took a mamuli from his wood purse and broke it in two. He gave one half to each snake. So then the snakes turned into humans (and gave him a chicken). . . . After a while that chicken laid an egg. That egg crowed from inside. Once hatched from the egg, that rooster crowed continuously. Once grown, it kept crowing, (the crowing carried) all the way to Java. Java over there already heard that rooster crow. Now the man came from Java to Bodutera (the village), wanting to buy that chicken. He wanted to buy it with money. Ubu Nyali didn't want to sell it. He said, "Better than that, give me that ring on your finger." The man from Java thought it over. He really wanted that rooster, so, like it or not, he gave the ring. Now he had the rooster, he brought it to Java. So that's why now the president is in Java. That ring is in Bodutera. It had child after child, until they put it in the granary. The granary filled up with gold. Ubu Nyali's slave Mùda ran off to Lewa with that ring. Arriving in Lewa Paku, the same thing happened, it kept having children, put it in the granary, it filled up, put it in another, that filled up too. Until there was no longer any place left. Put it in a cave, it kept having more children, til there was no more room. It's all gold in that cave. So now that's why in Java, it becomes the president, and in Sumba, it's rich in gold. So it's like that rooster: we hear the president wherever we are in Indonesia, otherwise why is the president always from Java?

The fate of Ubu Nyali's gold displays both the promise and the hazards of wealth. Reproducing on its own, it contains the possibility of autonomy and riches beyond the demands of social interaction. Yora, which can also refer to a lover, is (for a man) like a wife, a source of goods, but like a lover, does not embed the man in relations with affines. Nonetheless, it remains detachable from persons and thus vulnerable to loss. Finally, the loss of the rooster forms a microcosmic image of the colonial relation between Sumba and both Dutch and Indonesian rule. The form of the exchange already entails the possibility of loss, an act of straightforward barter that establishes no further relations. The result of this barter makes clear that local claims to wealth and fame now operate against a background of something that has been lost: the political control represented by the president (and linked to masculinity through the conventional figure of the rooster) will always lie elsewhere. By implication, political control is found where gold is not—and, as many Anakalangese tell me, vice versa: for many people, Sumbanese gold represents a source of value that eludes the control of the state. What the temptation and danger of yora suggest is that colonial and postcolonial orders, for all their power and historical specificity, pose problems that, in some respects, may not have been entirely unfamiliar to Anakalangese from the start.

## THE ACTIVITY OF PERSISTENCE

When Walter Benjamin (1969: 220) contrasts the "aura" of a singular work of art to the products of mechanical reproduction, he stresses the materiality that gives the artwork "its presence in time and space, its unique existence . . . (which) determined the history to which it was subject throughout the time of its existence." But if material persistence is necessary, it is not sufficient for an object to mark historical depth. The object must also be distinguishable from others of its kind. Iconism marks ancestral valuables as tokens of ancestral types. As tokens, however, they are interchangeable with other tokens of the same type. The fact that I have cash in my pocket today and likewise had cash a year ago says nothing about the ongoing state of my purse. To serve as present traces of particular pasts is an indexical function: valuables must be linked to *this* kabisu, *this* ancestor, *this* village. Since the majority of ancestral valuables are physically indistinguishable from the valuables that circulate in ordinary exchange, their objectual qualities alone are insufficient to grant them the individuality that marks persistence. Their distinctiveness is produced through spatial restrictions and by the talk that recalls their names and histories and attributes to them current misfortunes. Most authoritatively, it is the ritual acts directed at them that sets them apart.[19] The status granted to those who have been able to hold onto ancestral valuables from the beginning of time is not simply a matter of physical things. It requires ongoing representational practices and their capacity to construct for that authority a presupposable origin and a reproducible outcome. Ritual acts demonstrate that the living need recurrently to respond to the threat that ancestral valuables pose if ignored for too long. The agency of objects is acknowledged by offerings and anointings, acts that demand in turn that the objects, or the spirits they represent, recognize the legitimacy of the humans who claim to possess them. To be recognizable, this legitimacy requires ritual speech, the social cooperation that produces it, and the collective subject that it embodies, with all the costs and compromises these entail.

Despite the normative claim that ancestral valuables are permanent, everyone knows stories about losses. When I undertook a survey of ancestral valuables in 1993, I discovered a large proportion of them are now missing. Some were lost in fire, others as war booty. Some were even jarred loose from their repose by the demands of extraordinary marriage exchanges, as when, a generation ago, the regent married the daughter of the raja of Wanukaka. And increasingly the story is of theft and sale. Recommodified, they become ethnographic curiosities, works of art, or simply so much gold and silver (see Taylor 1994). Although people will portray such events as contingent and aberrant, the possibility of loss is implicit in the very materiality of valuables, which exposes them to alternative destinies. In the absence of ritual obligations, ancestral valuables, like kabisu P's R, are coming increasingly to be reducible to either "arbitrary" (i.e., conventional) symbols of social unity or containers of purely economic value, salable gold.

The effort to endow social identities with the stability and concreteness of valuables simultaneously exposes those identities to some of their vicissitudes. But this exposure is a function of the loss not just of objects but of the activity that binds them to social subjects. These practices involve people in never fully resolvable tensions between text and context, transcendence and contingency, expansiveness and limits. The materiality of objects and the active efforts of subjects expose each to the economic and historical vulnerabilities to which the others are prone.

# CHAPTER NINE

# Conclusion

Certain shared assumptions about the nature of human subjects and societies underlie the concepts of representation, objectification, and alienation found in many accounts of modernity and some criticisms of ethnographic practice. Humanist, Marxist, and poststructuralist writings alike often portray Western modernity as something distinguished by, for example, a radical split between subject and object, the reification of social processes, and self-misrecognition. Conversely, if usually more covertly, this self-portrait stands over against a presupposed background of more authentic alternatives.[1] Perhaps we, if we are "Western" readers, are like Anakalangese in speaking of their own ancestors, when we implicitly contrast our own world to one inhabited by humans endowed with greater efficacy, solidarity, and self-presence than we ourselves possess. Whether such contrasts serve ethical critique or are meant to recall us from the ethnographic present to a more historicized realism, however, they are not well served by oversimplification.

By placing representational practice at the center of this book, I have had several goals. First, taking a cue from the Hegelian tradition, I have sought to examine certain representational practices as forms of objectification, for evidence of how people constitute themselves and act as social subjects. In particular, I have tried to show how representations are embedded within and implicit to the demands of interaction, in circumstances quite different from those that have defined modern Western social and economic organization. The dialectic of interaction means not just that subjects produce themselves through objects, but that objects (and here I refer both to verbal and material forms) must in turn be reincorporated back into the subject. For example, it is not sufficient for a kaḅisu to speak in ritual words, it must also be heard and obtain a reply. That is, it must be recognized by an interlocutor, such as another kaḅisu. As they interact with one another, each kaḅisu evaluates the other's performance—as replicas of ancestral forms, as evidence of that kaḅisu's vitality, and as tokens of the respect that they themselves demand. However formalized, these performances are not just a matter of following rules. It is their semiotic and pragmatic effects that help portray them as actions of people who bear a practical mastery of ancestral ways. That practical mastery in turn depends on the ability to transform the resources of everyday speech and material production in ways that extend beyond the here and now, becoming the stuff of representations. It has therefore been important in this book to pay attention to the details of objects, words, and performances.

One of my goals has thus been to separate representation and objectification from their common associations with either self-estrangement or direct self-expression. At the same time, by emphasizing practice, I have resisted an older ethnographic tendency to see representations as instantiating cultural texts or rules that exist independent of ongoing activity. Thus, on the one hand, if the textualizing moment in ritual speech is not coextensive with action, it is nonetheless a critical component of it. On the other hand, texts and other forms of objectification are not things that we can see *through* or discard in order to arrive at a more authentic human subject or more immediate kind of act. I have thus sought to do justice to both the processual and objectifying dimensions of action. In doing so, I have attempted to provide an (admittedly partial) account of the complex relations both between speaking subjects and their words and between producing and transacting subjects and their objects. In particular, I have emphasized the way that people's relationships to words and things are shaped by the demands, dynamics, and risks of interaction with others.

Several elements of the dialectical model of interaction are crucial to this argument. One is that we cannot assume interaction is a matter of fully autonomous subjects coming together to transact goods with one another or to jockey for position by making strategic choices among linguistic tools that lie ready to hand before them. Ultimately, for example, it is not just the relative status of Anakalangese kaḅisu that is at stake in a given exchange, but the very identity of particular persons as living embodiments of immortal kaḅisu, their capacity even to enter a claim for status in the first place. Anakalangese scenes of encounter involve a potential, but never fully guaranteed, transformation of individual bodies into collective agents identified with ancestors, under the name of kabisu. I have traced out parallel verbal and objectual features of this transformation. In material terms, this includes a passage from the socially and temporally constricted circuit of household production and consumption, through more expansive networks of exchange, culminating in the collective, long-term possession of immobile ancestral valuables. In verbal terms, the transformation involves an increased delegation, distribution, and displacement of the voice from personal to ancestral authorship, from highly contextual and fluid to decontextualized and rule foregrounding. Under the demands of these transformations, relations of domination (like that between noble and slave), of hierarchy (like that between junior and senior), and of cooperative, if asymmetric, complementarity (like that between husband and wife) are enfolded within unitary agents (such as household, house, and kabisu), known through their representational practices. For example, the performance roles of wunang, respondent, and leader iconically, and very selectively, enact a version of the relationship of domination between a noble ancestral couple and their slave (who gives his name to the nobles as their kadehang), as if it were primarily one between representative and represented. So, too, the presence of women's work is indexed in goods whose symbolic and iconic character denotes their gendered origins with reference to ancestral principles of cosmological complementarity. In terms, then, of the implicated subject, both verbal and material media transform discrete, gendered, fully "present," and mortal bodies into collective, dual-gendered, partially "absent," and, in principle, immortal objects of representation.

This process of transformation, however, should not lead us to take the part for the whole, conflating the formal representation with that which is represented or that which is undertaking the representing. For example, we will not obtain a sufficient account of male and female in Anakalang by interpreting the couplets of ritual speech or scrutinizing the semiotics of prestations, if we overlook what happens in the garden, around the hearth, in the throes of childbirth, and so forth. At the same time, there is no reason to privilege the "productive" end of the scale, bodily labor, as the "real" infrastructure that is disguised by a cultural superstructure, or the individual speaker as the authentic source of a self-expressive voice. Some Anakalangese might suggest we could just as accurately portray individuals as beings that are *not yet* completely realized, insofar as they are not yet fully social actors engaged in the collaborative construction of everlasting, recognizable identities. But it is surely more realistic yet to grant both ends of the spectrum their privileges, and to see in their differences and the tensions between them the stuff of ambition, pleasure, anxiety, and struggle.

An important consequence of this argument concerns the role of material things in speech events and of speech in material transactions. By looking not for a disembodied "discourse" or "rhetoric" but at concrete forms and practices, I have sought to take seriously the articulation of representations with political economy and material vicissitudes. By insisting on the importance of material things in social existence, however, I do not intend to invite reductionism in through the back door. That economic needs in Anakalang are shaped by the demands of exchange, for example, should challenge any straightforward account of "objective interests." The interests of Anakalangese women and men are not given independently of the practices and sociality that construct those interests, nor do people have available to them an abstract position from which to evaluate their interests relative to all theoretically possible alternatives. For example, the economic value of buffalo in monetary terms cannot be understood in isolation from the interactive dimension of social life and the susceptibility of any act of giving or retaining to being evaluated by other people. This is why, for example, I hesitate to use the plausible locution that rank is "validated" or "legitimated" through exchange and ritual performance. To do so would be, I believe, to treat rank misleadingly as an abstract position whose meaning is fully distinct from the practices that constitute particular claims to it. Similarly, it is the interdependence between material practices and more abstract concepts of persons and actions that I have tried to bring out in my discussion of the concept of dewa in the previous chapter. At the same time, the variety of slippages I have pointed to should also challenge the opposite conclusion, that people are enclosed within a seamless cultural web, unquestioningly carrying out unvarying directives.

This view of the relationship among practices, discourses, and society makes it difficult to find purchase for the split that, for example, Scott (1985, 1990) posits between a public face of deceit and a "hidden transcript" behind the scenes, where the dominated speak the truth. In saying this, I do not mean to play down the rumbles and occasional shouts of complaint and dissension that one can hear in Anakalang. Nor do

I mean to reduce all discourse to a single, undifferentiated, and neutral "conversation." On the contrary, I have argued that we cannot understand even formal representations without the verbal clash of styles, movement among registers, slippage of frames; without the social dynamics of risk and dissidence. Rather, my doubt concerns the possibility of attributing to some kinds of discourse a privileged access to perspectives free of the context in which they are embedded. If normative discourse serves some interests at the expense of others, it is because of its role as a practice amid other practices, not because it suppresses an underground discourse that is in fact true. If the study of speech practices, genres, and the contest among speakers tells us anything, it is that the alternative to a literal-minded acceptance of official, normative accounts of tradition and custom is not to be found simply by shifting our allegiance to another account, unless we pay further attention to the practices of which *that* account is part, and to the transformative relations among these accounts.

A related difficulty can be found when Bourdieu speaks of the "euphemization" of kinship ([1972] 1977: 191). This term accurately captures a dimension of local strategy but risks underplaying how it is embedded within a constitutive set of practices. A wealthy master of exchange like Ubu Dongu (whose comments I record in chapter 7) is indeed quite capable of exploiting the language of kinship, but he does so for interests that do not exist entirely independently of the demands that kinship imposes on him. He is a shrewd and rational strategist, but he is not a transcendental subject. Ubu Dongu may well speak about his maneuvers very differently at home than in a public forum, and his dependents in turn may view his tactics with a cold eye. But neither he nor his dependents have available an alternative, fully objective language that shares nothing with the moral implications of kinship which "euphemism" would serve to disguise. To point this out is not to deny the workings of power, or the capacity of speakers to reflect on, criticize, and even alter the available terms of discourse. But it is to insist as well on the reality and powers of discourse. Euphemism must be understood as one among other possible ways of speaking within Anakalang. What it rephrases are other situated discourses.

A final difficulty arises in Bourdieu's famous expression "symbolic capital." To collapse the distinction between material and symbolic in this manner risks reducing the latter to the former—to seeing wealth as "the ultimate basis of power" ([1972] 1977: 195)—rather than exposing their dialectics. Again, think of the calculations and strategies of

Ubu Dongu. To reduce his carefully cultivated relations with supporters, dependents, and exchange partners to "symbolic capital" may lead us to overlook the ways in which those others confront him as subjects and in which at least some of them may in turn seek to enfold him into their own subjecthood. In different practical circumstances, for example, Ubu Dongu's yera faces him by turns as a challenging other, reckons him as a resource, threatens to ignore him, and counts him as a pragmatic component of his own agentive identity. This is not exactly the discreet capital that gathers interest quietly in the bank, nor is it the industrious capital that searches restlessly for untapped opportunities while its owner sleeps.

The first set of themes I have raised concerns the relations between the "symbolic" and "material"; the second concerns agents. The transformation of persons into kabisu is not performed by each kabisu on its own. The self-constitution internal to each kabisu in the scene of encounter is a function of relations kabisu collaboratively develop between them. Their mutual recognition is produced in representational actions, including delegated speaking parts, ritual speech, and ceremonial exchange. In such formal encounters, Anakalangese appear to dramatize a view of interaction similar to that expressed by V. N. Vološinov ([1930] 1973), that to speak is implicitly to elicit a reply from another speaker and that the reply completes the act initiated by the speaker (see Mead 1934). This has important consequences for where we are empirically to seek out agency. Take, for example, the socially recognized authorship of words. As Bakhtin (1981) argues, there is no simple and singular distribution of "voices" over bodies. By means of "double-voiced utterances," for example, individual speakers may incorporate the (attributed) voices of others, diffusing responsibility for or increasing the moral weight of their words. But if a range of voices can occur within the utterances of "single" speakers, those speakers themselves enter into wider interactional fields. The speaker herself may not be fully able to control the allocation of responsibility for the authorship of her words. Rather, this allocation may be the outcome of a collective activity and may end up "thinning out and socializing its central focus" (Hill and Irvine 1992: 13). A similar complexity holds for the "authorship" (whether by production or transaction) of objects. The subject of exchange, for example, is constructed over the course of multiple acts of giving. Like the authorship of words, the allocation of

responsibility for producing and for giving objects is the outcome of social interaction. As Strathern (1988) puts it, different people, even different internal aspects of "partible" individuals, may all be recognized
as sources of different components of the object. In practical terms, this
potential for multiple attributions is registered in the fallibility of memory, disputes over the proper intent of gifts, conflicts over ownership,
and the fact that debts are not created by inherent properties of objects
but are forged in the activities by which they are transacted. Whether
the focus is on verbal or material media, the social character of agency
entails quandaries similar to those I mentioned in discussing charisma in
chapter 1: the rhetorical displacement or delegation of agency threatens
to become estrangement.

Thus we cannot assume that the subjects of interaction are individual
persons, or that they are engaged primarily in reciprocity, self-expression
or communication, trafficking in signs and goods that are fully distinct
from them and over which they have full control. This raises a third set
of problems, concerning risk and hazard. To the extent that neither the
authorship of words nor the sources of goods are given but are functions of social interaction, claims to agency are potentially defeasible.
The result is the ever-present potential for alienation, slippage, or loss.
This slippage is in part a characteristic of the media themselves, put on
display and even compounded by high formality. In pragmatic terms,
speech acts are subject to misfire. More generally, the inscrutability that
Anakalangese attribute to signs presents a challenge to the hermeneutic
approach to cultural texts. The fact that "texts" are publicly accessible
does nothing to guarantee the security even of "natives'" interpretations.
The interpretation of representations involves collaborative, fallible constructions of texts. This is neither a mystical quality nor a technical de-
fect, but reflects the fundamentally social character of language. Insofar
as speech is socially produced and interactively construed, it is in any
instance identified with its speaker and that speaker's intentions only with
some potential for ambiguity. Similarly, the source, ownership, purpose,
and destination of material prestations are also subject to contestation,
confusion, forgetting, and subversion. Finally, the activities by which
the performance of speech and transacting of goods are effected show
similar vulnerabilities to slippage. The delegation of speaking parts may
fail, the event may slip out of its frame. The hazards to which I refer
have two chief sources. One is that the objectification, the distantiation,
and the expansiveness afforded by representation bear with them the
risk of total detachment from the subject. The other is that interaction

forces participants into mutual dependence, placing each, to an extent, at the mercy of the other.

Corresponding to these sources of hazard are sources of its relative obscurity in our own field of vision. By focusing on distinct agents of actions, anthropologists are sometimes inclined to overlook the effects each agent has on the other, not just as a source of external force (such as coercion and resistance) but for the very constitution of the agent in the first place (as in recognition). In addition, if anthropologists have tended to overlook the elements of slippage and risk, this is due in part to the long-standing (and highly productive) project of uncovering the order presumed to lie hidden behind the unfamiliar. In places like Anakalang, this project coincides with the great value that Anakalangese themselves place on pata and formal procedures. It would be a disservice to Anakalangese concerns to ignore this value, and analytically unwise to overlook the cultural patterns on which pata draws. At the same time, it would be deceptive to take the *appearance* of rules too much at face value. As I have argued above, Anakalangese themselves have ways of explicitly talking about, and metapragmatically of displaying, the processual character of apparently rule-governed actions and, more generally, the risks of interaction. These include the assertion that actual performances of pata are "shadows" of the full set of rules and the variety of iconic and indexical features of formal action that displace agency, presuppose semiotic difficulty, and imply agonistic circumstances. To read pata as an efficient cause of ritualized action (to say nothing of projecting pata as the totality of Anakalangese culture) is, from one perspective, to mistake the negotiation of values for the carrying out of directives. It is also to misconstrue the way in which the discourse of pata seeks to read present deeds with a retrospective eye, as actions that replicate something that has always already been completed. This may be part of the authority of ancestors: they project into cosmological time the completedness of action that, for example, Schutz ascribes to ordinary self-conscious activity and Bakhtin to "authoritative discourse." As people in eastern Sumba put it (Forth 1981: 212), in some circumstances the dead receive an even number of offerings, because " 'the dead are complete' and therefore 'do not request (or require) anything.' "[2] The problem is, of course, that those who say so are themselves compelled, for the moment, to remain among the living.

The materiality of words and things exposes actors and actions to the social world: as concrete media, words and things are accessible to a public, bearing formal properties that are open to the evaluative gaze of others. These material qualities also display points of articulation between the semiosis that is foregrounded in ritualized action and the wider political economy that remains a more taciturn presence offstage, whose workings elude any set of conscious intentions. By requiring that words and things be transacted in tandem, the formal rules of interaction effectively introduce an economic dimension to speech events, even as they lay stress on the semiotic features of valuable goods. In doing so, scenes of encounter dramatize an important assumption of Anakalangese cosmology, that wealth reflects good ties with ancestors and thus with the ultimate sources of authority. Being immanent in the very forms that action takes, this conjunction of wealth with ancestral authority need not depend entirely on explicit beliefs shared by all participants. It is quite possible for some Anakalangese to doubt either the general proposition that wealth comes from ancestors or the more specific claims that certain individuals or groups possess their wealth legitimately, without undermining the efficacy of the practices in which almost everyone is involved. This is in part because of the ways in which individuals, their sense of identity and self-esteem and to a large extent their livelihood, are enmeshed with the projects of others. In semiotic terms, it is also because the links between economic capacity and authoritative actions are, in part, indexes (thus both logical and causal) constructed in performance. The causal side of the logicocausal nexus integrates signification with political economy and material vicissitude. On the one hand, it means those who would inherit status must work to sustain it. On the other hand, it means that those who come into wealth must also work to legitimate it. Both the authority of representational practices and the powers supported by material resources are vulnerable to each other.

The integration of verbal activity with political economy thus has two sides. One implication is that, if linguistic analysis allows us to examine the interactive negotiation of authority, it should not lead us to overlook the limits to the negotiable. These limits are implicit in the poetic conventions, institutional structures, and other contextual circumstances that make certain kinds of conversation and conversational outcomes possible. But limits are also imposed by properties that cannot be discovered within the confines of spoken interaction or the temporal frame of the speech event. Material and social resources can be accumulated over time. Over time, they make certain outcomes more feasible, others less likely—they help structure (as Bourdieu puts it) what people will consider to be "realistic" possibilities, what can be attempted and questioned, what cannot. There come to be circumstances in which, in practical terms, it becomes hard to question someone's claims to authority due to their overwhelming resources. This was the case, for example, with Umbu Sappy's right-hand man, Ubu B. After spending his youth as a laborer in the port town of Waingapu, he was summoned back to Anakalang to oversee Umbu Sappy's herds and to engage, it seems, in the occasional strong-arm activity. Over the course of two decades, he accumulated a large herd and forged several strong marriage alliances. With his wealth he sponsored the schooling of several children and other kabisu members, many of whom went on to acquire positions in the civil service. Today, few Anakalangese would consider it wise directly to challenge Ubu B's descendants' claims to rank, political leadership in their kabisu, or ritual authority. But this does not prevent people from recalling Ubu B's less than impressive origins, or the means by which he rose, or even to impugn the character of his descendants. People say that when he died, his herds quickly evaporated due to a weakened dewa, manifested by a sudden spate of cattle rustling. It is significant that the most secure means by which he was able to reproduce his position was by diverting wealth from exchange to invest it in the institutional structures of education and bureaucracy.

By diverting goods into the market, Ubu B was acting on a potential alienability that was probably never entirely absent from Anakalangese exchange. What was novel, in his time, was the existence of the peculiar forms of objectified status made available by the state. I want to close by briefly suggesting that we cannot understand people's historical experience if we overlook the fracture lines and possibilities embedded within existing practices. Recognizing the slippages and alternatives that can be found even within the most formalized of activities may permit us to see historical transformations not only as entirely alien forces imposed from without, a matter of replacing whole cloth one society, economy, and set of values with another. It has been common, for example, to dichotomize societies between gift and commodity economies (Gregory 1982; but cf. Appadurai 1986; Parry and Bloch 1989). When markets introduce money and commodities into gift economies, the narrative proceeds, they quickly undermine or drive out the values and morality of exchange. But Anakalangese exchange already recognizes, if not the full-blown commodity form of capitalist economics, at least many of the alienable properties of commodities. What may be different is the set of ways in which the conversion of goods into cash can draw Anaka-langese into the webs of "foreign powers," the chief source and often the ultimate destination of cash in this part of Sumba (Vel 1994). By insist-ing on the moral value of pata, Anakalangese support the distinction between gift and commodity. Pata can become a defense of local society not as identity politics or cultural expression, but as a tacit way of re-sisting the power that goes along with dependence on other people's money. Once we realize that exchange valuables circulate among a range of alternative destinations, we can see how historical circumstances may configure and transform existing possibilities, or make real what had heretofore only been imagined.

A similar argument can be made for words. Elsewhere (Keane 1995a) I have argued that ritual speech is peculiarly available for reappropria-tion to new ends. As the contemporary Indonesian context encourages certain kinds of folklorization (Acciaioli 1985; Bowen 1991), it is of-ten the most textual dimensions of ritual speech that are foregrounded, largely at the expense of the interactive and performative dimensions. This is already signaled in Ubu Sebu's baptismal yaiwo, mentioned in chapter 3, in which the lack of offerings suggested that the speeches were not addressed to a spirit audience. When the demand for a response is lost, what is left can appear to be something like a virtual book of cus-tom, waiting to be written down. Because the textual dimension of rit-ual speech permits it to be treated as something independent of prac-tice, this can lead to a redistribution of authority. For example, it should not be surprising to discover that practitioners are often relatively inar-ticulate about their knowledge when discussing it out of a practical context. As I have mentioned, some ratus have difficulty remembering ritual knowledge, when, as they say, the gongs are not playing. Other wunangs and ratus simply find such reflections to be pointless and grow impatient when asked to recount or analyze ritual procedures in the abstract.

In contrast, it is sometimes people who are distant from ritual prac-tices and can draw on new sources of status, such as formal education, who seem most articulate about "tradition." One of these was a minor official who delighted in providing me with synoptic accounts of the pata of marriage and funerals and was remarkably good at interpreting couplets and coming up with etymologies. Nor should he be accused of complete infidelity to the true character of Anakalangese ritual, insofar as its strangeness and textlike properties do create the sense of distance that invites reflection. But when called upon to use this knowledge in practice in negotiating a marriage exchange (as I described at the beginning of chapter 4), he floundered, finally shifting from kajiàla into colloquial Indonesian. Those people who are adept at providing synoptic and decontextualized accounts of pata may undermine the authority of those who know how to act but cannot explain (see Briggs 1984; Hill 1985). Related to this is the experience of nostalgia and inauthenticity. When Anakalangese focus on the literal referents of couplets, or when they reify pata, they are liable to find a mismatch between text and world. Rather than negotiate this mismatch, in full recognition that only the ancestors could get it right, they may draw somewhat different conclusions. When the text is treated chiefly as evidence of a world to which it refers, the mismatch between text and material things (such as marriage payment or houses in an ancestral village) may support an increasingly common perception that "authentic Anakalangese culture" either is imperfectly realized in the given instance or had been perfectly realized once but only in the past.

This may help explain something that at first puzzled me. Many of the people most committed to what they see as modernity are also the most vocal about the loss of tradition. This was the case, for example, with one woman, a high school graduate and good Christian, who ran a small kiosk by the side of the main road and had little but scorn for the backward village people around her. She often expressed her astonishment that someone from a rich country like mine would waste his time among such ignorant and impoverished hicks. Yet she also frequently criticized these same village people for not getting their pata right. When her father was still alive, she insisted, he really knew how to do the rituals. This double vision was not unusual in my experience. She is one of those who are in the position to measure their vision of tradition against the imperfections of actual practices and the apparent inarticulateness of practitioners. Even those who promote "tradition" as a way of resisting the market, the church, or the state may end up presenting the "local" as a site of symbolic reserve. They may inadvertently limit tradition to being an expressive resource in the face of political and economic activity that is solely in the hands of external agents.

Yet few Anakalangese are likely to view pata without some degree of ambivalence and we should be cautious about the nostalgia that sees transformation as pure loss. Whether their view is overly optimistic or not (they may be unaware of the historical leap from frying pan to fire), many Anakalangese see their emerging circumstances to be liberating. The possibilities include escape from the demands of formal encounter.

When the minor official mentioned above fumbled during his attempt to negotiate the marriage between a Timorese orphan and a bride whose father was from Flores, he suggested that, since they were all part of one great "Christian family" (Indo. *keluarga Kristen*), they should switch to "Christian customary law" (Indo. *adat Kristen*). Although the suggestion was an obvious act of desperation and drew an angry rejection from his listeners, it also displays both the difficulty of pata and the appeal that contemporary alternatives can hold. To escape encounters also seems to promise, for some, a chance to elude dependency. Those men and women, especially the young and unmarried, who can get access to regular sources of cash may value the relative freedom this provides them from their seniors and other patrons. Several single women have been able to support themselves with positions in schools and the church, maintaining some freedom from the labor demanded by full involvement in exchange. One or two married women and several men of low rank find at least partial independence in small businesses. They continue to feel the pressures of kin, and the awkwardness of their marginal status. Still, increasingly, as one man put it to me with mixed disdain and envy, 'Now that we are in the free age (Indo. *masa merdeka*— an expression that in national discourse usually refers to liberation from colonialism), it's not rank that we defer to, but brains and money.' But as the account of representational practices I have essayed here suggests, if he means that rank was once a stable position in the world, untouched by the activity of brains and the movements of wealth, he may well be misremembering.

According to the old people, Ubu Paroru told me with a knowing chuckle, earth tremors are caused by a dispute between a cat and a mouse under the ground. The mouse says, 'I want to cut the navel cord of the earth,' but the cat says, 'No, don't, there are people up there.' The mouse says, 'No there aren't' and the cat says 'Go ahead, I'll shake the earth and you'll hear them.' So when there's a tremor we all beat drums, gongs, pots and pans, and we shout out 'I'm here! (*Ya ga!*).' I recalled reading of similar stories elsewhere in the region (e.g., Forth 1981: 124) and was tempted to take them as a way of imagining the ultimate consequences of going unheard. On reflection, it is further tempting to see in this story the materials for a new allegory of the quandary of self-representation as Anakalangese find themselves facing a host of new interlocutors, and look for a way in which they might speak recognizably, and receive recognizable speech in reply.

# Notes

## CHAPTER 1: INTRODUCTION

1. I leave this definition rather abstract at this point to bring out shared features between two very different sorts of events. The "encounter" is most evident between two groups of living people, as when clans negotiate marriage exchanges. Prayers and offerings to ancestors are also structured as encounters with others. To be sure, the audible speech and immediate material transaction are all on the side of the living: the dead reply through divinatory signs and future benefits such as good harvests. But the activity is still structured as an encounter in which the one party faces another who, though invisible, ought to be present, and the general principles of engagement remain the same as those with living persons. In speaking of both sorts of encounter together in this way, I wish to bring out the problems of representation they share.

2. What the political, legal, diplomatic, and artistic senses of "representation" have in common is the role of *absence*. In each case, representation is "the making present *in some sense* of something which is nevertheless *not* present literally or in fact" (Pitkin 1967: 8–9; emphasis in original). Pitkin adds that there must also be a third party who considers the relationship between the present and the absent to be one of representation (1967: 100–105). This suggests that representation is not objectively constituted, because that third party may deny or simply not perceive the relationship in question. Judith Butler (1990: 1) points out that much contemporary feminist theory tends to assume that political representation is a function in part of effects of mimetic representation and thus that effects on one will have consequences for the other. On the problematic consequences of conflating representation as political speaking-for (*vertreten*) and as signifying (*darstellen*), however, see Spivak 1988: 275 ff.

3. It is significant that some accounts of power, which stress relations among persons ("power-over"), exclude from consideration the merely practical advantages afforded by access to material resources ("power-to"; see Wartenberg

1990). Although it is important not to conflate the two analytically, we should not forget that the relations between them can be of great concern for the people involved. This can be seen, for instance, when people attribute supernormal physical powers to the holders of charismatic authority, and in the classic problem of legitimizing wealth obtained by illicit means.

4. Although Geertz's treatment of representation shares certain features with the Durkheimian tradition, his more explicit debt is to Weber. Of particular relevance here are the implications of a founding exclusion with which Weber begins *Economy and Society*. The definition of action with which he constitutes his object of sociological study rules out the nonmeaningful, even when things like demographic change and floods have social effects (Weber 1978: 7–8).

5. As with Geertz's discussion of Bali, I am not concerned here with the particular empirical status of Anderson's account of Java. It can be argued, for example, that Javanese concepts of power are inseparable from the effects of long domination by the Dutch. Even if this is the case, however, such concepts are persuasive and effective, in part by virtue of their logical and causal characteristics. Thus it might be instructive to compare a very different approach to a similar phenomenon, Bourdieu's ([1979] 1984: 54–55) explanation of "aestheticization" in contemporary France. In emphasizing the aesthetic over the practical value of possessions, the aesthete demonstrates an easy distance from the press of necessity. The power of this display is strengthened by the fact that it remains implicit—like the signs of Javanese power, it is imputed to the person's innate character, not to any intention to signify.

6. In making the distinction between natural and non-natural meaning, Grice aims to create a programmatic definition of linguistic meaning, grounded in the intentions of individual speakers as they interact with others. By citing him here, I do not mean to endorse this project. On the contrary, much of what I have to say here about the material and mediated character of signs runs counter to it. I do, however, find the distinction useful for the more limited task of showing one dimension of how people often *understand* signs to function.

7. Compare Durkheim's (1915: 380) assertion that ritual representations must be kept analytically distinct from action. Any belief that representative ritual acts on the *world* is simply a reflection of its *real* action, which is on the emotions and the mind (Durkheim 1915: 375). Its apparent powers are a projection from the individual's own experience of the power of society.

8. Compare Peirce's assertion that a person's "thoughts are what he is 'saying to himself,' that is, is saying to that other self that is just coming into life in the flow of time" (5.421). Similarly, according to Mead, "The 'I' of this moment is present in the 'me' of the next moment" (1934: 174). This seems, incidentally, to be part of Ricoeur's argument about the model of the text, which has influenced the anthropological effort to read cultures as texts. According to Ricoeur (1971: 538), experience is only knowable when it is transformed into something like a text.

9. "The individual is not a self in the reflexive sense unless he is an object to himself" (Mead 1934: 142), which according to Mead is only made possible by language. For the linguistics of the argument that selves and others are mutually constructed in dialogue, by virtue of the capacity of speakers to take

turns using the first- and second-person pronouns, see Benveniste [1958] 1971a (see also Urban 1989). Compare Vološinov ([1930] 1973: 86), for whom the word is "*the product of the reciprocal relationship between speaker and listener, addresser and addressee. . . .* I give myself verbal shape from another's point of view, ultimately, from the point of view of the community to which I belong. . . . A word is territory shared by both addresser and addressee" (emphasis in original).

10. The role of language in organizing experience has, of course, been familiar since the Romantics, taking classic form in the linguistic anthropology of Benjamin Lee Whorf and Edward Sapir. Foucault (e.g., [1969] 1972: 47–48) draws on similar theoretical foundations to emphasize the close relationship between the constitutive effects of language and the workings of power. My interest here is in showing the role of typification in the phenomenology of interaction, in order to counter the individualistic tendencies found in many phenomenological approaches. For instance, even though Schutz ([1932] 1967: 119) gives language a crucial role, he leaves its social implications undeveloped, perhaps because his own view of language places so much weight on the intentions of (individual) speakers. Compare this to Peirce, who says what makes something like the "act of giving" real conduct and not momentary happenstance is the fact that it is knowable because it is a general type, mediated by signs, and thus takes the form of knowledge that can guide our actions (1.175–176; 1.475); it is something that could happen again. For a discussion of "typification" as an objectifying moment in speakers' partial awareness of their own linguistic practices, see Errington 1988; Hanks 1993.

11. Reference to ancestral authority can be quite explicit. It resembles performative speech, words that accomplish what J. L. Austin ([1955] 1975) calls "illocutionary" acts by virtue of being said ("I hereby do thee wed"). Like explicitly performative speech, Anakalangese ritual action is often at once illocutionary (a form of action) and propositional (a kind of statement): it does things (such as create relationships between clans) in part—but only in part—by saying what ancestral type of action it is carrying out (see chaps. 5 and 6). As Emile Benveniste ([1963] 1971b) points out, even when language is "acting," it is also describing things. To say "I hereby do thee wed" effectively is not only to carry out an action, it is also, in the process, to make a true statement. Reflection *on* action, in this example, is put to the service *of* action. It does so by invoking a recognizable form, to say that "what is going on right now is an instance of a type of action" (namely, wedding). That speech acts in *both* illocutionary and propositional ways is an important component of the more general problem of representation.

12. The fact that strongly iconic signs—photographs, for example—appear forcefully to impress upon us their innate resemblance to their objects can be misleading. Resemblance requires recognition, some construction or selection: "for any two objects in nature resemble each other. . . . [I]t is only with reference to our senses and needs that one resemblance counts for more than the other" (Peirce 1.365). For some implications of this underdetermined quality for the meaningfulness of material objects, see chapter 3.

13. I stress here that what counts as an existential connection depends on

particular ontologies. Thus, for example, part of the theological defense of Christian icons against the iconoclasts was that the pictures were produced through *causal* effects emanating from the divine beings whom they portrayed. They were not simply the products of the intentional acts of painters (Belting 1994: 149–155).

14. Indexes have been of particular interest to linguists because of the role they play at the intersection of linguistic structure and the context of use. Thus the first-person pronoun refers to the person who utters it, and it is coordinated with the "here" and "now" of the moment of speaking (Benveniste [1958] 1971a). Because indexes can "direct the attention to their objects by blind compulsion" (Peirce 2.306), they are also of interest to sociolinguists. Such is the forcefulness of indexicality that conventions of politeness commonly avoid it (Errington 1988: 222–223): see chapter 4.

15. The particular shape that the sense of risk will take depends in part on socioeconomic background and in part on cosmological assumptions about what is possible. Thus people in Anakalang, as in other societies that practice divination and auspices, are likely to seek explanations for events that an American might attribute to accident. As a result, the Anakalangese sense of risk and slippage will differ from the American intuition, as characterized by Goffman (1974: 35): "Given our belief that the world can be totally perceived in terms of either natural events or guided doings and that every event can be comfortably lodged in one or the other category, it becomes apparent that a means must be at hand to deal with slippage and looseness. The cultural notions of muffing and fortuitousness serve in this way, enabling the citizenry to come to terms with events that would otherwise be an embarrassment to its system of analysis."

16. This problem of authorship and authority is the subject of the discussions of "monologism" and "heteroglossia" by Vološinov ([1930] 1973) and Bakhtin (1981). I return to this in detail in chapters 4, 5, and 6.

## CHAPTER 2: GEOGRAPHY, HISTORY, AND SOCIALITY

1. Thus, as Mauss says, speaking of Australia, the "exchange of things is at the same time the exchange of pledges of peace" ([1925] 1990: 86 n. 9). Similarly, Leach (1954: 153) associates the feud with debt, saying, "to the Kachin way of thinking co-operation and hostility are not very different," and de Josselin de Jong (1952: 179) speaks of the "'hostile friendship' characteristic of phratry dualism" in Sumatra. As Sahlins (1972: 182) observes, Mauss "transposes the classic alternatives of war and trade from the periphery to the very center of social life, and from the occasional episode to the continuous presence. . . . All the exchanges, that is to say, must bear in their material design some political burden of reconciliation."

2. The name "Anakalang," like many similar toponyms, refers both to a single village and, by synecdoche, to an entire region, whose people identify themselves as speakers of "the language of Anakalang" (*na hilu Anakalang*). Given the decentralized nature of precolonial Sumbanese societies, the structure

and boundaries of the "domain" or "landscape" (Dutch *landschap*) created perennial difficulties for the colonial administration (Couvreur 1914; Groeneveld 1931; Nooteboom 1940; Riekerk 1934; Waitz 1933). Even today administrative units may be in flux. In the 1980s, Anakalang was part of a multidialect district (kecamatan) called Katikutana, which incorporates the formerly distinct domains of Anakalang, Mamboru, Lawonda, and Umbu Ratu Nggai, but by 1993, there was talk of redistricting.

3. In 1986, the recorded population density of the wider Anakalang region (pop. 23,866) was about 33 persons per square kilometer (Kantor Statistik 1987). Access to resources varies dramatically across the island. In east Sumba, it appears that a small noble class controls most of the productive land and herds (Metzner 1977). In Lawonda, Anakalang's closest neighbor to the north, it has been estimated that about 10 percent of the population does not own enough land to be fully self-sustaining, but nearly everyone has access to some land through pawning or dependency relations (Vel 1987: 18). Land claims usually become a problem only in the case of wet rice fields, which are in far shorter supply than garden and pasture land and whose crop is important to ceremonial life. West of Anakalang, land pressure is greater, the distribution of wealth appears to be somewhat more even, and competition over resources is more vigorous (Kuipers 1990).

4. Hoskins (1993a: 211) estimates that in west Sumba two or three times as many buffalo are slaughtered in feasts as are sold for export.

5. Civil service is an exception. Since it endows the employee with an honorific title and the presumptive patronage of the state, it resembles long-term reciprocity more than the closure effected by wage labor. The most important sources of cash in Anakalang are the salaries of civil servants, of whom the vast majority are schoolteachers. According to statistics kept in desa offices, in the mid-1980s, one or two particularly favored desa reported a number of civil servants equivalent to 24 percent of households. Most desa, however, are closer to the figure of 5 percent. The number of people holding occupations such as craftsman and trader is nugatory. In 1987, the monthly salary of an elementary schoolteacher, the most common civil service position, began at about Rp 20,000 to 40,000 (about US $12–$24), supplemented with a rice allotment. Local civil servants cannot live off of their salaries alone, but also work the land.

6. Of course, the moral high ground claimed by critics of modernity should be kept in perspective. The contrasts have different values depending on one's point of view: for unmarried men and women, the market is often liberating. Exempt from many of the demands of propriety and social obligation, located on interstitial terrain, the market provides treasured opportunities for flirtation.

7. In east Sumba, the horse trade may have had even deeper consequences. A handful of leaders on the east coast seem to have maintained loose ties with Dutch and Arab traders, enough to provide them with sources of gold, silk, ivory, and the occasional cannon. It is likely that the rank system characteristic of east Sumba was greatly strengthened by control over these sources of wealth.

8. Thus Hoskins, for instance, says that certain ritual offices in Kodi are shaped by the effort to adapt to foreign rule (1993b: 138) and "appropriate an

incompletely understood external power" (1993b: 124; see Fox 1982). Evidence for a similar incorporation can be found in Anakalang. For example, one expression for high ritual office, *hagula—hangaji*, probably derives from titles, themselves apparently of Javanese origin, in the Bimanese sultanate that once claimed authority over Sumba. Nonetheless, Dutch and Indonesian interventions were dramatically more forceful than the largely titular assertions of Bima (and perhaps Majapahit before that) and less readily assimilated through representational practice alone.

9. The vast bulk of colonial sources on Sumba concerns, or was produced by, Christian missions. Much of the work of the most prolific writers was ethnographic (see references in the bibilography to Lambooy, Onvlee, Wielenga, and the visiting missionary-ethnographer Kruyt). A rich source of mission documents is van den End 1987; a good history, stressing the Catholic mission, is Haripranata 1984. For Christianity in Indonesia more generally, see Kipp and Rodgers 1987, which includes a discussion of missionization in west Sumba (Hoskins 1987).

10. In the 1920s and 1930s, nationalist sentiments were apparently restricted to a few government clerks in town (*Militaire memories* 1931–1933: 39). Retrospective efforts to find links to the national narrative are largely confined to the raja family, one member of which is said to have been killed during the Revolution while at school in Java. In terms of this narrative, however, the advantage provided to these leading families by their greater access to the national arena is offset by the strong personal interest they held in the continuation of Dutch rule.

11. The formal duties of desa heads, whose territory usually covers the land of several kabisu (which in turn often cross desa lines), include overseeing the collection of census figures, reporting changes in residence, registering cattle sales, carrying out small government-mandated work projects, such as fencing gardens, and transmitting information from higher authorities. Desa heads are also supposed to deal with most law and order matters, which is one area in which the boundaries between governmental and nongovernmental authority and agency become unclear. They try to stay out of disputes over exchanges and land rights, matters better left to kabisu elders and ritual experts (Vel 1994). For the conflict between *adat* and *dinas*, see Spyer 1996, Warren 1992.

12. One of the most direct means by which the state is able to influence and pressure people, once they are beyond school age, is through the civil service. Civil servants are exposed to the rationalized forms of the office and organizational hierarchy, to civic rituals and to regular indoctrination and training programs. They are also subject to sanctions by which the state seeks to enforce its policies concerning religion (such as adherence to a legally recognized religion), culture (such as the speaking of formal Indonesian), and ethics (such as undergoing civil marriages).

13. The kabisu has been described as a corporate unilineal descent group (Forth 1981; Mitchell 1981; Onvlee [1969] 1973d). The word *kabisu* also means "(interior) corner," as in a house or the crook of an arm (Onvlee 1984). The figure of the house corner brings out the mutual dependency among kabisu: there is no corner without a house and, therefore, without other corners.

This figure is very common in the Austronesian world: the Malay and Indonesian word *suku*, now commonly used to refer to ethnic groups, also means "one quarter" or "leg of an animal" (de Josselin de Jong 1952: 66–71), comparable, for instance, to Belau's "four cornerpost" chiefs (Parmentier 1987: 111–112). On mutual dependence among clans and the critical role of ritualized interaction, compare this observation from an island not far from Sumba: "If the clan were to be defined by its chief activity, the clan in Kédang would have to be called a bride-wealth exchanging group" (Barnes 1974: 238).

14. The identification of physical dwelling with social unity is common, especially in "house societies" (Carsten and Hugh-Jones 1995). There has been much discussion of the symbolic dimensions of house structure in eastern Indonesia (see, for example, Cunningham 1964; Ellen 1986; Forth 1981: 23–43; see also Fox 1993). For Anakalangese houses and the discourses surrounding them, see Keane 1995a.

15. For a discussion of tombs in Kodi, see Hoskins 1986. Anakalangese tombs are shown in Rodgers 1985, Rouffaer 1934, and the frontispiece of Wielenga 1932.

16. Similar patterns of relations between ritual centers and branch villages are common in eastern Indonesia; compare the accounts given in McKinnon 1991, Schulte Nordholt [1966] 1971, and Traube 1986.

17. Female bloodlines are given more emphasis in western Sumba, where clan allegiances conflict with a more strongly individualistic ethos. In Kodi, unlike Anakalang, bloodlines form named but covert lineages with distinctive identities (Hoskins 1990; van Wouden [1935] 1968).

18. Sumba has a remarkably low birthrate, which some people in Anakalang attribute to the "heat" generated by high marriage payments. In the 1950s, a birthrate of three-quarters to one percent was reported, and attributed to the late age of marriage, a result of high marriage payments (Sastrodihardjo 1957: 27). This gives a certain demographic urgency to the cosmologically loaded debt that kabisu are expected to feel toward their yera.

19. East Sumba, including Anakalang, is a locus classicus of asymmetric alliance and generalized exchange (Lévi-Strauss [1949] 1969: 70, 462). I cannot do justice here to the long debates to which these systems have given rise (for Indonesia, see Barraud 1979; Beatty 1992; de Josselin de Jong 1952; Lewis 1988; Singarimbun 1975; and the essays in Fox 1980). On the importance of the range of alternatives at play within "an asymmetric marriage system," see Barnes 1980, McKinnon 1991, and the discussion below in chapter 6.

20. Every kabisu is divided into a number of named houses. Houses are conceived of as descending from brothers, are identified with specific house sites in the Great Village, usually possess certain ritual prerogatives, and often give rise to their own offshoot villages. Whether the relevant unit in an exchange is the kabisu or the house is highly variable, depending on a host of factors such as population size, political factionalism, and exchange history. The more a house begins to act as an independent agent, however, the more like a kabisu it is becoming. At risk of some simplification, in this book I will always refer to the relevant agent in exchanges as "kabisu."

21. Discussing rituals in Kodi, Hoskins (1990) says "female" priests are

gender ambiguous. From a different angle, however, we can see this as an effect of the transformations at work in representational practice, a contrast between physical and social males at one plane and enactments of a more abstract "femaleness" at another. At least in Anakalang, no one confuses or conflates the two planes, for example, having the ratu marry a man. Note that, although representation remains the work of men (see Ardener 1975; Yanagisako and Collier 1987; see also Butler 1990; but cf. Ortner and Whitehead 1981), the fact that prestigious activities are carried out by (some) males does not in itself make them "male" games. For one thing, not all men hold the same stakes in these activities. Moreover, as will become apparent in subsequent chapters, the nature of Anakalangese representations raises fundamental problems for identifying the character of the "agents" behind them.

22. *Ngàba wini* (literally, "the side or direction of the seed") is a general term for the group that has received a wife. *Yera* is the reciprocal collective term, but can also refer more specifically to a wife's brother, for which the specific reciprocal, sister's husband, is *layewa*. The mutual relation between affines is "being as yera and layewa to one another" (*payera palayewangu*).

23. According to statistics from desa offices in the mid-1980s, about 20 percent of households owned at least one buffalo, with a desa-wide average of 1.52 to 2.67 buffalo per household (this pattern resembles that of the colonial period; see Versluys 1941). The average wet rice field holdings ran from 0.9 to 2.9 hectares per household. It takes 500 buffalo-hours and 100 man-hours to trample one hectare (Metzner 1977: 9). Such figures give at least a sense of the degree to which people find themselves in mutual economic dependence. For detailed discussion of economic relations and work networks, see Vel 1991, 1994.

24. The word *ata* in parts of west Sumba means "person" (*tau* in Anakalang). In Anakalang, a nonslave dependent is called "person in the house" (*tau ta uma*). Anakalangese distinguished among several kinds of slave. A "brought slave" (*ata ngidi*) entered the household in the company of a new bride, and was closely identified with the bride's status, in contrast to the unmarked class of slaves born within the household. A more problematic category was the purchased slave (*ata pahi*). Anakalangese accounts of the latter tend to be confusing. One reason that purchased slaves were dubious was probably their destabilizing effects on the definition of nobility, since wealthy commoners could buy them.

25. It is unlikely Anakalang ever had a large number of slaves, and the discussion of noble and slave status that follows should be taken to apply to that particular configuration. Specific attributions of rank are difficult to sort out in Anakalang; even the titles Ubu (Lord) and Rabu (Lady) reserved for nobility in east Sumba are, in contemporary Anakalang, politely used for nearly everyone. This reflects Anakalang's position midway between the highly rank-conscious domains of east Sumba and the less hierarchical west. Of a sample taken in the western domain of Weyewa, Kuipers (1990: 30) reports 22 percent noble, 67 percent commoner, 9 percent slave. By contrast, Forth's figures (1981: 426) for the eastern domain of Rindi (where rank pertains to clans, not persons) yield approximately 7 percent noble, 27 percent commoner, and 66 percent slave. Of

Lawonda, Anakalang's neighbor, Vel (1994: 100) estimates that fewer than 10 percent of the population was of noble rank in the 1980s but believes the figure to have been slightly higher in previous generations. The relative lack of domination by nobles in western Sumba was often remarked during the colonial period (e.g., Versluys 1941: 436–437). It seems likely that rank differences became more pronounced in Anakalang after the Dutch created the "kingship," which encouraged nobles to adopt a number of east Sumbanese rank markers and prerogatives. A reverse trend began with the introduction of national discourses since independence, which, although never very influential in Anakalang, disparage overt displays of rank as "feudal" (Indo. *feodal*).

## CHAPTER 3: THINGS OF VALUE

1. *Bahan na parangu waiḍa, na pakayi waiḍa.* It is suggestive that in this context, Ubu Bura uses one Indonesian word, *bahan* (material, substance) in place of the likely Anakalangese equivalents, *dati* (material media for a ritual act), *ngawu* (things, objects), or *ḅada* (possessions, especially exchange items and cattle)—as if to stress the modernity of the particular distinction between material and speech. The root *wai* indicates instrumentality, as in "What do you say that's used for?" (*Ga waingu wimi ya?*); "That machete's for cutting wood" (*Katopu nai papogu waingu aiya*).

2. A common reason men give for taking more than one wife is to increase the household's workforce, and women can be referred to ritually as "ladlers of rice." The close association between work and the meaning of female gender is revealed in people's attitudes toward male transvestites, "false females" (*kahala ḅai*). They dress and move like women, perform their dances, socialize with them, but, most important, do women's work. People usually speak of transvestites in reference to their appetite for work and not, for example, in terms of their own or others' sexual desire. Anakalang reflects the general claim that a deemphasis of sexuality is associated with the lack of strong concerns with female purity and pollution, or of suspicion or hostility between men and women (Ortner and Whitehead 1981).

3. The workings of the state in recent years call for some minor qualifications to this account. Since women have relatively equal access at least to the lower rungs of the civil service, they enter identical working situations with men. Some women seem to have taken advantage of the relative financial independence that allows them to remain unmarried. Some state-sponsored organizations, however, notably the desa women's association (PKK), tend to assume a middle-class model of women as primarily housewives (Warren 1992: 239). In Anakalang, however, organizations like the PKK are largely inactive, and employment reaches only a small elite.

4. As elsewhere in Southeast Asia, for Anakalangese the combination of betel pepper and areca nut is a common metaphor for courtship and sexuality, which seems to me to be contained within the more abstract model I propose here. It is perhaps significant that both ritual symbolism and ordinary conventions overlook the existence of the lime, portraying the betel quid as composed

essentially of only two elements. For example, when a host hands a guest a dish of betel, it must include both betel pepper and areca. But often the guest, if he or she wants to chew, must then *ask* for lime.

5. Form is crucial to the act of recognition. Anakalangese pay a great deal of attention to the manner by which tokens of hospitality are distributed. Like formal distributions of betel, rice and meat are served to each man and woman of a group on an identical plate, heaped with scrupulously equal portions. Thus people speak derogatorily of the two alternative styles of collective eating currently available. One is to share out of a single pot or platter, to eat "in the manner of Roja" (Florinese Muslims) (*parojangu*). The other is to serve a buffet. The latter is associated with high civil servants and contexts marked for their modernity; hence it is to eat "national style" (Indo. *cara nasional*) or, in reference to the story that it was introduced by President Sukarno, "presidential style" (Indo. *cara presiden*). What these styles have in common is that guests are not directly acknowledged by the host: the food is simply there for them to take. More important, because the size of the portion is left for each recipient to determine, it forces the guests to expose the degree of their desire. As a result, people can take affront even at being received with the buffet. Several people told me that they are always hungry afterward, since they wouldn't dare be seen taking enough to satisfy themselves.

6. As across Southeast Asia, rice in Anakalang is explicitly associated with women. It originated in the body of the eponymous ancestress, Rabu Pari (Lady Rice), young girls play a prominent part in planting and harvest rites, and the planting of seedlings is done by groups of women.

7. Vel (1994: 208) estimates that less than 10 percent of the rice harvested in Lawonda is sold, and unless that money is quickly used, it is subject to the same expectations of easy sharing as rice (1994: 54–55, 70).

8. The expression, as used by Appadurai (1986; cf. Bohannan 1955), refers to the exchange situations within which objects circulate, which may include cross-cultural contexts in which shared standards of value are quite limited. For an analysis of the political role of "traditional" cattle wealth in an African economy of constant labor migration and dependence on cash remittances, see Ferguson 1985.

9. Among the alternatives is theft (*kedu*), and several local fortunes are supposed to have had an initial boost from the sort of cattle rustling that is expected of restless young men. Less unilateral transactions include *hogu* (borrowing with interest) and *gadi* (pawning). For a comparable situation in Flores, see Barnes and Barnes 1989.

10. Symbolic analysis of material objects usually emphasizes their physical properties. Thus, for example, Weiner (1976, 1989) argues that the intrinsic properties of certain objects give rise to similar meanings across cultures. Strathern (1981), in criticizing her, points out that objective properties require culturally specific interpretations. In Peirce's terms, such properties or "qualisigns" bear only incomplete semiotic potential. Note here an implication for the concept of "use" as well. The particular utility of an object is not inscribed in its material properties. To the extent that any given object has a wide range of poten-

tial uses, the concept of "use value" points to the way in which things have a "structural openness to new contexts" (Keenan 1993: 160).

11. Chains, from one to several feet long, are of copper (*lolu amahu*), silver (*halaku lolungu*), and gold (*kanatar*). Other metal valuables are horn-shaped *làba*, crescent *tabelu*, circular *wula*, sproutlike *ladu*, flat twisted *maraga* and scalloped lumps called *madàka*, and the omega-shaped *mamuli* (see illustrations in Rodgers 1985). The best-quality mamuli, and sometimes maraga, tabelu, and wula, can be worn as a sort of brooch by male or female dancers on ceremonial occasions. Even more rarely, various gold valuables may be worn by ratus during important rituals (see fig. 3). In fact, however, most "ornaments" are not used as such in Anakalang, but serve only to circulate, to be buried with the dead, to be manipulated in ritual, or to be hidden away as the inalienable "ancestral portion" (see chapter 8).

12. The mamuli can be either plain (*lobu*) or decorated (*karagat*); see photographs in Keane 1988. In some parts of Sumba, people identify their omega shape with female genitalia (Forth 1981: 360). But the most elaborate, "those with feet" (*ma pawisi*), sport detailed figures on the base representing such things as roosters, cockatoos, horsemen, buffalo, and headhunting skull trees, which are conventional symbols of male greatness and bravado. In parts of east Sumba (Onvlee [1949] 1977: 154) and in Laboya to the west (Geirnaert-Martin 1992a: 238), decorated mamuli are considered to be male, undecorated ones female. In Onvlee's ([1949] 1977) structuralist logic, the gender of valuables is a function of their position relative to other valuables rather than of any inherent semiotic characteristics. Thus valuables form a series of recursive oppositions in such a way that the gender marking of the object can be reversed at the next level of generality. One virtue of this approach is that it recognizes that in specific contexts Sumbanese are able to treat valuables as gendered, even if these particular treatments do not add up analytically to form a single, overarching iconological system.

13. The actual fashioning of ornaments in the past was probably in the hands of itinerant smiths from the nearby islands of Roti and Sawu, some of whom, in the Dutch period, even came through Anakalang to take orders. In a sense, gold, silver, and ivory valuables do originate in the past, since at least the coins that served as raw materials most likely came to the east and north coasts of Sumba in the nineteenth and twentieth centuries in exchange for horses and slaves (Rodgers 1985). That the gold and silver that went into metal valuables ultimately derive from the sale of humans may influence their historical meaning, but today few people in Anakalang seem to be aware of this origin.

14. A related story concerns Ubu Sebu, Ubu Riri, and Ubu Kawolu, the three brothers from whom most of Anakalang's kabisu descend. At first they lived under the trees, because they had no tools with which to construct houses. One day, when they set out to hunt, their dog refused to go after the game. Instead it began to dig at a hill (with the same name as the cave mentioned above). For three days the dog worked at that hill. Unable to get it to stop, they asked for lightning from their mother's brother (who, recall, is their source of life's blood as well as a conventional recipient of metal goods), with which they

split open that mountain. Inside they found all the iron things that make civilized living possible, such as machetes, gongs, and gold valuables, and the celebrations they held while raising the first house initiated ritual.

15. Many observers of eastern Indonesia postulate an iconic association between the durability and hardness of spears, swords, and metal valuables and the enduring qualities to which the male links of clanship aspire (Adams 1980: 220; Traube 1986: 76–77). In contrast, argues McKinnon (1991), both cloth and bracelets have enveloping female qualities, the former also marked by its relative fragility. Although these interpretations are quite plausible, their apparent naturalness must be weighed against other evidence for the qualities locally attributed to genders. In Anakalang, for example, conceptually inherent ties of blood pass only through women and are more enduring than clan ties, which are vulnerable to disruption by political schism and other historical events. A different interpretation of the iconic qualities of metal is offered by Forth (1981: 126–127), who suggests that its radiance links it to divinity. Radiance also seems to be foregrounded in Anakalangese rituals in which inalienable metal valuables are polished with coconut oil, and in a ratu's remark to me that he used a gold valuable to light his way during a cave rite.

16. Two basic cloths enter exchange, the rectangular cloth (*regi*) worn by men and the tubular sarong (*rabi* or *lawu*) worn by women. In most cases either kind is suitable for exchange, although when even numbers are given, it is usually as pairs of regi and rabi. The men's headcloth (*rowa*), not normally used in exchange, sometimes plays a role in ancestral rituals. In the 1990s, the wearing of "modern" or "national" skirts and trousers was marked enough to be termed "foreign clothing" (*kalabi jiawa*) and was largely confined to civil servants and students.

17. Impermanence has been emphasized in several interpretations of textiles in other societies. For example, an interpretation of the cloth woven by Tamang women in Nepal finds it especially suited for representing their social identities, which are likewise "always in danger of becoming frayed" and need to be rewoven in each generation (March 1983: 737). A similar, iconic, link to mortality is found in Kodi, where the smell of indigo is said to be associated with that of rotting flesh (Hoskins 1989).

18. One common approach to cloth has been through iconography, for which there is a rich literature on Sumbanese cloth (Adams 1969, 1980; Geirnaert-Martin 1989, 1992a; Hoskins 1989). The self-evident iconographic richness of at least some of the cloth used in Anakalang, however, forms a striking contrast to the lack of an iconological discourse. Moreover, some of the most prized cloth there, *pagilung*, is plain white, with a geometrically twined border. Perhaps Anakalangese are less inclined than people accustomed to Western pictorial traditions to approach textiles as surfaces within which are contained discrete elements holding autonomous meanings. In both words and physical handling, Anakalangese usually treat textiles as unitary objects, to be understood in reference to larger actions.

19. Cotton and indigo grow on the coast but are easily transported inland. Some Anakalangese attribute the local absence of weaving to "laziness"—which is often a covert assertion of aristocratic status. According to Geirnaert-Martin

(1992a: 108), people in Laboya say that the weaving of ikatted (but not plain or embroidered) cloth is restricted to either extreme of the island, where it prevents the underground rivers from flowing out to sea. If it were done elsewhere, the flow of water throughout the island would be interrupted. The closest analogies to weaving in Anakalang are the plaiting of baskets and mats, done by women, and the twining of string, done by men.

20. Buffalo are perhaps even more central to ceremonial life in Kodi than in Anakalang, despite the fact that they are rarely used in agriculture there (Hoskins 1993b: 207).

21. The very existence of the procession presupposes a serious exchange. Animals under a certain value should not be accompanied by gongs, and the smallest animals should be discreetly conveyed in the dark and quiet after sundown. These matters can give rise to tensions between two groups. For example, in one case, a group of yera was reluctant to release the bride to live with her husband, because ngàba wini, being able to give only a few of the animals they owed, had not brought their gongs. Had they returned to their village with bride but no gongs, this would have implied to all within earshot that the bride's kabisu had not valued her but had given her up cheaply. This was resolved by a separate exchange by which yera loaned them their own gongs—which put the ngàba wini into further debt, since it would take another exchange to return them.

22. The killing of buffalo in Anakalang is much less competitive and expensive than the dramatic slaughters found in much of the rest of west Sumba (Geirnaert-Martin 1992a; Hoskins 1993a; Onvlee [1952] 1980) and some other Southeast Asian societies (e.g., Beatty 1992; Volkman 1985), but even the smallest funeral should climax with the public killing and butchering of at least one buffalo. The largest funeral I saw, for the burial of one of the widows of raja Umbu Sappy Pateduk and mother of the first regent of West Sumba, dispatched fifteen buffalo, to which should be added the dozen or so animals killed during the wake. Some Anakalangese claim that even this large a scale only began during the Japanese occupation, when people decided to gain status from their animals rather than lose them to the occupiers for nothing. In contemporary Anakalang, most ancestral rituals demand the sacrifice of only chickens. When larger animals are called for, pigs are far more common than buffalo.

23. In her analysis of Kodinese buffalo slaughter and men's identification with their animals, Hoskins (1993a) focuses on the display of youthful violence, to argue that sacrifice dramatizes struggles between junior and senior men. My own analytical approach is influenced in part by the relatively lesser role of buffalo slaughter in Anakalang. A good description of chicken entrail and pig liver divination in Weyewa, with diagrams, is given in Kuipers 1990: 100–107.

24. Anakalangese love meat, but none but the wealthiest civil servants ever eat meat that was not butchered for a feast or ceremony, something that struck the author of one of the first written accounts of the island (Kruseman 1836: 66). For the problems raised for Christians by the social and ritual role of meat, see Keane 1996.

25. Buffalo horns are perhaps the most overt conventional symbols among

the valuables we have considered. As icons of masculinity, the display of horns is echoed in everyday talk. The prized stone monoliths to which only a few kabisu can claim rights are "stone horns." But as icons, even horns are underdetermined: they are not only long, sharp, and potentially dangerous, they also come in pairs. It is this property that comes to the fore in the terms for the two wooden posts (identified as a male and female pair) called "house horns" that top off the peaked roof and for "horn partners," ritually matched but structurally identical houses (see Keane 1990: 97–100).

26. Pig measures range from one "carried under the arm" (*pahalili*) by a single man and on up by even numbers to an "eightsome" (*pawalungu*), which is borne in a bamboo cage on the shoulders of eight men. Horses fall into rough categories of age and gender, such as (literally) "young male horse" (*ana jara moni*) or the mature "female horse" (*jara bai*).

27. The most conventional measures for buffalo horns are as follows:

| Term and literal translation | Horn extends to |
| --- | --- |
| ana karabau (young buffalo) | (has no horn) |
| hakawilu (one candlenut) | first joint of index finger |
| duada kawilu (two candlenuts) | second joint of index finger |
| hadoduk (one pointing) | knuckle of forefinger |
| hahokal (one hollow) | beginning of thumb |
| hatabalu (one slap) | middle of palm |
| hamangaduku (one nodding over) | base of palm (where hand flaps) |
| hakaraja rewa (one bracelet place) | wrist |
| madidi gadung (ivory bracelet sits) | mid-forearm |
| hakabihu (one fullness) | fat part of forearm |
| tanga duada (worth two) | twice wrist-length |
| ta loku (at the furrow) | inside crook of arm |
| bera dolu (splits armlet) | lower part of bicep |
| pohi wira (wipe snot) | mid-bicep |
| tanga patu (worth four) | shoulder (four wrist-length) |
| tanga lima (worth five) | middle of chest (five wrist-length) |
| hadàpa (one arm span) | anything larger than tanga lima |

28. There are also markets in cloth and metal, a trade into which Anakalangese usually enter only as buyers. Probably most cloth in circulation comes from exchanges, otherwise the large volume of cloth transacted during a marriage negotiation would create a huge expense. One man told me that, besides at least seventeen cloths contributed by his supporters, he had drawn on the following reserves of his own household: two cloths woven by a kabisu sister who had married into a weaving district, one he had received several years earlier for overseeing another marriage negotiation, one given him by his brother three years earlier, and another he had received for supporting another marriage exchange three years earlier. In addition, as a civil servant, he had also been able to buy several cloths ranging in price from Rp 45,000 to Rp 15,000, totaling Rp 110,000 (at 1993 rates, about US $53), the price of a small buffalo or a large pig.

29. Some idea of the weight of exchange is shown by the market values for animals in 1987. At the time, the monthly starting salary of a schoolteacher was Rp 20,000 to 40,000 (about US $12–24). A steer with a horn length of "one finger" (about eight to ten months old) could bring Rp 60,000 to 100,000, a full arm-length ten-year-old, Rp 275,000 to 350,000 (lighter females bringing

less). A mature stallion could bring up to Rp 100,000, a mature mare Rp 60,000 to 75,000. The market for pigs was much less clear-cut, but some prices I heard ran from Rp 15,000 for a "two-man" (one-year-old) to over Rp 250,000 for the largest.

30. *Tanga* is a cover or top to something and is also used (as in the buffalo measures above) to indicate an equivalent measure or value. The *liḍi* is the lip or edge of the dish. One interpretation I was able to elicit was that, in contrast to baskets, which have lids, the offering dish is completed by its own lip, rather than by a separate piece, and so is self-contained. Ordinarily, the offering dish is a small woven dish with raised edges, although store-bought plates can also be used.

31. What is binding is less the actual object itself than its placement in the offering dish. At least, no effort is made to preserve the object as a visible sign of the obligation: most metal valuables are not individuated, and if coins or paper money are used in this role, they simply pass right back into circulation.

32. Nothing other than words can link metal or cloth with the cattle or pig that is standing outside the house or that is not yet in hand, or the gift with either intention or recipient. Beatty (1992: 141), speaking of exchange in Nias, notes "the perhaps obvious point that the objects of exchange are in nearly every case the same: pigs. Only the names of the prestations are different." The names are likely to be metapragmatic, that is, speaking of the actions they perform. This is implicit in Leach's (1954: 147) observation that the "titles" of Kachin fines specify both the problem in question and its resolution. In Anakalang, people commonly use the name of the prestation to refer to the action. For example, negotiating Ubu Dongu's son's marriage, his yera gave two pigs called "pig that is fostered" and "pursue the body," which implies that the couple had already slept together. At this, Ubu Dongu exploded in rage: "(He's) trying to ruin me! . . . It's as if the meat has already been taken from the shelf, as if the rice has already been scooped from the pot, when he 'foster pigs' my child, when he 'pursues the body,' when he 'bears' it 'on the lap.'" His rage concerns the way in which the gift impugns the good name of his household.

33. The risk that gifts will not be reciprocated is a widespread feature of exchange, but, as Weiner (1992) argues, it can operate in tandem with a second risk as well, that one will be forced to give what one wishes to hold on to (see chapter 8). On the consequences of these two risks for social identity, in a society of New Ireland, see Foster 1993.

34. Ubu Laiya's logic is not idiosyncratic. It mirrors, for example, one conventional way of disposing of a baby's navel cord. The parents should not intentionally throw it away. They store it until the child is old enough to play, then wrap it in cloth and give it to the child to use as a ball. In this way, it just becomes lost.

## CHAPTER 4: LOADED TERMS

1. My main interest here is in the register shift. For some other implications of using the Indonesian language in an Anakalangese context, see Keane in press.

2. I refer to "ritual speech" throughout. As Kuipers (1990: 58) points out,

the expression "ritual language" is somewhat misleading in the Sumbanese case, as it does not comprise a distinct lexicon and does not derive historically from a different language. For an introduction to ritual speech as a regional feature of eastern Indonesia, see the essays in Fox 1988; for comparable traditions in western Indonesia, see Bowen 1991; Metcalf 1989. The importance of ritual speech in Sumba was recognized early (Onvlee 1925; Wielenga 1909); the most thorough treatment to date is Kuipers's study of Weyewa (1990); see also Kapita 1979, 1987 for Kambera. I discuss some effects of the changing historical context for ritual speech in Keane 1995a.

3. *Lola* is to cut in strips. In reduplicated form, *lola-lola*, it is to divide up a garden, marking out its major divisions before planting. One ritual speaker explained *lola li panewi* to me as meaning 'to straighten out the talk, to say it has to be this way and that way.' *Teda*, the term mentioned above, means "arranged in close order" (as of rice fields). For *pata* (which I gloss here as "customary"), see chapter 7.

4. Other metalinguistic terms distinguish between phonological and pragmatic dimensions of language. They include *li* (word, intentional sound), *pulu* (the sound of a voice), *tiki* (to enunciate, pronounce), and *peka* (inform, tell, communicate). In the context of ritual, to "speak mistakenly" (*kajala panewi*) is to use an inappropriate couplet, to "utter mistakenly" (*kajala tiki*) is to mispronounce something. *Li* can refer to words or to the sound produced by a bird or gong. *Pulu* is restricted to the human voice. Metonymically it refers to speech more broadly: one might say of an imminent decision from an important man "we await his utterance" (*tenginya puluna*). Nominalized (*pulungu*) it can refer to the illocutionary force of an utterance.

5. Among the named genres of speech that I have heard are *papalang* (conveyance speech in exchange), *kajiàla* (negotiation speech), *wara* (challenge before war or directed at outsiders arriving at village), *hau ma mati* (women's keening songs), *loḍu* (male song for female dancers, with female chorus), *yaiwo* (male song for male dancers), *taungu li* (oratory performed along with either *loḍu* or *yaiwo*), *pawururungu* and *payoyelang* (ritual chants), *palaikung* (offering speech made before prayer), *nyàba* (prayer), *kaḅetahu rau nyau* (coconut leaf divination), and *uratu* (spear divination). For Weyewan ritual speech genres, see Kuipers 1990: 58.

6. Some women, however, are said to be the real brains behind their husbands' command of ritual speech. One important leader told me that he sometimes sends his wife, who is herself remarkably assertive and self-confident, to oversee certain minor ritualized negotiations. Women are also considered to be the most appropriate performers of certain genres of song, especially keening over the dead and some work chanties, in which the focus is on direct emotional engagement of the listeners (see Kuipers 1986).

7. I know of only one clear case of invention. Sometime in the 1980s, Ubu Laiya, a skillful but at times perilously brazen speaker, expanded on a familiar reference to hospitality, "quickly scoop water, quickly cook rice" (*wai geha lingi, auhu geha mami*) by interpolating the lines "like thermos water, like (a newly introduced strain of) short rice" (*ta wai termosu, ta auhu pari padak*). Criticizing him, people said this sort of hubris is just what you would expect

of someone as shamelessly aggressive as Ubu Laiya. As I explain below, however, although people faulted Ubu Laiya for too obvious an innovation, he was was in fact extrapolating from a legitimate principle that allows the speaker to lengthen the line.

8. Compare Gossen's (1974: 412) observation that in Mayan ritual speech the higher the register of speech, the greater the number of potential referents for given terms, and Errington's (1988: 191) finding that lexemes in "higher" speech styles of Javanese have multiple equivalents compared to those in "lower" styles—in these cases, the higher the register, the greater the semantic or referential ambiguity (see also Dixon 1971).

9. See Mannheim (1986) for a version of this argument in Quechua. Analysis of parallelism in search of cultural patterns need not be restricted to the lexicon. For example, Urban (1991) argues that grammatical parallelism in myth texts may consistently favor either agent or patient, revealing fundamental, but unconscious, cultural assumptions about agency.

10. Bauman (1977) argues that we should not assume a priori that poetic language is a deviation from a prior or more fundamental literal means of expression. In accepting this argument, I appeal to linguistic ideology as a means of getting at a locally shared, and *public*, understanding of what is or is not figurative. The dominant Anakalangese treatment of ritual speech is as a highly marked form of language. Thus, in east Sumba, the figures of ritual speech are spoken of as "disguised reference" (*hangindingu ngara*; alternatively, perhaps translatable as "screened-off name") (Adams 1974: 331; Forth 1988: 135).

11. It is also true, however, that when people in Anakalang refer to a couplet in ordinary speech, they often say only the first line. This suggests that they may see the couplet as composed out of two conceptually (but not, as I have noted, prosodically) independent lines, a common feature of Malay and Indonesian poetics (see Sweeney 1987: 130). Forth (1988: 315) reports that people in Rindi say one line is primary, the other a secondary comment on it (see Mannheim 1986). In Anakalang, the asymmetry seems to be rather weak, but to the extent it holds, couplets would seem to have some structural resemblance to similes, in which a figure is compared to a ground that is taken to be already given.

12. When I went over excerpts from three ritual speech genres with a man twenty-seven years old who, although a fluent native speaker of Anakalangese, had spent the last seven years of his education away from Sumba, he was unable to identify a significant number of words: oration—text of 111 lexemes (157 word tokens), 23 unknown; prayer—145 lexemes, 20 unknown, 16 known but not found in everyday speech; negotiation—110 lexemes, 11 unknown.

13. Compare use of different dialects of Rotinese (Fox 1974), of neighboring languages in Berawan (Metcalf 1989), and of Spanish in Mayan couplets (Bricker 1974). On the appropriation of Sanskrit and Old Javanese to form an elevated register in Bali, see Zurbuchen 1987: 16.

14. Deictics are indexical elements of language that "specify the identity or placement in space or time of individuated objects relative to the participants in a verbal interaction" (Hanks 1990: 5). In contrast to such words as "dog" and "cat," the differences between "here" and "there," "this" and "that," "now" and "then," require some reference to the actual circumstances in which they

are spoken. Hence the infinite deferral embedded in my landlord's ambiguous undated note, posted day after day on the front door: "The elevator will be fixed tomorrow." Tomorrow (relative to now) is always another day. For a foundational discussion of the importance of pronouns as indexical components of language, see Benveniste 1971a.

15. Limited reference to context is a common characteristic important to the authority of ritual speech (Du Bois 1986). Different genres of Sumbanese ritual speech vary in how much indexicality they permit (Kuipers 1990; see Forth 1988: 130). Negotiation speech is syntactically more rooted in context than speech directed at spirits, some of which presents couplets in minimal forms, without any affixing at all. This imparts to them a sense of strangeness, a certain incantatory abruptness, and syntactic ambiguity (for instance, it is affixing that most clearly distinguishes substantive from verbal functions). In addition to creating a sense of detachment from the here and now, the muting of indexicality is also a common way to show deference to the listeners. High Javanese, for example, uses fewer demonstrative pronouns than lower styles (Errington 1988: 210), for indexicals, as Peirce puts it, may produce the feeling of "forcibly intruding upon the mind" (cited in Errington 1988: 249).

## CHAPTER 5: TEXT, CONTEXT, AND DISPLACEMENT

1. Imperatives and requests are especially likely to appear nested in quotations, as if to separate the speaker from their force. It thereby creates a sense of temporal displacement: the imperative is portrayed as something that has already been uttered (Bakhtin 1981: 294, 331). The speaker thus is not directly present at the critical moment and her or his agency is not directly involved, blunting that part of the interaction in which one person's desires impinge most directly on another (Brown and Levinson 1978; Du Bois 1986; Sherzer 1983: 210). This reflects the fact that at the core of many ritual texts lie verbs of giving, injunctions to receive, requests for things to be given, and the names of donors and recipients, and of course performance itself can be an exchange valuable: in Anakalang, the term "reciprocation" (*pitaku*) can refer to either verbal or material exchanges. Indirection therefore also helps mute the indexical force and the danger of pragmatic misdirection, such as misconstrual of the nature of the act or misidentification of the agent. Similarly, as Errington (1988: 192) points out, the etiquette of Javanese speech styles bears especially carefully on acts of exchange.

2. The shift in key that I have described creates sound patterns whose authority is inseparable from their aesthetics. Orations may be proclaimed in stentorian tones or in soft, mournful cadences. A forceful delivery displays the vigorous and self-confident spirit of the speaker, a more modest delivery can express deference to the listener—or accent the speaker's own refinement (see figs. 11 and 12). Rising and falling speech is considered emotionally affecting. It is *panarungu*, the empathy-producing quality also possessed by the rising and falling volume of mortuary gongs. Sometimes the speaker may even break into

weeping—when the singer quotes the speech, he too will then weep. I watched one orator give a series of speeches in an almost inaudible voice, his back to the plaza, because, he later told me, he was ashamed to face the ancestors whose knowledge and wealth was so much greater than his own.

3. The possibility that a given event will be wrongly typified is especially at issue when dealing with spirits, with whom communication is always somewhat problematic. Thus, for instance, when the villagers of Prai Bakul held a cooling ritual after a fire, they staged the *kataga*, an exuberant dance by armed men. Since the same dance can be used in rites to declare war, the accompanying oratory stated explicitly that this was *not* intended. Quoting lines that would have been used when declaring war, the orators said, "I don't 'begin and give cause,' I don't 'twine and hammer.'"

4. The reverse can also be the case, that context can determine what the couplet denotes. For instance, "he of the red eyes, she of the blushing chest," when used in negotiation refers to gold exchange valuables but in worship denotes the marapu that they represent. In oration events, "Sawu betel, fashioned cover" is an offering made to the singer by an orator, but in negotiation it is a formal request for an interruption in the proceedings. Conversely, the same objects may be referred to by different couplets, according to context. Thus gongs are "father sun lute, mother moon flute" in major rituals but "asking voice lute, singing lap drum" in processions.

5. The following passages are from recorded performances, containing a few defective couplets and other errors. Speakers, in going over transcripts, usually correct these, but I have left the text here as it was spoken. The yaiwo oration here was performed by Ubu Pàda Buli Yora of kabisu Makatakeri in August 1986.

6. Although some lines are missing, including the first line of the offering speech, I have chosen this for its brevity and because it has reflexive functions of its own, its purpose to close a night of orations, taking up the words of the song from the plaza and stowing them in the house. These performances were part of the annual rites called "Descent to the Marapu Cave" in Parewatana, December 1986. I recorded them in the village of Deru. The offering speech was by Ubu Kana Dapa Namung (Paroru) of kabisu Awanang, the prayers by Ubu Longgi Wana, kabisu Makawawu.

7. This refers to the host spirit in the village where the event takes place—it awaits the offering on the mat along with the praying ratu who faces the man making the offering speech. The spirit receives this message from the praying ratu and will pass it on in turn. Anakalangese pronouns are not marked for gender, but when couplets explicitly refer to gender, they usually pair male with female (e.g., "mother" and "father").

8. A synecdoche for "mother-father," that is, the speaker, who, on behalf of the ritual's sponsor, addresses the praying ratu, who in turn represents the senior ratu of the village. He is spoken to as the one who receives this speech in order to pass it along to the spirits.

9. This form of address, which is somewhat intimate, is used for the immediate recipient of the offering, the most recently deceased ancestor of the ratu,

presumably his father, who will pass the message on to more distant ancestors. Unlike earlier ancestors, this spirit is in close physical proximity to the speaker. As another ratu put it, 'My father hears everything I say in the house.'

10. Epithets for the addressee, the spirit who guards the house in the host village into which the words are to be lifted.

11. Christians can be addressed by their baptismal name—but even this is still subject to some further operation, such as abbreviation (e.g., Kristof becomes Risto). That even the full Christian name is still a form of displacement is suggested by the fact that people often refer to the Christian name as either one's "foreign name" (*ngara jiawa*) or "school name" (*ngara sekola*).

12. Horse names are usually semantically transparent. Although some refer to physical characteristics of the horse itself ("White Eye"), they often allude to an event ("Breaks Off the Greater," referring to headhunting exploits), make boasts ("Puts Down Companions"), testify to social position ("Noble's Flank," who was owned by the raja's right-hand man), or even make an accusation ("Only Me," referring to a neighbor's selfishness) all of which allude back to the horse's owner.

13. That the association between hierarchy and representation may underlie the use of metaphor as well is suggested by one person's comment to me that in east Sumba, where rank is a serious matter, marriage negotiators will promise you one hundred head of cattle but only give you one. By contrast, the more vulgar west Sumbanese say just what they will give—as if literalism were a function of commonness.

14. The "good name" is usually taken from a recent ancestor, such as a great-grandparent. The naming procedure suggests that the ancestor in question actually selects the name. Evidence from similar procedures in Rindi (Forth 1981: 144–148) and Laboya (Geirnaert-Martin 1992a: 65–66) suggests that the relationship is not one of reincarnation but of patronage and protection.

15. Putnam's classic example concerns the meaning of the word "gold." I do not have to know the chemical description of gold, nor must I be able to prove whether something is gold, to use the word, but *some* speaker of my language must. My practical knowledge of the word depends on the expertise of others. This sort of difference is not restricted to scientific matters but reflects the fact that cultural knowledge is unevenly and hierarchically distributed.

16. For the distinction between presupposing and entailing (or creative) indexicality, see chapter 7.

17. As Metcalf (1989: 28–34) points out, societies vary greatly in how much they insist on the formulaic (hence, iconic and iterable) character of ritual speech. Anakalang lies between the improvisitory individualism of the Berawan described by Metcalf and the exactitude demanded of Navaho ritual (Reichard 1944). Reichard's (1944: 12) description of the latter makes apparent the relationship between iterability and danger: "there is the emotional pressure which ensues from the dictum that a single mistake not only renders the prayer void, but may bring upon the one praying the wrath instead of the blessing, of the beings implored." In Bakhtinian terms, one might suggest that the more "monologic" the speech genre, the greater the implicit danger. See below for an example of this wrath in Anakalang.

18. The general phenomenon of "internal translation" (Becker 1979; Zurbuchen 1987) is a significant feature of ritual or etiquette systems in many parts of Indonesia. For example, Javanese and Balinese ceremonial theater directly counterpose different languages, some characters paraphrasing in contemporary everyday speech the archaic language of others (see Sherzer 1983 on similar effects in Central America). In these forms of internal translation, alternative forms of expression are both present within a single set of utterances. Copresence, however, is not necessary for speakers to be aware of what is not being said. Java's famous "speech levels" work in part by self-conscious lexical substitution, which Errington (1988: 191) has analyzed in terms of avoidance of the "ordinary" word. For some of the implications of treating the relations among Javanese speech levels as translation, see Siegel 1986.

## CHAPTER 6: VOICES, AGENTS, AND INTERLOCUTORS

1. In some very large kaḅisu, constituent houses form the basic negotiating units. This is one indication that the kaḅisu may be starting to fission, and the capacity to act independently in this way is another constitutive power of the representational practices of negotiation. As will become clear below, however, such houses must still act under an ancestral name (kaḍehang) by which they are addressed in ritual speech. This makes it difficult for them to be recognized as acting independently of the full kaḅisu. For purposes of simplicity, I will speak here of "kaḅisu" as the groups that negotiate.

2. One form of marriage by capture, "snatching in the field," is still practiced on occasion. On rare occasions it is a real kidnapping, but at least by the 1980s it seems mostly to have been done by mutual agreement between bride and groom. It is a recognized, if risky, way of initiating negotiations when one or the other kaḅisu has resisted the marriage, to jump-start a negotiation that has stalled.

3. Writing of "headhunting rituals" in Sulawesi that now make use of coconuts in place of heads, Kenneth George (1996: 60) remarks that we need not assume the coconut is merely a poor substitute for a prior and more real head. The palpable artifice may itself have value.

4. An interesting comparison can be made to Maori formal encounters. According to Salmond (1975: 58), meetings between stranger groups have many of the characteristics of agonism and risk that I describe here. In contrast, meetings between "friendly groups and kinfolk" are marked by *aroha* (love, solidarity). In Anakalang, the rhetoric of solidarity works in tension with a pragmatic structure that suggests confrontation (see Beatty 1992: 236 on an analogous situation in Nias). Moreover, who counts as friendly is never fully given but requires continual practical reconstruction. For a useful comparison to the interplay of represented and implicit violence in poetic challenges in Yemen, see Caton 1990.

5. For an example of ḅatang talk, see the quoted speech addressed to Dedungara in the previous chapter, page 118.

6. Whether the visiting party is yera or ngàba wini depends on the history of the two groups up to that point. Although the woman should reside with her

family until the negotiations reach a resolution, circumstances such as elope-
ment make it very common for the final meeting to occur at the village of wife-
takers.

7. The mother-father does not go along in the first encounter, as when kabisu
N first brought betel to K. In part, this is evidently a matter of saving face, since
outright rejection is most likely at this stage. The mother-father only goes along
when there are women in the party and when they are permitted to enter the
host's house. Thus the presence of mother-father indexes the full engagement of
two collective social agents. Put another way, the existence of a mother-father,
in any instance, is a potential that is only realized and fulfilled as a result of
prior successful interactions.

8. According to Joel Kuipers (pers. comm.), the less hierarchical parts of
Weyewa do not emphasize the delegation of speech to nonprincipals. Nonetheless, as I argue later in this chapter, to the extent that they still speak in canonical couplets, Weyewans must be understood as delegating their voice to some degree. In this, they are less egalitarian, for instance, than the Berawan of Borneo,
in whose ritual speech "the speaker has no voice but his own" (Metcalf 1989:
34).

9. When responding to the shouted kadehang, màlo (an allophone of the
everyday welcome màla) is a high-pitched and drawn-out cry—in keeping with
the idiom of distances overcome, this is said to be because the two parties are
facing each other across a great space, like people calling from one ridge to another, and is thus a pragmatic icon of the metaphor of social distance. The serious consequentiality of proper form applies even to this task. People say that
if the respondent's cries do not match the intonation and length of the wunang
to whom he replies, or if he cries out at the wrong time, or—worst of all—if he
cries out the wrong name, he will fall sick or suffer some other misfortune.

10. This trope, part of the pervasive imagining of formal encounters as stylized warfare, is found in the very word kadehang, literally, a piece of wood used
as a chopping block or a pillow, a foundation or underpinning (see Mitchell
1981: 337; Forth 1988: 138). The most pertinent sense seems to be the first,
which portrays the words received from the other wunang as blows received by
the person who serves as kadehang.

11. Ritual speakers avoid eye contact, usually gazing down at the mat just
in front of them, or off to the side. As in Samoa (Duranti 1994: 78), this is
probably in part to allow the speaker and listener to concentrate on what they
are hearing. But it is also part of a more general embodiment of deference, what
Bourdieu ([1972] 1977) (probably following Mauss) calls "bodily hexis." It is
integrated with other forms of indirection such as the use of multiple intermediaries, the avoidance of "good names," the muting of indexicals, and the way
suppliants may sit at the edge of the veranda facing away from their host.

12. Ubu Laiya's insistence that he never studied ritual speech but that it just
came to him is very typical of ritual speakers in East Nusa Tenggara, who are liable to attribute their skills to an ancestral source (Fox 1988: 13–14). More
generally, it reflects the way in which practical know-how is often acquired, not
through self-conscious activities of teaching and learning but by picking it up as
a disposition (Bourdieu [1972] 1977; Lave and Wenger 1991). Another charac-

teristic diagnostic of this kind of learning is one ratu's comment, when he was unable to remember certain details of his kabisu history for me: 'Wait until the (ritual) gongs start playing, then it all comes out.' One can pick up the basic rhythms of the dialogue fairly quickly. I have seen small children play at being wunang, one crying out a kadehang, the other responding.

13. Normally, the principals make an initial prestation, a machete or a cloth, at the time they first approach the wunang for help. On arriving for the first stage of negotiations, a gift of a small rooster and, for yera, a mamuli, and, for ngába wini, money or a ring, invests the wunang with speaking authority. At the point when the exchanges have been settled, but the formal speech frame is still in place, the closing exchange is between wunang. Using valuables provided by their respective principals, yera's wunang gives a cloth to ngába wini's wunang, who reciprocates with a horse. In contrast to all that has gone before, it is a direct exchange between donor and recipient, unmediated by others, a step back out of the frame of formality. It is also performed without negotiation, as befits those who must themselves have no interests but speak only for others.

14. As in all honorable gain, however, there is an important temporal dimension to the wunang's reciprocation. The immediate payment is relatively light, but the gratitude he gains stands to come in handy in the long run. Ama Delu claimed that when his daughter married, he did not even have to ask people for help. As soon as they heard, people for whom he had served as wunang came from as far away as Lewa and Wanukaka to contribute: goods were simply attracted to him by dint of his personal powers.

15. Recorded in Lai Bodi, May 1986. Wunang for Palajangu is Ubu Hami Leli Dima; for Pàda Pari, Ubu Janga.

16. The couplet in lines 4 and 6 refers to the passage of a wunang across the space that separates the two parties. It also resonates with a common couplet that denotes the act of speaking formally, figured as a dog that leaps, a horse that jumps (see lines 59 and 61).

17. The couplets in lines 10–11 and 12–13 refer to two prestations as they are represented by tokens in the offering dish. Here the prestations formalize the invitation to eat.

18. This passage refers to the formal act of receiving a guest by giving a meal. The "granary" (the house attic) and benches are synecdoches for the house. Line 16 is a defective couplet, missing the second line.

19. An allusion to the process of making a spice from river shrimp, this rather obscure figure refers to the act of receiving and responding to a message. The speaker left out the couplet's second line. Note that the speaker has also reversed the order of lines 35 and 36.

20. Wanukaka and Laboya are two ethnolinguistic domains southwest of Anakalang. The figures of trail, thorns, and rotten wood play on the common image of ritual procedures as following a narrow path laid down by the ancestors ("men of old") without deviating into the brush on either side.

21. Like cattle that go astray: let these prestations not miss the mark or their purpose be misconstrued.

22. These are count terms alluding to objects in the dishes. Spears and

machetes come in "sticks," the flat metal maraga (as well as cloth) in "sheets," and mamuli in "mates."

23. Refers to the prestation made when ngàba wini first went to yera to bring the betel that opens negotiations.

24. As I noted in chapter 1, in ordinary conversations certain default assumptions about the relationships among voices, bodies, and agencies usually hold. But the formal character and language ideology of ritual speech work to disrupt such assumptions. This contributes to the sense of semiotic difficulty and social unease that pervades formal events.

25. The constructed nature of the collective subject, and the way in which even an overactive mother-father can destabilize it, can be illustrated with another incident. Guru Andreas, from kabisu B, was a teacher posted to a corner of Anakalang far from home. When his son decided to marry locally, Guru Andreas asked the local desa head, a man from kabisu L, to serve as mother-father for ngàba wini. When troubles arose during the negotiation, this desa head intervened directly, raising hackles on both sides. As one member of the yera complained, 'Hey, we don't receive cattle from L but from B!' Had all gone smoothly, no one would ever have made this distinction. The desa head would have been accepted as a member of kabisu B, whose actions would have been those of a single, undivided agent. It was when things began to go badly that yera discovered that they faced a congeries of particular persons. This also shows the extent to which *one party's* agency depends on the willingness of *another* to attribute responsibility to it.

## CHAPTER 7: FORMALITY AND THE ECONOMY OF SIGNS

1. The problem is not only posed by the state. For a discussion of the complex effort by Dutch missionaries to understand and disentangle what they saw as a mistaken conflation of spiritual and material, subject and object, words and things on the part of Sumbanese, see Keane 1996 and n.d.

2. The less authoritative "pata of life" (*pata moruku*), for example, can include minor variations of style and custom such as the various techniques of planting rice in different ethnolinguistic domains in west Sumba. A rarer term, *hùri*, perhaps borrowed from east Sumba, refers more narrowly to ancestral procedures. Ancestral rules are also sometimes identified with the dimly perceived, vaguely personified spirit Nuku-Sara (Kapita 1976a: 81). Nuku is apparently cognate with Indonesian *hukum*, "law," from Arabic, Sara with Indonesian *cara*, "manner, style," versions of which are found in local ritual or institutional terminologies across eastern Indonesia.

3. The word *adat* is of Arabic origin and its meanings were first formulated in the Malay-speaking world, apparently to distinguish non-Islamic from Islamic practices. Thus even in its precolonial context, its role in defining a contrast internal to society implies the existence of an outsider's perspective on the discursive object to which it refers. It is therefore not surprising that the concept of adat was readily adopted and manipulated by colonial and postcolonial pow-

ers, as a bolster for indirect rule, bulwark against Islam, and, most recently, "invented tradition" (Abdullah 1972; Acciaioli 1985; Rodgers-Siregar 1981). Early Indonesian nationalism often saw adat as a barrier to modernity and its freedoms. In contemporary Indonesia, the concept is ambivalent. On the one hand, both state and local societies seek in adat a source (albeit highly attenuated and reified) of primordial legitimacy. On the other hand, it also represents a hindrance to the rationalizing forces of development. In the process, adat in some parts of Indonesia has become increasingly about the display of a traditional order detached from surrounding events. In the latter sense, it is part of a semantic field that also includes "culture" (Indo. *kebudyaan*) and "tradition" (Indo. *tradisi*) (for a subtle discussion of this set of issues, see Pemberton 1994). On the reconfiguration of "culture" in contemporary Anakalang, see Keane 1995a.

4. Debates in Anakalang often concern rather arcane or technical questions, such as whether one prestation should come before or after another. Sometimes they concern the degree to which ritual speech is metaphorical or literal: one man told me how impressed he was that a group from east Sumba gave his kabisu an actual dog for a prestation called "the dog" that in Anakalang is usually a horse. As in Malagasy (Keenan 1975), debate can also be a way for one party to show its deference to the other: ngàba wini is more likely to be challenged and eventually to cede the point to yera than vice versa. But some differences are neither trivial nor matters of etiquette. For instance, during the long set of rituals to call back the spirit of a village that had burned, two ratus insisted on versions of the central rite that differed dramatically in their spatial orientation, physical performance, and speech. According to one, the ratus stand at the village gate, shred a chicken, and toss it outward in all directions while shouting a ritual summons to the wild lands where the spirit had hidden. The other held that a gold mamuli should be lowered by stages from top to bottom of a vertical post in the center of the village, drawing the spirit back down from the sky, which is its origin place, to which it had fled. In this case, colleagues envisioning entirely different ritual performances both supported their cases by appeal to ancestral rules they would *both* say they share.

5. In using the term "metapragmatics" to refer to talk about action in general, I am expanding somewhat on its original use, which is restricted to talk about the actions performed by language (as opposed, for example, to talk about syntax or semantics). This term occurs in trying to distinguish the various ways in which language relates to its contexts and has roots in the work of, among others, Bateson ([1955] 1972), Jakobson (1960), and Vološinov ([1930] 1973).

6. A similar insistence on inadequate knowledge, a widespread feature of ancestral ritual, plays an important part in Traube's (1986) account of the Mambai of Timor; for a millenarian version of the sense of depletion in Sulawesi, see Atkinson 1989. In addition to the features described here, disclaimers probably also have the effect of sustaining the shared assumption that an ideal order of pata exists, in the face of conflicting accounts, imperfect performances, and failed outcomes, by the same sort of self-justifying logic that Evans-Pritchard (1937) attributed to Azande magic.

7. When animals are killed, for example, the purpose must be enunciated in words, effectively announcing that the killing is not for nothing. The disclaimer has two aspects: the killing is situated within a larger ritual project, and it is compelled by the demands of ancestrally decreed formal action, not by the personal desires or intentions of the killers. If no prayers are spoken to frame the sacrifice, the animal dies startled (*katatak*), without any reason, and its dewa will run off into caves or trees, no one knows where. In this context, intentions are not personal purposes but rather that which links discrete actions to overarching and typifiable projects. The notion of creating and naming differences among otherwise indistinguishable items is reflected in the ritual epithet of the ratu who makes the offering speech, he "who tears the barkcloth, who apportions out the beads."

8. The importance of naming can be seen in its avoidance as well. For instance, certain marriage prestations that are given as a unit consist of several distinct components, each of which has its own name. If ngàba wini feels its own prestation is inadequate, it may ask to give all the components together, "together with their leaves, together with their vines" without publicly distinguishing the parts. A stubborn or hostile yera might try to force them to name the parts, shaming them into owing five buffalo instead of, say, five colts.

9. For a discussion of the separation and reincorporation of brides in Rindi, see Forth 1981: 377–381. For marriage prestations in other Sumbanese domains, see Geirnaert-Martin 1992a: 233–242; Hoskins 1993b: 21–22; Kapita 1976a: 124–128; Onvlee 1973e: 81–101. Perhaps most similar to Anakalang is Wanukaka (Mitchell 1981: 296–327). For the implications of variable affiliations see McKinnon 1991.

10. Thus, at any given moment, people may hold conflicting interpretations of the present status of a couple. For instance, a groom often spends several years in bride service living with his wife's parents. This man's status hinges on whether his kabisu eventually completes the exchanges. But until they actually do so, it can never be entirely certain if they will. In the meantime, whether the man is undergoing bride service or has become a dependent may be only retrospectively determined. Conversely, parents may release a bride to her husband's household before they are willing to declare themselves satisfied with the exchanges thus far. The kabisu affiliation of this couple may also be subject to debate.

11. Forth (1981: 390–394) argues that in Rindi (where rank is more prominent, status rivalry apparently absent, and marriage exchange much less expensive and contested than in Anakalang), completeness and expense tend to correlate with the social distance between the two parties. Because standing affines can be relied on to continue to support each other, the marriage exchanges that renew their ties are likely to be low or incomplete. In contrast, new alliances, being less reliable, are likely to be more costly to initiate. Two factors, however, bring Rindi closer to the kind of causal logic I describe for Anakalang. Marriages between poorer, lower-ranking, and smaller lineages—characteristics that, significantly, tend to covary—are less likely to form asymmetric (hence socially close) alliances (Forth 1981: 393), and asymmetric alliances among nobility

may be very expensive for prestige considerations. In addition, the expense of high-ranking marriages means that much larger numbers of people are involved. As a result, like dynastic marriages around the world, such marriages have broad consequences for political and structural relations across society.

12. Since Anakalang, like some other parts of Sumba (Mitchell 1981: 46), has a low birthrate, kabisu may even have to worry about biological as well as institutional reproduction. Several kabisu seem to have become extinct within the last century. This can be prevented by adrogation (a term used by McKinnon [1991] to describe a similar procedure in Tanimbar). An adult male is formally separated from his kabisu by exchanges called "jackfruit pith, citrus section," a metaphor for identical units that are easily separated. In contrast to "marriage-in," the man loses no status. This is one example of how even the physical reproduction of the kabisu is a function of its ability to engage in ritual speech and exchange.

13. The contingency on wealth of claims to rank is a familiar feature of exchange and feasting systems such as those in Nias (Beatty 1992) and highland Burma (Leach 1954). Within the limits of this book, my concern is less with the strategic maneuvers such claims involve than with the implications for how the interwoven meanings of wealth and rank articulate with the challenges inherent to formal interaction.

14. Upwardly mobile men can, at least to an extent, translate wealth into rank in the following generation by using high marriage payments to obtain brides of rank. If the difference in rank is too obvious, the extremely high payment that ruptures relations, mentioned above, may result, but the children will still be considered of higher rank than their father. Not surprisingly, such strategies are viewed with suspicion by more respectable folk; as in Kodi (Hoskins 1993b: 22), an upstart man is said to "wash himself off with gold."

15. Since at any given point people are often enmeshed in multiple exchanges, goods can disperse very quickly. For example, kabisu D received six horses and three buffalo from their ngàba wini. One buffalo went immediately to the bride's mother's brother, as was his due, two horses and two buffalo to her father's parallel cousin, who had directed the negotiation and made the greatest contribution of cloth and pigs. Two horses were given to members of the group who had pressing obligations to their own yera. These were handed over within a week. Three horses went to pay an outstanding marriage debt arising from marriage negotiation a few months earlier. They were sent over to the yera in question the very day they were received, without formality, since D considered them to be out of their hands right from the start, "fallen stem, broken base," that is, already committed. One horse I was able to trace passed through three exchanges over the course of a single week.

16. The bond between memory and material things is itself a highly valued form of regard, as suggested by the fact that to "remember" (namu) is also to "be concerned with someone," which Anakalangese often gloss as "love" (Indo. cinta). Both are commonly manifested in material forms: as one man told me, 'I know my mother loves me because when I come to visit, she sets aside food for me, even if I've shown up empty-handed.'

17. For the distinction between "presupposing" and "entailing," or "creative," indexicality, see Silverstein 1976, 1993. In language, the use of presupposing indexicals builds on shared assumptions between speaker and hearer in which the referent has already been established: to say "that chair" assumes that the particular chair being referred to has already been made clear earlier in the conversation or by some other feature of the context. Entailing (or "creative") indexicals make explicit and reframe or transform a reading of the circumstances in which they occur. A familiar example is the switch between *tu* and *vous* in French, which can redefine the degree of intimacy and respect between speakers.

## CHAPTER 8: SUBJECTS AND THE VICISSITUDES
##                     OF OBJECTS

1. The use of male "grandfather" (*boku*) is probably short for the more formal dual-gendered "ancient grandfather, ancient grandmother" (*boku dai, apu dai*). The pronouns (*duna, -na*) referring to the gold object are ambiguous for both gender and the animate/inanimate distinction. By calling it a "thing" (and switching into the modernity-coded register of Indonesian to do so) suggests he thinks of it as inanimate, but the term I translate below as "guy" (*oda*) usually refers to a person.

2. Cognates of the word *dewa* are found throughout the Indonesian archipelago, ultimately derived from Sanskrit, though presumably in most cases, as in Sumba, by way of some intermediate languages. Onvlee ([1957] 1973b: 211 ff.; 1984: 331) proposes that in translating the Bible into Kambera, *ndewa* be used for *psyche* and occasionally for *pneuma*. People seem to vary greatly in how they think of dewa, something that is surely exacerbated by differing assumptions on the part of Christians and non-Christians.

3. Dewa is not restricted to humans but may be attributed to solitary large trees, outstanding rocks, or other individual features of the landscape, or to villages, cattle, and other wild or domestic animals. Inalienable valuables manifest the dewa of the ancestral village, the "dewa of the village land, *ura* of the river mouth." Altars in the gardens receive offerings for the "work dewa, digging dewa," which assures that labor there will have productive results. Like English "spirit," dewa bears connotations of the nonphysical essence of something. For example, a person, upon meeting another and being able to offer only betel without the necessary areca, might use the word *dewa* either to denote the missing object, saying "chew its dewa" (*mama na dewana*) or agent, "let your dewa chew" (*mama na dewamu*).

4. There are several terms associated with dewa, but few Anakalangese seem confident about the distinctions among them. As Forth (1981: 77) rightly observes speaking of the Rindi cognate, "*ndewa* . . . is probably the most elusive term in the eastern Sumbanese metaphysical vocabulary." In Anakalangese ritual speech, *dewa* is most commonly paired with *ura*: vein, nerve, lines of the palm or sole, that is, marks by which personal fate is divined, and by metonymy, fate itself. Some people say the closely related term *hamangu*, like its cog-

nates in many other Indonesian languages, refers to the mortal parts of a person, identified with the breath (*hangahu*), in contrast to dewa that is immortal and has no particular location in the body. Associated with *hamangu* (see Forth 1981: 439 n. 3; Hoskins 1987; Onvlee 1984: 59) is the word *hamawu* (literally, "a shadow"), and one person told me it is the shadow of the dewa (on spirit and shadow in Laboya, see Geirnaert-Martin 1992a: 59–70). Both seem to emphasize ways in which persons are composed of distinct, potentially separable, components. It is the hamangu that registers the effects of being startled and that can be lost if one is thrown by a horse, suffers a sudden attack, falls from a tree, or undergoes a shaming experience.

5. A thriving house has a number of dewa, including those located at altars by the front door, the front pillar, and the back of the front room. The various dewa in the house are a continual presence that serves as the addressee for prayers and ritual song and, as people reminded me from time to time, an important audience for all other activities in the house as well (Keane 1995a). They not only mediate between effort and outcome but also provide a constant other to whom the living present themselves.

6. The power of prestations to detach and move the dewa is institutionalized in several forms. For example, after a senior man has directed an enterprise like a marriage negotiation or a tomb dragging, his main beneficiaries should give him a cloth lest his dewa remain behind in the house where the work took place. When ratu Kadi fainted during the ritual, one cause turned out to be that his predecessor's dewa had never been escorted home after *his* last ritual performance in that same house.

7. Anakalangese men and women are very sensitive to embarrassment. One woman who is normally very self-confident and assertive told me she always feels embarrassed (*makaya*) when walking into the church for services. This may reflect the peculiar nature of that gathering, which along with the marketplace is one of the only sites at which large numbers of unrelated people gather without any structured way of according one another recognition, even to the extent of sharing a betel pouch.

8. Certain possessions have strong metonymic links to persons. Among these are a man's or woman's betel pouch (Forth 1981: 74; Geirnaert-Martin 1992b) and a man's headcloth (Keller 1992). As the most common instrument of everyday sociality, the betel pouch seems to embody the boundary and mutual dependence between persons. The headcloth is wrapped across the forehead, where some people locate one's spirit. One ratu whom I knew well was famous for having been brought back to life, after a fatal childhood illness, by his father striking him with his headcloth. As Onvlee ([1952] 1980: 196) puts it, "A person recognizes that his possessions have a spiritual underpinning to which his entire existence is bound. Possessions do not exist on their own, nor can they be detached from their underpinning; a person's conduct is related to his possessions." The relationship may work both ways. In Rindi, for example, Forth (1981: 439 n. 5) reports that some people told him that "without the soul of the 'possessor' the object would not exist or assume its present form." It is interesting that the statement Forth mentions apparently arose out of someone's attempt to link a word for soul (*hamangu*) to that for "possessor" (*mangu*). This

suggests that for this person what requires explanation is the existence of a *relationship* between possessor and possessed.

9. To a lesser extent, the reverse is also the case. In funerals, for example, the amount of cloth in which the corpse is wrapped for burial should strike a balance between rank and actual wealth. When ratu Gani died, although he was a noble, and in theory could have been buried in twelve layers of cloth, his corpse took only eight. People told me this was because his survivors were not rich. Had they indulged in excess, they would be in danger of falling into deeper poverty later. One of the ways in which objectification works is that in later generations people may be more likely to remember actual amounts of cloth than abstract assertions of rank.

10. The extent to which people consider the objects to be identical to, metonyms of, or representatives of ancestors may be undecidable. Many Anakalangese told me that ancestral valuables are the bodies of the ancestors, some suggesting the ancestors were actually transformed into gold. In other contexts, especially when countering Christian accusations of idolatry, some people insist that valuables are merely a meeting place, a mat of honor, a horse for, a reminder of, or a symbol for the ancestors (see Keane 1996). The missionary Lambooy (1930: 281) reported that, although Tanggoe Marapoe was usually identified for foreigners as the Marapu itself, "sometimes I asked of a Sumbanese, 'is that now really the Marapoe.' Then he looks at me indignantly, for that was not the Marapoe, only the Tanggoe Marapoe, the possession of the Marapoe. 'But what is the "Marapoe" then?' 'We ourselves do not know the Marapoe, who is for us concealed.'" Lambooy thus concluded that the object is "the medium for coming into contact with the Marapoe." According to Kapita (1976a: 90), in east Sumba "this gold becomes, as it were, a replacement for the figure who has been worshipped, that is why this gold is considered as the Marapu itself." For the complexity of this problem, see Forth 1981: 94–97; Hoskins 1993b: 119–128.

11. The majority of ancestral valuables are gold ornaments, physically identical to the best of those that circulate in exchange, and old Chinese or Vietnamese trade porcelain. But all sorts of things become ancestral valuables, such as knives, pieces of cloth, even a child's marble. Many kabisu hold named ritual implements such as drums, gongs, and spears. Kabisu Hawu claims the tools used to smelt the first metal valuables. Unique items of which I have heard are a miniature metal boat and small gold representations of a bridle, a sea turtle, a spinning top, a rooster, and a pig. One kabisu possesses several small stones, said to have been born of women. Three kabisu in Anakalang and two in Parewatana, whose ancestors control lightning, hold a distinct class of valuables called "lightning stones." These are collections of smooth stones so dangerous they cannot remain in a human dwelling but are kept in their own houses or in caves outside the village. As is apparent, no single physical or formal characteristic unifies ancestral valuables other than that they be small enough to secret within the house and thus are potentially mobile.

12. In the 1980s, the two most important rituals in Anakalang, both involving multiple kabisu, were Lai Tarung's biannual Descent to the Ratu Valley and Ḍeru's annual Descent to the Marapu Cave (for details, see Keane 1990). The rites are complex and last several weeks, but the culminating, though hid-

den, moment in both includes the bathing of valuables. In addition to these calendrical rites, I also witnessed several rituals (including the one described below) that responded to more specific circumstances, such as burned houses, lightning strikes, and illness. All of these culminated in the bathing of valuables.

13. Weiner (1992: 40) argues that inalienable possessions make possible the accumulation of distinguishing marks and the monopolization of control over them that can lead to a centralization of power. Parmentier portrays objects in Belau as media by which the hierarchical structure of society is simultaneously reproduced as unvarying, while also gaining value from "cumulative weight of layered events" (1987: 15)—so that they serve both as signs *of* history and signs *in* history (1987: 11; see Hoskins 1993b: 118–141; Tambiah 1984: 263). One political effect in Anakalang is simultaneously to establish a hierarchy among settlements *within* the kabisu and a relative equality and autonomy *among* kabisu. Like early Christian relics, being highly localized permits a hierarchy of places in sacred and social geography (Brown 1981: 86). As will become apparent, Anakalangese valuables also resemble early Christian relics in maintaining a productive tension between proximity and distance. In all these cases, the *materiality* of the medium is important, to the extent that it permits accumulation, persistence over time, and localization. For a qualification of this point, however, see below.

14. As proofs of past events, ancestral valuables share a function with more ordinary objects in Anakalang. This can be seen in several stories in which one kabisu's ancestor tricks another one out of his rightful land. First the trickster secretly buries some objects on the land. Then he challenges the original owner's claim and, on revealing the hidden objects as proof, wins his case. That people feel a strong link between objects and narrative is shown by one incident I witnessed. At the funeral of Pak Yos, who had settled away from the village, a debate broke out over whether to place the tomb in front of the house or away from it, next to the road. The clinching argument came from one of his sons. Sitting on the veranda, he wept and gestured dramatically to the area in front of the house, exclaiming 'How can we put the tomb over by the road? If it's over there, how can I sit here and tell my son about his grandfather someday?' By the same practical logic, people sometimes say wistfully of more distant ancestors, 'I know of them only by hearsay—we don't know where their tombs are.'

15. This is a variation on a relationship familiar in Southeast Asia. See, for example, Heine-Geldern's (1956: 10) characterization of the Islamic kingdoms of southern Sulawesi—that "it is really the regalia which reign, the prince governing the state only in their name"—and the discussion in Errington 1983.

16. Similarly, Hoskins describes the effort of men in Kodi to escape the risks of exchange. Where the situation in Kodi seems most to differ from Anakalang is in the emphasis on individual glory. In Anakalang, the most valued ways of imagining the transcendance of exchange involve not only temporal eternalization, by becoming an ancestor (Hoskins 1993b: 140; see Bloch and Parry 1982), but also social and spatial expansiveness. By this I mean the capacity to transcend particular interests through identification with the kabisu, which extends beyond both the temporal "now" and the social "here."

17. Speculation about the money of foreigners began early in Sumba. One

visitor told of a "puzzle, which our host would like to have solved, which is why the 'taoe djawa' (= foreign man, Europeans) came to have much money. He was asked what he thought himself. He said that in the foreign land three trees must grow, one which bears goldpieces as fruit . . . another of silver (rijks-dollars) and the third of coppercoins" (Witkamp 1912: 115).

18. *Yora* in east Sumba can denote a friend, companion, lover, or opponent (Onvlee 1984: 562), and many yora stories echo more mundane trysts in wild places. Yora are only one of several sorts of spirits of the wild found across Sumba (Adams 1979; Forth 1981: 106 ff.; Hoskins 1993b: 224). In Anakalang, they are distinguished from other spirits of the wild by the fact that they form alliances with individuals.

19. The power of ritual practice to constitute a relationship between the living and their ancestral valuables is what makes it possible for a lost valuable like R to be replaced. One of the rituals I witnessed was in fact to induct a new valuable in place of one that had been lost in a fire. The circular logic of ritual indexicality is that it can creatively bring about that which will subsequently be presupposed.


CHAPTER 9: CONCLUSION

1. Thus Heidegger (1977), for example, characterizes modernity as uniquely given to "representation," and describes it as a move from being totally (and "authentically") embedded within the world to seeing it as containing represented objects.

2. On the other hand, Forth also observes, the clan ancestor receives an uneven, "incomplete" offering. But this is because the ancestor is treated, in this context, as one who requests prosperity and fecundity from God on behalf of the living. My description of ancestors as "complete" here must be understood to be a relative matter.

# Bibliography

Note: All references to Peirce 1931–1958 follow the standard citation form indicating volume and paragraph number (e.g., 1.175 for volume 1, paragraph 175).

Abdullah, Taufik. 1972. Modernization in the Minangkabau World: West Sumatra in the Early Decades of the Twentieth Century. In *Culture and Politics in Indonesia*, ed. Claire Holt. Ithaca: Cornell University Press.

Acciaioli, Greg. 1985. Culture as Art: From Practice to Spectacle in Indonesia. *Canberra Anthropology* 8: 148–172.

Adams, Marie Jeanne. 1969. *System and Meaning in East Sumba Textile Design: A Study in Traditional Indonesian Art*. Cultural Report no. 16. New Haven: Yale University of Southeast Asia Studies.

———. 1970. Myths and Self-Image among the Kapunduk People of Sumba. *Indonesia* 10: 81–106.

———. 1971. History in a Sumba Myth. *Asian Folklore Studies* 30: 133–139.

———. 1974. Symbols of the Organized Community in East Sumba, Indonesia. *Bijdragen tot de taal-, land- en volkenkunde* 130: 324–347.

———. 1979. The Crocodile Couple and the Snake Encounter in the Tellantry of East Sumba, Indonesia. In *The Imagination of Reality: Essays in Southeast Asian Coherence Systems*, ed. A. L. Becker and Aram A. Yengoyan. Norwood, N.J.: Ablex.

———. 1980. Structural Aspects of East Sumbanese Art. In *The Flow of Life: Essays on Eastern Indonesia*, ed. James J. Fox. Cambridge, Mass.: Harvard University Press.

Anderson, Benedict R. O'G. [1972] 1990. The Idea of Power in Javanese Culture. In *Language and Power: Exploring Political Cultures in Indonesia*. Ithaca: Cornell University Press.

Appadurai, Arjun. 1986. Introduction: Commodities and the Politics of Value.

In *The Social Life of Things: Commodities in Cultural Perspective*, ed. Arjun Appadurai. Cambridge: Cambridge University Press.

Ardener, Edward. 1975. Belief and the Problem of Women. In *Perceiving Women*, ed. Shirley Ardener. London: Malaby Press.

Aristotle. 1941. Ethica Nicomachea. Trans. W. D. Ross. In *The Basic Works of Aristotle*, ed. Richard McKeon. New York: Random House.

Asad, Talal. 1986. The Concept of Cultural Translation in British Anthropology. In *Writing Culture*, ed. James Clifford and George Marcus. Berkeley: University of California Press.

Atkinson, Jane Monnig. 1989. *The Art and Politics of Wana Shamanship*. Berkeley: University of California Press.

Atkinson, Jane Monnig, and Shelly Errington, eds. 1990. *Power and Difference: Gender in Island Southeast Asia*. Stanford: Stanford University Press.

Austin, J. L. [1955] 1975. *How to Do Things with Words*. Cambridge, Mass.: Harvard University Press.

———. [1956–1957] 1979. A Plea for Excuses. In *Philosophical Papers*, ed. J. O. Urmson and G. J. Warnock. 3d ed. Oxford: Oxford University Press.

Bakhtin, M. M. 1981. *The Dialogic Imagination: Four Essays*. Ed. Michael Holquist, trans. Caryl Emerson and Michael Holquist. Austin: University of Texas Press.

Barnes, R. H. 1974. *Kédang: A Study of the Collective Thought of an Eastern Indonesian People*. Oxford: Clarendon Press.

———. 1980. Marriage, Exchange, and the Meaning of Corporations in Eastern Indonesia. In *The Meaning of Marriage Payments*, ed. John L. Comaroff. London: Academic Press.

Barnes, R. H., and R. Barnes. 1989. Barter and Money in an Indonesian Village Economy. *Man*, n.s. 24: 399–418.

Barraud, Cécile. 1979. *Tanebar-Evav: Une société de maisons tournée vers le large*. Cambridge: Cambridge University Press.

Barthes, Roland. [1967] 1983. *The Fashion System*. Trans. A. Lavers and C. Smith. London: Jonathan Cape.

Bateson, Gregory. [1955] 1972. A Theory of Play and Fantasy. In *Steps to an Ecology of Mind*. New York: Ballantine Books.

Baudrillard, Jean. 1975. *The Mirror of Production*. Trans. Charles Levin. St. Louis: Telos Press.

———. 1981. *For a Critique of the Political Economy of the Sign*. Trans. Charles Levin. St. Louis: Telos Press.

Bauman, Richard. 1977. *Verbal Art as Performance*. Prospect Heights: Waveland.

Bauman, Richard, and Charles L. Briggs. 1990. Poetics and Performance as Critical Perspectives on Language and Social Life. *Annual Review of Anthropology* 19: 59–88.

Beatty, Andrew. 1992. *Society and Exchange in Nias*. Oxford: Clarendon Press.

Becker, A. L. 1979. Text-building, Epistemology and Aesthetics in Javanese Shadow Theatre. In *The Imagination of Reality: Essays in Southeast Asian Coherence Systems*, ed. A. Yengoyan and A. L. Becker. Norwood: Ablex.

Belting, Hans. 1994. *Likeness and Presence: A History of the Image before the Era of Art*. Trans. Edmund Jephcott. Chicago: University of Chicago Press.

Benjamin, Walter. 1969. The Work of Art in the Age of Mechanical Reproduction. In *Illuminations*, trans. Harry Zohn. New York: Schocken.

Benveniste, Emile. [1958] 1971a. Subjectivity in Language. In *Problems in General Linguistics*, trans. Mary Elizabeth Meek. Coral Gables: University of Miami Press.

————. [1963] 1971b. Analytic Philosophy and Language. In *Problems in General Linguistics*, trans. Mary Elizabeth Meek. Coral Gables: University of Miami Press.

Besnier, Niko. 1992. Reported Speech and Affect in Nukulaelae Atoll. In *Responsibility and Evidence in Oral Discourse*, ed. Jane H. Hill and Judith T. Irvine. Cambridge: Cambridge University Press.

Bloch, Marc. 1961. *Feudal society.* Trans. L. A. Manyon. Chicago: University of Chicago Press.

Bloch, Maurice. 1975. Introduction. In *Political Language and Oratory in Traditional Society*. New York: Academic Press.

————. 1986. *From Blessing to Violence: History and Ideology in the circumcision Ritual of the Merina of Madagascar.* Cambridge: Cambridge University Press.

Bloch, Maurice, and Jonathan Parry, eds. 1982. *Death and the Regeneration of Life.* Cambridge: Cambridge University Press.

Bohannan, Paul. 1955. Some Principles of Exchange and Investment among the Tiv. *American Anthropologist* 57: 60–69.

Boon, James A. 1977. *The Anthropological Romance of Bali, 1597–1972: Dynamic Perspectives in Marriage and Caste.* New York: Cambridge University Press.

————. 1990. *Affinities and Extremes: Crisscrossing the Bittersweet Ethnology of East Indies History, Hindu-Balinese Culture, and Indo-European Allure.* Chicago: University of Chicago Press.

Bourdieu, Pierre. [1972] 1977. *Outline of a Theory of Practice.* Trans. Richard Nice. Cambridge: Cambridge University Press.

————. [1979] 1984. *Distinction: A Social Critique of the Judgement of Taste.* Trans. Richard Nice. Cambridge, Mass.: Harvard University Press.

————. 1991. *Language and Symbolic Power.* Ed. John B. Thompson. Cambridge, Mass.: Harvard University Press.

Bowen, John R. 1991. *Sumatran Politics and Poetics: Gayo History, 1900–1989.* New Haven: Yale University Press.

Brenneis, Donald Lawrence, and Fred R. Myers, eds. 1984. *Dangerous Words: Language and Politics in the Pacific.* New York: New York University Press.

Bricker, Victoria R. 1974. The Ethnographic Context of Some Mayan Speech Genres. In *Explorations in the Ethnography of Speaking*, ed. Richard Bauman and Joel Sherzer. London: Cambridge University Press.

Briggs, Charles L. 1984. Learning How to Ask: Native Metacommunicative Competence and the Incompetence of Fieldworkers. *Language in Society* 13: 1–28.

Brown, Penelope, and Stephen Levinson. 1978. Universals in Language Usage: Politeness Phenomena. In *Questions and Politeness: Studies in Social Interaction*, ed. Esther N. Goody. Cambridge: Cambridge University Press.

Brown, Peter. 1981. *The Cult of the Saints: Its Rise and Function in Latin Chris-tianity*. Chicago: University of Chicago Press.

Butler, Judith. 1990. *Gender Trouble: Feminism and the Subversion of Identity*. New York: Routledge.

Caton, Steven C. 1990. *"Peaks of Yemen I Summon": Poetry as Cultural Prac-tice in a North Yemeni Tribe*. Berkeley: University of California Press.

Carsten, Janet, and Stephen Hugh-Jones, eds. 1995. *About the House: Lévi Strauss and Beyond*. Cambridge: Cambridge University Press.

Chatterjee, Partha. 1993. *The Nation and Its Fragments: Colonial and Post-colonial Histories*. Princeton: Princeton University Press.

Comaroff, John L. 1980. Introduction. In *The Meaning of Marriage Payments*, ed. John L. Comaroff. London: Academic Press.

Comaroff, John L., and Simon Roberts. 1981. *Rules and Processes: The Cul-tural Logic of Dispute in an African Context*. Chicago: University of Chicago Press.

Corner, Lorraine. 1989. East and West Nusa Tenggara: Isolation and Poverty. In *Unity and Diversity: Regional Economic Development in Indonesia since 1970*, ed. Hal Hill. Oxford: Oxford University Press.

Couvreur, A. J. L. 1914. Jaarverslag afdeeling Soemba 1914 tevens memorie van overgave. Typescript, Algemeen Rijksarchief, The Hague.

Culler, Jonathan. 1975. *Structuralist Poetics: Structuralism, Linguistics, and the Study of Literature*. Ithaca: Cornell University Press.

Cunningham, Clark E. 1964. Order in the Atoni House. *Bijdragen tot de taal-, land- en volkenkunde* 120: 34–68.

———. 1965. Order and Change in an Atoni Diarchy. *Southwestern Journal of Anthropology* 21: 359–382.

Derrida, Jacques. [1967] 1973. Speech and Phenomena: Introduction to the Problem of Signs in Husserl's Phenomenology. In *Speech and Phenomena and Other Essays on Husserls's Theory of Signs*, trans. David B. Allison. Evanston: Northwestern University Press.

———. [1972] 1982. Signature Event Context. In *Margins of Philosophy*, trans. Alan Bass. Chicago: University of Chicago Press.

Diffloth, G. 1980. To Taboo Everything at All Times. *Proceedings of the Sixth Annual Meeting of the Berkeley Linguistics Society*.

Dirks, Nicholas B. [1992] 1994. Ritual and Resistance: Subversion as Social Fact. In *Culture/Power/History: A Reader in Contemporary Social Theory*, ed. Nicholas B. Dirks, Geoff Eley, and Sherry B. Ortner. Princeton: Princeton University Press.

Dixon, R. M. W. 1971. A Method of Semantic Description. In *Semantics: An Interdisciplinary Reader in Philosophy, Linguistics, and Psychology*, ed. Danny D. Steinberg and Leon A. Jakobovits. Cambridge: Cambridge Uni-versity Press.

Doko, I. H. 1981. *Perjuangan kemerdekaan Indonesian di Nusa Tenggara Timur*. Jakarta: Balai Pustaka.

Du Bois, John W. 1986. Self-Evidence and Ritual Speech. In *Evidentiality: The Linguistic Coding of Epistemology*, ed. Wallace Chafe and Johanna Nichols. Norwood: Ablex.

————. 1992. Meaning without Intention: Lessons from Divination. In *Responsibility and Evidence in Oral Discourse*, ed. Jane H. Hill and Judith T. Irvine. Cambridge: Cambridge University Press.

Duranti, Alessandro. 1994. *From Grammar to Politics: Linguistic Anthropology in a Western Samoan Village*. Berkeley: University of California Press.

Duranti, Alessandro, and Charles Goodwin, eds. 1992. *Rethinking Context: Language as an Interactive Phenomenon*. Cambridge: Cambridge University Press.

Durkheim, Emile. 1915. *The Elementary Forms of the Religious Life*. Trans. Joseph Ward Swain. London: George Allen & Unwin.

Durkheim, Emile, and Marcel Mauss. [1903] 1963. *Primitive Classification*. Trans. Rodney Needham. Chicago: University of Chicago Press.

Ellen, Roy. 1986. Microcosm, Macrocosm and the Nuaulu House: Concerning the Reductionist Fallacy as Applied to Metaphorical Levels. *Bijdragen tot de taal-, land- en volkenkunde* 142: 1–30.

Emerson, Ralph Waldo. [1844] 1983. Gifts. In *The Collected Works of Ralph Waldo Emerson*, vol. 3, ed. Joseph Slater, Alfred R. Ferguson, and Jean Ferguson Carr. Cambridge, Mass.: Belknap Press.

Errington, J. Joseph. 1988. *Structure and Style in Javanese: A Semiotic View of Linguistic Etiquette*. Philadelphia: University of Pennsylvania Press.

Errington, Shelly. 1983. The Place of Regalia in Luwu. In *Centers, Symbols, and Hierarchies: Essays on the Classical States of Southeast Asia*, ed. L. Gessick. Yale Southeast Asian Monographs 26. New Haven: Yale University Press.

Evans-Pritchard, E. E. 1937. *Witchcraft, Oracles, and Magic among the Azande*. London: Oxford University Press.

Ferguson, James. 1985. The Bovine Mystique: Power, Property, and Livestock in Rural Lesotho. *Man*, n.s. 4: 647–674.

Firth, Raymond. 1975. Speech-making and Oratory in Tikopia. In *Political Language and Oratory in Traditional Society*, ed. Maurice Bloch. New York: Academic Press.

Forth, Gregory. 1981. *Rindi: An Ethnographic Study of a Traditional Domain in Eastern Sumba*. The Hague: Martinus Nijhoff.

————. 1988. Fashioned Speech, Full Communication: Aspects of Eastern Sumbanese Ritual Language. In *To Speak in Pairs: Essays on the Ritual Languages of Eastern Indonesia*, ed. James J. Fox. Cambridge: Cambridge University Press.

Foster, Robert J. 1993. Dangerous Circulation and Revelatory Display: Exchange Practices in a New Ireland Society. In *Exchanging Products: Producing Exchange*, ed. Jane Fajans. Sydney: University of Sydney.

Foucault, Michel. [1969] 1972. *The Archaeology of Knowledge and the Discourse on Language*. Trans. A. M. Sheridan Smith. New York: Pantheon.

Fox, James J. 1971. Semantic Parallelism in Rotinese Ritual Language. *Bijdragen tot de taal-, land- en volkenkunde* 127: 215–255.

————. 1974. 'Our Ancestors Spoke in Pairs': Rotinese Views of Language, Dialect, and Code. In *Explorations in the Ethnography of Speaking*, ed. Richard Bauman and Joel Sherzer. London: Cambridge University Press.

———. 1975. On Binary Categories and Primary Symbols: Some Rotinese Perspectives. In *The Interpretation of Symbolism*, ed. R. Willis. London: Malaby Press.

———. 1977. *Harvest of the Palm: Ecological Change in Eastern Indonesia.* Cambridge: Cambridge University Press.

———. 1982. The Great Lord Rests at the Centre: The Paradox of Powerlessness in European-Timorese Relations. *Canberra Anthropology* 5: 22–33.

———. 1989. To the Aroma of the Name: The Celebration of a Rotinese Ritual of Rock and Tree. *Bijdragen tot de taal-, land- en volkenkunde* 145: 520–538.

Fox, James J., ed. 1980. *The Flow of Life: Essays on Eastern Indonesia.* Cambridge, Mass.: Harvard University Press.

———. 1988. *To Speak in Pairs: Essays on the Ritual Languages of Eastern Indonesia.* Cambridge: Cambridge University Press.

———. 1993. *Inside Austronesian Houses: Perspectives on Domestic Designs for Living.* Canberra: Department of Anthropology, Australian National University.

Geary, Patrick. 1986. Sacred Commodities: The Circulation of Medieval Relics. In *The Social Life of Things: Commodities in Cultural Perspective*, ed. Arjun Appadurai. Cambridge: Cambridge University Press.

Geertz, Clifford. [1959] 1973a. Ritual and Social Change: A Javanese Example. In *The Interpretation of Cultures*. New York: Basic Books.

———. [1972] 1973b. Deep Play: Notes on the Balinese Cockfight. In *The Interpretation of Cultures*. New York: Basic Books.

———. 1973c. Thick Description: Toward an Interpretive Theory of Culture. In *The Interpretation of Cultures*. New York: Basic Books.

———. 1980. *Negara: The Theatre State in Nineteenth-Century Bali.* Princeton: Princeton University Press.

Geirnaert-Martin, Danielle C. 1989. Textiles of West Sumba: Lively Renaissance of an Old Tradition. In *To Speak with Cloth: Studies in Indonesian Textiles*, ed. Mattiebelle Gittinger. Los Angeles: UCLA Museum of Cultural History.

———. 1992a. *The Woven Land of Laboya: Socio-Cosmic Ideas and Values in West Sumba, Eastern Indonesia.* Leiden: Centre of Non-Western Studies.

———. 1992b. Purse-Proud: Betel and Areca Bags in West Sumba (East Indonesia). In *Dress and Gender: Making and Meaning*, ed. R. Barnes and J. B. Eicher. Oxford: Berg.

George, Kenneth M. 1996. *Showing Signs of Violence: The Cultural Politics of a Twentieth-Century Headhunting Ritual.* Berkeley: University of California Press.

Giddens, Anthony. 1979. *Central Problems in Social Theory: Action, Structure and Contradiction in Social Analysis.* Berkeley: University of California Press.

Gittinger, Mattiebelle. 1979. *Splendid Symbols: Textiles and Tradition in Indonesia.* Washington: Textile Museum.

Goffman, Erving. 1956. The Nature of Deference and Demeanor. *American Anthropologist* 58: 473–502.

————. 1974. *Frame Analysis: An Essay on the Organization of Experience.* New York: Harper and Row.

————. [1979] 1981. Footing. In *Forms of Talk.* Philadelphia: University of Pennsylvania Press.

Goodwin, Marjorie Harness. 1990. *He-Said-She-Said: Talk as Social Organization among Black Children.* Bloomington: Indiana University Press.

Gossen, Gary H. 1974. To Speak with a Heated Heart: Chamula Canons of Style and Good Performance. In *Explorations in the Ethnography of Speaking*, ed. Richard Bauman and Joel Sherzer. London: Cambridge University Press.

Greenblatt, Stephen. [1988] 1994. The Circulation of Social Energy. In *Culture/Power/History: A Reader in Contemporary Social Theory*, ed. Nicholas B. Dirks, Geoff Eley, and Sherry B. Ortner. Princeton: Princeton University Press.

Gregory, C. A. 1982. *Gifts and Commodities.* New York: Academic Press.

Grice, H. P. 1957. Meaning. *Philosophical Review* 64: 377–388.

Grimshaw, Allen D., ed. 1990. *Conflict Talk: Sociolinguistic Investigations of Arguments in Conversations.* Cambridge: Cambridge University Press.

Groeneveld, F. J. 1931. Memorie van overgave van den gezaghebber van West-Soemba. Typescript. Algemeen Rijksarchief, The Hague.

Hanks, William F. 1990. *Referential Practice: Language and Lived Space among the Maya.* Chicago: University of Chicago Press.

————. 1993. Metalanguage and Pragmatics of Deixis. In *Reflexive Language: Reported Speech and Metapragmatics*, ed. John A. Lucy. Cambridge: Cambridge University Press.

Haripranata, H. 1984. *Ceritera sejarah gereja Katolik Sumba dan Sumbawa: Dengan sejarah umum Sumba kuno sebagai latar belakang.* Ende: Arnoldus.

Hart, K. 1986. Heads or Tails: Two Sides of the Coin. *Man*, n.s. 21: 637–656.

Hefner, Robert W. 1990. *The Political Economy of Mountain Java: An Interpretive History.* Berkeley: University of California Press.

Hegel, G. W. F. [1807] 1977. *Phenomenology of Spirit.* Trans. A. V. Miller. Oxford: Oxford University Press.

Heidegger, Martin. 1977. The Age of the World Picture. In *The Question Concerning Technology and Other Essays*, trans. William Lovitt. New York: Harper and Row.

Heine-Geldern, Robert. 1956. *Conceptions of State and Kingship in Southeast Asia.* Southeast Asia Program Data Paper no. 18. Ithaca: Cornell Southeast Asia Program.

Hill, Jane. 1985. The Grammar of Consciousness and the Consciousness of Grammar. *American Ethnologist.* 12: 725–737.

Hill, Jane H., and Judith T. Irvine. 1992. Introduction. In *Responsibility and Evidence in Oral Discourse.* Cambridge: Cambridge University Press.

Hoskins, Janet. 1986. So My Name Shall Live: Stone Dragging and Grave-building in Kodi, West Sumba. *Bijdragen tot de taal-, land- en volkenkunde* 142: 31–51.

————. 1987. Entering the Bitter House: Spirit Worship and Conversion in West Sumba. In *Indonesian Religions in Transition*, ed. Susan Rodgers and Rita Kipp. Tucson: University of Arizona Press.

———. 1988. Etiquette in Kodi Spirit Communication: The Lips Told to Pronounce, the Mouths Told to Speak. In *To Speak in Pairs: Essays on the Ritual Languages of Eastern Indonesia*, ed. James J. Fox. Cambridge: Cambridge University Press.

———. 1989. Why do Ladies Sing the Blues? Indigo, Cloth Production, and Gender Symbolism in Kodi. In *Cloth and Human Experience*, ed. Annette Weiner and Jane Schneider. Washington: Smithsonian Institution Press.

———. 1990. Doubling Descent, Deities, and Personhood: An Exploration of Kodi Gender Catgories. In *Power and Difference: Gender in Island Southeast Asia*, ed. Jane Monnig Atkinson and Shelly Errington. Stanford: Stanford University Press.

———. 1993a. Violence, Sacrifice, and Divination: Giving and Taking a Life in Eastern Indonesia. *American Ethnologist* 20: 159–178.

———. 1993b. *The Play of Time: Kodinese Perspectives on Calendars, History, and Exchange*. Berkeley: University of California Press.

———. 1993c. Snakes, Smells, and Dismembered Brides: Men's and Women's Textiles in Kodi, West Sumba. In *Weaving Patterns of Life: Indonesian Textile Symposium 1991*, ed. Marie-Louise Nabholz-Kartaschoff, Ruth Barnes, and David J. Stuart-Fox. Basel: Museum of Ethnography.

Hugh-Jones, Stephen. 1990. Yesterday's Luxuries, Tomorrow's Necessities: Business and Barter in Northwest Amazonia. In *Barter, Exchange, and Value: An Anthropological Approach*, ed. Caroline Humphrey and Stephen Hugh-Jones. Cambridge: Cambridge University Press.

Hymes, Dell. 1972. Models of the Interaction of Language and Social Life. In *Directions in Sociolinguistics: The Ethnography of Communication*, ed. John J. Gumperz and Dell Hymes. New York: Holt, Rinehart, and Winston.

———. [1975] 1981. Breakthrough into Performance. In *'In Vain I Tried to Tell You': Essays in Native American Ethnopoetics*. Philadelphia: University of Pennsylvania Press.

———. [1977] 1981. Discovering Oral Performance and Measured Verse in American Indian Narrative. In *'In Vain I Tried to Tell You': Essays in Native American Ethnopoetics*. Philadelphia: University of Pennsylvania Press.

Irvine, Judith. 1974. Strategies of Status Manipulation in the Wolof Greeting. In *Explorations in the Ethnography of Speaking*, ed. Richard Bauman and Joel Sherzer. London: Cambridge University Press.

———. 1979. Formality and Informality in Communicative Events. *American Anthropologist* 81: 773–780.

———. 1989. When Talk Isn't Cheap: Language and Political Economy. *American Ethnologist* 16: 248–267.

Jakobson, Roman. 1960. Closing Statement: Linguistics and Poetics. In *Style in Language*, ed. T. Sebeok. Cambridge: MIT Press.

———. 1966. Grammatical Parallelism and Its Russian Facet. *Language* 42: 399–429.

de Josselin de Jong, P. E. 1952. *Minangkabau and Negri Sembilan: Sociopolitical Structure in Indonesia*. The Hague: Martinus Nijhoff.

Kantor Statistik. 1987. *Sumba Barat dalam angka 1986*. Waikabubak: Kantor Statistik Kabupaten Sumba Barat.

Kantorowicz, Ernst H. 1957. *The King's Two Bodies: A Study in Medieval Theology.* Princeton: Princeton University Press.

Kapita, Oe. [Umbu] H[ina]. 1976a. *Masyarakat Sumba dan adat istiadatnya.* Waingapu: Panitia Penerbit Naskah-Naskah Kebudayaan Daerah Sumba Dewan Penata Layanan Gereja Kristen Sumba.

―――. 1976b. *Sumba di dalam jangkauan jaman.* Waingapu: Panitia Penerbit Naskah-Naskah Kebudayaan Daerah Sumba Dewan Penata Layanan Gereja Kristen Sumba.

―――. 1979. *Lii Ndai: Rukuda da kabihu dangu la pahunga lodu (Sejarah suku-suku di Sumba Timur).* Waingapu: Panitia Penerbit Naskah-Naskah Kebudayaan Daerah Sumba Dewan Penata Layanan Gereja Kristen Sumba.

―――. 1987. *Lawiti luluku Humba/Pola peribahasa Sumba.* Lembaga Penyelidikian Kebudayaan Selatan Tenri.

Keane, Webb. 1988. Ombres des hommes et des esprits: Les *mamuli* de Sumba Shadows of Men and Spirits: The *Mamuli* of Sumba. *Art tribal* Musée Barbier-Mueller 2: 3–15.

―――. 1990. The Social Life of Representations: Ritual Speech and Exchange in Anakalang (Sumba, Eastern Indonesia). Ph.D. dissertation, University of Chicago.

―――. 1991. Delegated Voice: Ritual Speech, Risk, and the Making of Marriage Alliances in Anakalang. *American Ethnologist* 18: 311–330.

―――. 1994. The Value of Words and the Meaning of Things in Eastern Indonesian Exchange. *Man,* n.s. 29: 605–629.

―――. 1995a. The Spoken House: Text, Act, and Object in Eastern Indonesia. *American Ethnologist* 22: 102–124.

―――. 1995b. Religious Change and Historical Reflection in Anakalang, West Sumba. *Journal of Southeast Asian Studies* 26: 289–306.

―――. 1996. Materialism, Missionaries, and Modern Subjects in Colonial Indonesia. In *Conversion to Modernities: The Globalization of Christianity,* ed. Peter van der Veer. New York: Routledge.

―――. In press. Knowing One's Place: National Language and the Idea of the Local in Eastern Indonesia. *Cultural Anthropology.*

―――. n.d. From Fetishism to Sincerity: On Agency, the Speaking Subject, and Their Historicity. Unpublished paper.

Keeler, Ward. 1987. *Javanese Shadow Plays, Javanese Selves.* Princeton: Princeton University Press.

Keenan, Elinor. 1974. Norm-makers, Norm-breakers: Uses of Speech by Men and Women in a Malagasy Community. In *Explorations in the Ethnography of Speaking,* ed. Richard Bauman and Joel Sherzer. London: Cambridge University Press.

―――. 1975. A Sliding Sense of Obligatoriness: The Polystructure of Malagasy Oratory. In *Political Language and Oratory in Traditional Society,* ed. Maurice Bloch. New York: Academic Press.

Keenan, Thomas. 1993. The Point Is to (Ex)Change It: Reading *Capital,* Rhetorically. In *Fetishism as Cultural Discourse,* ed. Emily Apter and William Pietz. Ithaca: Cornell University Press.

Keesing, Roger M. 1984. Rethinking *Mana. Journal of Anthropological Research* 40: 137–156.

Keller, Edgar. 1992. Head-dresses as a Medium of Self-Expression in Laboya: Sumbanese Attire in Historical Perspective. In *Weaving Patterns of Life: Indonesian Textile Symposium 1991*, ed. Marie-Louise Nabholz-Kartaschoff, Ruth Barnes, and David J. Stuart-Fox. Basel: Museum of Ethnography.

Kipp, Rita, and Susan Rodgers, eds. 1987. *Indonesian Religions in Transition.* Tucson: University of Arizona Press.

Kopytoff, Igor. 1982. Slavery. *Annual Review of Anthropology* 11: 207–230.

———. 1986. The Cultural Biography of Things: Commoditization as Process. In *The Social Life of Things: Commodities in Cultural Perspective*, ed. Arjun Appadurai. Cambridge: Cambridge University Press.

Krul, J. M. 1984. *Pengolahan Tanah dan Pemakaian Luku di Pulau Sumba, Indonesia.* Leusdan: Algemeen Diakonaal Bureau van de Gereformeerde Kerken in Nederland.

Kruseman, J. D. 1836. Beschrijving van het Sandelhout Eiland. *De oosterling* 2: 63–68.

Kruyt, Alb. C. 1921. Verslag van eene reis over het eiland Soemba. *Tijdschrift van het Koninklijk Nederlandsch Aardrijkskundig Genootschap*, 2d ser. 37: 513–553.

———. 1922. De Soembaneezen. *Bijdragen tot de taal-, land- en volkenkunde van Nederlandsch-Indië* 78: 466–608.

Kuipers, Joel C. 1986. Talking about Troubles: Gender Differences in Weyéwa Speech Use. *American Ethnologist* 13: 448–462.

———. 1988. The Pattern of Prayer in Weyéwa. In *To Speak in Pairs: Essays on the Ritual Languages of Eastern Indonesia*, ed. James J. Fox. Cambridge: Cambridge University Press.

———. 1990. *Power in Performance: The Creation of Textual Authority in Weyewa Ritual Speech.* Philadelphia: University of Pennsylvania Press.

Lambooy, P. J. 1930. De godsnaam op Soemba. *De macedoniër* 34: 275–284.

Lanze, C. E. 1919. Memorie van overgave van de afdeling Soemba. Typescript. Algemeen Rijksarchief, The Hague.

Lave, Jean, and Etienne Wenger. 1991. *Situated Learning: Legitimate Peripheral Participation.* Cambridge: Cambridge University Press.

Leach, E. R. 1954. *Political Systems of Highland Burma: A Study of Kachin Social Structure.* Cambridge, Mass.: Harvard University Press.

Lederman, Rena. 1986. *What Gifts Engender: Social Relations and Politics in Mendi, Highland Papua New Guinea.* Berkeley: University of California Press.

Lévi-Strauss, Claude. [1956] 1963. Do Dual Organizations Exist? In *Structural Anthropology*, trans. Claire Jacobson and Brooke Grundfest Schoef. New York: Basic Books.

———. [1949] 1969. *The Elementary Structures of Kinship.* Trans. James Harle Bell, John Richard von Sturner, and Rodney Needham. Boston: Beacon Press.

———. [1975, 1979] 1982. *The Way of the Masks.* Trans. Sylvia Modelski. Seattle: University of Washington Press.

Lewis, E. Douglas. 1988. *People of the Source: The Social and Ceremonial Order of Tana Wai Brama on Flores.* Dordrecht: Foris Publications.

Lindstrom, Lamont. 1992. Context Contests: Debatable Truth Statements in Tanna (Vanuatu). In *Rethinking Context: Language as an Interactive Phenomenon*, ed. Alessandro Duranti and Charles Goodwin. Cambridge: Cambridge University Press.

Lucy, John A., ed. 1993. *Reflexive Language: Reported Speech and Metapragmatics*. Cambridge: Cambridge University Press.

Luijendijk, P. J. 1946. *Zeven jaar zendingswerk op Soemba (1939–46)*. Groningen: Niemeijer.

Mannheim, Bruce. 1986. Popular Song and Popular Grammar: Poetry and Metalanguage. *Word* 37: 45–75.

March, Katherine. 1983. Weaving, Writing, and Gender. *Man*, n.s. 18: 729–744.

Marx, Karl. [1887] 1967. *Capital: A Critique of Political Economy*. Trans. Samuel Moore and Edward Aveling. New York: International.

Mauss, Marcel. [1925] 1990. *The Gift: The Form and Reason for Exchange in Archaic Societies*. Trans. W. D. Halls. New York: Norton.

McCracken, Grant. 1988. *Culture and Consumption: New Approaches to the Symbolic Character of Consumer Goods and Activities*. Bloomington: Indiana University Press.

McKinnon, Susan. 1991. *From a Shattered Sun: Hierarchy, Gender, and Alliance in the Tanimbar Islands*. Madison: University of Wisconsin Press.

Mead, George H. 1934. *Mind, Self, and Society from the Standpoint of a Social Behaviorist*. Chicago: University of Chicago Press.

Merlan, Francesca, and Alan Rumsey. 1991. *Ku Waru: Language and Segmentary Politics in the Western Nebilyer Valley, Papua New Guinea*. Cambridge: Cambridge University Press.

Messick, Brinkley. 1987. Subordinate Discourse: Women, Weaving, and Gender Relations in North Africa. *American Ethnologist* 14: 210–226.

Metcalf, Peter. 1989. *Where Are You Spirits?: Style and Theme in Berawan Prayer*. Washington: Smithsonian Institution Press.

Metzner, J. 1977. *Studi ecology tentang daerah Sumba dan Timor Timur*. Trans. Ny. S. Syah. Kupang: Biro Penelitian Universitas Nusa Cendana.

*Militaire memories van de afdeling Soemba, Omvattende de patrouillegebieden Waingapoe en Waikaboebak, 1931–1933*. Memories van Overgave Nederlands-Indië. Typescript. Algemeen Rijksarchief, The Hague.

Miller, Daniel. 1987. *Material Culture and Mass Consumption*. Oxford: Basil Blackwell.

Mitchell, David. 1988. Method in the Metaphor: The Ritual Language of Wanukaka. In *To Speak in Pairs: Essays on the Ritual Languages of Eastern Indonesia*, ed. James J. Fox. Cambridge: Cambridge University Press.

Mitchell, Istutiah Gunawan. 1981. Hierarchy and Balance: A Study of Wanokakan Social Organization. Ph.D. dissertation, Monash University.

Munn, Nancy D. 1983. Gawan Kula: Spatiotemporal Control and the Symbolism of Influence. In *The Kula: New Perspectives on Massim Exchange*, ed. Jerry W. Leach and Edmund Leach. Cambridge: Cambridge University Press.

———. 1986. *The Fame of Gawa: A Symbolic Study of Value Transformation in a Massim (Papua New Guinea) Society*. Cambridge: Cambridge University Press.

Nakagawa, Satoshi. 1988. The Journey of the Bridegroom: Idioms of Marriage among the Endenese. In *To Speak in Pairs: Essays on the Ritual Languages of Eastern Indonesia*, ed. James J. Fox. Cambridge: Cambridge University Press.

Needham, Rodney. 1980. Principles and Variations in the Structure of Sumbanese Society. In *The Flow of Life: Essays on Eastern Indonesia*, ed. James J. Fox. Cambridge, Mass.: Harvard University Press.

———. 1983. *Sumba and the Slave Trade.* Melbourne: Monash University.

Nooteboom, C. 1940. *Oost Soemba: Een volkenkundige studie.* The Hague: Martinus Nijhoff.

Ochs, Elinor. 1979. Transcription as Theory. In *Developmental Pragmatics*, ed. Elinor Ochs and Bambi B. Schieffelin. New York: Academic Press.

Onvlee, Lois. 1925. *Eenige Soembasche vertellingen: Grammatische inleiding, tekst, aanteekeningen.* Leiden: A. Vros.

———. [1933] 1973a. Na huri hàpa. In *Cultuur als antwoord*. Verhandelingen van het KILTV, 66. The Hague: Martinus Nijhoff.

———. [1957] 1973b. Over de weergave van pneuma. In *Cultuur als antwoord*. The Hague: Martinus Nijhoff.

———. [1936] 1973c. Eenige opmerkingen aangaande taal en literatuur. In *Cultuur als antwoord*. The Hague: Martinus Nijhoff.

———. [1969] 1973d. Kabisu—Marapu. In *Cultuur als antwoord*. The Hague: Martinus Nijhoff.

———. [1969] 1973e. Uit de Levensgang van de mens. In *Cultuur als antwoord*. The Hague: Martinus Nijhoff.

———. [1949] 1977. The Construction of the Mangili Dam: Notes on the Social Organization of Eastern Sumba. In *Structural Anthropology in the Netherlands*, ed. P. E. de Josselin de Jong. The Hague: Martinus Nijhoff.

———. [1952] 1980. The Significance of Livestock on Sumba, trans. James J. Fox and Henny Fokker-Bakker. In *The Flow of Life: Essays on Eastern Indonesia*, ed. James J. Fox. Cambridge, Mass.: Harvard University Press.

———. 1984. *Kamberaas (Oost-Soembaas)—Nederlands woordenboek.* Dordrecht: Foris Publications.

Ortner, Sherry B. 1981. Gender and Sexuality in Hierarchical Societies: The Case of Polynesia and Some Comparative Implications. In *Sexual Meanings: The Cultural Construction of Gender and Sexuality*, ed. Sherry B. Ortner and Harriet Whitehead. Cambridge: Cambridge University Press.

———. 1984. Theory in Anthropology since the Sixties. *Comparative Studies in Society and History* 26: 126–166.

Ortner, Sherry B., and Harriet Whitehead. 1981. Introduction: Accounting for Sexual Meanings. In *Sexual Meanings: The Cultural Construction of Gender and Sexuality*, ed. Sherry B. Ortner and Harriet Whitehead. Cambridge: Cambridge University Press.

Parmentier, Richard J. 1987. *The Sacred Remains: Myth, History, and Polity in Belau.* Chicago: University of Chicago Press.

Parry, Jonathan, and Maurice Bloch. 1989. Introduction: Money and the Morality of Exchange. In *Money and the Morality of Exchange*, ed. J. Parry and M. Bloch. Cambridge: Cambridge University Press.

Patterson, Orlando. 1982. *Slavery and Social Death: A Comparative Study.* Cambridge, Mass.: Harvard University Press.

Peirce, Charles Sanders. 1931–1958. *Collected Papers of Charles Sanders Peirce.* Ed. C. Hartshorne, P. Weiss, and A. W. Burks. Cambridge, Mass.: Harvard University Press.

———. 1986. *Writings of Charles Sanders Peirce: A Chronological Edition,* vol. 3, ed. M. Fisch et al. Bloomington: Indiana University Press.

Pemberton, John. 1994. *On the Subject of 'Java.'* Ithaca: Cornell University Press.

Pitkin, Hannah Fenichel. 1967. *The Concept of Representation.* Berkeley: University of California Press.

Purwadi, Suriadiredja. 1983. Simbolisme dalam disain kain di Watu Puda. Thesis, Padjadjaran University, Bandung.

Putnam, Hilary. 1975. The Meaning of 'Meaning.' In *Mind, Language, and Reality: Philosophical Papers,* vol. 2. Cambridge: Cambridge University Press.

Reichard, Gladys A. 1944. *Prayer: The Compulsive Word.* Monographs of the American Ethnological Society VII. New York: J. J. Augustin.

Reid, Anthony. 1974. *The Indonesian National Revolution 1945–1950.* Hawthorne: Longman.

———. 1983. Introduction: Slavery and Bondage in Southeast Asian History. In *Slavery, Bondage, and Dependency in Southeast Asia,* ed. Anthony Reid. St. Lucia: University of Queensland Press.

———. 1988. *Southeast Asia in the Age of Commerce 1450–1680,* vol. I: *The Lands Below the Wind.* New Haven: Yale University Press.

Ricoeur, Paul. 1971. The Model of the Text: Meaningful Action Considered as a Text. *Social Research* 38: 529–562.

Riekerk, G. H. M. 1934. Grenregeling Anakalang, Oemboe Ratoe Nggai. Typescript, no. H975 (2). Koninklijk Instituut voor Taal-, Land, en Volkenkunde Leiden.

———. [1941] n.d. Dagboek. Typescript, no. H975 (2). Koninklijk Instituut voor Taal-, Land, en Volkenkunde, Leiden.

Rodgers, Susan. 1985. *Power and Gold: Jewelry from Indonesia, Malaysia, and the Philippines.* Geneva: Barbier-Mueller Museum.

Rodgers-Siregar, Susan. 1981. *Adat, Islam, and Christianity in a Batak Homeland.* Athens: Ohio University Center for International Studies.

Roos, S. 1872. Bijdrage tot de kennis van taal, land, en volk op het eiland Soemba. *Verhandelingen van het Bataviaasch Genootschap van Kunsten en Wettenschap* 36: 1–160.

Rosaldo, Michelle Z. 1973. 'I Have Nothing to Hide': The Language of Ilongot Oratory. *Language in Society* 2: 193–223.

———. 1980. *Knowledge and Passion: Ilongot Notions of Self and Social Life.* Cambridge: Cambridge University Press.

———. 1982. The Things We Do with Words: Ilongot Speech Acts and Speech Act Theory in Philosophy. *Language in Society* 11: 203–237.

Rossi-Landi, F. 1973. Commodities as Messages. In *Approaches to Semiotics (18): Recherches sur les systèmes signifiants, Symposium de Varsovie 1968,* ed. J. Rey-Debove. The Hague: Mouton.

Rouffaer, G. P. 1934. *Ethnographie van de Kleine Soenda Eilanden in beeld.* 's-Gravenhage: Koninklijk Instituut voor de Taal-, Land- en Volkenkunde van Nederlandsch-Indië.

Rubin, Gayle. 1975. The Traffic in Women: Notes on the 'Political Economy' of Sex. In *Toward an Anthropology of Women*, ed. Rayna R. Reiter. New York: Monthly Review Press.

Rumsey, Alan. 1990. Word, Meaning, and Linguistic Ideology. *American Anthropologist* 92: 346–361.

Ryle, Gilbert. 1946. Knowing How and Knowing That. *Proceedings of the Aristotle Society* n.s. 46: 1–16.

Sabarua, Y. O. 1976. Marapu dan kebudayaanya dalam kepercayaan masyarakat Anakalang di kecamatan Katiku Tana, daerah Tingkat II Sumba Barat. Thesis (skripsi), History Faculty, Universitas Nusa Cendana (Kupang).

Sacks, Harvey, Emanuel A. Schegloff, and Gail Jefferson. 1974. A Simplest Systematics for the Organization of Turn-taking in Conversation. *Language* 50: 696–735.

Sahlins, Marshall. 1972. *Stone Age Economics.* Chicago: Aldine.

———. 1985. *Islands of History.* Chicago: University of Chicago Press.

Salmond, A. 1975. Mana Makes a Man: A Look at Maori Oratory and Politics. In *Political Language and Oratory in Traditional Society*, ed. Maurice Bloch. New York: Academic Press.

Sastrodihardjo, R. Soekardjo. 1957. Beberapa tjatatan tentang daerah Sumba. Mimeo. Djakarta: Pusat Djawatan Pertanian Rakjat.

Schegloff, Emanuel A., Gail Jefferson, and Harvey Sacks. 1977. The Preference for Self-Correction in the Organization of Repair in Conversation. *Language* 53: 361–382.

Schulte Nordholt, H. G. [1966] 1971. *The Political System of the Atoni of Timor.* Trans. M. J. L. van Yperen. The Hague: Martinus Nijhoff.

Schutz, Alfred. [1932] 1967. *The Phenomenology of the Social World.* Trans. George Walsh and Frederick Lehnert. Evanston: Northwestern University Press.

Scott, James C. 1985. *Weapons of the Weak: Everyday Forms of Peasant Resistance.* New Haven: Yale University Press.

———. 1990. *Domination and the Arts of Resistance: Hidden Transcripts.* New Haven: Yale University Press.

Scott, Joan W. 1991. The Evidence of Experience. *Critical Inquiry* 17: 773–797.

Sherzer, Joel. 1983. *Kuna Ways of Speaking: An Ethnographic Perspective.* Austin: University of Texas Press.

Shore, Bradd. 1982. *Sala'ilua: A Samoan Mystery.* New York: Columbia University Press.

Siegel, James T. 1986. *Solo in the New Order: Language and Hierarchy in an Indonesian City.* Princeton: Princeton University Press.

Silverstein, Michael. 1976. Shifters, Linguistic Categories, and Cultural Description. In *Meaning in Anthropology*, ed. Keith H. Basso and Henry A. Selby. Albuquerque: University of New Mexico Press.

———. 1979. Language Structure and Linguistic Ideology. In *The Elements: A*

*Parasession on Linguistic Units and Levels*, ed. Paul R. Clyne et al. Chicago: Chicago Linguistic Society.

———. 1981. Metaforces of Power in Traditional Oratory. Unpublished paper.

———. 1993. Metapragmatic Discourse and Metapragmatic Function. In *Reflexive Language: Reported Speech and Metapragmatics*, ed. John A. Lucy. Cambridge: Cambridge University Press.

Simmel, Georg. [1907] 1990. *The Philosophy of Money*, ed. David Frisby, trans. Tom Bottomore and David Frisby. 2d ed. New York: Routledge.

Singarimbun, Masri. 1975. *Kinship, Descent, and Alliance among the Karo Batak*. Berkeley: University of California Press.

Spivak, Gayatri Chakravorty. 1988. Can the Subaltern Speak? In *Marxism and the Interpretation of Culture*, ed. Cary Nelson and Lawrence Grossberg. Urbana: University of Illinois Press.

Spyer, Patricia. 1992. The Memory of Trade: Circulation, Autochthony, and the Past in the Aru Islands (Eastern Indonesia). Ph.D. dissertation, University of Chicago.

———. 1996. Diversity with a Difference: Adat and the New Order in Aru (Eastern Indonesia). *Cultural Anthropology* 11: 25–30.

Stallybrass, Peter. 1996. Worn Worlds: Clothes and Identity on the Renaissance Stage. In *Subject and Object in Renaissance Culture*, ed. Margreta de Grazia, Maureen Quilligan, and Peter Stallybrass. Cambridge: Cambridge University Press.

Steedly, Mary Margaret. 1993. *Hanging without a Rope: Narrative Experience in Colonial and Postcolonial Karoland*. Princeton: Princeton University Press.

Strathern, Marilyn. 1972. *Women in Between*. London: Seminar.

———. 1981. Culture in a Netbag: The Manufacture of a Subdiscipline in Anthropology. *Man*, n.s. 16: 665–688.

———. 1984. Marriage Exchanges: A Melanesian Comment. *Annual Review of Anthropology* 13: 41–73.

———. 1988. *The Gender of the Gift: Problems with Women and Problems with Society in Melanesia*. Berkeley: University of California Press.

Sweeney, Amin. 1987. *A Full Hearing: Orality and Literacy in the Malay World*. Berkeley: University of California Press.

Tambiah, S. J. 1968. The Magical Power of Words. *Man*, n.s. 3: 175–208.

———. 1984. *The Buddhist Saints of the Forest and the Cult of the Amulets*. Cambridge: Cambridge University Press.

Taussig, Michael T. 1980. *The Devil and Commodity Fetishism in South America*. Chapel Hill: University of North Carolina Press.

Taylor, Charles. 1992. The Politics of Recognition. In *Multiculturalism and the "Politics of Recognition."* Princeton: Princeton University Press.

Taylor, Paul Michael. 1994. *Fragile Traditions: Indonesian Art in Jeopardy*. Honolulu: University of Hawaii Press.

Thomas, Nicholas. 1991. *Entangled Objects: Exchange, Material Culture, and Colonialism in the Pacific*. Cambridge, Mass.: Harvard University Press.

Traube, Elizabeth. 1986. *Cosmology and Social Life: Ritual Exchange among the Mambai of East Timor*. Chicago: University of Chicago Press.

Tsing, Anna Lowenhaupt. 1990. Gender and Performance in Meratus Dispute

Settlement. In *Power and Difference: Gender in Island Southeast Asia*, ed. Jane Monnig Atkinson and Shelly Errington. Stanford: Stanford University Press.

——. 1993. *In the Realm of the Diamond Queen: Marginality in an Out-of-the-Way Place*. Princeton: Princeton University Press.

Urban, Greg. 1989. The 'I' of Discourse. In *Semiotics, Self, and Society*, ed. Benjamin Lee and Greg Urban. Berlin: Mouton de Gruyter.

——. 1991. *A Discourse-Centered Approach to Culture: Native South American Myths and Rituals*. Austin: University of Texas Press.

Valeri, Valerio. 1980. Notes on the Meaning of Marriage Prestations among the Huaulu of Seram. In *The Flow of Life: Essays on Eastern Indonesia*, ed. James J. Fox. Cambridge, Mass.: Harvard University Press.

——. 1985. *Kingship and Sacrifice: Ritual and Society in Ancient Hawaii*. Trans. Paula Wissing. Chicago: University of Chicago Press.

van den End, Th., ed. 1987. *Gereformeerde zending op Sumba: Een bronnenpublicatie*. Alphen aan den Rijn: Raad voor de Zending der Ned. Herv. Kerk, de Zending der Gereformeerde Kerken in Nederland en de Gereformeerde Zendingsbond in de Ned. Herv. Kerk.

van Wouden, F. A. E. [1935] 1968. *Types of Social Structure in Eastern Indonesia*. Trans. Rodney Needham. The Hague: Martinus Nijhoff.

Vel, Jacqueline. 1987. *Lawonda: Een dorpsbeschrijving*. Leusden: Propelmas GKS Lawonda/Algemeen Diakonaal Bureau GKN.

——. 1991. *Tussen ruilen en rekenen: Agrarisch sociaal werk in de veranderende economie van Sumba*. Kampen: Kok.

——. 1992. Umbu Hapi versus Umbu Vincent: Legal Pluralism as an Arsenal in Village Combats. In *Law as a Resource in Agrarian Struggles*, ed. F. von Benda-Beckmann and M. van der Velde. Wageningen: Agricultural University.

——. 1994. The Uma-Economy: Indigenous Economics and Development Work in Lawonda, Sumba (Eastern-Indonesia). Thesis, Agricultural University, Wageningen.

Versluys, J. D. N. 1941. Aanteekeningen omtrent geld- en goederenverkeer in West-Soemba. *Koloniale studiën* 25: 433–483.

Volkman, Toby Alice. 1985. *Feasts of Honor: Ritual and Social Change in the Toraja Highlands*. Urbana: University of Illinois Press.

Vološinov, V. N. [1930] 1973. *Marxism and the Philosophy of Language*. Trans. Ladislav Matejka and I. R. Titunik. New York: Seminar Press.

Waitz, E. W. F. J. 1933. Bestuurs-memorie van de gezaghebber van West Soemba. Typescript. Algemeen Rijksarchief, The Hague.

Warren, Carol. 1992. *Adat and Dinas: Balinese Communities in the Indonesian State*. Kuala Lumpur: Oxford University Press.

Wartenberg, Thomas E. 1990. *The Forms of Power: From Domination to Transformation*. Philadelphia: Temple University Press.

Watson-Gegeo, Karen Ann, and Geoffrey White, eds. 1990. *Disentangling: Conflict Discourse in Pacific Societies*. Stanford: Stanford University Press.

Webb, R. A. F. Paul. 1986. The Sickle and the Cross: Christians and Communists in Bali, Flores, Sumba and Timor, 1965–67. *Journal of Southeast Asian Studies* 17: 94–112.

Weber, Max. 1978. *Economy and Society: An Outline of Interpretive Sociology.* Trans. Ephraim Fischoff et al. Berkeley: University of California Press.

Weiner, Annette B. 1976. *Women of Value, Men of Renown: New Perspectives in Trobriand Exchange.* Austin: University of Texas Press.

———. 1983. From Words to Objects to Magic: Hard Words and the Boundaries of Social Interaction. *Man,* n.s. 18: 690–709.

———. 1989. Why Cloth? Wealth, Gender, and Power in Oceania. In *Cloth and Human Experience,* ed. Annette B. Weiner and Jane Schneider. Washington: Smithsonian Institution Press.

———. 1992. *Inalienable Possessions: The Paradox of Keeping-While-Giving.* Berkeley: University of California Press.

Whitehead, Harriet. 1981. The Bow and the Burden Strap: A New Look at Institutionalized Homosexuality in Native North America. In *Sexual Meanings: The Cultural Construction of Gender and Sexuality,* ed. Sherry B. Ortner and Harriet Whitehead. Cambridge: Cambridge University Press.

Wielenga, D. K. 1908. Soemba: Op reis (Van Pajeti naar Memboro). *De Macedoniër* 12: 167–174, 257–269.

———. 1909. *Schets van een Soembaneesche spraakkunst (naar 't dialect van Kambera).* Batavia: Landsdrukkerij.

———. 1911. Reizen op Soemba. *De Macedoniër* 15: 166–172.

———. 1912. Reizen op West-Soemba (IV). *De Macedoniër* 16: 169–174.

———. 1923. Doodencultus op Soemba. *De Macedoniër* 27: 297–310.

———. 1932. *Marapoe: Een verhaal uit Soemba.* Kampen: J. H. Kok.

Witkamp, H. 1912. Een verkenningstocht over het eiland Soemba. *Tijdschrift van het Koninklijk Nederlansch Aardrijkskundig Genootschap* 29: 744–775; 30: 8–27, 484–505, 619–637.

Wittgenstein, Ludwig. 1953. *Philosophical Investigations.* Trans. G. E. M. Anscombe. New York: Macmillan.

Woolard, Kathryn A. 1992. Language Ideology: Issues and Approaches. *Pragmatics* 2: 235–249.

Yanagisako, Sylvia Juko, and Jane Fishburne Collier. 1987. Toward a Unified Analysis of Gender and Kinship. In *Gender and Kinship: Essays toward a Unified Analysis,* ed. Jane Fishburne Collier and Sylvia Juko Yanagisako. Stanford: Stanford University Press.

Zurbuchen, Mary Sabina. 1987. *The Language of Balinese Shadow Theater.* Princeton: Princeton University Press.

# Index

|            |                        |
|-----------:|------------------------|
| Compositor: | Prestige Typography |
| Text and Display: | Sabon |
| Printer: | Braun-Brumfield, Inc. |
| Binder: | Braun-Brumfield, Inc. |